WITHDRAWN

THE POLITICS OF
TORCH

THE POLITICS OF TORCH

The Allied Landings
and the Algiers *Putsch*
1942

by
ARTHUR LAYTON FUNK

THE UNIVERSITY PRESS OF KANSAS
Lawrence/Manhattan/Wichita

© Copyright 1974 by The University Press of Kansas
Printed in the United States of America

Library of Congress Cataloging in Publication Data
Funk, Arthur Layton, 1914-
    The politics of TORCH; the Allied landings and the Algiers Putsch, 1942.

    Bibliography: p.
    1. Operation Torch. 2. World War, 1939-1945—Diplomatic history. I. Title.
D766.82.F86   940.54′23   74-2020
ISBN 0-7006-0123-6

Contents

	Introduction	vii
1	Before Pearl Harbor	3
2	After Pearl Harbor: The Rise and Fall of GYMNAST	27
3	The French	45
4	The TORCH Decision	65
5	The Planners: Washington and London	89
6	The Planners: France and Algiers	123
7	General Clark's Secret Mission	149
8	Last Minute Preparations	171
9	The Algiers Landings—8 November 1942	203
10	Negotiating with Darlan	231
11	The Clark-Darlan Agreement	249
	Appendices	
	A. Text of the "Soft" Armistice Terms and the Final Version of the Clark-Darlan Agreement	265
	B. Note on the Assassination of Admiral Darlan	275
	Notes	279
	Bibliography	
	Bibliographical Note	303
	Basic Books Cited by Abbreviated Title	304
	Selected Bibliography	308
	Index	315

Introduction

What this book attempts to do, and in this it is unique, is to describe the North African occupation from the point of view of political, not military, considerations, taking into account the French as well as the Anglo-American interests. Most writers of books in English have glossed over the French position and have seen the operation only from the American side. Most books do not deal adequately with the *Putsch* in Algiers—of significance today because of new-found emphasis on guerrilla warfare. Nor do most books cover the variety of developments. The approach in this volume enables one to follow what was happening in Washington, London, Algiers, and Vichy as the invasion was prepared and finally launched. It is not a military history; and it refers only briefly to operations at Casablanca and Oran which, however important they may have been to the history of amphibious warfare, possessed no significance politically. Algiers was the political center, and it remains the center of emphasis in this book.

Some of the material may be novel to those who have not delved into the French books on the subject. For example, it may surprise some who know of General Mark Clark's famous secret mission (for which he was decorated) to learn that the French participants considered the conference to be not only counter-productive but an unsavory example of American duplicity.

The book calls attention to several other matters. It shows that the decision to deal with Vichy officials—including Darlan—had been made three weeks before the landings. The terms of the Clark-Darlan Agreement were not negotiated on the spot; they were drawn up in London before the invasion. Robert Murphy never knew of these terms, and received virtually no guidance from Washington. He had to plead for a directive. When he received one, it turned out to be extremely vague. The blame for the Darlan deal (if it is to be considered a political error) lies in Washington, not with Murphy.

In 1959, I published a study of what happened in North Africa *after* the Darlan deal in a book published by the University of Oklahoma Press: *Charles de Gaulle: The Crucial Years, 1943–1944.* For a long time I hesitated to write the book for which the earlier volume would be a sequel, but the availability of new materials has led me to believe that such an effort would have merit.

I am greatly indebted to many who gave advice, made materials available to me, and read parts of the manuscript; especially to Clifton Child of the British Cabinet Historical Office; General Mark W. Clark; Dr. Hervé Cras, distinguished naval historian who writes under the pen name of Jacques Mordal; F. W. D. Deakin, formerly warden at St. Antony's College, Oxford; Louis Gottschalk of the University of Chicago; Henri Michel, president of the International Committee on the History of the Second World War; Robert Murphy, the diplomat among warriors; Bernard Pauphilet, secretary of the Association de la Libération Française du 8 Novembre 1942, who brought me into contact with comrades of the *Putsch*; Forrest Pogue, director of the George C. Marshall Foundation; Claude Sturgill, colleague at the University of Florida; Robert Wolfe of the National Archives.

A. L. F.

Gainesville, Florida
October 1973

THE POLITICS OF
TORCH

1

Before Pearl Harbor

Washington, September–October, 1940
Dangers and possibilities in North Africa[1]

On 24 July 1942, the Combined Chiefs of Staff, with the enthusiastic blessings of Prime Minister Churchill and President Roosevelt, reached the decision to launch Operation TORCH, a landing in North Africa. Gen. Dwight D. Eisenhower would be named commander in chief, and his staff, already headquartered in London, immediately began its complicated work.

Within the week, on 1 August, Robert Murphy, special representative of the president, received orders to report in Washington. Having lived in Algiers for over a year, Murphy held a key position: he was the one person whose knowledge of the North African French could conceivably lead to an unopposed landing. No one else had the wide, high-level contacts and the intimate understanding of how the resistance organizations worked. He was absolutely essential.

That Murphy had entered North Africa in the beginning resulted from the imagination and insistence of Franklin D. Roosevelt. When France collapsed during six turbulent weeks in 1940, Roosevelt reacted with indignation that a country so glorious and a people so talented should have surrendered ignominiously to Nazi violence. Publicly Roosevelt placed the blame on Axis aggression, but privately he had come to the shocked realization that France had revealed itself as weak, impotent, and completely demoralized. Admiring the country and priding himself on his understanding of French language and culture, the president readily reached the conviction that his influence and wisdom could help shore up the tattered fragments which remained.

Roosevelt saw no reason to break relations with the Vichy regime of eighty-four-year-old Marshal Philippe Pétain. The American people had not risen up to demand belligerent moves against Hitler and his quislings in Europe. In 1940, with the third-term campaign looming ahead and with the transfer of fifty old destroyers to Britain bringing queries and protests, isolation gripped most of the country. The United States could scarcely break with Vichy when it kept representatives at Berlin, Rome, and Tokyo.

There still existed, in accordance with the Franco-German armistice, parts of France and of the French Empire which remained theoretically free and outside Axis control. All of southeastern France, a square some 300 miles across, including Lyons, Vichy, Marseilles, Toulouse, and the Mediterranean coast, maintained an uneasy independence; and across the Mediterranean, Tunisia, Algeria, Morocco, and French West Africa remained virtually as they had been before the war. In the fall of 1940 the future status of these African areas posed complex questions not only for the belligerents but for the United States as well.

President Roosevelt and his military advisers examined carefully, with due regard for American interests, the implications of a free versus an occupied North and West Africa. First of all, they argued, the United States must be defended from potential Axis aggression. The danger of Hitler crossing the Atlantic was remote; but the president and chiefs of staff would have been criminally negligent to ignore any possible avenue of attack. In the north, so long as England and Iceland remained in friendly hands and so long as control of air and sea was ensured, the dangers seemed minimal. In the south it was different.

After the devastation of France in 1940, Hitler's panzer divisions could have pushed on to the Mediterranean. Generalissimo Francisco Franco, an Axis sympathizer since German planes helped him during the Civil War, might offer free passage through Spain. Suppose Hitler, with or without Franco's cooperation, should march across the Pyrenees, seize Gibraltar, and take possession of a helpless French North Africa. Occupation of the Azores and the Canary Islands might soon follow. The British Eighth Army, blocked and hard pressed by Mussolini's Italian forces in Libya, would be incapable of hindering the Germans, who would then hold Morocco and French West Africa, a 2,000-mile coast facing the Atlantic, together with the Azores and Canaries. Installed in the Senegalese port city of Dakar, they could maintain and refuel U-boat packs which could then blockade the 1,500-mile stretch of ocean between Africa and Natal in Brazil. With the Mediterranean closed at Gibraltar and the long route around Africa rendered hazardous, no American ship could ever have reached Egypt. The entire Middle East could fall into Axis hands.

The danger posed by German possession of Dakar might have been eliminated if the British had seized the port. They had tried. A joint expedition of British forces and a Free French contingent led in person by General Charles de Gaulle had attempted a landing in September 1940. The failure not only left Dakar under Vichy control, but it aggravated the bitterness many Frenchmen felt toward their former allies.

So the problem remained, and President Roosevelt looked apprehensively at this African bulge which curved menacingly into the Atlantic. Even though the United States remained isolated from the European conflict, theoretically at peace, the president could not throw off the uneasiness he felt about Dakar.

Another carry-over from the defeat, the French navy, fascinated Roosevelt, whose long-time passion for ships made him more conscious than many observers that the French fleet had come through the 1940 debacle untouched. Admiral of the Fleet Jean François Darlan had been prepared: his naval units had been alerted and fueled in readiness for their turn. Their turn never came. The armistice left the fleet intact, anchored or docked in various ports—in the West Indies, at Oran, at Dakar, at Alexandria, and at the principal Mediterranean base in southern France, Toulon. Some French ships at Mers-el-Kebir, the naval installation near Oran, had been destroyed by an impulsive British action; but the remainder of the French navy might still play a decisive part in the war. Admiral Darlan had declared that so long as he retained the power, he would keep his fleet out of Axis control.

In the fall of 1940, heavily involved in the presidential campaign, President Roosevelt had not the slightest intention of employing military force on behalf of France. Yet it was imperative, as the president viewed American interests, to help the French hold on to their fleet and to deny North Africa to the Axis.

Roosevelt noted certain developments in France and decided on an exploratory line of action. The president had read with intense interest a report which Commander R. H. Hillenkoetter, then naval attaché at Vichy (he would later become head of CIA), had written after a trip to North Africa. Hillenkoetter found virtually no Axis activity there.[2] This could possibly mean that Hitler did not intend to adopt a Mediterranean strategy or at least was not preparing the ground for military penetration.

At that time, in September 1940, no one could have told what Hitler's plans would be, especially as the military and political situation changed from day to day. Hitler entertained a variety of possible moves—an invasion of England, a move through Spain to Morocco, a complete turnaround to the east and attack on Russia. Basically an infantry soldier, the führer did not understand naval strategy, and he did not want to get involved in the Mediterranean. He had been impressed by the way General Boisson repulsed British and Gaullist units at Dakar. If he could be sure that France would defend her colonies, Hitler could afford to abandon ideas of German occupation.

The fate of North Africa was influenced also by a Vichy cabinet shuffle which occurred early in September. At that time, Pétain, weary of the argumentative parliamentarians who surrounded him, decided to eliminate them. To balance the dismissal of the politicians, he also dismissed his minister of defense, General Maxime Weygand, for whom he envisaged more significant employment. He immediately appointed Weygand as delegate general in French North Africa.

General Weygand was known to be tough, efficient, and uncompromisingly anti-German. After a long and distinguished military career—he had served on Foch's staff in World War I and later became vice-president of the Army Council—he had been recalled from retirement after World War II broke out. When Hitler's panzers began slicing through the northern defenses in May, 1940, Weygand had been hurriedly named, at the age of seventy-three, as commander in chief. The appointment came too late; but, while he was forced to preside over the defeat, Weygand had managed to avoid blame for the woeful shortcomings of French defense. He thus held a reputation, not entirely deserved, as a staunch proponent of resistance. There was no question of his loyalty to Marshal Pétain; but he detested Prime Minister Pierre Laval, and he had no great love for Admiral Darlan. In spite of his age, Weygand's dynamic energy was extraordinary, and his diminutive size was more than compensated by his austere, domineering military posture. He was an impressive man: bantam-weight but accepting no nonsense. As delegate general in North Africa with headquarters at Algiers, General Weygand would have limited official power; but his enormous prestige and personal reputation, second only to that of Marshal Pétain, lent him an authority which stood in notable contrast to the ambivalent mediocrity at Vichy.[3]

The combination of Weygand's new appointment and the apparent Axis shunning of North Africa suggested some alluring possibilities to President Roosevelt. The French government had already put out feelers regarding American economic assistance. If Hitler intended to avoid penetration of North Africa, he left there an opportunity which only the United States, still recognizing the Vichy government, could exploit.

If a vacuum were to exist in North Africa and if the United States possessed the best capacity for filling it, the question arose: how to get there? In one sense the question was academic; the United States already had representatives in Africa: a consulate in Tunisia, consulates at Algiers and Oran in Algeria, a consulate in Tangiers, at Casablanca in Morocco, and at Dakar. But consular officers had limitations in terms of duties and experience; the wartime crisis demanded more agents with military training and representatives with higher rank, suitable for negotiation at top levels. For example, the governor general of Morocco, Gen. Auguste Noguès, a full general since 1930 and a member in 1940 of the Superior War Council, operated like Weygand in the highest echelons of the French government. If something more than routine official relationships were to develop, the United States would need someone near ambassadorial rank in North Africa.

There was also the possibility of entering North Africa clandestinely, just as British Intelligence was doing.[4] (Having broken with Vichy, Great Britain kept only one official British representative in the area: at Tangiers.) If the ultimate purpose of infiltrating North Africa was to rally it as a military base, some means of reinforcing French troops with modern equipment would have to be found. While Vichy might approve the appointment of additional vice-consuls, it could not very easily accept military attachés. Agents of this sort would have to be disguised as consuls—a device foreign to

American diplomatic traditions at that time—or they would have to operate clandestinely with some other type of cover.

Both the president and the chiefs of staff needed more information. They decided to send special representatives to North Africa.

Washington and North Africa, October 1940–March 1941
The Murphy mission[5]

The president's choice for this delicate mission was Robert D. Murphy. At the time of France's fall, Murphy had been counsellor of embassy at Paris, the highest ranked diplomat serving under Ambassador William C. Bullitt. When Bullitt left, Murphy, then forty-five, had become chargé d'affaires at Vichy. Then relatively unknown, Murphy would later become General Eisenhower's political adviser. His energy and competence, and above all his capacity to work congenially with soldiers and statesmen in difficult circumstances, would bring him after the war to high positions of responsibility: abroad as political adviser with rank of ambassador in Germany and as ambassador to Japan; at home as undersecretary of state for political affairs.

Although he spent a good fraction of his professional life in contact with diplomats and aristocrats, Murphy himself claimed neither diplomats nor aristocrats among his forebears: he had sprung from a solid, middle-class, Irish family which had settled in Milwaukee. Entering the foreign service, he came rapidly up the ranks through his own perseverance, charm, and all-round ability. With ten years' service in Paris, he spoke French fluently, had a wide circle of friends among Frenchmen, and had experienced at first hand all those phenomena—the February riots of 1934, the Popular Front, the reoccupation of the Rhineland, Munich—which epitomized the apathetic prewar failures of the Third Republic.

Tall, slightly stoop-shouldered, Murphy radiated a congenial warmth and sympathy which was disarming. It would have been difficult to dislike him. Well-informed himself, he was a good listener and projected a courteous, smiling reception of other people's views. To some this characteristic could even be deceptive, leading them to believe that Murphy agreed with them when in fact he was simply acknowledging what they had to say.

One of his close associates in 1941 and 1942, Kenneth Pendar, has written of Murphy:

He had a gaiety that brought out gaiety in others, a tremendous gift for friendship, affections that were almost too easy-going and warm. He wanted to, and inclined to, believe the best of everybody. He was, I found, a devout Roman Catholic, and something of his deep faith seemed to be reflected in the loyalty and liking he showed toward acquaintances, colleagues and even the men with whom he negotiated.

. . . Though he had a hot Irish temper, which came in occasional lightning-like flashes, he was in general too indulgent, too loyal, too fair-minded, in a way, for a diplomat, whose main job is, after all, to sell a national bill of goods.[6]

In October 1940, Undersecretary of State Sumner Welles escorted Murphy, who had been specially called in from Vichy, to the White House. President Roosevelt had a large map of French North and West Africa spread out on his desk. After a few casual remarks, he elaborated his thinking for Murphy's benefit.

Perhaps North Africa, the president wondered, could become the focus of French anti-German activity; perhaps French army units stationed there, though now impotent, could be secretly rearmed. Perhaps General Weygand would choose to break with Vichy and rally, so much more effectively than Charles de Gaulle could, the thousands of officers and men who still wanted to fight Germans. How much more impressive would be a movement headed by Weygand, with his five stars and extraordinary prestige, than that organized by a brigadier general in London who had bungled the effort to take Dakar. If such a movement could develop and if it could be supported by the French fleet, France might yet play a consequential role in the war.

But first of all the president needed information. He wanted Murphy to get into North Africa—this would require Vichy's permission—and assess the situation. He should explore the possibility of shipping American food and clothing, with General Weygand's approval, for the civilian population in Africa. Murphy must get to know Weygand. "You might even go to Church with him," the president suggested, knowing that both Murphy and the general were Catholic. As Murphy was leaving the president's study, Roosevelt added a final instruction: "If you learn anything in Africa of special interest, send it to me. Don't bother going through State Department channels."[7]

The career diplomat in Murphy was somewhat taken aback to

learn that he had become one of President Roosevelt's "personal representatives," free to bypass his nominal chiefs. "Embarrassing as that was," Murphy later wrote, "it was a situation which had to be accepted as one of the occupational hazards of Roosevelt's special assignments. And there was always the consolation that the President, though he might let one down in a public utterance, gave very stanch support in private."[8]

Murphy carried out his mission quite rapidly, joining General Weygand at Dakar on 20 December. In principle, an understanding presented no difficulty. Weygand firmly had dedicated himself to the defense of Africa; he wished to avoid dependence on German supplies, and yet he realized that oil, sugar, clothing, and other commodities must come from abroad. A commercial arrangement with the United States would provide the obvious and logical solution. As negotiations for such an arrangement had started before either Weygand or Murphy came to North Africa, a tentative accord was quickly reached. President Roosevelt's personal representative and the French delegate general initialed the document, to be known as the Murphy-Weygand Agreement, on 26 February 1941.[9]

The French government at Vichy could not tell what price they might have to pay for the Murphy-Weygand Agreement. If Hitler insisted on pressing into North Africa, the French army obviously could not prevent him. Marshal Pétain, for all his misguided defeatism, never conceded to Berlin more than he felt essential to preserve what little French autonomy was left. Badgered by the threat of Germanophile collaborators on one side and of Free French adventurers on the other, for the moment he placed hopes on Admiral Darlan and General Weygand. Darlan would collaborate, Weygand would resist; but they were both military men and he could count on their allegiance. But in the spring of 1941, the old marshal gave the edge to collaboration: by 10 March, when he approved the Murphy-Weygand Agreement, Darlan had become the most powerful person in the government: deputy premier, heir-apparent, minister of foreign affairs, interior, and marine, and commander in chief of the navy.

To have approved American supplies to North Africa involved for Vichy a delicate, calculated risk, based on the assumption that Hitler would become so involved in central Europe that he would leave France alone. If Weygand became too strong, his pro-Ally stance might provide exactly the provocation Hitler needed to redeploy his divisions southward. There was a gamble here, but scarcely an American one: Hitler was betting that France would view its interests as aligned with those of the Axis; Pétain was gambling that between Darlan's collaboration and Weygand's independence, he could achieve maximum security for France.

So Vichy, with German approval, tendered no objection to the Murphy-Weygand supply arrangement and agreed that the United States should assign additional consular personnel to supervise the shipments. The way had been paved for America's first venture, even before declaring war, in espionage.

North Africa, February–May 1941
U.S. military appraisals of Africa

At the same time that Robert Murphy was reaching his understanding with General Weygand, U.S. Army Intelligence sent an observer into North Africa. This was Lt. Col. Robert A. Solborg, a naturalized American citizen of Russian extraction who for years had been director of European operations for the ARMCO Steel Company.[10]

With German divisions at the Pyrenees, the United States Chiefs of Staff, as well as President Roosevelt, were giving anxious attention to Africa. What were the possibilities, the army wanted to know, of holding Morocco against a German assault? While Murphy made official contact at the diplomatic level, Solborg, posing as an ARMCO representative, could reach the military people and assess the resistance capabilities of the colonial Armistice Army.

Colonel Solborg flew into Algiers, ostensibly on business, in February 1941, soon after Murphy and Weygand had initialed the economic accord. Solborg was shortly introduced by Consul General Felix Cole to a young captain, André Beaufre, who then served on the staff of the Algerian governor general. Part of Beaufre's duties consisted of building up, clandestinely, a native army in North Africa; and ever since the Murphy-Weygand rapprochement he had been alerted to expect an American military attaché in Algiers. Although he was not appointed as an attaché, Solborg let Beaufre understand that he represented the first wave of American military intervention and that he was in Algiers to ascertain French needs.

Beaufre went to work on a plan. At that time he lived at Dar Mahieddine, a villa which by reason of its privacy lent itself well to secret discussions. Beaufre found several junior officers who shared his enthusiasm for an ultimate strike against Germany: in particular, Maj. Léon Faye, then heading the North African air force's G-3 (Troisième Bureau de l'Air), and Maj. Emile Jousse, in charge of the XIX Corps G-3. Faye would later become one of the great heroes of the French resistance, head of the ALLIANCE underground network. He was ultimately caught by the Gestapo and executed. Jousse, a quiet, dedicated career officer, would later play an instrumental role in seizing Algiers for the Allies when the landings finally took place.[11]

The threat and the opportunity, as the French officers saw it, lay in the Italo-German campaign then being waged in Libya. If the British Eighth Army could press the Italian army, recently reinforced by Rommel's still inexperienced Afrika Korps, back against southern Tunisia, a French army, properly equipped and supported by Allied naval units, could strike from the rear and place the Axis forces in a deadly vise. A detachment would be needed to stop a possible German advance through Spain toward Morocco.

Beaufre, Faye, and Jousse drew up detailed lists of military supplies required for such resistance and submitted them to Solborg, who undertook to transmit the information to Washington. The young officers, knowing that General Weygand could not officially approve their deliberations, did not seek out any confirmation from his headquarters. On the American side, while Solborg could relay the requirements to Washington, he could give no guarantee concerning American intentions. In March 1941, eight months before Pearl Harbor, no one knew what American policy in North Africa would be.

The lack of response from Washington frustrated the young officers and embarrassed Solborg. Even though many of his advisers were urging the president to strike some positive note, President Roosevelt was unwilling to call attention to America's sympathy for the French; he knew the state of public opinion and he contented himself with economic promises and encouraging but insipid pronouncements.

Captain Beaufre wondered if his group's efforts were worthwhile, and he confided his discouragement to one of his friends, Jacques Lemaigre Dubreuil, a businessman who also was acquainted with Solborg. As a reserve officer, Lemaigre Dubreuil had served for a while with Beaufre on Weygand's staff. He also knew Murphy.

North Africa, December 1940–May 1941
A key Frenchman in African politics,
Jacques Lemaigre Dubreuil[12]

As Lemaigre Dubreuil would play a very controversial part in North African politics, more than a little attention must be given to his personality and background. A friend of Laval's, he would be castigated in Gaullist propaganda as pro-Nazi; a wealthy industrialist, he would be accused of serving only his own economic interests; a friend of Robert Murphy's, he would be charged with duping the American diplomat into a fascist conspiracy.

In fact, the most transparent quality of Jacques Lemaigre Dubreuil was his passionate enthusiasm, his emotional, almost childlike ambition to rehabilitate France and to restore the country to a position of dignity and responsibility. Unquestionably he viewed the world through lenses that were conservative. Rightist, property conscious, suspicious of communism and socialism, he admired the nondemocratic socio-political structure of Marshal Pétain's national revolution. But he feared and opposed German dominance. He hoped for resistance first by Pétain and Laval, then by Weygand. When these leaders demonstrated their unwillingness to break the armistice, he turned elsewhere.

Once committed to a cause, Lemaigre Dubreuil threw himself into it with the emotional intensity of a crusader, using every means he could find—sometimes quixotically, sometimes passionately—to achieve his end.

Jacques Lemaigre Dubreuil did not spring from one of the great families of France, but he married into a prominent one. In 1926, when he married the daughter of Georges Lesieur, he became associated with the direction of the country's most important peanut-oil producer, Huiles Lesieur. But during the 1930s, while Hitler was maneuvering to power in Germany, and France was wracked with scandal, misgovernment, and financial abuse, Dubreuil put most of his energies into a rightist taxpayers' lobby, the Fédération Nationale des Contribuables, of which he became president in 1935, the year after the famous February riots. In the hurly-burly of French politics during and after the war, Lemaigre Dubreuil was accused of being fascist and pro-Hitler. But like many political accusations based on some fragment of fact, the charges had more froth than substance. What Lemaigre Dubreuil wanted was an ordered, disciplined France, financially solvent, with the resources of the state used honestly in its best interests. When the Bank of France, transformed into a national institution by the Popular Front, opened its directorship to candidates elected by the shareholders, Lemaigre Dubreuil campaigned for one of the seats and won. Later this association with the Bank would be turned against him to imply that he was one of the "two hundred families," or a "synarchist," plotting for control of the government. More accurately, Lemaigre Dubreuil must be seen as a gadfly, continually embarrassing the Bank with his well-publicized attacks on the board's policies. His charges carried a particular sting because, with experienced insight into the techniques of French political infighting, he made sure his voice was heard through the taxpayers' organ, *L'action contribuable*. Later, seeking a wider audience, in 1939 he bought *Le Jour-Echo de Paris* which, under the able direction of Jean Rigault, continued to appear in unoccupied France until 1942.

When Germany invaded France in the spring of 1940, Lemaigre Dubreuil volunteered, only to find defeat, be captured, and finally escape back into the central part of France, now administered from Vichy. A further military career struck him as pointless, and he could see no meaning any more to the political flurries related to taxpayers and the Bank of France.

Meanwhile the family business interests needed attention. The main Huiles Lesieur processing factory stood a few miles from Dunkirk, now under German occupation. Shipments of raw materials—peanuts from West Africa—had tapered off as a result of the British blockade. Lemaigre Dubreuil saw two possible solutions: either convert the Dunkirk factory to production of soap and detergents or transfer the peanut processing operation to West Africa. The latter proposition proved interesting to both Vichy and German authorities: the Germans would take 25 percent as their share, and the French saw advantages in a commercial enterprise which, guaranteeing food, could make use of shipping and capital. With a passport permitting him to go back and forth from Africa to France, Lemaigre Dubreuil went to Morocco in December 1940 to look over the situation.

At that time he became acquainted with Robert Murphy, who was then carrying out his first inspection tour.[13] The fact that Murphy, an American, was examining North Africa interested Lemaigre Dubreuil very much. As Murphy was trying to work out arrangements to ship goods into North Africa and as Dubreuil was endeavoring to transfer his factories to Morocco, the two men clearly possessed a concert of interests. But Lemaigre Dubreuil's horizons were large, and his thinking not restricted to short-range business interests: he was a crusader, a fighter for causes, more than he was businessman. Almost intuitively he could see a potential chain of events: if Murphy surveyed North Africa it was because Washington envisaged some potential employment of North Africa. Ultimately the armed forces of the United States might intervene. Lemaigre Dubreuil visualized the military and political possibilities: a combination of Weygand, 125,000 French colonial soldiers in North Africa, and American material support. This was a concept to conjure with. It far surpassed another combination: de Gaulle, 20,000 volunteers, and British support. With these embryonic thoughts in mind, Lemaigre Dubreuil began to try to implement his concept with the emotional fervor of a true convert.

Lemaigre Dubreuil, therefore, took the trouble, when on trips to Algiers or Casablanca, to keep in touch with Murphy and with Solborg. He was also accustomed to exchange views with Major Beaufre. Although the businessman had put aside his uniform, he shared Beaufre's realization that only American material reinforcement could give the North African army a fighting potential. Lemaigre Dubreuil was a frequent visitor at Dar Mahieddine, where he enthusiastically discussed North Africa's future with Beaufre and his friends. He worked out a simple code with Beaufre so that the two could communicate between France and Algiers.[14]

North Africa, May–August 1941
Premature military planning

During this spring of 1941, Hitler's intentions regarding North Africa still remained uncertain to Allied observers. It appeared that the führer had abandoned his plans of marching through France or Spain. In April, concentrating his attention on eastern Europe, he ordered the Wehrmacht into Yugoslavia and Greece. While the occupation of the Balkans, accomplished by the end of May, eased German pressure in the west, the Germans now threatened the entire Middle East, where France, with its mandate over Lebanon and Syria, had vital interests.[15]

Under these circumstances, Admiral Darlan stood ready to make virtually any concession to Hitler—passage through Syria, use of French North African ports—in order to preserve what vestiges of independence remained in France itself. Weygand bitterly and forcefully opposed the Darlan policy, which he saw might lead to such a creeping infiltration that the whole Empire might be jeopardized.

The Darlan-Weygand conflict came to a showdown in May, at precisely the time that Beaufre's rearmament negotiations received unfortunate publicity. An informer reported the military plans which Beaufre, Jousse, Faye, and another officer, Major Loustaunau-Lacau, had been discussing a bit too freely at the Villa Dar Mahieddine. Lemaigre Dubreuil was implicated because the code linking the industrialist to Beaufre had been found. Even Robert Murphy was involved because, having been invited to dinner at Beaufre's on the day of the arrests, he later showed up at Dar Mahieddine.

The evidence was brought to the attention of André Achiary, chief of the Brigade Spéciale de Surveillance du Territoire.

Achiary was an energetic and patriotic young man. He held a post which gave him wide powers of investigation throughout Algeria. Ostensibly he served the Vichy government, but in actual practice he quietly supported the insurgent movement in North Africa. He realized that he could render greater services to the Allied cause if he held his official position, and he maneuvered with supple dexterity between fascist sympathizers and clandestine resisters. Where possible he simply overlooked information filed against underground groups, or warned them, providing Vichy with a minimum of information. Because he had authority throughout Algeria, he actually became a coordinator of resistance groups, occasionally putting one unit into contact with another.

The evidence against the French officers was, unfortunately, too blatant to be ignored. However sympathetic Weygand may have been to their ultimate goal, he was furious that his subordinates should have involved themselves in a conspiracy on the eve of his departure for Vichy, where he intended a confrontation with Darlan. The general's autonomous position in North Africa would have been weakened, possibly even destroyed, if Darlan could demonstrate that Weygand had disloyally conspired with the Allies. Weygand was embarrassed enough by British and American news reports that he intended to act counter to Pétain.

In Algiers, the little nucleus of military resistance which had hopefully negotiated with Colonel Solborg simply fell apart. Achiary was able to drop the charges against Major Jousse, and he turned his back while Loustaunau-Lacau escaped; but he could not avoid turning over Beaufre and Faye to the Vichy authorities. In France they were tried and given relatively light sentences. After his release, however, Beaufre was forbidden to return to North Africa. Meanwhile he had donated his villa to Lemaigre Dubreuil, who later moved his family to Algiers and made Dar Mahieddine his wartime residence. Beaufre and Lemaigre Dubreuil continued to communicate regularly with each other.[16]

Against Lemaigre Dubreuil the police possessed nothing but the code reference to him found among Beaufre's papers. Achiary called the industrialist in for questioning. During the examination each carefully explored the beliefs held by the other, coming hesitatingly to the conclusion that they were both on the same side, working for the same ends. They agreed that Lemaigre Dubreuil would have better cover if Achiary reported to Vichy that Lemaigre Dubreuil had been picked up for expressing pro-German opinions at the Hotel Aletti bar. He was then released. Significantly, the two men shook hands.

With the elimination of the Beaufre group, Solborg was left without significant contacts in the Algiers area. But he continued to travel and observe.

The immediate German threat to French North Africa seemed to have passed. Early in June the British, reinforced by some of General de Gaulle's Free French, had defeated the Vichy commander in Syria, General Dentz, and had placed Syria and Lebanon under effective occupation. The danger of a German pincer movement through Turkey and Syria for the moment had been averted. Then, on 22 June, Hitler invaded the Soviet Union and soon became so immersed in that vast campaign that he could spare few moments for intensive analysis of Mediterranean problems.

Weygand returned to his command post at Algiers assured of Pétain's continuing support, and by July he could assure himself with reasonable certainty that German occupation, at least in the immediate future, was out of the question. But whether he could guarantee his own security was another matter. The showdown had intensified his rivalry with Admiral Darlan, and if pressures from collaborationists and Germans continued to mount, the ancient marshal might find himself unable to pursue his policy of balancing

Darlan with Weygand. Where could Weygand find support? Military resistance would be possible only with serious reinforcement of his pitifully under-equipped African army. The United States might provide such reinforcement, but Weygand had few illusions about this source of assistance. In spite of the economic agreement he had made with Murphy, only dribbles of food and petroleum supplies had so far arrived.[17]

By August 1941, Colonel Solborg had learned all he profitably could about conditions in North and West Africa. Supplied with information about economic and military needs, and having made scores of potentially useful contacts, Solborg flew to Washington to report his findings.[18]

Algeria, August–September 1941
The French underground and Murphy

So long as the United States remained out of the war, its North African policy remained vague and contingent. Murphy knew that his primary responsibility required a continuous relationship with Weygand—cautious, diplomatic, not so close as to alarm the Axis but sufficient to reassure the French that the United States would sooner or later help in defeating Hitler. A tangible gesture would soon manifest itself, Murphy hoped, in shiploads of food and clothing which would let the United States contribute to North Africa's tenuous independence. Murphy was even authorized by the president to tell Weygand that military supplies would be forthcoming. In relaying this information to Weygand, Murphy did not strengthen but actually weakened the general's independence: the American diplomatic code had been broken by Germany, and Murphy's messages, which frequently assessed Weygand's defiance, were regularly circulated in Berlin. A month before Pearl Harbor, Weygand was forced into retirement. With his disappearance the United States, because of its own impetuosity and naive confidence in its antique ciphers, lost its key to a logical North African policy.[19]

Several months before Weygand's recall, the American presence began to manifest itself concretely when the special vice-consuls, approved under the Murphy-Weygand Agreement, began to arrive. Ostensibly to verify the American shipments (none of which had yet appeared), the vice-consuls in fact constituted a corps of secret agents, making contacts and forwarding economic, military, and political information to Washington. By the end of 1941 they had all arrived: Kenneth Pendar, David King, Sydney Bartlett, Stafford Reid, and Franklin Canfield in Morocco; Ridgway Knight and Leland Rounds at Oran; John Boyd and John Knox at Algiers; Harry Woodruff and John Utter in Tunisia.[20] They sent volumes of reports, mostly on ship movements, but they included also certain information on troop and battery dispositions which later helped the landing operations. They also created occasional embarrassment to those French officials who tried to maintain, under the eyes of the German and Italian Armistice Commissions, a posture of collaborationist loyalty.

During 1941 Murphy widened his acquaintance with Frenchmen who agonized over Vichy defeatism and who hoped that France and the United States could share in an ultimate victory over the Axis. One of these, Jacques Tarbé de Saint-Hardouin, was a fellow diplomat and a member of Weygand's staff with whom Murphy had worked to develop the economic agreement. When Weygand left, Saint-Hardouin obtained leave from the diplomatic corps but remained in Algiers where he undertook to extend the Murphy-Weygand Agreement into an understanding whereby, if the United States ever occupied North Africa, the French would retain some sovereign rights.

Murphy also kept in touch with those who had developed a military program for Lieutenant Colonel Solborg early in 1941 but who had been dispersed by Weygand's disapproval. The only officer now left in Algiers was Colonel Jousse, who had not abandoned his belief that some sort of clandestine military operation could hamper Rommel or aid the Allies in the Mediterranean. From time to time Murphy saw Lemaigre Dubreuil, now living in Beaufre's former home, Dar Mahieddine. Continually attempting to develop his Huiles Lesieur vegetable oil factories in West Africa, Lemaigre Dubreuil traveled back and forth from France to Algiers, Casablanca, and Dakar. He talked with Murphy when the occasion permitted and kept in touch also with Colonel Jousse, Saint-Hardouin, and with Achiary, the police security officer who had protected him.

Through Achiary, Murphy extended his contacts outside of Algiers. In Oran, close to the French naval base at Mers-el-Kebir and not far from Spanish Morocco, a small group began to meet with the idea of resisting a hypothetical German push through Gibraltar. The group was heterogeneous, including Catholic priests like Father Théry and the Abbé Cordier; army officers, like Henri d'Astier de la

Vigerie, Lt. Bernard Karsenty, and Colonel Tostain; and young Jews, militantly opposed to Vichy anti-Semitism, like Roger and Pierre Carcasonne. In May 1941, this group became acquainted with Colonel A. S. Van Hecke, North African commissioner of the Chantiers de la Jeunesse.

With Van Hecke's affiliation the movement[21] developed a truly North African aspect. Van Hecke, then fifty-one, originally Belgian, had run away from home at age eighteen to join the Foreign Legion. A dedicated soldier, he had worked his way through the ranks, adopted French citizenship, and fought against the Germans in 1940. At the end of that year he became one of the six regional commissioners, under General de la Porte du Theil, of the Vichy youth movement: Chantiers de la Jeunesse (Youth Workshops), a group not unlike the American Civilian Conservation Corps of the 1930s. Recruits in the Chantiers wore a smart, distinctive uniform—baggy trousers, blue-green beret, short jacket—and, while unarmed, occupied themselves with exercise, service projects, and military-type training. With his patriotic enthusiasm, Van Hecke viewed the five North African groups—one in Morocco, three in Algeria, and one in Tunisia—as constituting shock troops which, if provided with weapons, could augment the regular army. Van Hecke's optimism, however, overestimated his organization's value: some of the leadership was mediocre and the rank and file so heterogeneous that no serious reliance could be placed on the shock battalions. Van Hecke, however, possessed ideal qualifications for organizing a clandestine movement: he controlled transport and gasoline, had authorization to travel, and developed contacts with the military and civilian leadership. But this enthusiasm was not counterweighed with that circumspection necessary for underground conspiracy, and he had several close calls with security officers.

Through the Oran resistance group, Van Hecke met Commissioner Achiary, who made it possible for him to reach Robert Murphy and Lemaigre Dubreuil. By the end of 1941 these Frenchmen were meeting irregularly, sometimes with Murphy and his vice-consuls, at various places in Algiers. To the Algiers group was later added Henri d'Astier de la Vigerie, whom Van Hecke had met in Oran and who impressed him as the person to organize his young men into a resistance shock group.

D'Astier was probably the most fascinating of all the personalities brought together in the underground movement. He had two brothers, Emmanuel, head of the resistance group Libération in France, and François, an air force general with de Gaulle in London. Henri d'Astier has been described as a character from the Italian Renaissance, a brilliant, persuasive charmer, fascinated with intrigue, at heart a royalist, who exercised an almost hypnotic influence on the young men he led.[22] He resigned from his position in Oran and came to Algiers as Van Hecke's assistant in the Chantiers.

By the end of 1941 one more insurgent had moved to Algiers. Lemaigre Dubreuil had been instrumental in attracting Jean Rigault. Editor of the newspaper *Le Jour*, which Lemaigre Dubreuil owned, Rigault brought to the group a first-rate mind and capacity for organization. Thin, rather saturnine in appearance, with a seeming frailty that belied an ability for hard work, he conjures up the vision of a French Harry Hopkins, the pragmatic administrator who pierces superficiality to grasp the essential core of a problem. According to Rigault, France needed to preserve the authoritarian structure it had achieved under Pétain but to divest itself of German control. He was least Gaullist of all the conspirators and he feared that de Gaulle in power would revive the parliamentary regime which, with socialist and communist political agitation, would bring France again to chaotic feebleness. If these qualities characterize fascism, Rigault was a fascist; but he had no sympathy with Hitler's New Order.

Although Murphy discussed the possibility of American assistance with many Frenchmen, it should be borne in mind that he was an official diplomatic representative of the United States government. His principal contacts, therefore, were administrators of the Vichy government—men like General Weygand, General Noguès, and the officials on their staffs. It was natural that he should have become well acquainted with members of Weygand's entourage, such as Saint-Hardouin and Admiral Fenard, secretary general of Weygand's administrative office, the Délégation Génerale. There was always the possibility that a "legitimate" resistance movement might take shape within the government itself.

Vichy, August–December 1941
The policies of Admiral Darlan[23]

Through Admiral Fenard, Murphy began to receive from time to time, beginning around October 1941, unofficial and veiled intimations that Admiral Darlan wished to keep in touch with the Americans. It is necessary to assess briefly what role Darlan played at Vichy and what he wanted from the United States.

Since Laval's dismissal in December 1940, Admiral Jean François Xavier Darlan had held the highest posts, under Marshal Pétain, in the Vichy government. He was not only deputy prime minister, but also commander in chief of all French armed forces—land, sea, and air. In this double vantage point of dominating both the civil and military administrations, he held the key position from which to swing France into collaboration or into resistance.

A man of great capability and vast personal ambition, Darlan played his political cards with so little fanfare and revealed his inner thoughts so rarely that the word "enigmatic" has frequently been applied to him. Basically Darlan and de Gaulle had much in common: both sought power and both delighted in the exercise of it. But their techniques of obtaining power and using it were 180° apart. De Gaulle believed that a leader should establish a principle, should adhere to it, and should determine his actions in accordance with this principle. Idealist that he was, like Joan of Arc, de Gaulle would achieve the summit or be overwhelmed in magnificent defeat. Darlan, on the other hand, was the pragmatist, the negotiator, the compromiser, taking an advantage here, surrendering one there, edging his way into authority, always protecting his flanks, always ensuring an avenue of retreat. He calculated his chances with precision and cynically observed the fluctuations of power in order to press his own career at the expense of others who were less discerning and less careful. Had he chosen politics instead of the navy he probably would have succeeded, like Laval, in surviving the erratic party alliances of the 1930s. That he had risen to top rank in the navy during this period reveals that in fact he *was* a politician—a superb one—and he operated successfully in the corridor-deal atmosphere of prewar France. Many who knew him disliked and distrusted him, but they acknowledged his abilities.

With his skill in maneuver Darlan brought a life-long Anglophobia. He enjoyed explaining that this attitude stemmed from his ancestors' defeat at Trafalgar, for which he had never forgiven the British. During the blitzkrieg in 1940, as he watched the French army collapse, Admiral Darlan stood by, as supreme commander of the French fleet, ready to block Axis penetration into the Mediterranean. He was not prepared, like de Gaulle, to violate the armistice by ordering the French navy to take independent action. He was deeply embittered, consequently, when the British fleet bombarded French units at Mers-el-Kebir to keep them, presumably, out of Axis hands. Darlan never intended to surrender his fleet, and the British action only intensified his distrust of anything emanating from London.

With his anti-British orientation, Darlan guarded no thoughts whatsoever of attempting to support Great Britain, in 1941, in its lonesome defiance of the Axis. Neither his background nor military bent would lead him to support a crusade for the democratic way of life. Darlan bore no great affection for Germans or Italians, but he recognized with complete dispassion that with neither Russia nor the United States throwing its potential influence into the conflict, Hitler controlled the military and political destinies of continental Europe. Eliminating all thoughts of further French resistance, Darlan faced two alternatives: remain in power and collaborate with the Axis or resign. For a man to whom power and authority had been the inspiriting urge throughout a lifetime, the thought of retirement at the peak of his career was simply unacceptable. Darlan chose to follow Marshal Pétain and to attempt, through collaboration, to preserve what little remained of French autonomy.

As the chief architect of Pétain's policy, Darlan exerted his utmost skill to convince the Axis of France's willingness to cooperate with the Nazi New Order. No attempt is made here to vindicate Admiral Darlan: he pursued exactly the same policies for which Laval, Pétain, and other Vichyites were later indicted and for which Laval was hanged. To the French resister Darlan became the epitome of collaboration and surrender: on posters one saw frequently the word *vendu* ("sold") scribbled across the admiral's face. He courted favor in Nazi circles and attempted to fortify his own position by proposing that France offer Tunisian facilities to Rommel. It was this effort, incidentally, which Weygand vociferously opposed in May 1941 and, by opposing, revealed to Darlan how little control Vichy exerted over a quasi-independent North Africa nurtured by the United States. From then on Darlan maneuvered for Weygand's recall.[24]

The fact that Darlan collaborated does not prove that he was pro-Axis or fascist. He collaborated because he believed, from a coldly analytical assessment of power relationships, that, under the terms of the armistice, cooperation at that time served the best interests of France. But Darlan had no faith that a given structure would prevail indefinitely; if he had any political genius at all it was in the capacity to sense intuitively shifts in the direction and force of his opponent's power.

Such a shift occurred in June 1941, when Hitler attacked the Soviet Union. As it became evident, in July, that the German blitz might not succeed in Russia as it had in France, Darlan began to assess a changing set of possibilities. He always sought an alternative contingent plan, believing, as he once told his son, Alain, that "a leader must have given thought to any problem which might come up before it actually does come up."[25] Darlan could envisage the possibility that Germany, having penetrated deeply into Russia, would become vulnerable in the western Mediterranean. Then, if the United States should be brought into the war, the combined weight of America, Russia, and England might ultimately bring about Germany's collapse.

In July 1941, such thinking was extremely long-range: at that time the United States still held on to an uncertain neutrality. What Darlan feared more than anything was precipitous action. In his thinking, France had extracted three trump cards from the armistice: the southern part of France unoccupied, the French fleet at Toulon, and a virtually independent North Africa. France could not resist an Axis decision to seize any of these assets, and Darlan's policy attempted to placate Germany so that Hitler would hold meticulously to the armistice terms. Darlan was furious at Weygand because he feared that inept and premature dealings with the Americans would produce a German occupation of North Africa. Having good intelligence of what Murphy and Weygand were discussing, Darlan wanted to make sure that he controlled all contacts with the United States. He made this clear to Ambassador Leahy on 1 August 1941, when he told him: "When you have 3,000 tanks, 6,000 planes and 500,000 men to bring to Marseilles, let me know. Then we shall welcome you."[26]

Darlan did not intend this statement as sarcastic or humorous; he meant it very much in earnest and he repeated it many times to American representatives. The statement did not suggest that Darlan was ready to conspire with the United States; it simply conveyed a plea that if Washington had in mind the long-range interests of France it would not do anything so stupid that North Africa and southern France would be occupied or the fleet would be jeopardized.

As Germany became further immersed in Russia, Darlan continued to make overtures to the United States. Through his friend Admiral Fenard, he reached out in October to Robert Murphy in Algiers, intimating to the American diplomat that he was changing his views and interested in exploring new possibilities. A month later, through the American Embassy, he even ventured a suggestion to President Roosevelt that he might become a useful intermediary.[27]

It was during this period, in the fall of 1941, while American relations with Japan rapidly deteriorated, that Darlan redoubled his efforts to remove his rival, General Weygand, from North Africa. Maneuvering adroitly with the Germans and exerting masterful pressure on Marshal Pétain, in November Darlan succeeded in getting Weygand recalled. With unswerving loyalty to the marshal, Weygand accepted the decision and went into retirement. Thereafter no single individual possessed authority for the whole of North Africa. The Algiers office of the Délégation Générale remained open, but without Weygand it retained, under the supervision of the secretary general, Admiral Fenard, only minor administrative responsibilities. Darlan had succeeded in eliminating a rival, but he kept in the office a close personal friend.

Weygand's recall forced Murphy and the United States to reconsider the entire North African policy. If, as Murphy could not help but suspect, American leaks and carelessness had rendered Weygand vulnerable, a comparable approach by United States representatives to other French officials might also produce effects counter to those expected. A vulnerable and harrassed Pétain might authorize greater restrictions on North Africa, and his government could well purge its administrative staffs of everyone who showed the least sympathy for the Americans. Murphy believed that increased Axis infiltration into North Africa was inevitable unless the United States could formulate a new, forceful Mediterranean policy. He opposed cancellation of the economic-aid program, which Washington had suspended when Weygand left, and agreed with Ambassador Leahy that both he and the ambassador should be recalled for consultation.[28]

At this juncture everything changed. On 7 December, the Japanese bombed Pearl Harbor and the United States entered the war. Roosevelt and Churchill were now allied in a common venture and would inevitably have to formulate a joint policy regarding Europe and the Mediterranean.

2

After Pearl Harbor
The Rise and Fall of GYMNAST

London, December 1941
Prime Minister Churchill's reaction to Pearl Harbor[1]

The bombs dropping on Pearl Harbor conjured up before Winston Churchill's eyes a vast and enthralling vista. He intuitively knew then that the war was won. Inevitably Germany and Italy would declare war on the United States, and in the protracted severe fighting which must follow, the unlimited resources of America would finally grind the Axis to defeat. But, knowing precisely where he most wanted American assistance, Churchill did not wish to give the Americans time to formulate their own plans before they had given their full attention to the British appreciation of strategy. In spite of earlier understandings, the Americans might fix all their energies against Japan. Britain, too, had its stake in the Far East—the *Prince of Wales* and the *Repulse* had been sunk only hours after Pearl Harbor—but the British needed reinforcements preeminently in the Mediterranean, an area which the American Joint Chiefs of Staff might too casually repudiate as not involving America's most vital interests.

In Churchill's strategic architecture, Egypt, the Suez Canal, and Syria, together with Gibraltar and Malta, all filled key positions because if they were lost not only did the sea lane to India and the Far East become vulnerable but a crucial gap would remain in the great geographical ring he hoped to loop around Axis-held Europe.

Incapable of attacking the Axis directly, Great Britain had to dominate the perimeter of that great circle which swung across the Arctic, continued down the coast of Norway, the English Channel, and the Iberian Peninsula, extended across North Africa through the Middle East, finally joined up through Iran with the immense Russian front that sprawled from the Black Sea to Finland. Along the arc of this gigantic ring were many vulnerable sectors. The Russian defenses might be penetrated, or Spain might serve as a highway that would guide German panzers into Morocco. But the greatest threat, as seen in London, resided in the possibility that the German Afrika Korps, commanded by the unpredictable and daring General Erwin Rommel, might break into Egypt, open the ring, and become master of the entire Middle East.

At the moment of Pearl Harbor, British spirits were buoyed up by the prospect of Rommel's imminent defeat. On 18 November, the British Eighth Army had launched a counterattack against Rommel. Just three days after Japan bombed Hawaii, the Afrika Korps withdrew from the Tobruk area, closely pursued by the British. If the momentum of the offensive could be maintained it might just be possible to occupy all of Libya and to force Rommel back to Tunisia.

In the event of a German defeat, some critical questions would arise: would Tunisia, still loyal to the French government at Vichy, provide asylum for Axis troops? Would the French army in Tunisia turn against the Germans and Italians and defend the area against them? In this case, could British forces land in Tunisia and strike at Rommel's rear in alliance with the French? Would the Americans help?

If these questions found no easy and rapid answer, it was because the key to their solution lay in Washington. Washington maintained diplomatic relations with Vichy; London did not. Perhaps Ambassador Leahy could force, persuade, or cajole the venerable Pétain into permitting—even inviting—Allied forces to enter Tunisia and other parts of North Africa. Perhaps the United States would be willing to send some divisions into Morocco, a move which would pin down an Axis advance through Spain or Portugal. Churchill suspected that President Roosevelt, who for months had been receiving special, personal reports from North Africa, might turn out to be very sympathetic to some proposal regarding Morocco, Algeria, or Tunisia.

Washington, December 1941–January 1942
The First Washington Conference[2]

It was surely no surprise to President Roosevelt when, minutes after the news of Pearl Harbor became public, he received a phone call from Churchill. He may have been somewhat taken aback, however, when two days later he had to face up to the prime minister's insistent proposal for a full-scale Anglo-American conference. The president confronted an almost insurmountable number of decisions and might have preferred a short delay; but Churchill tenaciously labored his point. On 11 December, the president gave in, graciously invited the prime minister to stay at the White House, and spread the word among his advisers to prepare themselves for a probing reappraisal of grand strategy.

Within three days of Roosevelt's invitation, Churchill had embarked aboard the *Duke of York* with a small staff. While on board ship, the prime minister drew up four remarkable surveys of the war situation, including a projection of what might transpire in 1943. These studies, weighing factors in the Atlantic, in the Pacific, on the Russian front, and in conquered areas, spanned the entire spectrum of the global struggle. Churchill anticipated that by 1943 the United States and Great Britain would have recovered naval superiority in the Pacific; that the British Isles would remain intact; and that "the whole West and North African shores from Dakar to the Suez Canal, and the Levant to the Turkish frontier would be in Anglo-American hands."[3]

His proposals concerning the last of these goals are particularly instructive, and worth studying, because they establish a basic plan from which the prime minister, although hard-pressed in argument by the American chiefs of staff, never deviated. He wrote, on 16 December 1941 (Churchill's italics):

> *We ought ... to try hard to win over French North Africa, and now is the moment to use every inducement and form of pressure at our disposal upon the Government of Vichy and the French authorities in North Africa.* . . . Now is the time to offer to Vichy and to French North Africa a blessing or cursing. A blessing will consist in a promise by the United States and Great Britain to re-establish France as a Great Power with her territories undiminished. It should carry with it an offer of active aid by British and United States expeditionary forces, both

from the Atlantic seaboard of Morocco and at convenient landing-points in Algeria and Tunis, as well as from General Auchinleck's forces advancing from the east. Ample supplies for the French and the loyal Moors should be made available. Vichy should be asked to send their fleet from Toulon to Oran and Bizerta and to bring France into the war again as a principal. . . .

. . . We hold ready in Britain (Operation "Gymnast") about fifty-five thousand men, comprising two divisions and an armoured unit, together with the shipping. These forces could enter French North Africa by invitation on the twenty-third day after the order to embark them was given. Leading elements and air forces from Malta could reach Bizerta at very short notice. *It is desired that the United States should at the same time promise to bring in, via Casablanca and other African ports, not less than one hundred fifty thousand men during the next six months.* It is essential that some American elements, say twenty-five thousand men, should go at the earliest moment after French agreement, either Vichy or North African, had been obtained.

. . . .

A campaign must be fought in 1942 *to gain possession of, or conquer, the whole of the North African shore including the Atlantic ports of Morocco. . . . Plans should be set on foot forthwith.*[4]

The prime minister had good reason to place heavy emphasis on Vichy and North Africa. He knew perfectly well that ever since the French disintegration in 1940, the French possessions in Africa had held for President Roosevelt a special charm. Churchill could sense, with that incredible intuition of his, that the correct line with the president should be North Africa, and again North Africa, and again and again North Africa.[5]

When the prime minister reached the United States, he lost no time in getting down to work. He was flown with members of his party from Hampton Roads directly to Washington; and in a matter of minutes, during the evening of December 22, he was in conference with President Roosevelt. At his side were Lords Halifax and Beaverbrook, while with the president the participants included Secretary of State Cordell Hull, Harry Hopkins, and Sumner Welles.

Most of the talk related to North Africa. Roosevelt had become increasingly excited about prospects there, and in spite of the pressing needs of the Pacific he entertained the hope that the United

States could do something quickly to reinforce the British campaign in Libya. Churchill sensed the president's wish to pull benefits out of the American recognition of Pétain and skillfully encouraged Roosevelt to commit himself to action. The two chiefs wondered whether some advantages could still be salvaged from America's longtime patience with Vichy. They agreed that another appeal to General Weygand might induce the disspirited general to emerge from retirement and lead a North African resistance.

But while Weygand's support would provide enormous advantages, the Anglo-American planners could not count on it. They had to be prepared with alternate plans and first of all had to assess whether possession of the Mediterranean littoral from Morocco to Egypt was so vital to western interests that it must be occupied at all cost. To Churchill, and to most British planners, there was no question: what England had been bleeding and struggling for, what the embattled garrison on Malta was tenaciously suffering for, was to hold that traditional life line to the east. And President Roosevelt, unlike his military advisers, sympathized with this position. He therefore agreed, two weeks after Pearl Harbor, that planning should be started, whether or not Weygand cooperated, for occupying North Africa.

A measure of the earnestness with which Roosevelt and Churchill took the North African venture was their immediate action, next morning, to get a message off to Weygand. They agreed that a rather formal New Year's greeting should go to both Pétain and Weygand, but that a personal appeal should be delivered, orally, to Weygand by an American official. This would prove to be a vain hope. When the message was delivered, in January 1942, Weygand told the emissary that under no circumstances would he lead a dissident movement in North Africa.[6]

Meanwhile in Washington, British and American planners debated the prospects of an early move into North Africa. Churchill at first steadfastly argued that the GYMNAST operation, now with American cooperation called SUPER-GYMNAST, was feasible; but after two weeks of discussion he had to admit that failure to break the Afrika Korps made the prospects more formidable than they had appeared earlier in December. By 14 January 1942, when the prime minister left Washington, GYMNAST had not been given a clear approval. Both British and American staffs were to develop con-

31

tingent plans, but neither really saw a prospect of moving into the Mediterranean before March.

The policy regarding North Africa thus remained tenuous and confusing during January and February. Clearly Roosevelt and Churchill favored some sort of action there, but the military staffs, who began to examine the problems in detail, could not develop much enthusiasm. General Marshall, backed by Secretary of War Stimson, consistently stood against peripheral ventures and argued that the main American effort should be directed at Berlin. Thus, although the Joint Planning Staff, now directed by Gen. Dwight D. Eisenhower, began to work on GYMNAST, it first nevertheless had to formulate a more immediate scheme to build up American forces in Great Britain. Once these men were transported and trained, a decision could be made on their deployment. But to move them into the Mediterranean when France lay only a few miles across the channel seemed to the American officers wasteful and pointless.

Washington and Lisbon, January–April 1942
The Office of the Coordinator of War Information[7]

If the Joint Chiefs of Staff had to function without a clear-cut directive, it was even more difficult for other agencies to pursue logical and cooperating policies. One Washington agency, created in July 1941 and heavily involved in the North African problem, labored especially under the handicap of inadequate direction. This was the Office of the Coordinator of Information (COI), the predecessor of OSS, directed by Col. William J. Donovan. "Wild Bill" Donovan, a personal friend of President Roosevelt's, was a man of enormous energies, with wide-ranging interests, ready to leap into untried but exciting experiments. In 1941 he was tapping his circle of friends to form the nucleus of what would become OSS, the Office of Strategic Services. It was only reasonable that Donovan would want to set up a section to probe North Africa and to touch possibilities forbidden to regular diplomats and military attachés.

Donovan especially wanted to organize within COI a "special operations" section, patterned on the model of the British SOE—Special Operations Executive. SOE devoted itself not to information-gathering (except perhaps as a by-product) but to sabotage and to support of guerrilla armies. What Donovan needed was a structure, operating parallel to the information and intelligence sections, which would concentrate on subversion and clandestine military interventions. United States agents had little experience at this time in "black" espionage but were learning rapidly from the British who, confronted with desperate need since 1940, had developed skills and weapons especially suited for resistance groups.

Donovan was making plans for special operations activities in Spain and North Africa just at the time, in the fall of 1941, that Lt. Col. Robert Solborg, having completed his observations in Africa for Military Intelligence, returned to Washington. Donovan believed that Solborg, after a short period of schooling in England, would be the ideal person to organize undercover activities for COI in the Iberian Peninsula and North Africa. Solborg's task would be to establish headquarters in Lisbon while Lt. Col. William Eddy would set up a subsidiary office, concentrating on North Africa, in Tangier. Eddy, a Marine Corps officer in World War I, expert in Arab studies, sometime professor at Dartmouth College and president of Hobart, had volunteered for military service at the war's outbreak and had been serving as attaché at Cairo. Both Solborg and Eddy would serve ostensibly as assistant military attachés, but in reality would recruit agents and organize clandestine communications networks.

Inevitably there would be some conflict of jurisdiction between Solborg, working for COI, which was attached to the Joint Chiefs of Staff, and Murphy, operating with his vice-consuls for the State Department. But theoretically there was none. Murphy was a legal diplomatic representative (as were the vice-consuls) and his function was to provide information and intelligence. Solborg and Eddy were agents who normally would not enter French territory and who would organize networks not for intelligence but for sabotage and for clandestine military action. No matter how involved Murphy might become with resistance leaders, he had no capability for bringing them equipment and arms. Even money for subversive operations remained a responsibility of COI, although it is true that the consulates did become somewhat involved in financial transactions. (Murphy also ultimately brought in several radio transmitters through the diplomatic pouch; but he did this at personal risk and only because OSS failed to provide what it promised.)

Actually Murphy would have been only too pleased to find the military side of his negotiations handled by a competent army officer. He pleaded for a military expert to be sent, but Washington never saw its way clear to assign one.[8] As a result, Colonel Eddy and Colonel Solborg, both of them World War I reservists unskilled in modern military techniques, had forced upon them military responsibilities for which they were ill equipped.

Algiers, December 1941–February 1942
Murphy and the North African French

If the United States's entry into the war brought new enthusiasm to Churchill, it also inspired the North African resisters to increase their efforts. Murphy could anticipate a new freedom to express anti-German sentiments although he could not, at such a distance from Washington, know with any precision what direction Allied grand strategy was taking. On 9 January, he wrote personally to James Dunn in the State Department. Without identifying them specifically, he referred to groups of officers in Morocco and Oran, to Colonel Van Hecke's Chantiers de la Jeunesse, and to Lemaigre Dubreuil, who wanted from American representatives some indication whether the United States government would approve "a plan of independent French North African action, in principle." Murphy went on to express his need for guidance:

> Now, frankly, I am at sea, but I have the feeling that under the changed conditions we should not ignore and discourage responsible elements who are actuated by a desire to resume hostilities. That desire, of course, always revolves around the question of American military support, that is, material, munitions, and technicians. As matters now stand, I simply tell these people what the President has said in his public declarations of our desire to aid all those who offer resistance to Axis aggression. I should be very grateful if you would tell me that is as far as I can go or whether our policy now may contemplate more specific intervention.[9]

Murphy was in the process of forwarding rather detailed proposals which the principal French group, including Lamaigre Dubreuil, his former editor Jean Rigault, and Colonel Jousse, had furnished him. Basically, the group had urged that the United States cooperate with them, if Vichy did not turn against the Axis, in declaring North Africa an independent political entity. They reasoned that if Washington could provide them with arms, together with three divisions, they could then neutralize whatever Vichy and Axis measures developed and turn over at least Morocco and Algeria to the Allies as a base for operations against the Axis.[10]

For the conspirators, American entry into the war had opened enormous possibilities, but these were almost completely negated by Weygand's departure and noncommittal attitude. With Weygand absent, North Africa had become fragmented into its component parts. There was no individual who exercised command over all the armed forces, land, sea, and air, or whose authority overrode that of the governor generals in Morocco and Tunisia. Nor had the underground group found any widespread resistance sentiment among the Armistice Army officers, most of whom apathetically carried out their duties, posting photographs of Pétain in their quarters, content that the marshal should make the decisions. With the possible exception of General Emile Béthouart in Morocco, no French officer above colonel rank, and very few below, hinted at anti-German and anti-Vichy sentiments.

In early 1942 the resistance groups became stronger and more active. By this time Lemaigre Dubreuil had been instrumental in bringing Jean Rigault to Algiers, and Van Hecke had recruited young Lt. Henri d'Astier into the Chantiers de la Jeunesse, with a transfer to Algiers from Oran. Toward the end of January 1942, these four, together with the diplomat Tarbé de Saint-Hardouin, affiliated themselves into a group which thereafter came to be known simply as "The Five." They agreed to work together in extending contacts throughout the civilian and military population, in organizing resistance cells, and in maintaining relations with the Allies. Although no member of the group was a regular army officer, they kept in close touch with military circles through Colonel Jousse, who served on the staff of General Alphonse Juin, commander of North African ground and air forces. Colonel Van Hecke, with his quasi-military position as head of the Chantiers, regularly conferred with officers in Morocco, Algeria, and Tunisia.

The Five agreed to elect no leader and to make their decisions unanimous. One of The Five's functions, indeed, was to locate a leader, someone with the authority, rank, or prestige which General Weygand had possessed. It did not seem possible that anyone then in North Africa could emerge as such a figure. Lemaigre Dubreuil would not do; he had political ambitions but insufficient prestige; and he recognized the fact that he would have to ride the coattails of someone else. Van Hecke, with command over 10,000 regulars and 10,000 veterans of the Chantiers, considered himself the most powerful of the conspirators, but in spite of his energy and authority, he lacked the qualities of leadership which could enable him to carry off the enterprise.[11]

So the search went on. The conspirators made plans and recruited volunteers, hoping that the Allies would help them and that they would find someone whom the Allies would support. Robert Murphy meanwhile could do nothing except to plead to Washington for shipments under the economic agreement and to make note of such plans as came to his attention. It did not surprise him that his contacts included all shades of political opinion; as a diplomat he was required to assess conditions as he found them, and he reported the overtures of Admiral Darlan in Vichy with the same impartiality that he reported those of The Five.

Vichy and Algiers, January–April 1942
Murphy and the Vichy French

When Germany declared war on the United States, the Vichy government had to reappraise its position and decide whether or not to sever diplomatic relations with Washington. For Admiral Darlan, there was no question about the line he would take. He could see no immediate Anglo-American victory; therefore, he would continue to collaborate with Germany. But with America in the war, the ultimate chances of German defeat increased; consequently he wanted at all costs to preserve his lines of communication with the United States.

In February 1942, on the occasion of a visit by Admiral Fenard to Vichy, Darlan authorized his friend to continue his congenial relations with Murphy. At the same time he asked his son, Alain, to meet Murphy. Alain was a naval officer on active duty whose cover as an insurance agent enabled him to travel back and forth between France and North Africa. Fenard arranged a meeting at a dinner party in Algiers soon afterward.[12]

During the spring of 1942 Darlan's position in relation to Germany gradually changed. With their failure in Russia, the Germans had to tighten their organization, intensify their economic controls, and exploit sources of labor throughout Nazi-held Europe. They increased their pressures on Vichy to a point where Darlan found himself unable to meet their demands. By April it was clear that if Darlan could not provide labor and goods, an opportunity was being created for Pierre Laval to reemerge as the instrument of all-out collaboration. Faced with possible eclipse and fearful of his waning influence, Darlan more than ever was anxious to keep open his avenues to Murphy.

At a dinner with Murphy on 11 April, Admiral Fenard and Alain Darlan tried to convince the American that Darlan wanted to open up conversations with the Allies regarding a secret resistance plan in southern France. Darlan would go further, they reported, but he was afraid that secret conversations would leak out to the Axis. Darlan knew full well that the Germans had learned of Murphy's conversations with Weygand; he did not wish to risk similar exposure.

A week later Laval succeeded in his bid for a comeback; he eliminated Darlan from the cabinet and replaced him as deputy prime minister.[13] A new crisis developed in French-American relations: the Murphy-Weygand Agreement was abrogated and Admiral Leahy was recalled. There was serious discussion in Washington whether relations should not be broken completely with Vichy, even though this would mean closing all the consulates in North Africa and ending the contacts Murphy and his vice-consuls had laboriously built up.

The reinstatement of Laval might have ended Darlan's career if Pétain had not insisted on retaining the admiral as commander of all military forces. Thus, although his civil power had been curtailed, Darlan could still exercise absolute authority over the navy, army, and air force. Darlan wanted to make sure that this fact was not lost on the Americans. By way of his son and Admiral Fenard, he informed Murphy that "the Laval Government is a temporary affair" and that "the power still lies with Pétain and Darlan."[14] This intelligence was forwarded meticulously by Murphy to Washington, but it did not stimulate any enthusiastic response. North Africa had lost, temporarily, its appeal to the military strategists.

Algiers, March–April 1942
The dilemma of Robert Murphy

Murphy was later criticized for his support of collaborationists such as Darlan and "fascists" such as Lemaigre Dubreuil and Rigault. The fault did not lie entirely with Robert Murphy, who had to deal with what anti-German elements he could find in North Africa, either among civilians or among the military. Clearly, Murphy would have avoided either group if he had been so instructed; certainly he would have ferreted out Gaullists—or cold-shouldered them completely—if Washington had told him to. But he had no precise instructions, much as he pleaded for them, and he was left no choice but to keep in touch with whatever bona-fide resistance movement he could identify.[15] This he did. But in 1942, with Weygand removed from the African scene, he could not report to Washington that any important official French administrator had revealed himself as clearly anti-German. In retrospect, however, one might charge Murphy with dereliction in not attempting more energetically to approach Gen. Alphonse Juin, commander of all North African land and air forces.

General Juin would play an important part in the invasion; and afterward, cooperating with Mark Clark in the Italian campaign, he would so distinguish himself as to be ultimately rewarded with a marshal's baton.[16] But in 1942 he was not well known to the Americans, and, because he had been captured by the Germans, he labored under a handicap: no one could be certain he would fight against an enemy which had voluntarily liberated him. Furthermore, it was well known that he had conferred with Goering in December 1941. Nevertheless, Juin in reality was a tough, staunch patriot, a man of great integrity and spirit; that Robert Murphy had not been able to confer with him secretly would turn out to have been a political error of the first magnitude. Certainly Murphy later blamed himself for just this oversight, but in the context of 1942 a Murphy friendship could have been a kiss of political death. No one knew exactly at the time why Weygand had been recalled, but there were plenty of guesses in North Africa that his dealings with Murphy had evoked German counterpressures on Vichy. We know now, of course, that Murphy's code had been broken and that Nazi authorities were aware that military talks had taken place between the American diplomat and the French proconsul. Murphy had every reason to believe that he had gone too far, and he was loathe to embarrass Juin and Noguès in the same way. He was somewhat like the ardent suitor who looks for hints from his beloved as to just how far he may go.

The question has often been raised, why did not Murphy conspire with the Free French? He himself frequently explained that there were few Gaullists in North Africa. This is correct. There were Gaullist representatives in Algiers, like Professor René Capitant, but they were more interested at that time in propagandizing for de Gaulle than in conspiring. In any case, Murphy was acquainted with Capitant and the group of university students who aligned themselves with him.

It should be emphasized that there were two kinds of Gaullists: first, those who had specifically affiliated with the Free French, and second, those who supported de Gaulle's symbolic leadership and who would back him against Vichy when the time came. Many civilians were Gaullists of the second type, and one could even argue that in a sense The Five was more Gaullist than not. Tarbé de Saint-Hardouin had resigned his position under the Vichy administration and certainly sympathized with de Gaulle; Henri d'Astier, while a royalist, was considered a Gaullist and kept in touch with the London headquarters through his brother, an air force general with the Free French; Van Hecke admitted his intention of supporting de Gaulle and of bringing his youth group with him. Most of the young men, the 300 or 400 hard-core resisters led by Henri d'Astier, were Gaullists in the second sense. If the Allies had brought de Gaulle, not Giraud, in their train, Murphy could have lined up a certain amount of enthusiasm and support among the young men but not among officials and military personnel.[17]

Among The Five neither Lemaigre Dubreuil nor Rigault accepted Gaullism, nor could they have compromised with any sort of Free French administration. These two thought—more than the others—in political terms, and they deplored communist and socialist tendencies which they saw in the Gaullist movement. Lemaigre Dubreuil was a patriot and he detested the German infiltration; but all his life he had fought for exactly what Pétain represented: law and order, discipline, business-like methods in industry and government. For him the ideal resistance would be directed and authorized "legally," by Pétain, Laval, and Weygand. He undoubtedly saw himself, with Allied victory, as a figure in whatever government emerged. Rigault did not seek publicity and would have been content to influence events from behind the scenes. His *nom de guerre*, "Friday" (to Lemaigre Dubreuil's "Crusoe") belied his character and capacities: he was more "Grey Eminence" than servant, and acute differences sometimes developed between him and Lemaigre Dubreuil.

But they both fervently opposed tendencies toward the Left, and they used what influence they had to prevent Gaullist encroachments.

Even though there may have been some pro-Gaullist sentiments in North Africa, it would in any case have been impossible to foment or develop a Gaullist slant to the North African enterprise. The reasons, which had little to do with Robert Murphy or his personal inclination, were basically two: the Washington decision to maintain relations with Vichy and the presence of over 100,000 French troops in North Africa.

To help understand the situation, let us hypothesize a case in which the United States had broken relations with Vichy. In that event the consulates in West Africa, Morocco, Algeria, and Tunisia would have closed, and the nearest American officials would have been located in Tangier, Gibraltar, and Lisbon. Even as British Intelligence and SOE retained contacts with dissident elements, so Colonel Donovan's COI, and Army Intelligence, would have clandestinely but with difficulty kept in touch with anti-German elements, probably with The Five who, in fact, at one time planned to shift from the Americans to SOE. The French underground would have continued its training and preparations and, once the landings began, would have cooperated with the Allies. The French Vichy forces would have resisted.

The only significant difference, then, was the physical presence of Robert Murphy and the vice-consuls. To be sure, the vice-consuls produced a high order of intelligence, especially on army strengths and battery locations; but this was also duplicated partially through information sent to London by other means. Did the fact that Murphy resided in Algiers make an outstanding difference? Because of his rank and position as the president's personal representative, Murphy could indeed attract exchanges at the highest levels and could make it seem worthwhile for eminent Frenchmen, such as Darlan and Pétain, to keep in touch with the Americans. If relations had been broken, this would not have been possible.

American recognition and the continued presence of Murphy in North Africa had little effect on the 120,000-man Armistice Army. Vichy—that is, Pétain, Laval, and Darlan—maintained standing orders that the North African forces should fire on anyone whatsoever who tried to invade French territory. This order was unaffected by American recognition or nonrecognition, and at no time did Pétain issue secret instructions moderating its applicability to the Allies. A handful of French officers and men did, to be sure, cooperate with the Americans during the night of November 8; but this cooperation would probably have been forthcoming whether or not American consulates continued to function.

The question raised here is not whether contacts with resistance elements were desirable—clearly they were—but whether it was necessary to recognize Vichy in order to have such contacts. The White House obviously believed that it was and, even after Pearl Harbor, saw advantages in continued recognition of the Pétain regime. Once the United States entered the war, such recognition brought no clearcut advantages. The arguments given—that it provided intelligence, that it bolstered French morale, that it kept the French fleet intact at Toulon, that it blocked economic disaster from North Africa, that it permitted espionage in Morocco and Algeria—can all be questioned. The intelligence out of Vichy was rendered dubious by German plants and rumors fed into the American Embassy; United States support of Vichy, while it may have boosted morale among some Frenchmen, depressed others, especially those who admired de Gaulle; Darlan had sworn that the Germans would never take the fleet intact and there is no incontrovertable evidence that American recognition either helped or hindered him in this resolve; United States economic aid to North Africa was slight and nullified in any case by the British blockade and by incredible obstacles amassed by the American Board of Economic Warfare; finally, the intelligence from North Africa, mostly of a high order, would have been obtained, although to a lesser extent, through other channels.[18]

Washington and London, March–April 1942
The demise of GYMNAST

The whole question whether American recognition helped or hindered in North Africa almost became academic in April 1942, when the Allied governments came close to placing their plans for GYMNAST back in the file drawers. For a short while, in January and February, North Africa had possessed a high priority. SUPER-GYMNAST was being explored; green lights shone in Washington and London; and Murphy had some reason to believe that he had been moving in the proper direction. Then quickly the proposal soured, poisoned by military defeats and naval disasters which reduced the availability of landing craft. Taking advantage of a chang-

41

ing situation, General Marshall pushed with all his energy for a change in grand strategy, for a frontal attack across the channel at the expense of peripheral end runs in Norway and Morocco. By March 1942, GYMNAST had died, and Murphy agonized over what he should do with the enthusiastic schemes which The Five were developing.[19]

Ironically enough, the resistance group had been working hard and had brought out a new and elaborate set of plans which matured early in March. They now saw that three Allied divisions would scarcely suffice: they called for seven motorized and five armored divisions—in other words, a full-scale amphibious operation. Murphy and Eddy (who was energetically trying to procure small arms and money for the insurgents) forwarded the new projects to Washington.[20] Somewhat querulously Murphy cabled Sumner Welles:

> May I respectfully urge that you give me a directive in this connection. Do you wish me to continue these conversations, or do you wish them dropped? Do you wish the conversations conducted by someone else? . . . You will probably advise me when practicable of your ideas regarding the political possibilities and what form, in your opinion, the future political set-up in this area should assume to facilitate the accomplishment of whatever policy you may determine. . . .
>
> The time has arrived, I believe for you to give me a directive. . . .[21]

In far away Algiers, neither Murphy nor his colleagues could guess how rapidly the strategic thinking in Washington and London had veered from North Africa to the English Channel. With GYMNAST buried, the chiefs of staff could only consider diversionary guerrilla actions in North Africa; all their attention was now concentrated on new code names: BOLERO—to build up forces in England; SLEDGEHAMMER—to hit the French coast in 1942; ROUNDUP—a major thrust cross-channel in 1943. So Murphy received no directive, and Eddy learned to his disappointment that the request for guerrilla-type weapons had been turned down. Yet such was the secrecy of high-level planning that Washington did not reveal, even to its own agents, the new direction of its plans. Eddy surmised that Washington did not trust him; Murphy wondered whether someone else—possibly Colonel Solborg, newly arrived in Lisbon—had been authorized to negotiate with the French. Solborg himself believed that the British, for reasons of their own, had sabotaged the American effort.

At this confused juncture, a new dimension was added to the North African picture. A distinguished general, Henri Honoré Giraud, ranking among the highest half-dozen French officers, escaped from imprisonment in Germany and began to make clandestine approaches, from a hideout near Lyons, to Allied agents and to members of the French underground.

3

The French

Lyons, April–June 1942
The activities of General Giraud[1]

On 17 April 1942, General Giraud escaped from the ancient fortress of Königstein, a castle which after the debacle of 1940 had been converted into a prison for French officers of general rank. Henri Giraud at that time was sixty-three; he had been a full general since 1934 and had been a member in 1940 of the fifteen-man Superior War Council. Of the army officers available for service in 1942, only a few, like General Noguès, outranked him. He was far senior to General de Gaulle and General Juin.

Giraud had once before escaped from the Germans, when he was a captain in the First World War. But most of his early military reputation was made in the Riff campaigns in North Africa, where in 1925 he fought against Abd-el Krim. By 1930 he had become a general, in large part responsible for pacifying the Moslem tribes in Algeria and Morocco, and had gained widespread notoriety as a daring, even reckless exponent of rapid action and offensive tactics. In 1936 he became commander of the Metz military region, which he organized in rigid, autocratic fashion, neither playing politics nor making conciliatory gestures toward the Popular Front government. At this period of his career, Charles de Gaulle, then colonel of an armored regiment, was under Giraud's orders.

Giraud had always been a man of action, a daring decisive soldier. Not a thinker, certainly not a politician, he had built his career on courage and risk, firm in the faith that good fortune, the Islamic baraka, would stand by the officer who vigorously pressed his advantage. Tall and muscular, with full mustache, he was the very model of the French soldier. One of his close collaborators later said of him: "Giraud was the sort of French general, from oak leaves to fine mustache, that is typical Hollywood. Thus the Americans couldn't help but accept him."[2]

When the Germans invaded France, Giraud had commanded the French Seventh Army, and later, very briefly the Ninth. With his almost arrogant self-confidence, Giraud had hoped to encircle the German thrust by a movement north through Belgium. But the swift enemy onslaught soon left Giraud giving orders to nonexistent divisions; he was surrounded and captured.

The defeat in no wise lessened Giraud's rather pretentious trust in his own capacities. He still had faith in his baraka. He assured himself that the Germans were overestimated, that with better leadership the French could still outfight them, and that it was not too late to redeem French honor. Isolated from France and world events for two years, he was oblivious to the defeatism and double-faced machinations of Vichy. He worked, therefore, with unextinguishable perseverance, aided by his wife and a devoted band of conspirators on the outside, to escape from Königstein, hopeful that once free he could rally military forces in some way against the Axis.

The group of conspirators who formulated the escape plan were not motivated purely out of personal friendship for Giraud. What they sought was a legitimate military resistance movement, operating underground on French soil, that would appeal to the thousands of patriotic Frenchmen who could give their wholehearted allegiance neither to Pétain nor to de Gaulle. Most French officers could not accept de Gaulle: he was too junior in rank, too closely involved with the British. So long as General Weygand remained in Algiers many officers saw the possibility of his leadership in a strategic uprising to be coordinated with some future anti-German operation, presumably when the United States had entered the war. But after Weygand had been forced into retirement, they knew no French officer with the will, the prestige, and the rank around whom to build a non-Gaullist military resistance.

Once Giraud reached unoccupied France he soon became something more than simply a general who had escaped. With his seniority he would be entitled to a position near the top of the army hierarchy—he had been promoted to general, for example, four years earlier than the current Vichy chief of staff. Because of his daredevil escape, Giraud enchanted Frenchmen everywhere who sought guiltily for some French manifestation of strength and verve to counter the shabby humiliation of Vichy. Here was a possible leader—anti-German credentials unimpeachable, not tainted by Vichy collaboration or by an oath to Pétain, not embroiled in politics or indebted to the British like de Gaulle. Pure French, pure bravado, pure defiance.

Nor was he, nor could he possibly be, simply an individual. Those who had engineered his escape from the outside—General Baurès, General Chambe, and Colonel de Linarès— formed an unofficial staff which already had established contacts in many directions. And Giraud brought with him his own plans, based on his imperfect calculations of German weakness, his misguided conception of what French élan could do, his instinctive enthusiasm for surprise and attack, and a surprisingly ingenuous approach to logistics.

For many reasons, Giraud was the man of the hour. His escape could serve as a symbol of French resistance and this symbol possessed enormous value. Germany had to destroy it, and Laval, if he were to remain in power, had to be the instrument of that destruction. Great Britain wanted to exploit it, even at the expense of duplicating the Gaullist symbol already in London. De Gaulle would also welcome it if it could be subordinated to himself.[3] And the United States greeted this new expression of resistance as a possible replacement of Weygand.

The Germans confronted an embarrassing problem. Hitler had expressed himself forcefully to his entourage on the same day that Giraud crossed the Swiss frontier into France.

"We must do everything possible," argued the führer, "to recapture this man. As far as I know, he is a General of great ability and energy, who might well join the opposition forces of de Gaulle and even take command of them."[4]

Hitler ordered that Giraud was to be returned to Germany. For several days diplomatic leverage was applied to Vichy. Pétain, secretly admiring Giraud's exploit, tried to keep aloof; and he left the brunt of convincing Giraud to Laval and Darlan. Laval was furious. He was getting off to a bad start. He had been in office only two weeks and the Germans had already been pressuring him for labor battalions. How could he persuade them that France was firmly behind Hitler's crusade against bolshevism when this lummox, this caricature of a 1914-type French general, kept spouting about French honor and military glory. The practical, shifty, Auvergnese peasant that was Pierre Laval spit in disgust.[5] Darlan said very little. He let Laval do the grumbling, not at all unhappy at the prime minister's discomfiture and perhaps secretly admiring Giraud's audacity.

Failing to cajole Giraud back to Germany, Laval shifted to another tactic. If Giraud placed so much weight on an officer's word of honor, he would see if Giraud would at least pledge himself to neutrality. He drafted a letter for Giraud's signature:

> May 4, 1942
>
> Monsieur le Maréchal:
>
> Following your recent instructions, and to eliminate any ambiguity as to my attitude, I undertake to express to you my feelings of complete loyalty.
>
> You have indeed explained to me, and the Prime Minister has also, the policy which you intend to follow *vis-à-vis* Germany.
>
> I am fully in agreement with you. I give you my word as an officer that I will do nothing which might in any way whatsoever disturb your relations with the German Government, or hamper the work which you have charged Admiral Darlan and Prime Minister Pierre Laval to accomplish under your high authority.[6]

With his customary swagger, and without seriously considering its implications, Giraud copied out the letter in his own hand, added the phrase: "My past is guarantee of my loyalty," and signed it.[7] He did not bother to keep a copy.

This testimonial would bring Giraud considerable grief, but it was characteristic of the man that he could walk so blindly into a trap without sensing its dangers. Most likely the general considered only the French and personal aspects of his communication: that it was only a letter, not an oath; that it involved purely his own interpretation of what Pétain's policy was, which he undoubtedly took as basically resisting, not collaborating, with Germany. Giraud later would argue that when Laval publicly stated, on 22 June 1942, "I desire the victory of Germany," the prime minister's shocking policy statement automatically released him from whatever obligations his letter entailed.[8] Clearly General Giraud could not anticipate the propaganda effect which Gaullist publicists would ultimately squeeze out of this unfortunate letter, so impetuously and heedlessly signed.

Residing for the moment near Lyons, not far from Vichy, Giraud soon received feelers from the British, from the French underground, and from the Americans.

First, however, Giraud tried to exert what influence he could on a purely French, military resistance. At Königstein he had worked out plans which involved establishing a secure perimeter in southern France. If the Armistice Army could keep this toehold, and if Hitler became fearfully entangled in Russia during the winter of 1942-43, and if the Anglo-Americans could coordinate a landing on France's Mediterranean coast, it might be possible to press northward against the Axis and push into the German heartland. Giraud's plan has been frequently maligned as completely unrealistic, but the French general must be given credit where he deserves it: he wanted to hit the Germans directly in France, which is exactly what Marshall and Eisenhower wanted to do; and he gauged such an attack as feasible only in 1943, which coincided with the views of most American and British planners. Giraud did not wish to be deployed in a North African adventure any more than Eisenhower did. It was a peculiar confluence of events indeed which brought the two generals together, not in Europe in 1943, but in Algiers before the year 1942 was out.

Giraud's thinking also coincided with Roosevelt's in an interesting way. He believed that General Weygand was the only one with sufficient stature to lead a vigorous army resistance. Within two weeks of his arrival Giraud had sought out the old general, now living in retirement at Grasse, near the Mediterranean coast. The intermediary was General Chambe, an old friend of Weygand's and Giraud's. Chambe approached Weygand on 8 May. Weygand was cordial, sympathetic, but gave no inkling, any more than he had to President Roosevelt's proposal, that he would lead a resistance movement without Marshal Pétain's specific instructions. But he was happy that Giraud had become available. "General Giraud's escape," he told Chambe, "has been, through the tears, the first smile of pride for France."[9]

Algiers and Lyons, April–May 1942
Contacts with Giraud

At almost the same moment that news of Giraud's escape reached Algiers, The Five had sunk to a low point in despair so far as Allied assistance was concerned. Their grandiose proposal, forwarded by Murphy on 14 March, had received no acknowledgment.

They concluded that the United States had no real intention of promoting a European operation and that they would be best advised to turn to the British, whose SOE (Special Operations Executive), functioning from Gibraltar and Tangier, might provide them with sten guns and explosives. On 1 May they delivered to Murphy a sort of ultimatum to the effect that if no response was obtained in three weeks they would seek out other alternatives.[10]

The possibility that The Five might turn to SOE alarmed Colonel Solborg even more than it did Murphy. Solborg's primary mission was to develop resistance chains and to support clandestine fighters with arms and money. Murphy's mission, basically diplomatic and economic, was to observe. Murphy had never been specifically authorized to organize resistance, and in spite of his appeals, he had received no directive regarding American policy in North Africa. Solborg had received quite different instructions, and it appeared to him that the British were about to prevent him from doing his job. Having learned of these threats, Solborg flew to London on 25 April. After several weeks of negotiation with high-level British authorities, he believed he had scotched the SOE undercutting efforts and had reached an understanding that American and British agents would work together for a common end. While he was in London, incidentally, Solborg conferred with General de Gaulle, whom he admired and who he thought might ultimately play a role in North Africa.[11]

Solborg returned to Lisbon on 15 May. Meanwhile The Five had taken a momentous stride: they had made contact with General Giraud.[12]

A week previously Lemaigre Dubreuil had flown from Algiers to Lyons to seek out Giraud's hideaway. By coincidence this was the same day that Admiral Fenard revealed Admiral Darlan's resistance plan to Robert Murphy.

Several days later, on the nineteenth, Lemaigre Dubreuil had made clandestine contact with Colonel de Linarès and with General Chambe, whom he had known many years ago in Limoges. He was able to have a long, confidential talk with Giraud. He informed the general what his group had been doing in North Africa. He then discreetly inquired as to Giraud's own plans.

Giraud's own plans, still vague and rather unrealistic, were beginning to take more specific shape as he learned more about conditions in Europe. While in prison he had wondered whether resistance movements all over Europe, in Yugoslavia, in Poland, in the Low Countries, could not be coordinated with an uprising in France, particularly if Germany found herself foundering in Russia and if the Allies could support these uprisings from the encircling ring. He envisaged the Armistice Army holding the southern half of France while Anglo-American forces poured material and reinforcements through La Rochelle, or Sète, or Toulon. With the same disdain for peripheral distractions that marked the strategic thinking of Stimson and Marshall, the general could not find much in North Africa to interest him. If Hitler could be struck hard in Europe, the rest would come along of its own accord.

But Giraud did not want to turn down any opportunities, particularly in an area which he knew better than any other. He began to ask technical questions for which Lemaigre Dubreuil did not have the documentation to answer. Lemaigre Dubreuil suggested that The Five arrange for a mission to come from North Africa. Then the details could be examined at leisure. At the same time, with rather cavalier trust, General Giraud named a dozen officers in the colonial army who he was sure would be ready to fight with the Allies. Principal among these figured his former prison-mate at Königstein, now chief of staff of the XIX Corps in Algiers, Gen. Charles Mast.[13] Giraud undertook to designate Mast officially as his personal representative and agreed to write to him at once. He would send the letter by Madame Mast, then en route to join her husband.

General Mast had been released from Königstein the previous September, seven months before Giraud's escape, so that he could represent Vichy at Tokyo as military attaché. A short man, but carrying himself with confidence, Mast was then in his early fifties. He retained bitter memories of the French collapse in 1940 when, as commanding officer of the Third North African Infantry, he had been overruled by General Flavigny and forced to surrender. Imprisoned from June 1940 until September 1941, he had avoided the contaminating defeatism at Vichy, and he believed ardently, like General Giraud, that the French army must vindicate itself by reentering the war. If Germany's defeat were indeed inevitable, any Frenchman who could associate himself with the Allies would in the long run not only help bring France to victory but could further his own career. Mast chose his line of action, just as another brigadier general, Charles de Gaulle, had chosen his, as a way to fulfill conscientiously his dedication as an officer. Both were collaborating with the Allies, one within the framework of Vichy, the other outside. Certainly both felt that in addition to serving glory and honor, they were serving their personal futures as well.

General Mast assumed his new command in April. In spite of standing regulations which discouraged contacts between army officers and foreign diplomats, Mast soon was able to have a long talk with Robert Murphy. He made his convictions clear to the American: "I believe that a Frenchman has an obligation to facilitate the arrival of a British or American relief army and, so far as I am concerned, I will do everything I can to make such an Allied operation possible."

Murphy was impressed. General Mast was the highest ranking officer he had met who so frankly expressed a willingness to work with the Allies.

"What person," asked Murphy, "do you think could take the leadership in such a liberation movement?"

Mast had no doubts in that area. He had already given assistance to those who had succeeded in bringing Giraud to Lyon. And he did not find in North Africa any strong Gaullist movement which could serve as an alternate basis for military action. Mast told Murphy that he couldn't give much advice in the political area, but now that Giraud had escaped he could confidently recommend him as a potential leader. Giraud would be qualified to take command in Africa, he believed, if the Vichy commanders hesitated to cooperate.

On 23 May, having just flown back to Algiers from Lyon, Lemaigre Dubreuil excitedly tried to call on General Mast at XIX Corps headquarters. Mast knew something of the industrialist's association with Vichy, and he refused to see him pending an intelligence checkup. He soon had the information he sought:

> LEMAIGRE DUBREUIL, Jacques. Important industrialist, travels a great deal on business; has wide contacts among German services in Paris and at Vichy in several ministries. In particular, frequently received by Laval.[14]

Mast refused to see him.

Next day Lemaigre Dubreuil returned and insisted that the general verify his credentials in the letter from Giraud. Mast's wife had reached Algiers only that morning. With Giraud's letter in hand Mast altered his disdainful attitude and listened carefully to what Lemaigre Dubreuil had to say. Within a week Mast had become well informed on the status of the resistance movement.

For the first time in the long evolution of the North African underground, a general officer, in a key position, had expressed his willingness to help the Allies. Beaufre and Jousse had certainly brought military skill to the conspiracy, but without rank or influence they would not have been able to sway the course of events as General Mast could. In any case, Beaufre was now living in Marseilles and Colonel Jousse had been sent on temporary duty to Tunisia in connection with the turnover of French material to the Afrika Korps.

Mast was not clear on what steps had to be taken. His military mind automatically registered suspicion when he was informed that The Five could count on 5,000 men in Algeria. Who were they? What kind of training did they have? What kind of arms? He realized that one of the group, Colonel Van Hecke, as local director of the Chantiers de la Jeunesse, could probably direct several thousand young men into some sort of activity. But could one count on these boys in an emergency?

What was first needed, Mast told himself, was time. Time to make contacts, time to hide arms, time to train. Most of all, time to get in touch with the Allied military commanders in order to work out plans together.

Algiers, June 1942
The protocols drawn up by The Five

In spite of the new, secret friendship developing between Mast and Murphy, The Five still undertook to keep in touch with SOE, and they planned a conference. When he learned of this, Murphy immediately informed Solborg, who was greatly disturbed at evidence that his negotiations in London had apparently been meaningless. On 29 May Solborg cabled Donovan that if a meeting took place an American representative should be present. Donovan had already indicated that he had no objection to Solborg's attending such a meeting, but he had questioned the suitability of holding such a conference at Lisbon. To the new request, however, Donovan did not reply. Solborg felt uneasy about traveling without specific authorization but, convinced of his mission's importance, decided to go on his own initiative.¹⁵

Solborg waited for a specific rendezvous point to be designated but received none. After an uneasy day without news, Solborg anxiously queried Murphy, then in Casablanca, about it. Murphy had no further information but, in response to Solborg's query, affirmed that he would be delighted to confer with him. Solborg left at once and reached Casablanca on 4 June.

How crucial his timing was, Solborg could not possibly have known. He knew of course that Africa had become a military focal point once again when Rommel opened his offensive in Libya on 26 May; but he could not have known that Commissar of Foreign Affairs Molotov was then on mission to London and Washington exerting all his influence to promote an early Anglo-American front. He could not have known that at the highest levels GYMNAST was being nudged, revived, and reexamined in the light of new developments. Nor could Solborg have guessed at Donovan's indignation when the head of COI learned, during a conference with SOE officials in London, that his Lisbon representative had moved, without authorization, into a very sensitive area.

In Casablanca, Solborg met not only Murphy but also Lemaigre Dubreuil, who had just returned from France. Solborg assured the Frenchman that American aid would not be long in coming and, recalling his conversations with de Gaulle, reiterated the need of a leader around whom the resistance could rally.

"We now have such a leader," announced Lemaigre Dubreuil.¹⁶ He solemnly bound Solborg to a written promise that the name should be divulged to no one but General Marshall and President Roosevelt. He then informed the agent of General Giraud's acquiescence in principle to work with the Algiers group.

To Solborg this was an exciting prospect. A month ago no French leader seemed available. Now there was the possibility of two. Radiating a sense of official authority which in reality he did not possess, Solborg concluded that he must review the whole complex set of understandings and contacts in order to put the affair in order. Although Donovan wired him at Casablanca to drop everything and report to England, Solborg decided that meeting the underground leaders in Algiers was more important than seeing Donovan in London. Murphy concurred and relinquished his seat on the plane so that Solborg could meet with The Five as soon as possible.

Two other members of The Five, Jean Rigault and Colonel Van Hecke, had also just returned from France, where they had discussed thoroughly with General Giraud the problems associated with his coming to North Africa. When he presented Giraud's position to Solborg, Rigault considerably exaggerated the general's affirmation and enthusiasm. He did not frankly transmit Giraud's reservations as to the strategic value of North Africa. On the other hand, Solborg managed to convey the impression that the American chiefs of staff could scarcely wait to move into the Mediterranean. There was an unfortunate double deception. If both sides had kept more soberly to established facts some later recriminations and difficulties might have been avoided.

By 15 June, after a week of discussions, an elaborate draft agreement in three parts had been drawn up. The first part dealt with military affairs and simply reiterated the points that Colonel Jousse had developed in his memorandum of the previous March. This protocol insisted on the need for early conferences by responsible military personnel. If such insistence appears unrealistic, one should realize that organization of such a conference was not impossible: such a meeting did take place later, in October, two weeks before the landings. But one should also bear in mind that in June the decision to invade North Africa had not yet been made; and no one, neither Roosevelt, nor Churchill, nor General Marshall, could have told, on 15 June, what the ultimate decision would be.

The second part of the draft related to political positions which would be confirmed upon completion of a successful landing. Later on, in October, Murphy and Saint-Hardouin, The Five's diplomatic expert, would revise the political agreement which, because it was ultimately repudiated by President Roosevelt, caused a multiplicity of misunderstandings. The later agreements, made on the eve of the invasion, have been criticized as last-minute improvisations which Murphy conjured up. But they were not. The seeds exist in the 15 June protocol, and if the appropriate authorities in Washington had examined them carefully, they could have given Murphy precise guidance in adequate time.[17]

The draft agreement affirmed first of all that French questions were to be handled by the French without foreign pressure, and it also recognized The Five as possessing an exclusive mandate of action regarding Frenchmen and natives in North Africa. This clause alone possessed explosive implications. It not only affirmed a break with Vichy and the exclusion of de Gaulle, but it violated a sacred dictum of President Roosevelt's—not to recognize new regimes until after the war.

Surely such an experienced diplomat as Robert Murphy should have foreseen difficulties here. But it was not Murphy who was handling this particular set of negotiations. Murphy at this time had been granted no special powers to negotiate, and he had to assume that Solborg, presumably representing the United States Army, possessed adequate authorization. The irony of the situation lies in the fact that not only had Solborg overstepped his mandate but that, uninformed about President Roosevelt's attitude toward the Free French, he even suggested to the French that they should start negotiations with de Gaulle after the landings.

The third and final part of the draft agreement concerned financial and economic matters: it posed questions to Washington regarding extension of Lend-Lease, sending of food and other materials, establishment of an independent franc in North Africa. The exchange-rate modification registered a high priority on The Five's list of requirements. In March the Free French had worked out an evaluation of French currency versus the pound which pegged the franc at 43.8 to the dollar, whereas in non–Free French colonial areas the exchange worked out closer to 125 to the dollar. The Five asked whether the United States would support a rate equivalent to the British/Free French agreement. The problem was urgent but complex: it would not ultimately be resolved until the Casablanca Conference, in January 1943.

With a detailed agreement negotiated and with a leader, General Giraud, agreed upon, all that remained was for Solborg to take the protocols to Washington, in utmost secrecy, and secure his superiors' approval. On the French side, The Five would obtain Giraud's acquiescence. Rigault left immediately with the documents for France.

Solborg flew from Algiers on 19 June, but his departure was surrounded by omens that suggested the negation of everything he had done. General Donovan had wired him on the twelfth and fourteenth that he had violated an order expressly designed to keep him out of North Africa. Solborg protested that he had acted within the framework of War Department and OSS directives, but he did not persuade Donovan, who on the fifteenth wired: "I informed you before and you had already given us your word that you would carry on no activity of any kind in North Africa. I direct you at once no matter what you are doing to return to Lisbon and await further word from me." Murphy interceded on Solborg's behalf and on the sixteenth tried to persuade Donovan that it was considered "urgently necessary that he continue his conversations with several French authorities. . . . Both he and I consider it important. . . . He is encouraged that results . . . will be fruitful and should be discussed with you."[18]

By the time Solborg reached Lisbon it was too late to rendezvous with Donovan in London, and he proceeded directly to Washington. Once there, on 8 July he sent Donovan a long memorandum analyzing the North African situation. Donovan found Solborg's proposal unacceptable, but his argument against it (in a memorandum to his deputy) does not explicitly reflect his pique at Solborg for disobeying orders:

> I have read carefully the report of Colonel S. It is not a statement of observed facts. It is in a large part a statement of opinions and conclusions without supporting data. It is an assumption that the French Army in North Africa will follow the leadership of Colonel S. Also an assertion that the French will probably follow the unnamed General. It is a statement that Colonel S. has been given confidential information about Spain and Spanish Morocco but no proof of this. If it is possible to make a report in which he would not obtrude, but would deal wholly with facts, I would be glad to have it. It is important to have it quickly. But this report cannot be forthcoming unless Colonel S. is closely affirmed by someone competent to do so. Even if his conclusions are not correct, it would be important to know where his opinions have been affected by the retreat of the British in Libya. If you feel you have no one there to conduct a detailed examination of Colonel S., I will designate someone to do it. As it stands now, I do not want to submit it to any competent military authority.[19]

Thereafter Donovan refused to concern himself with further reports and dropped Colonel Solborg from the roster of OSS agents.

With Solborg no longer handling OSS operations in Lisbon, the responsibility of arranging for clandestine French assistance fell on Robert Murphy and Colonel Eddy. It is ironic that during all of

Solborg's negotiations there had been no official decision to move into North Africa. Yet this decision, the adoption of Operation TORCH, was made on 24 July, only two weeks after Solborg brought The Five's master plan to Washington.

Southern France, June–July 1942
The plans of General Giraud

As General Giraud began to sense that some army officers, indignant or shamed by the 1940 defeat, shared his conviction that French units should fight again, he decided to take a swing around southern France. He would talk personally to officers he knew, some of them inactive, some holding posts in the emasculated Armistice Army. He would sound them out, lay out his tentative plan of holding bridgeheads in cooperation with the Allies, and get a true sampling of the resistance spirit.

First of all, he would make another attempt to persuade General Weygand that he ought to assume leadership. General Chambe, who had served as Giraud's emissary to Weygand in May, agreed to go once more, early in June, to seek out the old general. Chambe arranged that Weygand and Giraud should meet near Aix-les-Bains on 17 June.

The interview, when it took place, was disappointing. Giraud expressed his opposition to Vichy's defeatism, his anxiety to see France involved in the war, his convictions that patriots must break with Marshal Pétain. Before the older officer, he laid out his plan for a bridgehead. Weygand essentially agreed but denied that he could accept the leadership: he claimed old age, but more convincingly he pointed out as usual that, having accepted a Vichy appointment, he could not now disloyally oppose the marshal.[20]

Weygand's rejection struck Giraud hard but did not keep him from pursuing his plan. He was Giraud, the man with the baraka, ordained by his successful escape for some sacred mission. How similarly Giraud's aims matched those of de Gaulle: both courageously unwilling to accept defeat, both ready to break with officialdom, both charged with faith in French valor and glory, both moody and quick-tempered, nurtured in that close, inbred society of French militarism, the tradition wedded to imperial arrogance. Yet how different in execution: de Gaulle always looking five years ahead, instinctively understanding his own and France's weaknesses and strengths, the master politician fashioning to his own ends those fragments of power that reached him; Giraud on the other hand impetuous, spoiling for action, wanting to grip the present in his powerful hands and mold it through sheer strength, never really sensing the long-range implication of his actions, believing, with unwarranted faith, that the god of war would bring him blessings once the battle started. Out of touch with the war since 1940, he had no practical comprehension of what a Panzer III Special could do. Giraud sincerely believed that in French generalship, supported by hardware which the Americans would somehow provide, lay not only a reasonable, but the best, formula for victory.

It was up to General Giraud now to find out who among his former companions-in-arms shared his views and his enthusiasm. With General Chambe and Commander Viret, of the Secret Service, as companions, immediately after his talk with Weygand, Giraud set off on a tour of southern France.[21]

After visiting Toulouse, the general's car turned east, and on 21 June, the same day that Tobruk fell, he reached Montpellier, where General Jean de Lattre de Tassigny—a charismatic, hard-hitting, broad-ranged man, whose 14th Infantry had fought one of the toughest withdrawals in 1940—commanded a strategic area in southern France: the low, sparsely populated ground that circled the Mediterranean west of the Rhône. This arc of land facing the Gulf of Lions, with Sète as a possible port, formed an essential part of Giraud's strategic plan to build a bridgehead in cooperation with the Allies.

But de Lattre had doubts about this scheme. Giraud had to be considered as a sort of maverick: he had refused a post in the Armistice Army and therefore had no official place in the chain of command. But Giraud's scheme had possibilities, particularly if the general had lines of contact with the British and Americans. De Lattre would mull it over. "I had the impression," Giraud later wrote, "that he had already reflected on the problem, but that he did not yet wish to reveal his thinking."[22] The two generals agreed to keep in touch with each other, and to go into the matter more thoroughly.

At the moment there did not seem to be an inordinate hurry. The news from neither Libya nor the Eastern Front showed Hitler ready to crumble—but if Russia could hold through another winter and if Rommel overextended himself, the next spring might bring with it an entirely different picture.

Neither general then could look into a perverse and ironic future, when de Lattre would assume command of Giraud's own North African divisions and lead them triumphantly, as the First French Army, up the Rhône valley in 1944. Nor could either of them see then that de Lattre would one day wield a marshal's baton; while Giraud, shunted aside by de Gaulle's inexorable march to power, would pass grudgingly into retirement, almost unremembered, certainly unsung.

Leaving Montpellier, Giraud swung east, visited other former colleagues, and finally returned to Lyons. Finding himself under annoyingly close surveillance by Vichy police, the general quickly moved into a villa owned by a friend. It was at this villa, La Fromente, not far from Lyons, that Giraud developed lines of communication with the United States.

It was only normal that the United States should get in touch with so celebrated a figure as General Giraud. If the Vichy policy could ever justify itself, it would do so by having enabled American diplomats to remain in contact with anti-German, pro-Ally Frenchmen, politicians like Edouard Herriot, president of the Chamber of Deputies, Albert LeBrun, former president, Jules Jeanneney, president of the Senate, or with officers—other than General Weygand—like Admiral Darlan, General de la Laurencie, and General Requin.[23] So it happened that Miss Constance Harvey, the American vice-consul in Lyons, had made contact through the Red Cross representative, Léon de Rosen, with General Giraud. In case Giraud wished to communicate with the United States, he could do so, she gave him to understand, by means of the embassy pouch or via Berne.[24]

In early July, Giraud received a secret message from the Deuxième Bureau in Vichy that an important communication awaited him. Fearful of his own security, he sent General Baurès to represent him. The Deuxième Bureau arranged a rendezvous in the nearby Forest of Randan: at the appointed time Baurès met, so Giraud records in his memoirs, a representative of the American Embassy. The message was simple: "Is General Giraud inclined to work for the liberation of France with President Roosevelt, and if so, under what conditions?"

By the time Giraud received this proposal, he had brought his own plans to a fairly definite point. Knowing that neither General Weygand nor General Georges, the only available officers in France who were senior to himself, stood ready to lead an anti-German revolt, he accepted the fact that this leadership must be his. He had in his possession of course the "Protocols of June 15" which The Five in Algiers had worked out with Colonel Solborg. He did not particularly care for the idea of a North African landing, but he saw the point of certain political and economic proposals. Taking all these matters into account, he wrote out a reply for Baurès to take back:

> General Giraud accepts the President's proposal under the following conditions:
> (1) French boundaries, both for France and outside France, will be reestablished as of 1 September 1939.
> (2) French sovereignty will be maintained in all French territory where French troops fight alongside American troops.
> (3) General Giraud will be commander in chief of Allied forces in the Theater of Operation where French troops fight.
> (4) The exchange rate of the franc to the dollar will be equal to that arranged by England with General de Gaulle in respect to the franc and the pound.[25]

Baurès returned this note to the American representative, whom he met once more secretively in the Randan woods. This contact with the Americans, it must be understood, took place through different channels from those arranged by The Five via Robert Murphy and the Algiers consulate. As a matter of fact, when he learned of Giraud's unilateral exchange through the Vichy Embassy, Lemaigre Dubreuil became extremely upset and admonished the general about violating the unity of command. Already perhaps Lemaigre Dubreuil saw himself in the role of prime minister, to Giraud's chief of staff.

While awaiting a reply from the Americans, Giraud gave his full attention to perfecting his plans. To help him, he was able to engage the services of Captain Beaufre, the young officer who had schemed in Algiers with Colonel Jousse and Major Faye until they were arrested in 1941. Beaufre's sentence had been light; but he was forbidden to return to North Africa and in early 1942 he had taken up residence on the Mediterranean coast at Sanary, near Toulon. He kept in touch with Faye and was informed about the activities of Faye's ALLIANCE underground group. He also occasionally saw Lemaigre Dubreuil, to whom he had given the keys to his villa outside Algiers. Through Dubreuil he had met Jean Rigault.

In early June, before Giraud made his swing around the south,

Rigault and Van Hecke had thoroughly discussed resistance strategy with the general, who had then deprecated the value of North African landings. Rigault suggested that Beaufre might further clarify The Five's thinking and might serve as liaison between Giraud and the Algiers group. Several days later Giraud's aide, Colonel de Linarès, located Beaufre in Toulon and asked him to come see the general. This he had done early in July.

Beaufre found himself impressed by Giraud, if not by his planning. This "devil of a man," Beaufre saw, was "direct, ardent, imaginative, disdainful of contingencies." He shared certain traits with Winston Churchill, a boyish love of adventure, a willingness to act, whatever the consequences; he was filled with bold schemes but unconcerned with the logistics which would make them possible. Beaufre asked him where 800 tanks, indicated in the plan, would come from. Giraud had a ready answer: "Oh, we'll get them from the Allies." Beaufre's task would be that of Sir Alan Brooke's with Churchill, or Marshall's with Roosevelt: to try to reduce vast imaginative enterprises to the dimensions of reality.[26]

Beaufre took the Giraud concept back with him to Sanary and began to work on details.

Offhand, one might tend to dismiss the Giraud Grand Design as an adventure fantasy devoid of feasibility. But one must go back to 1942. In this same July 1942, General Marshall and General Eisenhower were arguing with the British chiefs of staff as powerfully as they knew how for a modified Operation SLEDGEHAMMER which would land Anglo-American troops in the Cherbourg area. Eisenhower later admitted the scheme's impracticability, possibly recalling the nightmare of Anzio in 1944.

But Giraud's plan included certain assumptions which become obscured when critics dig into the North African landings:

1. His operation was planned for *1943* (just like ROUNDUP) before which a build-up in Ireland and Gibraltar would have enabled men, ships, and planes to be assembled.
2. It assumed an operation in *unoccupied* France, with the calculation that forty-eight hours would elapse before Axis troops could close on the bridgehead.
3. It assumed French underground cooperation, which would open up ports and airfields in a thirty-mile arc along the Mediterranean from the Pyrenees to Marseilles.

Given these assumptions, the Giraud plan was no wilder than SLEDGEHAMMER or some of the Churchill-Mountbatten schemes for commando raids. It is certainly not fair to compare Giraud's concept with Operation ANVIL, the landings in southern France which took place in 1944. ANVIL had to face a coastline which Germany had almost two years to fortify. A better comparison might be the landing which actually took place at Algiers, where a small amount of French cooperation enabled troops to get ashore and planes to become immediately land based.

What Giraud could not know, of course, was the logistic capability of his overseas allies. He and Beaufre planned for 50,000 troops to be flown in by 660 transports. Could this be done? He could not tell, either, whether Spain would remain neutral. Obviously, these were matters for discussion. All Giraud sought, in July 1942, was to establish contact with the Allies so that exploration of means would begin.

Possibly the greatest weakness in Giraud's plan was Giraud himself. He had no official authority over any of the units which he sanguinely assumed would cooperate. Only one man in France possessed such authority: Admiral Darlan. And Darlan had in the back of his scheming mind a grandiose conception strikingly similar to that of Giraud. But the Allies doubted the wisdom of dealing with the enigmatic admiral, whose policies followed such aberrant patterns that he had undermined his own credibility. They trusted Giraud, who possessed no authority; yet they winced at the prospect of negotiating with Darlan, the only one who could deliver the remnants of French military might. And Weygand, whom they trusted and who could possibly have delivered, refused to commit himself.

Whatever the merit of Giraud's proposals, the plans became meaningless on 24 July, when the Combined Chiefs of Staff agreed that Anglo-American forces would occupy North Africa in 1942 with or without the French. Nobody informed General Giraud that this decision had been made. But the general did receive, at the end of July, an answer to the communication which he understood had gone directly to the president himself. He was given to believe that his conditions had been accepted.

How genuine was this reply? The only evidence concerning it comes from Giraud himself, who wrote in his memoirs that the president's response came to General Baurès in the Forest of Randan by the same agent who had first communicated with him. In Giraud's papers was found the text of the message, copied in his own handwriting, with the indication that his conditions had been approved by Roosevelt. But where did the contact originate? It seems unlikely that the State Department was involved, because negotigations on the exchange rate between franc and dollar had already been started with The Five and no final decision was made until the Casablanca Conference in January 1943. Certainly no one in U.S. Army headquarters would have granted the position of commander in chief to a French general who could not be a party to the months of preliminary planning. And the guarantee on French boundaries runs absolutely counter to President Roosevelt's often repeated dictum that there should be no political settlements until after the war. No such document has turned up among the Roosevelt, or Hopkins, or Leahy papers. Douglas MacArthur II, described by some writers as the embassy's agent, denied he carried any such message. Nor does it seem to have been initiated by OSS. Thomas J. Cassady, assistant naval attaché at Vichy and OSS representative, has stated that he had nothing to do with it.[27]

But General Giraud believed in the communication's authenticity, and he patterned a good deal of his activity on the assumption that it was genuine. Undoubtedly there was some failure in communication, but Giraud had every reason to believe that he was being considered as the key French representative in American operational planning. It was the first misunderstanding between Giraud and the Americans. It would not be the last.

4

The TORCH Decision

London, Washington, May–June 1942
The Molotov mission[1]

To those in touch with North Africa—Solborg, Murphy, Lemaigre Dubreuil, Eddy—an operation there furnished a great opportunity for the western Allies.

To the staff officers in London and Washington, North Africa covered but one small wavelength in the spectrum of strategic alternatives.

Planners divorced from reality in a map-filled room could talk about optimum conditions—plenty of time for build-up, followed by a strike where the odds for success looked greatest. But time inserted itself relentlessly into the decision-making requirements, forcing the question as to what power, the Allies or the Axis, would be better served by striking early or by waiting.

No one expressed the problem more succinctly at the time than Soviet Commissar for Foreign Affairs Molotov, when, at the end of May 1942, he reviewed global strategy in the presence of Roosevelt, Hopkins, General Marshall and Admiral King:

> The Russians [Molotov explained] might hold and fight on all through 1942. But it was only right to look at the darker side of the picture. On the basis of his continental dominance, Hitler might throw in such reinforcements in manpower and material that the Red Army might *not* be able to hold out against the Nazis. Such a development would produce a serious

situation which we must face. The Soviet front would become secondary, the Red Army would be weakened, and Hitler's strength would be correspondingly greater, since he would have at his disposal not only more troops, but also the foodstuffs and raw material of the Ukraine and the oil-wells of the Caucasus. In such circumstances the outlook would be much less favorable for all hands, and he would not pretend that such developments were all outside the range of possibility. The war would thus become tougher and longer. The merit of a new front in 1942 depended on the prospects of Hitler's further advantage, hence the establishment of such a front should not be postponed. The decisive element in the whole problem lay in the question, when are the prospects better for the United Nations: in 1942 or in 1943.[2]

This analysis came at a crucial time in 1942, late in spring, when Russian defeats and losses marked the failure of Timoshenko's premature offensive, but before Hitler had unleashed his own summer campaign in the East.

Molotov's commentary made a great impression on President Roosevelt, now faced with implementation of the most recent decision: BOLERO, the build-up in England, and ROUNDUP, its follow-up across the channel in 1943. Neither of these plans could counter the dire contingency which the Soviet commissar for foreign affairs had so dolefully envisaged. And while they brought no help to Russia, they did nothing to stimulate the enthusiasm and morale of the American people, still depressed by the Pearl Harbor debacle of six months earlier. The president's sensitive political antennae, so continuously aware of changes in opinion, warned him that something dramatic and stimulating must soon take place, before the November elections if possible, but at least before the year's close.

But the problem contained many more complexities, the untangling of which required the greatest wisdom, forbearance, and cooperation on the part of American and British planners. In the long run, the British could do nothing without the Americans. But for the immediate future, the Americans could accomplish little without the British. London must take into account the view from Washington, and Washington had to extend its horizon across the Atlantic.

The decisions facing Churchill and the British chiefs of staff in one sense were simple: British forces faced attack—in Libya especially—and the Suez Canal must be defended. In early May a brief lull had descended on the desert. Auchinleck held Tobruk and Gazala, and even if Rommel could mount a new offensive he would have strong defensive positions to assail. For the moment, Churchill could accept the April decisions for a cross-channel attack; in fact, his vivid imagination had been kindled by the Saint-Nazaire raid of 28 March, which had produced devastation to shipyard facilities in France. With Lord Louis Mountbatten, head of Combined Operations, he plotted sallies onto the continent, commando raids the daring of which was matched only by their impracticality. The chief of staff, Sir Alan Brooke, wasted much time and energy bringing the prime minister back to earth.

By the third week in May, conditions had seriously changed. In an effort to estimate their capabilities for cross-channel operations, the British chiefs had tallied up a sober assessment of their landing craft. They found themselves faced with inexorable fact—destructive both to the prime minister's ebullient plans and to General Marshall's passion for the short route to Berlin: available landing craft could transport a maximum of 4,000 men to France.

The chiefs' efforts to make Churchill face the reality of this grave logistic limitation ironically coincided with the Soviet Union's attempt to press the western Allies into more vigorous action. Molotov had reached London on 20 May and soon found that the British evaded all the basic questions: not only on territorial issues but even on the date for the continental front. The cold fact of landing-craft shortage had brought Churchill to frustrated silence. Molotov had not survived in the tough environment of Soviet politics for nothing: he readily sensed that the core of power lay not at 10 Downing Street but in the White House. He had not too much time to waste: he already knew that the Soviet spring attacks on Kerch and Kharkov had failed. If Hitler soon moved successfully from counterattack to major offensive, the Germans might conceivably force Russia across the last narrow margin of possible resistance. Without pressing for the political agreement, the commissar for foreign affairs quickly signed a Treaty of Alliance with Great Britain on the twenty-sixth and took a plane for the United States.

In Washington, Commissar Molotov sat down to secret deliberations with President Roosevelt and his military staff on 30 May and 1 June.

After his effective initial exposé of the Russian position, Molotov could see that he had reached the president. He capped his argument by emphasizing how much more difficult a second front would be in the following year.

Roosevelt turned to General Marshall: "Are developments clear enough so that we can say to Mr. Stalin that we are preparing a second front?"

"Yes." Marshall's reply, masterful in its simplicity, nevertheless summarized all that he believed strategically and everything that he had been working for since Pearl Harbor.

The president then turned to Molotov. He authorized him to inform Stalin that a second front could be expected this year.

This decision, it should be noted, was made by the president without qualification and without consulting London. It meant in fact that with the British, or without them, American soldiers would somewhere, somehow, exchange shots with Axis troops before 1942 was out. The commitment was not, like some of the president's decisions, offhand or flippant. It was confirmed throughout the Molotov visit.

On Sunday, 31 May, the president called in Harry Hopkins, General Marshall, and Admiral King. They discussed the decision and how it should be broken to Churchill. The telegram which they agreed on stated in part:

> Molotov has clearly expressed his anxiety concerning the next four or five months. I think that this is sincere and that it is not put forward for the purpose of forcing our hand.
>
> I am, therefore, more anxious than ever that BOLERO shall begin in August and continue as long as the weather permits.[3]

The next day, at the final meeting with Molotov, the president reiterated his assurances, at the same time making it clear that the shipping requirements of a second front would necessarily subtract from the tonnage allocated for Russian convoys. Molotov expressed some distressed uneasineess at this point: "I have brought a new Treaty of Alliance from England. What answer shall I take back to London and Moscow on the general question that has been raised? What is the President's answer with respect to the second front?"

The tough Soviet diplomat could not have asked for anything more specific, but his long experience warned him that the promises of a chief can be whittled away by subordinates and allies. In the next few days he rejected a State Department draft of what the president had said, replacing it with his own: "In the course of the conversations full understanding was reached with regard to the urgent tasks of creating a Second Front in Europe in 1942." General Marshall opposed such a draft, which strangled the possibilities of military surprise, but the president insisted on accepting the Russian version. Giving Molotov time to return to Moscow, Roosevelt agreed to hold back release of the communiqué until 11 June. On that date the United States publicly and officially committed itself to engage in European battle earlier than January 1943.

This announcement carried with it implications of the most momentous sort. In the first place, London had not been consulted, and the timing, from the British view, could not have been more disastrous. Every day confirmed the shipping weaknesses which had been thoroughly reviewed by the British chiefs of staff in May. At the very moment that Roosevelt and Molotov conspired together on the second front, Mountbatten was flying to Washington, harbinger of British shortages, to prepare the awful blow which his chief would soon officially administer, that no cross-channel attack could be seriously entertained.

What could Churchill tell Molotov when he returned to London? Barely a week earlier Great Britain and the Soviet Union had solemnly clasped hands in a twenty-year military assistance pact. Russia then waited for the second deadly year of Nazi advance, facing millions of Hitler's forces on a thousand-mile front stretching from the Black Sea to the Gulf of Finland; England geared herself in Libya for Rommel's spring offensive, an operation which in Russian terms could be considered a minor diversion. The new ally, the United States, had committed itself without reservation. What would England do?

One of Churchill's great virtues was his ability and willingness to face up to unpleasant tasks. Sometimes petulant, sometimes exasperatingly naive, frequently buoyed up with schemes for implausible and impractical adventures, always difficult to handle, the prime minister nevertheless could recognize, when he had to, distasteful necessity. Churchill was too shrewd, too far-seeing, to permit himself to fall into the attractive trap of underlining the American pronouncement. He covered himself with a careful disclaimer, which he presented to Molotov in writing:

... it would not further either the Russian cause or that of the Allies as a whole if, for the sake of action at any price, we embarked on some operation which ended in disaster.... It is impossible to say in advance whether the situation will be such as to make this operation feasible when the time comes. *We can therefore give no promise in the matter,* but provided that it appears sound and sensible we shall not hesitate to put our plans into effect.[4]

The British *aide-mémoire* ended with an optimistic appraisal, but in fact neither the chiefs of staff nor the War Cabinet entertained any hopes for such operations. On 8 June, the chiefs had definitely committed themselves to the position implicit in the surveys made earlier in the month—that an early assault on the continent had to qualify not as a raid but as a landing, with every intention of establishing a bridgehead. And the military experts foresaw no chance of success for such an operation, unless Germany completely collapsed. There was no evidence that Hitler was close to defeat.

Indeed, the reports from Libya revealed exactly the contrary. Every day brought new evidence of Rommel's masterly tactics as he ranged his panzers against the southern defenses of Gazala. Clearly, any available planes, ships, tanks, and men must reinforce the Middle East until such time as Egypt could be considered secure. On 11 June, the British War Cabinet confirmed the chiefs' decision to hold off an attack on France until 1943.

The next step could await Lord Mountbatten's report on his conversations in Washington.

The implications of President Roosevelt's second-front commitment came into sharp focus during his long conversation with Lord Mountbatten on 9 June. By this date a new element had imposed itself into the overall strategic outlook: the Battle of Midway. With the Japanese defeat, the navy wanted a follow-up and a move to the offensive, all of which would deplete supplies for European action and reduce the chances of a really adequate build-up in the British Isles. The president above all feared that thousands of American soldiers, shipped to England, would serve no more significant war objective than the release of British troops to Africa. Better that the American soldiers go directly, if that were the case, to Morocco or Algeria, as the mothballed SUPER-GYMNAST had envisaged. Roosevelt had not missed Churchill's hint, in a recent communication: "We must never let 'Gymnast' pass from our minds."[5] Where else could Americans fight, if barred from Normandy, than in Africa or Norway?

Mountbatten made it unmistakably clear, in his five-hour after-dinner conversation, that Britain could not provide landing craft for anything more than a raid. Postponing the operation beyond August, the president's target date, would make little difference and would add the complicating hazards of holding a bridgehead in midwinter.

Circumstances tended to force decisions into limited tracks. The great enigma lay in Russia, or rather in Hitler's wild, isolated headquarters, the Wolf's Lair, in Prussia. If Russia collapsed, Hitler would control unlimited oil and could send twenty divisions back to the west. But if Russia held, Hitler might arrange an armistice which, practically speaking, for England and the United States, would have the same result. One way or the other, 1942 was the crucial year. Yet an intervention across the English Channel seemed to be ruled out. What remained? Norway? It was important to the prime minister, because it symbolized the 1940 defeat of England and vitally supported his "Closing the Ring" strategy, but action there did not bring strategic benefits to the United States. Africa? This was much more harmonious to the president's thinking. From the beginnings of the war, Dakar and Morocco had fascinated the president; he had paved the way for American intervention by the Vichy policy and the Murphy-Weygand Agreement: he could not lament if events once more unfolded the map of North Africa on his desk.

The direction of the president's thinking soon became apparent beyond the confines of the White House. One line would reach as far as Lyons, where General Giraud busied himself with his own strategic plans. Another would extend to the War Department, where General Marshall and Secretary of War Stimson would wonder whether the president had found another primrose path along which they would be forced reluctantly to tread.

Washington, June 1942
The second Washington conference—revival of GYMNAST[6]

The day following his long after-dinner talk with the president, Lord Mountbatten met with the Combined Chiefs of Staff in Washington. For the chiefs' benefit he summarized the conversation, and

General Marshall caught the trend of the president's thinking. BOLERO needed firm underpinning, for it was easy to see that Roosevelt's glance was turning again toward North Africa, the magnet whose attraction never failed.

General Marshall now faced two formidable obstacles to his personal strategic convictions: first, the presidential commitment to Molotov that a second front would be opened in Europe in 1942; second, British opposition to risking what landing craft there were in a cross-channel attack. Suppose, in the final showdown, an agreement with London could not be reached and the United States had to fulfill the president's commitment by itself. Then an attack on North Africa, the American part of the old SUPER-GYMNAST plan, remained as the only feasible operation.

Marshall ordered his staff, at highest priority, to rework the GYMNAST plan and bring it in line with the current situation. By 13 June, Roosevelt and Churchill had agreed that the prime minister and his staff should come over within the week. The president had wired:

> I find I must be in Hyde Park 19th 20th and 21st. If you land any time before noon of Sunday the 21st come to Hyde Park and we can leave for Washington that night getting to White House Monday morning.[7]

Thus it worked out that Roosevelt, Churchill, and Hopkins held some private deliberations at the president's estate on the Hudson while the Anglo-American military staffs battered out their positions in Washington. The divergence of views would produce some heavy strains at the decision-making level.

By 16 June, Marshall and his staff had completed a position paper on the North African operation. Available to the Joint Chiefs was the expert testimony of Colonel Eddy, now in Washington making full personal reports on the underground movements and political atmosphere of North Africa. Eddy exaggerated resistance capabilities, but at least he hedged his optimistic summary by pointing out that Laval, now two months in power, was rapidly installing subordinates whose loyalty to Vichy could be counted on.[8]

Marshall's paper set forth a plan in which the Americans, unaided by the British, would attempt to land 220,000 men at and near Casablanca. But Marshall considered such a plan risky and impractical, only feasible if French cooperation, a very uncertain factor, could be guaranteed. But his principal concern, which he would consistently argue, related to BOLERO, the build-up in England for a cross-channel attack. He did not believe, and correctly so, that the Allies could venture into Morocco or Algeria and still prepare for ROUNDUP in 1943. If the North African gamble were ventured, a direct attack became impossible in 1942, improbable in 1943, and too late in 1944.

Marshall had an opportunity to elaborate his views on 17 June, when the president, in anticipation of Churchill's imminent arrival, convoked his chief of staff along with Secretary Stimson, Secretary Knox, Admiral King, and General Arnold. It was clear that Roosevelt had GYMNAST on his mind, although Stimson hoped that "in his foxy way" the president wanted an airing of views "to forestall trouble that is now on the ocean coming toward us in the shape of a new British visitor."[9]

Next evening Churchill and his advisers, having flown the Atlantic nonstop in the Boeing flying boat *Bristol*, put down on the Potomac. After spending the night at the British Embassy, the prime minister flew on to Hyde Park for a weekend with Roosevelt and Hopkins. The remainder of the party, General Alan Brooke and General Ismay, joined Field Marshal Dill for preliminary talks with their American counterparts.

While the political chiefs labored at Hyde Park, the Combined Chiefs of Staff met in Washington. Sir Alan Brooke outlined the problems and possibilities that faced them. Brooke had not been overly impressed by Marshall as a strategist, and Marshall deplored Brooke's emphasis on the Mediterranean; but they found themselves curiously united against the Churchill-Roosevelt enthusiasm for reviving GYMNAST. After the formal session, Dill, Brooke, and Ismay sat down with Marshall, Eisenhower, and Bedell Smith (U.S. chief of staff's secretary) for an informal survey of BOLERO and GYMNAST. They all agreed that "the fundamental reasons that led to the adoption of BOLERO as the principal offensive effort of the United Nations are still sound. Accomplishment of the BOLERO plan should constitute the basis of our future strategy." They believed that spring 1943 should be the target date and that operations in 1942 should be undertaken only in an emergency, or provided they helped—or did not hinder—the build-up for 1943. Neither group showed much faith in the work that Murphy, Solborg, and Eddy had been pushing—to develop French official or clandestine cooperation in the landings. "The operation," said the combined chiefs, "depends upon the existence of certain psychological conditions in North Africa which are impossible to predict. If these conditions should be definitely unfavorable at the time of attack, the effect would be most serious both militarily and politically."[10] This was an understatement which events would reveal to have been most prescient.

The Combined Chiefs reviewed various operations and then drew certain conclusions, succinct and to the point:

> (a) That GYMNAST should not be undertaken under the existing situation.
> (b) That United States and Great Britain should adhere firmly to the basic decision to push BOLERO with all possible speed and energy.
> (c) That the locality, strength and availability of means for any 1942 attack on Western Europe should be studied further. . . .[11]

Next day, 20 June, the Combined Chiefs met once more and, with astonishing unanimity, confirmed what the small group had decided. They elaborated somewhat on what might happen if Russia collapsed, but their discussions only confirmed them in their conviction that BOLERO—cross-channel in 1943—provided the best chance of defeating the Axis.

Meanwhile, at Hyde Park, the president and the prime minister had traversed vast horizons, but they concentrated also on the immediate matter of the channel and the Mediterranean. Churchill felt impelled to pinpoint the crucial issues and to formalize them in a paper. He conceded the points on which most everyone agreed: that BOLERO should continue, that cross-channel emergency arrangements (SLEDGEHAMMER) should be available for September, and that this emergency plan must succeed. So far, there was no wide discrepancy. But assume it is not feasible to execute SLEDGEHAMMER:

> Can we [the Prime Minister queried] afford to stand idle in the Atlantic theatre during the whole of 1942? Ought we not to be preparing within the general structure of "Bolero" some other operation by which we may gain positions of advantage, and also directly or indirectly to take some of the weight off Russia? It is in this setting and on this background that the French Northwest Africa operation should be studied.[12]

Here was astute argumentation on Churchill's part. So many of the prime minister's wily maneuvers, his roundabout and subtle approaches, were lost on less agile minds. He never forgot how powerfully committed the president was for American action in 1942; but he could not afford to let that action go its own way, especially if it meant concentration in the Pacific.

Realizing the position of the military chiefs, Roosevelt and Hopkins had been putting their heads together in a search for ways to relieve the hard-pressed Russians. They wanted quick answers from Marshall and King. At one point their draft note contemplated action on the assumption that "American ground forces supported by air—in a direct attack on the German forces, *with or without British assistance*—can force a withdrawal of German forces from the Russian front." This sentence was later deleted and the question finally asked not only what American forces could do, but could "British forces in the same area or in a different area aid in the same objective?"[13]

Had Churchill intervened? Had he conveyed to the president the idea that unilateral American action would *never* be necessary, that British strategy could and would conform, ultimately, to American concepts? Interestingly enough, Churchill's memorandum invoked GYMNAST, not JUPITER, the Norway enterprise. There was a good chance for cooperation with GYMNAST, none with JUPITER.

The discussion at Hyde Park had been earnest and long. Ultimately the two leaders decided they could not wait until Monday for the conference with their military advisers. Cutting his weekend short, Roosevelt ordered his special train for Saturday night and set up appointments for the following day.

On Sunday morning, 21 June, General Brooke hastened to the White House, where the prime minister waited to take him to meet President Roosevelt. They went in to see the president and, together with Hopkins and later with Marshall, went over the whole turbulent ground of operations in 1942 or 1943, of cross-channel attacks, and of North African diversions. Churchill raised the questions he had memorialized: if no responsible British military authority could contrive an adequate scheme, could the Americans? "Have the American Staffs a plan? At what point would they strike? What landing-craft and shipping are available? Who is the officer prepared to command the enterprise? What British forces and assistance are required?"[14] With petulant tenacity, Churchill refused to let GYMNAST sink out of sight, viewing it as the best, possibly the only means of involving the United States in the Mediterranean. Churchill admitted as much: "I had made a careful study of the President's mind and its reactions for some time past, and I was sure that he was powerfully attracted by the North African plan."[15] Stimson believed that Churchill had "taken up GYMNAST, knowing full well I am sure that it was the President's great secret baby."[16] But, however much the president may have secretly delighted himself with the American special position in French North Africa, of which he fundamentally was the architect, he was not prepared to force an issue with Marshall or Stimson. He was inclined to let the battle rage about him, prodding here, hinting there, but never shifting his allegiance or support from his own military advisers. Nevertheless tempers came very close to flaring.

After lunch, with the argument hotly resumed, news came which shook Churchill hard. Brooke later wrote:

> I can remember this incident as if it had occurred yesterday. Churchill and I were standing beside the President's desk talking to him, when Marshall walked in with a pink piece of paper containing a message of the fall of Tobruk. Neither Winston nor I had contemplated such an eventuality and it was a staggering blow. I cannot remember what the actual words were that the President used to convey his sympathy, but I remember vividly being impressed by the tact and real heartfelt sympathy which lay behind these words. There was not one word too much nor one word too little.
>
> Marshall at once got to work to see what he could do to furnish some tangible signs of their sympathy in the shape of active assistance. . . . It was decided to send three hundred Sherman tanks and a hundred self-propelled guns at once to the middle East. . . .
>
> I always feel that the Tobruk episode in the President's study did a great deal towards laying the foundations of friendship and understanding built up during the war between the President and Marshall on the one hand and Churchill and myself on the other.[17]

Churchill was barely able to pull himself together during the remaining four days of the visit, and no basic decision was reached that altered the BOLERO strategy. Yet the prime minister would not let go of his fundamental conviction that the alliance between Washington and London could be consummated only by the actual commitment of American troops to battle. When Roosevelt proposed that an American division go to the Middle East, Churchill brightened momentarily but was persuaded—Brooke and Marshall stood together on this—that tanks and guns could shore up Auchinleck's defenses more effectively than American soldiers. At one point, during the late evening debate at the White House, Roosevelt voiced the disquieting proposal that "we might throw a large American force into the Middle East and cover the whole front between Alexandria and Teheran." Marshall was so disgruntled at this wild idea that he walked out of the room.

But GYMNAST did not die. Churchill had breathed life into it and found the president ready to nurture the secret baby in face of military hostility. The conclusions which the Combined Chiefs had reached, "that GYMNAST should not be undertaken under the existing situation," never received approval by the heads of government. After the stormy talks at the White House, General Ismay drew up a statement, quite different from that which the Combined Chiefs of Staff had earlier approved. It read:

> Provided that political conditions are favourable, the best alternative in 1942 is operation GYMNAST. Accordingly the plans for this operation should be completed in all details as soon as possible. The forces to be employed in GYMNAST would in the main be found from BOLERO units which had not yet left the United States.[18]

But this statement proved to be too strong for Marshall and finally the controversial passage was altered to:

> The possibilities of operation GYMNAST will be explored carefully and conscientiously, and plans will be completed in all details as soon as possible. Forces to be employed in GYMNAST would in the main be found from BOLERO units which had not yet left the United States. The possibility of operations in Norway and the Iberian Peninsula in the autumn and winter of 1942 will also be considered by the Combined Chiefs of Staff.[19]

GYMNAST had been revived and would be kept alive. But the official opinion at the close of the Washington Conference, on 24 June, still favored BOLERO in 1943, plans and preparations for which were "to be pushed forward with all speed and energy." If something had to be done in 1942, "operations in France or the Low Countries would, if successful, yield greater political and strategic gains than operations in any other theatre."[20] GYMNAST officially still had to content itself as an alternative, as a diversion. It was a feeble baby, but it was watched over tenderly by two nurses in very high places.

Washington and London, July 1942
Toward North Africa

The month of July 1942 brought Prime Minister Churchill and the British more setbacks and discouragement. Rommel had not stopped at Tobruk but within a week had battered down the improvised defenses at Mersa Matruh, and by the first of July he was deploying his tanks for an assault on El Alamein.

Churchill had to defend his strategy and his leadership in the House of Commons, where a "no confidence" motion had been filed against him. Although the motion was defeated, 475 to 25, the prime minister had become acutely aware that his war ministry could not weather another disaster such as the fall of Tobruk. Auchinleck unquestionably had to hold the Egyptian frontier, and every resource must be made available to enable him to succeed.

Were there sufficient resources, the British chiefs of staff inquired, to reinforce Auchinleck and simultaneously mount a cross-channel attack? They gloomily surveyed the prospects:

— No more than 238 landing craft could be located in the United Kingdom. A full-fledged attack on the French coast would require more than 2,000.
— A cross-channel operation would tie up 250,000 tons of shipping. With these vessels used for SLEDGEHAMMER, no additional supplies could be sent to Eighth Army in Egypt.
— Amphibious training would come to a halt. Where would crews needed for future operations obtain their skills?
— Malta was under siege. On 15 June the remains of convoy HARPOON from Gibraltar had limped into Malta with only 15,000 tons of supplies, while at the same time another convoy, loaded at Beirut and Alexandria, failed to break through the Italian fleet. Malta had to be held no matter what the cost, for without it, Axis convoys could provision the African coast almost unopposed. How

could Malta be saved if shipping were diverted into SLEDGE-HAMMER?

— Shipping and warships would have to be pulled away from the northern convoy route to the Soviet Union. In early July an important convoy of thirty-three ships was plodding toward Murmansk. Russia needed all the supplies the Allies could possibly send to her. Sevastopol had fallen on 2 July. If Russia surrendered, the Middle East could be lost by a German thrust through the Caucasus.[21]

To Churchill the answer to all these problems was relatively simple because it reinforced the strategy he had continually advocated, in the First World War as well as in the Second: if the front cannot be broken, the flanks must be turned. Give up, therefore, the cross-channel approach and concentrate on a giant pincer—either through Norway on one side or in North Africa on the other. At the moment, with the Eighth Army jeopardized by Rommel's offensive, the balance tipped toward North Africa.

On Sunday, 5 July, the prime minister found his first opportunity to elaborate his views to the new American general commanding the European theater of operations, Dwight D. Eisenhower, who had installed himself in London only ten days earlier. Churchill invited Eisenhower and General Mark Clark, commanding the II Corps (the first contingent of American troops, expected to arrive shortly in England), to spend the night at Chequers. Greeting his guests in smock and slippers, he lost no time in pressing his arguments as to why a cross-channel attack should be abandoned and why the North African operation, GYMNAST, should be revived. Eisenhower, fresh from his planning desk in Washington, shared with Marshall a conviction that to get to Germany's heart one should point an arrow at Berlin and follow it. At that time he had not yet experienced the prime minister's forensic powers, nor could he have yet comprehended the obstinacy with which Churchill could pursue an objective once convinced of its benefits. But Eisenhower did not become then—or later—a convert to the Churchillian strategy.[22]

Three days later the British War Cabinet formally accepted the view, already propounded by the British chiefs of staff, that SLEDGE-HAMMER was dead. Churchill lost no time in awakening Roosevelt's slumbering preoccupation with North Africa.

I am sure myself [he wrote the president on 8 July] that French

> North Africa [GYMNAST] is by far the best chance for effecting relief to the Russian front in 1942. This has all along been in harmony with your ideas. In fact, it is your commanding idea. Here is the true second front of 1942. I have consulted Cabinet and Defence Committee, and we all agree.

Further on he continued:

> It must be clearly understood that we cannot count upon an invitation or a guarantee from Vichy. But any resistance would not be comparable to that which would be offered by the German Army in the Pas de Calais. Indeed, it might be only token resistance. The stronger you are, the less resistance there would be and the more to overcome it. This is a political more than a military issue.[23]

However much in sympathy President Roosevelt may have been with this point of view, he did not find his views shared by his principal advisers, General Marshall and Admiral King. Marshall even went so far as to argue that concentration on the Pacific would be a better alternative than GYMNAST.

At Hyde Park, where he and Harry Hopkins were escaping the heat of the capital, Roosevelt mulled over these questions. He planned to return to Washington on 15 July, a Wednesday. By that time he must have made a decision. He could comprehend well enough the military validity of Marshall's arguments, but as president he had to cope with many other intangibles—public opinion, the possible collapse of Russia, the importance of the British alliance.

Roosevelt quickly ruled out Marshall's ploy of shifting American emphasis to the Pacific. That was a naval war, and the navy could only be rebuilt in time. Also he had no inclination whatsoever to wait until 1943 before American troops went into action. It was only a month since he had publicly committed the United States to a 1942 second front, and he feared the country's apathy if the war news consisted only of training and defeats. Franklin Roosevelt possessed a keen sense of the public's craving for excitement and drama. He also possessed imagination enough to visualize the consequence of Russian defeat, which could release so many German divisions for redeployment that the Allied ring might never be closed.

When General Marshall came to the White House the morning of 15 July, the president had already let his chief know that he was not going to use the Pacific threat as an ultimatum to the British.

By this time the president had decided to send Marshall, along with Harry Hopkins and Admiral King, to London. The president said he wanted a definite decision—his envoys were to battle it out with the British until something certain had been decided. He wanted American forces in action, somewhere, before the end of 1942, and he wanted a commitment in one week.[24] Next day the American team flew to England.

London, July 1942
The TORCH decision[25]

The outcome of the London meetings with the British staff, held during the week of 20 July, might have been forecast. The British could not and would not accept SLEDGEHAMMER. Roosevelt had specifically ruled out the Marshall ploy of abandoning Europe for the Pacific. This left ROUNDUP for 1943. But the president insisted on something European in 1942. So the real issues were simply:

1. Where?
2. Could ROUNDUP be preserved?

On the afternoon of 22 July, at the Combined Chiefs of Staff meeting, Marshall finally abandoned SLEDGEHAMMER. Eisenhower told his diarist, Harry Butcher, that the day could well go down as the "blackest day in history."[26] Eisenhower later revised this opinion when he came to realize how green American troops were and how inadequate the available air cover was.[27] But at the moment the American contingent was thoroughly depressed.

The time had come, Marshall announced, to cable the president for further instructions. On the twenty-third, President Roosevelt amplified his earlier instructions by insisting on any one of five possibilities, which he listed in order of his own preference:

1. A British-American operation against French North Africa (either Algeria or Morocco or both)
2. An entirely American operation against Morocco
3. Combined operations against northern Norway
4. The reinforcement of Egypt
5. The reinforcement of Iran.[28]

Having given Marshall complete freedom to obtain a cross-channel operation if he could, the president could now exert more and more pressure on his chief of staff. He had not ordered Marshall to support the North African adventure, but he had gradually narrowed down the alternatives. To give further emphasis to his first preference, the president forwarded new intelligence from North Africa, received via Berne. According to this report the French would soon be strengthening their defenses and air establishments in Morocco, but it was estimated that 150,000 Allied troops could obtain control of all French air bases in North Africa. The report stated (correctly as it turned out) that in Morocco General Noguès would probably at first resist but would cooperate if the Allies made a successful landing.

Roosevelt cabled the prime minister at the same time, secretly informing him that he was for the North African decision and was influencing his chiefs in that direction.

Marshall hated to give in. He remained convinced that some day his armies must fight their way across the European littoral toward Berlin: if he had lost SLEDGEHAMMER, how could he save ROUNDUP? He saw, perhaps more clearly than anyone, that the required magnitude of a North African operation would cut drastically into the 1943 cross-channel attack.

In any case, he would try. All day long on 23 July, Eisenhower and his staff labored to create for Marshall a workable plan which might save ROUNDUP. At the heart of this new project lay the idea that preparations for both a cross-channel landing and a North African landing would go along simultaneously, but no final decision for either would be made before 15 September, by which time the western strategists could tell with greater certainty whether or not Russia could hold on.

By evening the new proposal had been put into written form. A summary was wired to President Roosevelt. Marshall intended to present it the next day to the Combined Chiefs of Staff.[29]

It was at this point in the Allied deliberations that General de Gaulle attempted to reach Marshall.[30] Ignored for many months by Washington, de Gaulle had reason to believe that the United States might be reorienting its policy away from Vichy and toward the Free French. No ambassador had replaced Leahy, and, on 9 July, the Free French were approved as recipients of Lend-Lease. De Gaulle wondered whether the United States might be prepared to accept some further overtures from him.

As de Gaulle pondered over what sort of gesture he might make, he learned that General Marshall had come to London for high-level talks with the British. If he could talk to Marshall, demonstrate to him the strategic usefulness of those parts of the French Empire under Gaullist control, and offer to cooperate with him in the second front, he would be able to tell from Marshall's reaction how his group was held in American circles. On 21 July, de Gaulle had drawn up a detailed exposition, addressed to the three allies, setting forth the value of French aid. In this note he pointed out that the Free French could furnish one division, one brigade, and a few miscellaneous units. He "considered it likely" that eight divisions and fifteen air force groups could be recruited in French Africa. (He did not emphasize that these latter elements took orders at present from Vichy.)

General Marshall extended an invitation to the French general to call on him at Claridge's on 23 July. Uncertain as to Anglo-American strategic decisions and extremely wary of dabbling in the uncertain waters of French politics, Marshall intended to keep the discussion formal and noncommittal. He invited King and Eisenhower, among others, to join him. Marshall delivered polite and gracious speeches, but he gave de Gaulle no encouragement and no specific information. As soon as courtesy permitted the French leader stood up, dryly announced that he did not wish to take up more of General Marshall's time, and withdrew.

The implication to de Gaulle was clear enough. If there was to be an operation on French territory, he was not going to be consulted. As de Gaulle later recollected:

> By the end of July I foresaw what would happen. Although their intentions were carefully concealed from us, it seemed extremely likely to me that the Americans would limit their year's effort to seizing North Africa, that the British would willingly comply with this plan, that the Allies would employ General Giraud in its accomplishment, that they would exclude me from the operation altogether, and that thereby these preliminary steps to our liberation, auspicious though they were from many points of view, would nevertheless confront us as Frenchmen with inner torments that would raise fresh obstacles to national unity.[31]

Under the circumstances General de Gaulle could only persevere in his convictions and have trust that the unfolding of events would bring him ultimately to the position of influence that he believed he deserved.

Within two weeks, de Gaulle left London for the Middle East.

At the next meeting of the Combined Chiefs, on Friday, 24 July, General Marshall placed his new proposal before his colleagues and the prime minister. As the plan broke the deadlock it was seized eagerly by the various chiefs and with some amendments it was quickly adopted. The crux of Marshall's proposal, of course, was really to delay the final go-ahead on North Africa until 15 September. It is not certain that everyone at the council table perceived the implications of this postponed decision.

But Harry Hopkins saw it. Hopkins had a way of shedding the nonessential embellishments from an issue and of tackling the central problem. "Lord Heart-of-the-Matter," Churchill liked to call him. Hopkins recognized that the Marshall approach lacked decisiveness. With its idea of waiting to see what would happen on the Eastern Front the plan would certainly not convey to Stalin that sense of determination which in itself might serve as the vital buoy to the Soviet will to resist. Nor did the plan provide anything dramatic for the American people. What it did was to give Marshall time to expand his arguments for ROUNDUP; and this very extension could just possibly counteract what the president must have: action in 1942. Hopkins believed that Roosevelt could not afford to take chances. Much as the president might have preferred to maneuver rather than force his chief of staff into alignment with his views, he could not permit himself, in Hopkins's judgment, to be trapped by a proposal foreign to his objectives. Hopkins cabled the president, and suggested that he express his ideas on an expanded GYMNAST. This the president did, abandoning indirection for a message which placed his support solidly behind a North African landing even if ROUNDUP had to be temporarily bypassed.

Without delay the London proposal, docketed as CCS-94, was cabled to President Roosevelt for his reaction. Hopkins still worried about the 15 September date. He cabled the president his view of the decisions made and pointed out:

> What I fear most is that if we do not now make a firm decision on GYMNAST and fix a reasonably early date there may be procrastinations and delay.[32]

He urged the president to specify a date for the operation, suggesting that D-Day should come no later than 30 October. It was reasonable to suppose that three months at least would be required to develop specific plans once the basic decision was reached. (A time lapse of three months was later supported as a "flash estimate" at a Combined Chiefs of Staff meeting.[33]) Thus, if the decision were held off until 15 September, the operation could scarcely be launched before December, when winter storms might render the whole enterprise impractical. Using the three-month formula with 30 October as target date, the Combined Chiefs would be required to make a decision early in August—in other words, almost at once.

The president followed Hopkins's suggestion. In cabling his recommendation that D-Day come no later than 30 October, he implied that the decision had in fact been made. He told Hopkins in his message that he was "delighted" with the results; it was now "full speed ahead."[34]

Hopkins received the president's cable on 25 July, the same day that the Combined Chiefs agreed to call the new North African invasion by the code name TORCH. They also agreed that the supreme commander should be American.

Was the question now settled or was it not? Marshall could not accept the president's cable as a definitive approval. Surely the president would not have had time to study the new plan. While entertaining luncheon guests at Claridge's, Hopkins got through to Roosevelt on the phone and learned that he had not even received the text of CCS-94.

Later in the day the summary of Marshall's proposal had become available in Washington. Early that evening, President Roosevelt summoned several of his military advisers—Secretary of War Stimson, Admiral Leahy, General Arnold, and General McNarney—to the White House. There was, however, no intensive discussion of CCS-94, and the president did not ask for opinions. He had made up his mind. He had called them in simply to inform them that he had decided to give his approval to TORCH.

After the meeting President Roosevelt phoned Hopkins. As Harry Butcher records it:

> . . . Harry, who had been receiving numerous callers, and had been ducking in and out of parlor and bedroom doors, and trying to be host while conducting an international negotiation

via transoceanic telephone, poked his head out of a bedroom door and said:

"O.K., boys, we're going home."[35]

The president now had his African enterprise, and he was not inclined to let loose of it.

When General Marshall returned to Washington he felt obligated to dissipate the cloudiness that surrounded President Roosevelt's attitude toward TORCH. He wanted to know whether in fact a decision had been made and whether the decision makers understood the implications of their action. So far as Marshall was concerned, his proposal as set forth in CCS-94 was the only plan that had been under discussion. This plan called for studies to be made on *two* possible operations, ROUNDUP in 1943 and TORCH in 1942. Tentative agreement had been reached that he would be supreme commander and that Eisenhower would be deputy, actually responsible for planning to start at once in England. Then, on 15 September, the final decision would be made: TORCH or ROUNDUP. In Marshall's judgment it would have to be one or the other; there was insufficient shipping and matériel for both.

Such was the substance of CCS-94, and at the Combined Chiefs' meeting of 30 July, chaired by Admiral Leahy, General Marshall maintained that these were the prospects and terms to which both American and British chiefs had agreed in London. Sir John Dill voiced the opinion that in his considered judgment the prime minister assumed that the decision had already been made. Admiral Leahy, who was closer to the president than any one present, expressed a similar belief in connection with Roosevelt. Leahy agreed that he must accept the unenviable charge of going to the president, of explaining General Marshall's position, and of obtaining from the president a straightforward and unambiguous response.

That evening he had it. To make the issue categorically clear Roosevelt convoked Admiral Leahy, General Arnold, and General Smith to the White House at 8:30 P.M. Marshall was not there, but the president spoke to his objections. President Roosevelt stated explicitly that he, as commander in chief, had made the decision that TORCH would be undertaken at the earliest possible date. He referred to CCS-94 and pointed out that according to that document a decision was to be made by 15 September. Very well, the decision had been made. The president then advised that a message be sent immediately to Churchill to make sure that Great Britain concurred.[36]

This decision had not been made by the president in cavalier fashion, even though some of the president's messages to Churchill and to Hopkins may have sounded light-hearted. Roosevelt did not run counter to his chiefs of staff or to Secretary Stimson without reflection. If Marshall had succeeded in persuading the British to accept SLEDGEHAMMER, Roosevelt would have accepted it. He had given Marshall a free hand. Then, when the cross-channel proposal went aground, he had suggested an alternate. When the suggestion was rebuffed he had recommended. Now, when his recommendation seemed to be taken lightly, he had finally, but only when forced into it, overruled his military chiefs. He knew what he was doing.

For better or worse, TORCH was the president's baby.

5

The Planners
Washington and London

London and Algiers, July–August 1942
The decision and The Five

At this moment Eddy received orders to proceed immediately to London, where the decision on TORCH had just been made. He had been summoned by Col. Ned Buxton, who served under Donovan as assistant director of OSS. Buxton, representing Donovan during the Combined Chiefs' deliberations, knew about the work Solborg and Eddy had been doing; and he believed that Eddy could make an effective presentation to men who would be heavily involved in planning, for example to Gen. George V. Strong, head of Army Intelligence, and to General Patton, who would ultimately lead American forces entering Morocco. Buxton introduced Eddy to Strong and Patton. Taking in Eddy's many campaign ribbons and empty sleeve, Patton burst out with characteristic bluntness: "The son-of-a-bitch has really been shot at, hasn't he!"

During this session, which General Doolittle later joined, Eddy was able to set forth everything he knew about the North African situation. He described the Resistance groups, the negotiations with The Five, the possibilities of French Army support, the arrangements developing with General Giraud. He gave no more information than Solborg possessed, but the moderate tone of his comments and the sincerity of his delivery impressed the officers. This was a fortunate development because it gave Eddy personal and direct contact with General Strong just at the moment when the liaison by way of Colonel Solborg had been broken.[1]

In London, Eddy learned that an operation in North Africa was going to be approved, although he obviously had no conception of its scope, its timing, or its objectives. But when he came to Algiers, on 28 July, he was at least able to report the good news: something big was in the offing, and it would be directed at North Africa.

On 1 August, Robert Murphy received orders to report to Washington.[2]

With Eddy's news that a military operation in North Africa had been agreed on and with Murphy's orders to report to Washington, a new optimism began to permeate the Group of Five. Lemaigre Dubreuil left immediately for France to buoy up General Giraud's spirits with the intelligence that the Allies had finally committed themselves to an operation—although not to the French Riviera occupation which Giraud advocated. Lemaigre Dubreuil would remain in France for almost two months, coming back to North Africa on 25 September, only two weeks before Murphy himself returned.

The remaining four members of The Five pressed Murphy to transmit to Washington the same instruments which they had drawn up for Solborg's benefit in June. Tarbé de Saint-Hardouin especially wished to make certain that the French would not move from a German occupation to an American one: he wanted commitments in writing from the United States that the French would be treated as equal allies and would have a voice in future decisions. What the French diplomat wanted was exactly what de Gaulle wanted: recognition of French sovereignty; and with his training in foreign affairs Saint-Hardouin saw, perhaps more clearly than the other members of The Five, how closely sovereignty relates to power, and how cynically great powers treat small allies. He could not know, but could guess, that the American military commanders would want to exert sovereign authority in whatever areas they occupied. He was entirely correct: General Marshall, for example, did not sympathize with the idea of pre-invasion agreements with the French; he consistently advocated some form of military government in occupied areas.

If Saint-Hardouin was perturbed about political aspects of the operation, General Mast was concerned about the military part. Colonel Eddy had brought news that there would be a North African landing, but he could reveal nothing more: no one, not even Eisenhower, knew at that time when the invasion would take place, where, or in what force. Mast needed to confer with qualified officers of the invasion force, and Murphy, before leaving, assured him he would try to arrange a meeting for 15 September. Mast provided Eddy with an estimate of French forces in North Africa, but the French general could not affirm that most of the French forces would cooperate.

The extent to which the French military would assist in the landings remained a great question mark. Mast was certain on one point: if the British and Free French participated, there would be strong opposition. Memories of the British operations against Vichy French at Mers-el-Kebir, at Dakar, and in Syria were strong; furthermore, many officers and men, defeated by the Anglo-Gaullist forces in Syria, had been transferred to the North Africa Armistice Army. If the expedition were entirely American, Mast and the others believed, there would be some hope, provided the United States came in sufficient force, that the high commands would cooperate or, at the most, offer only token resistance. Both Murphy and Eddy understood this reasoning and assured The Five that they would explain the situation to their superiors.[3]

Having discussed all aspects of the problem with the conspirators, Murphy finally left Algiers on 10 August. His plan was to spend a few days in Casablanca, to move on to Lisbon, and to reach Washington by the middle of the month. Unfortunately for TORCH planning, Murphy fell ill in Casablanca: his itinerary was consequently thrown back by two weeks. One is tempted to wonder if problems might have been reduced if Murphy's schedule had been maintained as originally planned. In Murphy's absence, Colonel Eddy had to fill in the gaps as best he could, first in London around the tenth and then in Washington, which he reached about the twentieth. Eddy made full reports on the status of the resistance movements, on the need for small arms, and on the anti-British prejudices circulating in North Africa; but he could not replace Murphy, who alone could convey information at the highest echelons in Washington and London.

London and Washington, August 1942
The transatlantic essay contest[4]

While Murphy lay ill at Casablanca, Eisenhower was running into problems. The planning for TORCH, so enthusiastically initiated in July, churned in circles because neither the American nor the British strategists were able to impose their views on the other.

On 4 August the small TORCH planning group had moved into Norfolk House on St. James's Square, where the ROUNDUP planners had already been working for a month. Ultimately TORCH absorbed most of the Anglo-American military talent in Norfolk House and the merged ROUNDUP and TORCH officers, numbering over 1,000, provided the nucleus that evolved into AFHQ: Allied Force Headquarters. Later established at Algiers, AFHQ remained Eisenhower's base of operations until early 1944, when he returned to London to become supreme commander of OVERLORD. Soon after the move to Norfolk House, Gen. Mark W. Clark, who had come to England as commanding officer of the U.S. II Corps, became deputy commander, and a month later, Brig. Gen. W. Bedell Smith joined the planning group as chief of staff. It was not until 14 August that Eisenhower himself received a signed directive from the Combined Chiefs of Staff naming him the TORCH commander. He had known since Marshall's visit to London in July that he had been designated as commander of the *expeditionary* force, but he assumed that he would serve under Marshall's overall command of a larger operation to include not only TORCH but BOLERO and ROUNDUP as well. As time passed it became clear that ROUNDUP, the cross-channel venture in 1943, would be phased out and that Marshall would remain in Washington as chief of staff. The principal responsibility for overall planning thus lay completely with Eisenhower.[5]

Very quickly—by 9 August—Eisenhower's new staff had created a preliminary plan which pleased both the Americans and the British. As the new allies, about to engage in their first cooperative venture, held rather different strategic views, it is worthwhile establishing what those views were. They can be tabulated quite readily:

The British: Saw the operation as a strike at Rommel's rear, to assist the hard-pressed Eighth Army backed up against Cairo. Tunisia is the objective. If Tunisia is not grasped, the operation not only makes no sense but might precipitate a German countermove into Tunisia. With the Axis then holding Bizerte, Rommel would be aided rather than hindered. Crucial landings therefore: Algiers, Philippeville, Bône, Bizerte.

The Americans: Agreed that Tunisia was an important objective but also saw the operation as neutralizing possible Axis penetration into Morocco and Dakar. Feared Germans striking through Spain. Until convinced that Spain and Spanish Morocco would remain neutral, the Americans were unwilling to put major forces through the Straits of Gibraltar. Crucial landings therefore: Casablanca, Oran.

British and American intelligence differed regarding Spain. The British felt sure that Hitler, fully committed in Russia, would not spare the divisions to cut through Spain; and they were convinced that Franco would steadfastly hold to his policy of neutrality. The map-oriented American planners refused to accept the same information available to the British and looked with apprehension at those areas on their charts which showed them how narrow and how vulnerable was that aperture which led into the Mediterranean.

Both British and Americans agreed, however, that precautionary measures to ensure free passage through the straits must be made, and Eisenhower authorized planning for Operation BACKBONE, a move into Spanish Morocco. Fortunately for the Allies, neither Franco nor Hitler was anxious to involve the Iberian peninsula in military operations, and Allied assurances of respecting Spanish neutrality, presented to Franco by British Ambassador Sir Samuel Hoare, successfully persuaded the Spaniards to take no action.[6]

The 9 August plan included operations in both Morocco and Algeria, but it envisaged no landing farther east than Bône, about 100 miles from Bizerte. Almost immediately the project ran into that difficulty which would hamper all subsequent plans: a shortage of transports and a shortage of aircraft carriers and planes to protect adequately the debarkations. The British could provide only enough for one landing, and the Americans scarcely enough for one. Eisenhower had no alternative but to reduce his perspective and to think in terms of no more than two major assaults.

The reduction in scope caused Eisenhower to develop some severe misgivings. His doubts were reinforced by new intelligence brought to London by Colonel Eddy around 10 August. Eddy had received a complete breakdown of French dispositions from General Mast, and this information enabled Eisenhower to form a picture of what he might expect. On the fifteenth, he elaborated in a pessimistic cable to Marshall:

> In the region now are some fourteen French divisions rather poorly equipped but presumably with a fair degree of training

and with the benefit of professional leadership. If this army should act as a unit in contesting the invasion, it could, in view of the slowness with which Allied forces can be accumulated at the two main ports, so delay and hamper operations that the real object of the expedition could not be achieved, namely the seizing control of the north shore of Africa before it can be substantially reinforced by the Axis.

. . . .

We believe . . . that we will encounter very considerable resistance from certain sections of the French forces. We believe the area in which the French will be most favorable to us is around Algiers with the areas in which we will probably encounter resistance those between Oran and Casablanca and near Tunis.

We believe that the chances of effecting initial landings are better than even but that the chances for overall success of the operation, including capture of Tunis before it can be reinforced by the Axis, are considerably less than 50 per cent.[7]

Faced with a reduction in anticipated naval support, Eisenhower produced by 21 August a modified plan which emphasized an attack on Oran; but this seemed to jeopardize any chance of seizing Tunisia and the proposal ran into strong British opposition.

Eisenhower's planning during August also faced formidable difficulties because he could not obtain a precise answer to basic questions from the two highest authorities: Prime Minister Churchill and President Roosevelt. Churchill was completely out of reach: he had been traveling outside England during almost the whole of August, first to Cairo, where he revised the Middle East command, and then to Moscow, where he announced to an unenthusiastic Stalin that the second front in 1942 meant an occupation of French North Africa.[8] Churchill returned to London on 25 August convinced that TORCH must become an outstanding success, not only because he had to prove western integrity to the Soviets, but because he knew more clearly than ever how slim were the possibilities of a successful cross-channel assault. The commando raid on Dieppe, launched the previous week on 19 August, had shown that only enormous aggressive power would be able to crush German coastal defenses. The prime minister swung into action. Taking rapid note of the American concepts, he began to exert his considerable influence in pulling the divergences together.

President Roosevelt, on the other hand, revealed no alarm at the centrifugal forces that were causing TORCH to become two separate operations, an American one centering on Morocco and the Atlantic coast and a British expedition pointing toward Tunisia. Neither Roosevelt nor the American Joint Chiefs could accept the Churchillian estimate: "Spain: will do nothing, France: resistance will be negligible and Germany: reaction will be encountered only through Tunis."[9] This appraisal, reported by Eisenhower on 27 August, turned out to be 100 percent correct, yet it did not conform to the Joint Chiefs' conviction that leaving passage through Gibraltar at the mercy of Franco's good will would be utmost folly.[10]

The president held on to the American concept with a tenacity that purely military considerations cannot wholly explain. He hoped that TORCH would be launched before the November elections.[11] From this point of view the operation had to be successful and had to be clearly American. The president could not risk having the United States, in its first commitment to battle, appear as ancillary to a British plan which possessed only 50 percent chance of success. The president did not share Eisenhower's great feeling for an operation in which Americans and British subordinated their national differences to an Allied objective. Thus, during August, while Eisenhower tried to work out joint planning in the best sense of the word, Washington had been edging toward a project in which American identity would be clearly manifested.

It should be mentioned that in February the administration had authorized Hadley Cantril of Princeton to conduct a survey of Moroccan opinion regarding an American invasion. By 16 July the results of the poll had become available: the conclusions, gathered from 142 interviews, suggested that 70 percent of the civilian population would not resist but that two-thirds of the military would. More important, the poll confirmed the view that resistance to British forces and to de Gaulle's Free French would be firmer than resistance to Americans alone.[12]

This opinion was strongly reinforced by the information available to Colonel Eddy who, after his conferences with Eisenhower, went on to Washington, where on 22 August he testified to the Joint Chiefs regarding a long report he had drafted on the thirteenth. He argued that strong American pressure should be brought to bear to exclude the British and Free French from landing on French territory; he feared that otherwise the United States would forfeit the benefit of general cooperation by the French army.[13] It may be presumed that the Cantril report and Eddy's intelligence were available and known to the president, who must also have considered the strong opinions of General Handy, chief of operations, regarding TORCH.

On 22 August, Handy, who had just returned from a visit to Eisenhower's headquarters, expressed the view that TORCH as now set up "involves an unjustifiable hazard and should be abandoned entirely or revised and directed toward a less ambitious objective." After setting forth some possible alternatives, Handy then argued that if TORCH could not be executed, the best move would be to "revise the existing directive by limiting the purpose and provide for the U.S. Task Force to land on the West Coast [i.e., Morocco] and the British Task Forces (with U.S. troops attached) to land in the Mediterranean." Such an operation, he believed, "would have a reasonable chance of tactical success and would not present the possibilities of the major debacle that might well result from the present TORCH."[14] As a copy of the Handy report exists in the president's map room file, it is likely that Roosevelt had read it and had reflected upon its contents.

Faced with a variety of opinions about the anti-British feeling in North Africa, the president moved toward the conclusion that the presence of British troops would vitiate the possibility of obtaining French cooperation. By this time, also, Admiral Leahy had moved into the routine of his new job as the president's personal chief of staff; he was thus able to comment on the Anglophobic views which had prevailed at Vichy, and he was in a position to add the weight of his own opinion regarding British participation.[15] By 25 August, the president had concluded that Eisenhower's modified plan, which would concentrate on American activity in the west, would best serve the interests of the United States. The Joint Chiefs supported this view.

The American decision to go it alone, whether or not the British cooperated, came just at the moment when Churchill, back from Moscow, had concluded that TORCH, so vital to General Montgomery's imminent counterattack against Rommel, must at all costs develop into a major success. It did not take the prime minister long to guess that some change in the American position had been developing. General Clark recalled that the Joint Chiefs' recommendation to stop planning for Algiers and Bône had reached him at 3:00 A.M. on 25 August in a top-secret message. That night, he and

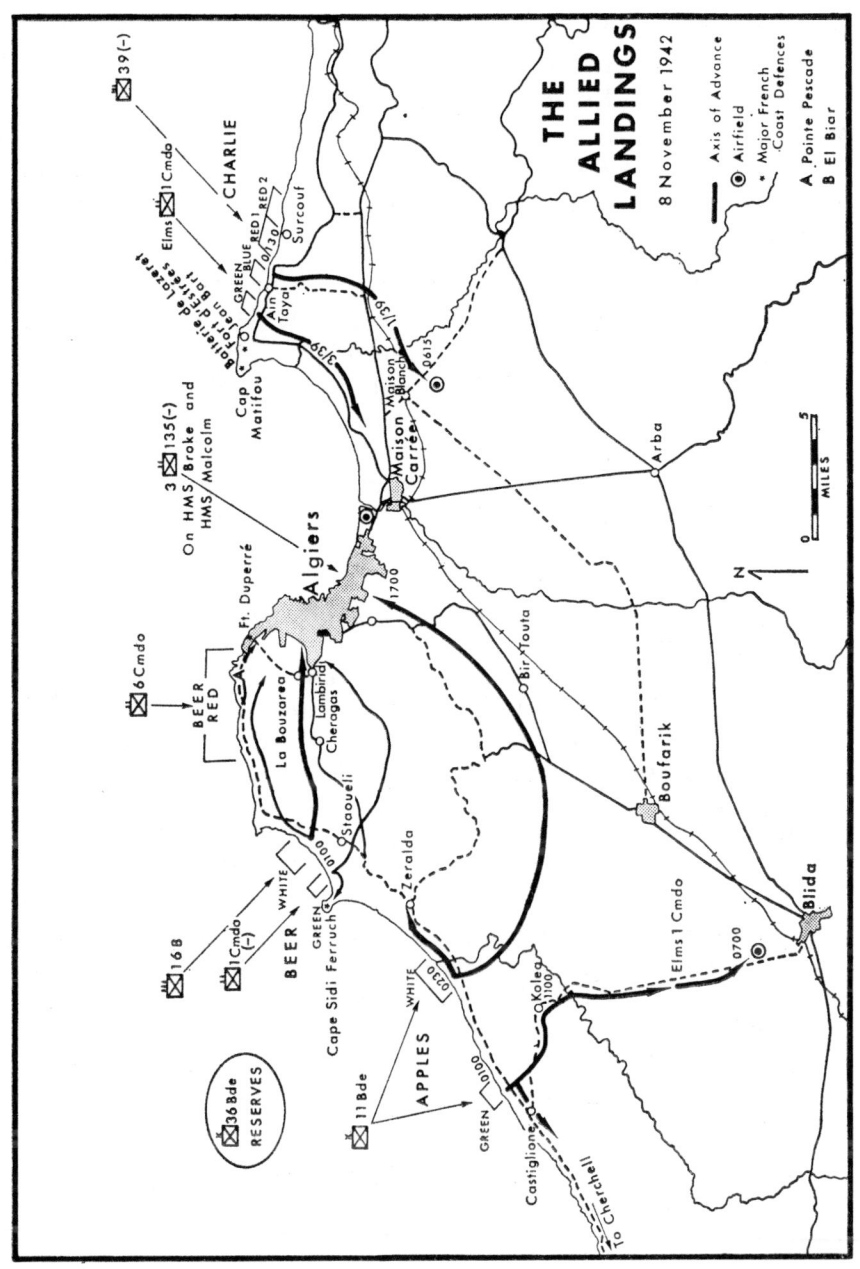

Map by Lewis Armstrong

Eisenhower, uneasily guarding their highly classified information during dinner with the prime minister, noted how anxiously Churchill pleaded for attack at the earliest possible moment.[16] Churchill on his part sensed an American cooling off. He immediately dispatched an urgent cable to Roosevelt arguing for an operation at least as far as Algiers.[17]

Roosevelt was not persuaded. On 28 August, Marshall sent off a long message to Eisenhower in which he tried to explain the president's position:

> I have just completed a conference with the President. He is informing the Prime Minister that reply will be made to his Torch messages in a few days, probably Monday. The President appears to have definitely repeat definitely decided that the initial operation must be a purely American one except for British Naval forces, air forces and shipping, including combat loaders. Presumably the operation would necessarily be restricted to Oran and Casablanca. British troops are not to come in until at least a week after our landings. The President believes that if he has a week after we land he can arrange matters with the French so that there will be no complications to landings of British troops later. He feels that joint landings even though led by American troops will not suffice. The President is apparently unwilling to accept the hazards of a single line of communications through Gibraltar. He does not accept the British argument that the action indicated will mean the loss of Tunisia and possibly Algiers to the Germans. He also is impressed with the necessity from the U.S. viewpoint for safeguarding the South Atlantic. This consideration should not at any time be communicated to the British. The President is convinced that naval resources are not sufficient for the support of more than two landings. The President pictures the landing of some 80,000 men in the two assault convoys and thinks such a number would be necessary to his political purposes.
>
> I am convinced that the President has fully made up his mind as outlined above and that he intends to dictate that procedure.[18]

Marshall's reference to the president's "political purposes" accurately appraises an important element of Roosevelt's thinking—that TORCH had not been conceived primarily for its strategic advantages, but for its role in domestic and international policy. Whether or not the North African occupation provided a true second front, it at least made a gesture toward Stalin; but more important it served as a fillip to the flagging morale and war spirit of the American people. As he became increasingly aware that British cooperation might endanger rather than enhance the United States's reputation, the president became more and more willing that the operation should shrink, so long as it could be both successful and American. This view thus obscured the true strategic objective, control of Tunisia, which could have been obtained only with complete British cooperation and with acceptance of the British position that in the eastern Mediterranean, rather than in the straits and on the Atlantic coast, was to be found the focal point of anti-Axis endeavor. From a strategic point of view all of these decisions were completely wrong: (1) an attack on Tunisia *was* feasible, would probably have succeeded, and would have placed Rommel in a vise which might have destroyed him; (2) the idea that the North African French were pro-American but anti-British, while true, did not make that much difference to French cooperation or hostility. All of the naval craft in the Mediterranean assault force had been identified by Axis and Vichy intelligence as British; and when the attack on Algiers began, on 8 November, the first elements to be identified were two British destroyers bursting into the harbor. When Darlan signed the cease-fire he did so not because the attackers were American but because they had overwhelming strength.

Yet it may still be argued that Roosevelt, superb politician that he was, with a sensitive finger on American attitudes, realized that for vaster purposes than strategy, namely American long-range support for the total war effort, he needed immediate involvement and certain victory. For these he bargained away an assault on Tunisia, and in return he obtained the dubious advantage of sole responsibility for the entire enterprise. Undoubtedly news of the invasion, when broadcast in November (too late for the fall congressional elections), did engender a patriotic sense, throughout the country, that the United States was finally and inextricably involved in the European war. But this was bought at the cost of prolonging the Mediterranean operation and ultimately destroyed any possible argument, so long and energetically sustained by General Marshall, for a cross-channel assault in 1943.

President Roosevelt's critical and historically significant decision became official on 30 August, the same day that Robert Murphy arrived in Washington. On that date the president sent off a cable to

Churchill asserting, as Marshall had forewarned Eisenhower, that TORCH must be an American operation and that American forces should be ventured only at Oran and Casablanca. But Churchill was not prepared to accept the idea of two separate operations. To permit the Americans to go their separate way would have defeated his basic strategy of getting the United States wholly committed and blooded in the western theater. Although the British chiefs were reluctant to give up landings at Philippeville or Bône, and even sensed that to abandon eastern Algeria was to lose Tunisia, they accepted Churchill's brief that a combined operation must be preserved. The prime minister proposed a simple compromise: he would accept Casablanca if the Americans would accept Algiers. The U.S. Joint Chiefs met on 2 September and concurred. On the next day, Churchill and the British chiefs met with Eisenhower and Clark, debated the whole issue, and reached agreement that landings could be made at Oran, Algiers, and Casablanca, especially if the troops assaulting the last port were reduced by about 10,000. Roosevelt split the difference, agreeing to reduce the Casablanca assault by 5,000. But he insisted on confirmation of the political arrangement that the United States be granted sole responsibility for North Africa, while Great Britain had Spain.[19] He cabled his final agreement on the fourth, thus ending what Eisenhower had called the "Transatlantic essay contest."[20]

On this same day Robert Murphy was flown to Hyde Park for a conference with the president.

Washington, September 1942
Murphy in Washington

During the entire month of September Robert Murphy talked, negotiated, and explained the French political situation to officials in Washington and London. The reception he personally received was friendly and sympathetic, but his proposals met with lukewarm approbation in many quarters, with hostility in some, and with enthusiasm in very few. Among the most enthusiastic listeners was President Roosevelt himself, who conferred with Murphy during a long, hot afternoon on 4 September. The president understood in general the situation in North Africa and in Vichy and no doubt wished to justify his two-year-old policy of recognizing Pétain's government. If indeed a French invitation would bring American soldiers into North Africa without casualties, he could boast of achieving the most remarkable diplomatic achievement of the twentieth century. At the same time a curious anomaly underrode the president's policy: he wished to violate French neutrality but he was loathe to recognize any dissident pro-Allied French regime to which anti-Vichy Frenchmen could rally. He was extremely clear about this in his conversation with Murphy: "You will restrict your dealings," he said, "to French officials on the local levels, prefects, and the military. I will not help anyone impose a Government on the French people."[21]

In his memoirs, Murphy remarks how alien this policy stood in relation to the aspirations of General de Gaulle; but Murphy does not point out that it was equally antipathetic to the program worked out by The Five, who also assumed that an independent North Africa might be recognized by the Allies.

While in Washington Murphy was much concerned about the diverse opinions he encountered. The president may have favored his work, but Murphy had to recognize that important implementing agencies, the War Department, the Joint Chiefs of Staff, and the Board of Economic Warfare, held indifferent and hostile views regarding cooperation with the French. In conversations with Stimson and Marshall, he gained the impression that they both wished to avoid entangling political involvement. The secretary of war had argued eloquently against the North African venture and still believed the whole operation should be shelved in favor of a 1943 assault on France. (His views here coincided exactly with those of General Giraud.) General Marshall was exerting all of his considerable ability to make TORCH a success, but he was convinced that armed strength plus surprise outweighed the uncertain benefits of exposing military plans to any Frenchman. With hard, pragmatic realism, both Stimson and the chief of staff believed that military superiority would shortly bring political and civil affairs into line. Murphy also took note of a decision, made by the Joint Chiefs of Staff on 9 September, that there should be no staff talks with the French separatists.[22]

The strongest opposition to Murphy's proposals came from the Board of Economic Warfare (BEW), which had never supported the Murphy-Weygand Agreement and which felt that an economic boycott of North Africa should be imposed. BEW could argue that the State Department's policy had accomplished little. Suspended from time to time, the Murphy-Weygand Agreement had indeed run an uneven course and had never given rise to such an abundance of shipments as to make an appreciable impression on North African opinion. Murphy felt that if the scheduled shipments could be authorized in time to reach Algeria or Morocco before the invasion, they might create some psychological advantages. He spent an inordinate amount of time, while he was in Washington, trying to assure BEW representatives that shipments would favor Allied interests and would not assist Rommel in Libya.

Faced with a great variety of opinions, Murphy redoubled his efforts to obtain the directive he had been seeking ever since Pearl Harbor. He was keenly aware of the difficulties Colonel Solborg had encountered in negotiating without clear-cut authorization. Murphy had been in the diplomatic game too long not to appreciate its complexities, and he needed to know just how far he could go in committing the United States government, whose contradictory policies left Murphy himself bewildered. Between the time he saw the president, 4 September, and ten days later when he left to see Eisenhower in London, Murphy supervised the drafting of a directive which was tentatively approved by the president and the chiefs of staff.[23] Significantly, the draft was not circulated in the State Department, which did not know officially of the TORCH operation or of Murphy's secret mission.

According to the directive, Murphy would be permitted to tell those Frenchmen whom he trusted that the United States planned to occupy North Africa. This, of course, he had already done. He was not to reveal the points of landing until he was told to do so, nor could he count on more than a two-day notice. (This was later extended to four.) He could assure the French that the expedition would be American—no Free French—and that the United States would welcome French assistance. To assuage fears of an armed occupation, he could assure the French that "no change in the existing French Civil Administration is contemplated by the United States." The directive said nothing about The Five, or General Giraud, or Admiral Darlan, all of whom had to be encompassed in the vague expression: "those French nationals whom you consider reliable." There was nothing which suggested avoidance of administrators associated with Vichy; on the contrary, the stipulation that no change in administration was contemplated categorically approved of negotiations with Vichy officials.

General Marshall saw future problems in Murphy's designation as the president's personal representative, presumably with authority to bypass both State and Army Departments. The chief of staff wanted to have a precise definition of Murphy's role vis-à-vis Eisenhower and those agencies—the Political Section and Civil Affairs Section—already established in the TORCH commander's headquarters. Marshall cabled Eisenhower on 15 September, the day before Murphy arrived in London, about his concern, and he invited Eisenhower to question the command relationships: "Do not let the fact that the President has given approval to this draft defer you from proposing alterations."[24]

London, August–September 1942
Civil Affairs planning at TORCH headquarters

When Eisenhower heard Murphy, on 16 September, describe the complex political situation in North Africa, he listened, Murphy later reported, "with a kind of horrified intentness to my description of the possible complications."[25]

If the TORCH commander registered concern, it was not because the snarl of foreign politics had been brought to his attention for the first time by Murphy's revelation. Eisenhower had been confronted with politics from the first day he installed himself in Norfolk House. He had actually inherited a political section. Among the administrative divisions functioning in connection with ROUNDUP and transferred to TORCH had been a Political Affairs Section headed by W. H. B. (Hal) Mack, a career diplomat in the British Foreign Service who in 1940, as a staff member of the British Embassy in Paris, had witnessed the French collapse. As soon as he joined the TORCH staff, Mack immediately set to work on plans associated with political and economic warfare which bore a marked British approach and did not seem to jibe entirely with American policy so far as Eisenhower understood it. Yet Eisenhower could not very well drop Mack without creating the sort of inter-Allied friction he deplored. He hit upon another device. As his administrative policy was to balance a chief of one nationality with a deputy of the other, the Allied commander looked for an American to become Mack's deputy. Then, going a little further, on 21 August, he proposed to set up a Civil Affairs Section, which would parallel the Political Section but would have an American in charge.[26] With an uneasy awareness of men like Murphy, who operated as the president's personal representatives, Eisenhower wanted it made clear to the candidate "that he will be a member of my staff and will have no independent avenue of official communication to any individual or office in the U.S."[27]

No one was more qualified to head a civil administration division than Robert Murphy, but he could not suit Eisenhower's requirements about being on the TORCH staff if that meant remaining in London. Yet in view of the complex political situation the Allied commander needed an American with recent experience in North Africa and with rank equal to the tremendous responsibilities he would have to bear. He required someone also who could authoritatively interpret the president's North African policy and debate it effectively with the British. Because the president had decided to insulate Secretary Hull and the State Department from the TORCH operation, the United States possessed no machinery comparable to that of the British Foreign Office for establishing and implementing policy. No one in the United States really knew what American policy was except Roosevelt; but, much as the president enjoyed elaborating his views to his immediate entourage, the White House simply did not possess at that point in time the machinery to carry out day-to-day requirements.

The British were baffled by the American system—or non-system. It was very well for Churchill to reach great agreements in principle with Roosevelt, but the prime minister and the president, in spite of their vast and frequent correspondence, could not resolve every detail. The British held to positions which differed markedly from the Americans':[28] they had a special commitment to de Gaulle and to the Free French; they did not recognize Vichy and held Pétain and Darlan in suspicion; they believed in an economic blockade of France and French Africa; they had no commitment to Lemaigre Dubreuil or to General Giraud; they believed, unlike Murphy, that contact should be made with General Juin; and, while their SOE alone possessed the small arms and explosives needed by the resistance, they chafed under a recent decision which enabled Colonel Eddy of OSS to designate the recipients.[29]

Foreign Minister Anthony Eden found no pleasure in the fact that, while Great Britain was providing 40 percent of the men and most of the naval support inside the Mediterranean, Churchill was content to let President Roosevelt dominate the political scene.[30]

Earlier in the summer Eden had chafed under a reprimand from the prime minister, who considered his anti-Vichy views too simplistic. "The position is so anomalous and monstrous," Churchill had written, "that very clear-cut views, such as you are developing, do not altogether cover it. There is much more in British policy towards France than abusing Pétain and backing de Gaulle."[31] Acquiescing to the fact that Allied policy was about to accept negotiations with Vichyites, Eden tried to anticipate future difficulties. On 20 August, the Foreign Office had completed the draft of a proposal looking toward a joint Anglo-American policy on North Africa. Eden sent this on to Lord Halifax, the British ambassador in Washington, with instructions to discuss it with Hull and the president. But the *démarche* had arrived at a bad time, just at the moment when Roosevelt was pulling the whole North African problem into his own hands. When finally Halifax saw the president, on 10 September, the matter had been decided. The ambassador could extract no specific information and gathered that Roosevelt would not permit the State Department to play its normal role as opposite number to the Foreign Office; he concluded that the best plan would have to be to negotiate directly with Eisenhower.[32]

Eisenhower by that date possessed only the rudiments of a Civil Affairs Section staffed with American experts. But he did not want to commit himself to Murphy as chief of that section until he had met the man and had convinced himself that there was no danger of losing ultimate control over some aspects of the operation; he also needed assurance that his civil affairs adviser could remain in London.

By the time Murphy reached TORCH headquarters a compromise had been worked out: Murphy would ostensibly head the Civil Affairs Section but would be represented by an acting chief or deputy until such time as the occupation took place. The deputy selected was H. Freeman Matthews, known as "Doc" to his intimates, an experienced foreign service officer who had served with Murphy at Vichy and had succeeded him there as counsellor of embassy. At the time of his new appointment, Matthews was assigned to the United States Embassy in London. He was fully informed on French developments.[33]

As the distinctions between the Civil Affairs Section and the Political Section had not been clearly delineated, the consequence of Matthews's appointment would be to balance British political influence more effectively than the appointment of an American as Mack's deputy would have done. Matthews later recalled the appointment thus:

> I was detailed to General Eisenhower's staff by order of the President . . . as a Political Adviser and opposite number to Hal Mack of the Foreign Office. (There was some anxiety on the President's part lest Eisenhower get all his political advice from the British: hence my appointment.)[34]

Matthews had scarcely begun his work on Eisenhower's staff when Murphy flew in to London on 16 September; only the day before had the new Civil Affairs Section been officially established.

London, September 1942
Murphy's directive[35]

Murphy came to London in cloak-and-dagger secrecy to avoid the possibility that anyone might recognize him at Eisenhower's headquarters. He traveled in uniform as Lieutenant Colonel McGowan.[36]

During the afternoon and evening of 16 September, Murphy elaborated on political aspects of the TORCH operation to General Eisenhower and to a select group of whom only two were British. The American officers included the TORCH deputy, General Clark; the chief of staff, General Bedell Smith; Captain Harry Butcher, Eisenhower's aide; and Col. Julius Holmes, formerly of the State Department and currently serving in the newly established Civil Affairs Section. Holmes, incidentally, spoke perfect French. Three American civilians were present, Ambassador Winant; Averell Harriman, in England on special assignment for the president; and the recently designated acting head of the Civil Affairs staff, Freeman Matthews. The only British representatives were Brigadier Mockler-Ferryman, head of the TORCH G-2 (intelligence) section, and the political adviser, Hal Mack.

Murphy explained in detail the negotiations he had carried on with The Five, the possible availability of General Giraud as French leader, and the chances of French cooperation in Morocco, Oran, and Algiers. In turn, Eisenhower told Murphy something about the military arrangements.

Murphy never obtained a detailed and complete briefing on

Operation TORCH. Before he arrived in London there had been discussion at TORCH headquarters whether all the details should be given to him. Certainly Murphy convinced his auditors of his trustworthiness, but Murphy later wrote that he had never received an official briefing. Presumably he was told what Eisenhower and his officers believed he "needed to know," even though the information he received was somewhat misleading. For example, Murphy was told, so that he could relay the information to his French friends, that the landings would include 150,000 troops with rapid build-up to 500,000. (Actually there were 107,453 in the initial assault, and in three weeks 253,213 had come ashore.) He knew there would be three major areas of attack, Casablanca, Oran, and Algiers, but he also gained the impression that there would be landings in Tunisia. A thorough briefing might have provided Murphy with greater appreciation for the monumental effort and precise timings required; such an explanation would have prevented his embarrassing request, at D-Day minus eight, to postpone the entire enterprise. A detailed briefing might also have enabled him to see in more accurate perspective the French role relative to the Anglo-American effort.[37]

A certain amount of time during the London meeting was devoted to discussion of the draft directive Murphy brought with him. General agreement was reached on the Civil Affairs arrangement so that the directive finally read:

> Upon the occupation of French North Africa by American Military Forces you will act as the Operating Executive head of the Civil Affairs Section and Advisor for Civil Affairs under General Eisenhower. Prior to the arrival of Military Forces in the Area, you will have the status of the Personal Representative of the President.
>
> You will work in close cooperation with General Eisenhower . . . in the preparation and execution of plans of a civil and political nature for the occupation of French North Africa by American Military Forces. . . . All communications between the President and you and between General Eisenhower and you will be carried out through such channels as General Eisenhower and you may arrange.

The directive also stated that:

> As Political Advisor to General Eisenhower you will prepare and submit to the President for approval: (a) Recommendations regarding policies to be followed by the American

Government in the area, including economic supply and financial support, and such additional matters as you may deem appropriate.[38]

Eisenhower and Marshall had made certain that Murphy would communicate via military channels, and this arrangement gave the Joint Chiefs some control over developments. Murphy was also supposed to work on various proclamations and state messages, of which drafts had already been prepared. These drafts were brought to Washington later by Colonel Holmes, and Murphy had some opportunity to check them before he returned to Algiers. But the major economic and financial policies were worked out at Eisenhower's headquarters by Matthews and Mack in the weeks following Murphy's departure. No one in London had much knowledge of The Five's proposals, already prepared by Tarbé de Saint-Hardouin in Algiers. Nor could Murphy know accurately what his Civil Affairs Section was doing.

It should be noted again that no French nationals were identified in Murphy's directive except as those "whom you consider reliable." Murphy explained to Eisenhower and the others what communications he had exchanged with General Giraud and with Admiral Darlan, but he received neither encouragement nor strictures regarding his revelations. Mack and Mockler-Ferryman may well have entertained severe reservations about both Giraud and Darlan, but they were outranked and outnumbered. When a key phrase in Murphy's directive, already approved by President Roosevelt, stated categorically: "No change in the existing French Civil Administration is contemplated by the United States," it scarcely behooved two fairly low-echelon Englishmen to protest that Vichy collaborators should be replaced with Gaullists. Murphy had no reason to question that he had been pursuing a path generally acceptable to his superiors.

In discussing General Giraud, Murphy and Eisenhower necessarily broached the question of command. In two world wars, Allied forces fighting on French soil had served under French supreme command and, as Murphy reported, his French contacts expected General Giraud to exert such authority. To Eisenhower such a thought edged toward the absurd—a commanding officer had to participate in preparation of a major expedition, and in any case supreme command was awarded by the Combined Chiefs of Staff.

Eisenhower would concede that once French forces had received up-to-date equipment and were loyally serving under an Allied commander in chief, they might remain under the command of a French general. This was not a question to be settled at once.

All in all, Murphy made an excellent impression on Eisenhower and his staff. Captain Butcher conjured up a pleasant picture of the discussions at Eisenhower's cottage hideout near London:

> Murphy, I saw, was tall, slightly stoop-shouldered, and talked more like an American businessman canvassing the ins and outs of a prospective merger than either a diplomat or a soldier. . . . All of us sat on the lawn for a couple of hours, enjoying the sun and hearing from Murphy detailed information on the situation in Algeria and French Morocco and the plans for French co-operation. Murphy impressed all of us as an honest reporter who delivered his story objectively. If all that he anticipates in the way of French co-operation comes to pass, many of our worries will have been needless.[39]

Three days after Murphy's one-day conference, Eisenhower wrote Marshall that if the directive were revised so that final authority in the African theater rested with him as supreme commander, there would be no misunderstandings regarding a division of authority between American military and civil officials. Of Murphy, Eisenhower wrote:

> . . . I have the utmost confidence in his judgment and discretion and I know that I will be able to work with him in perfect harmony. . . . I am sure that Murphy will agree with [the revisions] and with the necessity of presenting the French with a clean cut and single authority.[40]

Murphy had been equally impressed by General Eisenhower and was relieved "to find that although Eisenhower had been as displeased as Marshall about the shift in operational plans, he did not share Marshall's indifference to help from Frenchmen in Africa."[41] Murphy was, therefore, encouraged to hope that with his new directive, which he received on 22 September, he could get back immediately to North Africa to work on the final plans for the invasion, now set definitely for 8 November, only six weeks in the future.

Murphy was delayed in Washington for two more weeks, however, before he could free himself from further consultations with Task Force commanders, with General Clark, who made a quick trip to Washington late in September, with Colonel Holmes regarding the proclamations, and, most tedious of all, with Board of Economic Warfare representatives who were determined to hinder transport of civilian supplies. It was not until 4 October that Murphy finally left Washington, and he did not reach Casablanca, his first stop in French North Africa, until the ninth. The invasion was just one month away.

London and Washington, 17 September–4 October
TORCH planning[42]

Between the date that Robert Murphy left London for Washington, 17 September, and the time he departed for North Africa, 4 October, most of the important military decisions and plans were made. During this period D-Day was finally and definitely set for Sunday, 8 November. All of the complex arrangements for moving troops and equipment to loading points, for assigning ships, and for developing cover plans now focused on a specific requirement: that convoys must leave the United States and England between 22 and 26 October. Work in Washington and London proceeded at the frantic pace needed to make up the time lost in obtaining a top-level decision on objectives. This decision, to strike at Casablanca, Oran, and Algiers under American supreme command, had only been reached on 5 September, forty-seven days before the first convoys had to sail. Later in the war a "recommended schedule for preparation of a Task Force" was worked out by the War Department: before sailing date there should be 180 days after the basic decision, 150 after troop assignment, and 40 after completion of pre-invasion maneuvers.[43] In the case of TORCH, troops were being assigned up to 16 days of departure, and final maneuvers were observed by Eisenhower on 19 October, only a few days before embarkation.

Planning for the Algiers attack had become complicated when Churchill acquiesced to Roosevelt's insistence that TORCH become essentially an American enterprise. Throughout August the staff in Norfolk House had assumed that Algiers would come within a British zone and that Gen. Kenneth A. N. Anderson, as commander of the Eastern Task Force (essentially the British 1st Army), would plan and carry out the operation. Then, in September, the British planners suddenly found themselves incorporated into the American staff and, although United States forces would number about 10,000 against the British 23,000, they had to acquiesce to an American ruse placing General Anderson in the background. By early October the machinery of this device, which thereafter changed only in minor details, had been worked out. Gen. Charles W. Ryder, the lanky commanding officer of the U.S. 34th Division, then training in Scotland, was placed in command of the Eastern Assault Force. He would remain in charge of the Algiers area until troops were ashore and ready to move toward Tunisia, at which time General Anderson would replace him. To make the transition more palatable, much of the planning was supervised directly by General Clark, who as TORCH deputy commander was senior to both Ryder and Anderson.

The attack plan called for an envelopment of Algiers from east, south, and west. Algiers lies on the western edge of a broad semicircular bay some ten miles across, protected at either side by formidable batteries, those of Fort d'Estrées and Lazeret on the east and Fort Duperré on the west. The Allied landings were scheduled for beaches several miles farther out on both sides, at Ain Taya and Surcouf on the east, and west of Algiers along twenty miles of shore from Pointe Pescade to Castiglione. About midway along this coastline lies the fortified point of Sidi Ferruch, which would be of special interest to the Americans because General Mast believed he could arrange a friendly and cooperative reception to troops who might land there. An American regimental combat team, the 168th, from Ryder's 34th Division, together with a British commando, was scheduled to land about three miles from Sidi Ferruch, but the remaining forces on the west, commandos at Pointe Pescade and the 11th Brigade Group to the south, were all British. The forces landing on the other side of Algiers were partly American: the 39th Combat Team of the Ninth Division; and partly British: one commando unit.

If all went well the landings would begin after midnight, 8 November, and as soon as possible forces would move toward the city and toward the airports at Blida and Maison Blanche. Two British destroyers, H.M.S. *Malcolm* and H.M.S. *Broke*, after ramming the boom guarding the southern entrance to Algiers port, were scheduled to tie up at one of the quays and land commandos. The latter operation had been forcefully urged on Eisenhower by British naval officers, especially by Admiral Bertram Ramsey, who apparently believed that the raids on Saint Nazaire and on Dieppe had proved its feasibility, even though it violated the age-worn axiom that warships should not challenge shore batteries of superior calibre and range. The introduction of British ships into the Algiers port would furthermore reveal at the very beginning that the operation was not purely American. If anything could have been conceived to energize the French will to resist, it was this direct naval confrontation, which unnecessarily evoked memories of Dakar and Mers-el-Kebir.

As Oran had from the beginning been considered an American area, a certain amount of thought had already been expended on ways to assault that city and its important naval base at Mers-el-Kebir. For several weeks in August, Eisenhower had assumed that the major thrust of General Patton's Western Task Force would be directed at Oran. After the final decision on 5 September, Patton was ordered to limit his assault to Casablanca,[44] while planners associated with Clark's II Corps were given responsibility to develop blueprints for occupying Oran.

The assault plan for Oran, objective of the Center Task Force, was similar to the scheme for Algiers: landings at three points outside the city, seizure of the air facilities, and encirclement. This operation would be essentially American, with fewer than one-tenth of the 40,000 troops, to be commanded by Gen. Lloyd R. Fredendall, being British. The British, however, would provide transport together with naval and air protection.

While both the Algiers and Oran operations would be mounted in Great Britain, the Casablanca assault force would be entirely trained and equipped in the United States and would be transported directly to Morocco in the largest amphibious operation the world had yet seen. From his headquarters in Washington General Patton, working closely with Adm. Henry Kent Hewitt, who commanded the Naval Task Force, drew up plans to land some 33,000 men at Port Lyautey and Fedala, north of Casablanca, and at Safi, a port 140 miles to the south. Most of the transports would be loaded at Hampton Roads, at the mouth of Chesapeake Bay, and would start putting to sea on 23 October. Later, at sea, the transport would rendezvous with the flagship, the cruiser *Augusta*, and with the aircraft carriers, battleships, cruisers, destroyers, and other craft which constituted the covering group. The whole convoy, over 100 ships, would be carrying an army for direct attack 3,000 miles away, a task unique in military history.

London, September–15 October 1942
Political and Civil Affairs planning

With the signing of Murphy's directive, Eisenhower possessed a clearer picture of his powers in political matters, and with the arrival of Matthews at Norfolk House, he oriented the overall TORCH policy even more specifically along American lines. Ultimately Mack's political section was absorbed into a larger civil affairs division. As Butcher recorded it:

> Mack, because he is British, has gracefully stepped aside after most of the hard work has been done, so that an American front may be given to the political activities....
>
> ... Mr. Mack will be the Supreme Commander's personal adviser on political matters, and at his own suggestion, his title will be British Civil Liaison Officer.[45]

What had begun on Churchill's part as acquiescence to American dominance, largely to make sure that the United States became fully involved in Europe, now solidified into official policy to the extent that when the six-page political directive for TORCH was issued on 11 October it stated clearly:

> It has been agreed between the United States and British authorities that civil administration of controlled territory shall be entirely under American control.
>
> Parleys and negotiations will be conducted by United States officers, with the assistance of the Political Officer attached to each force....
>
> In the assault stage the fact that the operation is predominately American and under American command must always be kept in the forefront. The participation of British Naval and Air Forces from the outset cannot be concealed.[46]

At the same time that the political directive was issued the text of President Roosevelt's proclamation—to be delivered to Pétain and the governors of North Africa, as well as broadcast—became available to authorized planning personnel, including the British Foreign Office.[47] However willing the prime minister may have been to submerge the British effort, Foreign Minister Eden could not suppress a feeling of indignation that no gesture had been made to acknowledge the considerable British contribution.[48]

On 12 October, TORCH General Order No. 5, a summary of civil-administration policies, was issued. This document, together with the previous day's political directive, served as the basic statement of political aims. It reflects completely the American Vichy policy. A fundamental declaration is found in its first paragraph (italics added):

> PURPOSE OF THE CIVIL AFFAIRS SECTION
> ... To maintain and control for the Commanding General the civil governments of the territories of French North Africa as soon as military control of those territories is secured; *to retain the existing form or forms of government* in the territories under control, and *to retain the civil governments and their officials* and employees in their present positions, insofar as they are willing to continue in office, and as is consistent with the military mission and the policy of the Commanding General; to supplant those persons not in accord with the war aims of the United States, and its supporting ally [i.e., Great Britain], with other capable and efficient local personnel; or, with military personnel in the event there is hostile action on the part of the armed forces of the territories to be occupied, or by the inhabitants after the control is secured.[49]

A certain ambiguity exists in the authorization to "supplant those persons not in accord with" the Allies' war aims. One could argue that virtually every official in North Africa, having been appointed by Vichy, held reservations about Allied war aims and that the only Frenchmen who concurred in them had associated themselves with The Five or with de Gaulle. But the Free French, having been barred from participation by American policy, were prevented from providing a pool of "capable and efficient" replacements. And the resources of The Five were small. Even then, many insurgents recruited by The Five were later arrested by the Vichy officials who remained in office with American sanction.

A very curious anomaly of the civil and political directives lay in the fact that Robert Murphy, who would head the Civil Affairs Section after the landings, never studied them. Murphy continued to negotiate with insurgents as the president's personal representative, but he had no way of ascertaining the detailed provisions that were emerging from TORCH headquarters. Most of these details, referring to control of utilities, courts, police powers, and the like, hold no great political significance; and to examine the directives item by item—they run to fourteen single-spaced legal-size pages— would not be especially instructive. It will suffice to point out the politically significant aspects in a summary which will quickly reveal similarities and differences between the military, political, and economic objectives of The Five and those of the American planners.

	The Five	*The Americans*

Military

1. Occupy North Africa with forces sufficient to maintain control, estimated at seven (French-size) motorized divisions and five armored brigades (700-800 tanks) or approximately 190,000 troops.

1. Occupy North Africa with as powerful a force as available, estimated at the equivalent of six American and three British divisions, or approximately 108,000 troops in the initial wave, building up rapidly to over 250,000.

2. Landings at Oran, Algiers, Bizerte.

2. Landings at Casablanca, Oran, Algiers.

3. Operation to be entirely American: no British or Free French.

3. Operation given appearance of being American. No Free French, but 25 percent of initial landings to be British troops, building up to 40 percent of total Allied force within three weeks.

4. Total operation to be under a French commander in chief. General Henri Giraud to be given this command.

4. General Eisenhower, named supreme commander by the Combined Chiefs of Staff, never had any intention of relinquishing his command. He was willing to consider a French command over cooperating French forces.

5. The French Armistice Army in North Africa, numbering over 120,000, would be furnished modern arms and equipment.

5. The United States agreed to rearm the French army to fight against the Axis.

6. Small arms and explosives to be smuggled in to the French

6. The United States agreed to provide small arms but, lack-

115

The Five	The Americans

Political resistance prior to the landings.

ing means, had to rely on the British SOE, placed under Eisenhower's command, for deliveries. (For reasons not clear, the arms were never delivered.)

1. The United States should authorize a representative with full powers to negotiate military, political, and economic arrangements with The Five.

1. Under the directive signed by President Roosevelt on 22 Sept. 1942, Robert Murphy was named personal representative of the president. He was authorized to give certain information to Frenchmen he considered reliable and to recommend political, economic, and financial policies *for the President's approval.*

2. American relations with Vichy should be maintained if possible.

2. The United States continued to maintain relations with Vichy although no ambassador remained in France after May 1942.

3. If Vichy breaks relations, the United States should accept the installation of an *independent French government* in North Africa. Recognition of such a government would imply:

3. The United States had no intention of recognizing any independent regime. Roosevelt wanted local administrators to continue under American supervision. Recognition of new regimes would await the end of the war.

   (a) Treating the French in North Africa as equal allies.

   (a) Until France could carry its own weight, the United States had no intention of recognizing equal sovereign rights. Roosevelt thought of North Africa as occupied territory.

(b) Recognizing the integrity of the French Empire.

(c) Dealing with the Arab native population of North Africa only through the French administration.

(d) Issuing public announcements, leaflets, radio broadcasts, etc., only with prior approval of the French administration.

(b) President Roosevelt was unwilling to give any guarantees. Some French overseas territories were administered by Vichy, some by de Gaulle. In private conversations, the president implied he saw no reason to give some colonies, like Indochina —then occupied by Japan—back to the French. His policy was to deal individually with the administration of each colony, even though some public speeches spoke grandiloquently of the "restoration of France."

(c) Various edicts and proclamations prepared by Civil Affairs staff were printed in Arabic as well as in French. Practically speaking, the U.S. civil administrators would have to work through the French, but they did not officially concede this.

(d) Proclamations, edicts, leaflets, recorded announcements were prepared by the Civil Affairs staff. A high priority objective of TORCH was seizure of local radio broadcasting stations. There is no evidence that consultation, except for practical reasons, was considered necessary.

117

| The Five | The Americans |

Economic

1. The United States should guarantee the economic stability of North Africa by granting credit, by making appropriate shipments of goods, by extending Lend-Lease, by making reciprocal trade agreements, by regulating inflation, etc.

    1. The United States considered economic stability in North Africa vital to its own interests and to the war effort. It was prepared to cooperate in all areas, and also to guarantee wages and benefits to those who became employees of the United States after the landings.

2. The exchange rate should be pegged at 43.8 North African francs to the dollar. (This rate had been arranged by the British in areas controlled by the Free French. The free rate was around 125 to the dollar.)

    2. The United States was prepared to peg the franc at 75 to the dollar. (In 1943 the exchange rate was set at 50 to the dollar.)

When he returned to North Africa, Murphy would have to negotiate with The Five on the basis of what he surmised represented a policy the president would support. On certain points of difference, like the exchange-rate question, Murphy obtained some clarifications from Washington, but on others he made no headway at all.

Another plan which affected Murphy, but of which he knew very little, was the formulation of two contingencies: No. 1, "if the Allied Forces have been met with only slight or token resistance," and No. 2, "if the resistance has been considerable or prolonged." In the second contingency "a most stringent form of control," tantamount to a military government, would be imposed. For each of these conditions, three basic documents were prepared, a set of armistice terms, a proclamation, and a set of ordinances. When the landings took place, all of the task force commanders considered that only token resistance had been met and that consequently Armistice No. 1 should be the basis of a cease-fire. During the first weeks of the occupation, the "soft" armistice thus became the subject of negotiations which resulted in what came to be known as the Clark-Darlan Agreement. Inasmuch as the armistice terms include certain conditions quite alien to the spirit of Murphy's negotiations with The Five, it is worth setting forth the terms of this fundamental document to emphasize the differences between the thinking in North Africa and that at Eisenhower's headquarters. One should realize that Murphy did not see the document until after the French had surrendered.

Summary of the Terms of Armistice No. 1
(The "Soft" Armistice)[50]

1. All opposition to the landings and to Allied operations must cease.
2. Status, command, and functions of French forces will remain under French direction and will continue in the service of internal security.
3. French governmental personnel will continue in the performance of their functions.
4. Control and command of landing fields, ports, defenses, fortifications, and arsenals will be placed at the disposal of the American command.
5. Full information will be given as to location of all facilities, installations, equipment, and devices which may be a hinderance or useful to the Allied forces.
6. All telecommunication services essential for the maintenance of law and order will be maintained intact. Other services will be temporarily closed down. All telecommunication services will be placed at the disposal of the American forces.
7. French warships will continue to fly the French colors and will retain enough fuel to provide electric power. Explosives, ammunition, and critical gun parts will be landed. Such machinery parts as would prevent ships from putting to sea in less than twelve hours will be landed. Wireless offices will be sealed. Onboard crews will be reduced to one-third. Warships will proceed when so instructed to ports designated by the United States.
8. Crews of French merchant vessels will be disembarked as may be required by the American authorities. Those who so wish may work for the United Nations. Merchant vessels will be employed in the service of the United Nations to take part in the war effort against the Axis.
9. All port facilities, harbor and naval installations and establish-

ments will be placed intact at the disposal of American forces, and such assistance as they may require will be rendered.

10. Requisition of billets, supplies, lands, buildings, transportation, and services for military needs is authorized. Payment will be made at once in cash. Prices will be the fair market value.
11. The French authorities will provide a list of all persons arrested because of their sympathies with the United Nations. Those under detention will be released when the American authorities so direct.
12. All Allied merchant seamen who have been interned in French North Africa will be released.
13. The authorities in French North Africa will take such measures as the American commanding general may deem appropriate with regard to the control of foreign property.
14. No tax, direct or indirect, will be collected upon American property or representatives.
15. Civilian and military representatives of the Allied forces shall enjoy extraterritorial privileges.
16. Areas deemed to be of importance may be declared to be military areas in which the maintenance of order and administrative and public services shall come under the direct control of the commanding general.
17. If the internal situation endangers lines of communication or threatens disorder, the commanding general may take such administrative and other measures as may be necessary for the protection of military interests.
18. Such military, naval, air, and economic missions as may be required to administer the provisions of these arrangements will be appointed by the American commanding general.
19. The arrangements are drawn up in English and in French. The English version is authoritative.

From the TORCH political directives and from the proposed armistice terms, several conclusions can be reached. First, the decision-making process would be essentially American, with no more than consultation with the British; second, the United States was determined to see its North African exploitation as a benefit—or payoff—of its controversial Vichy policy; and third, cooperation with Vichy officials after the landings was a basic assumption. In none of the papers or correspondence can be found the slightest suggestion that the United States would consider recognition of some insurgent regime. There were no warnings or hints that certain Vichy officials might be less acceptable as allies than others.[51] The United States was quite prepared (although Eisenhower realized it would destroy his already meager prospects of seizing Tunisia) to impose a military government. No matter how essential Murphy may have gauged clandestine French cooperation, his judgment found no clear counterpart in Washington or London. The feeling about the French resistance among Allied planners is summed up in Eisenhower's somewhat cynical words (italics added):

> We consider that the operation has more than fair chances of success provided Spain stays absolutely neutral and the French forces either offer only token resistance or are *so badly divided by internal dissension and by Allied political maneuvering* that effective resistance will be negligible.[52]

6

The Planners
France and Algiers

Algiers, October 1942
Robert Murphy back in North Africa

The long absence of Robert Murphy from Algiers had caused a backlog in the diplomatic clearing house. Everyone knew the Allies were up to something, and the president himself had publicly emphasized that the "something" would take place in 1942. The build-up of forces in England, Scotland, and at Gibraltar could not be concealed. Paris newspapers ran daily stories that North Africa had been chosen as the target. Pétain and Darlan became very concerned at these rumors, as well they should have been, for an Allied invasion—even an unrepulsed commando raid—would inexorably trigger operation ANTON, the complete occupation of France. Hitler could not afford to leave the French Riviera unguarded if American and British forces held Oran, Algiers, and Bizerte.

The responsible French army and navy commanders in Africa became nervous: General Juin and Admiral Moreau at Algiers, General Noguès and Admiral Michelier in Morocco, General Boisson and Admiral Collinet at Dakar. All of them shared in apprehension, but they did not necessarily see eye to eye on action to be taken. The naval officers by and large unanimously curdled at the thought that the British navy might again inflict some ignominious disaster upon French units. Army officers were split, some believing in German victory while others wished to bring France back into the war. But almost all of them loyally supported Marshal Pétain. Their allegiance to him rested on either conviction or discipline. Those whose convictions bound them to Pétain—and General Noguès would be numbered among these—feared that collaboration with the Allies would bring not military victory but only a further disintegration of French authority. If authority collapsed, Arab nationalists would rise in North Africa and communists would dominate the resistance movement in France. Then, if Germany won, France would be gauleitered; if Germany lost, France would become communist and her Empire shattered. French officers must consequently hold on, at whatever apparent disdain for Anglo-American war aims, to the cardboard façade of authority which the armistice left them.

Other officers, perhaps less subtle in logic but more democratic in outlook, aspired to fight Germans but were not prepared to undermine military discipline and loyalty in order to do it. A French officer in 1942 had few choices: he could break his oath and join de Gaulle, reasoning that great moral issues released a soldier from habitual loyalties. But to do this struck at the heart of military discipline without which an army became a mob, a tool of partisan interest. De Gaulle would later reap the harvest of this disintegration which he himself had seeded in 1940.

Or an officer could go into retirement, releasing himself from the need to choose. Many of them did.

Or an officer could serve Marshal Pétain, praying that the leadership in defiance would come from this venerable soldier, bypassing Laval's civil collaboration and subservience and placing France back in the belligerent ranks. If an officer made this latter choice, clearly he could not accept de Gaulle—an officer in "dissidence"—nor Giraud either. Many officers knew of camouflage plans, plans to delay collaboration, secret contingency plans to exploit evidence of German weakness; they expected Pétain or Darlan to someday give the sign and they would respond. Many believed that General Weygand was being held in reserve, so to speak, and would be called forth at the appropriate moment.

Vague plans for anti-German action existed, but they all contemplated 1943 as the year of potential resistance. Admiral Darlan, who in spite of Laval's return still possessed supreme authority over French ground, sea, and air forces, held the key post which could unleash and coordinate the fragmentary remnants of French power. And in North Africa, it was General Juin, in command of ground and air forces, who could bring the Armistice Army into action.

Yet neither Darlan nor Juin could see much future in an unaided rising. Without air cover, without gasoline, without sufficient ammunition, the French risked complete annihilation unless backed by Allied military and logistic support. It was essential to sound out the Americans. If the United States's Vichy policy had any justification at all, it must be in having established a pipeline through which France could reach the western powers who defied the Axis. This must have been the purpose, and Darlan believed he had demonstrated his understanding of this purpose when he told Admiral Leahy to return with 500,000 men.[1]

But the summer and fall of 1942 had slipped by, and American encouragement, estranged by collaboration, had faltered. Admiral Leahy had left Vichy in May, not to return; Murphy had disappeared from Algiers in August. How could one reach the Americans? The United States Embassy at Vichy was too closely watched, and, in any case, one had to be sure the contact came at a level high enough to ensure reaching the decision-making authorities in Washington. However competent they may have been, Chargé d'Affaires Pinkney Tuck at Vichy and Consul General Felix Cole at Algiers could not negotiate at the highest levels.

Thus Robert Murphy's return to North Africa in October possessed, from the French point of view, a considerable significance. Three men—Darlan, Juin, and Giraud—were anxious to reestablish contact with him through their confidential agents.

Murphy did not come directly to Algiers. Knowing that the principal American attack would be launched at Casablanca and Port Lyautey, and appreciating (unlike many of his American colleagues) the dominant position held by Governor General Noguès, whose rank made him senior to anyone else in Africa, Murphy stopped first at Rabat. He saw General Noguès on 9 October.

Noguès by inclination tended toward the position of those who feared chaos and collapse if the Vichy false front were to crumble. He was no longer young and his inclinations for hazardous adventure had been frozen, some people thought, by the untimely death of his son before the war. Noguès appreciated only too keenly how vulnerable Morocco was to German and Spanish attack; and yet, with great Atlantic swells pounding the western shore, he knew how difficult the coast would be to assail from the sea. If Hitler came to Africa through Spain, Morocco would be the first French possession slated for occupation.

Noguès provided a serious challenge to Murphy's diplomacy. If the president's representative could sense in Noguès some hopeful sign, some hint of cooperation, he might get Patton ashore without casualties. Yet Noguès had never been cooperative, and Murphy could not say too much without the danger of tipping off Vichy and, with some probability, the German command. In Murphy's own words:

> On this particular occasion he invited me to dine with Mme. Noguès and himself, and after dinner for a quiet talk in his library. The key question I put directly to him was "Supposing *next spring* the United States would be prepared to land in North Africa with several hundred thousand men and proportionate tanks and planes and equipment, what would be your reaction?"
>
> He replied with cutting emphasis—"Ne faites pas ça. C'est trop tard" and went on to say that France was out of the war, would remain out of it and not risk the loss to Germany of its African possessions. To my reminder of what Admiral Darlan had said to Admiral Leahy in August he gave a simple brush-off.
>
> That was my last effort to bring him around, and of course I keenly regretted it. With his assistance Torch would have been a dream.[2]

Noguès left no doubt as to his stand. He would take orders from Pétain. "I will meet you," he had said, "with all the fire power I possess." Although Murphy reproached himself for his failure to rally Noguès, it is difficult to see what more, within the limits of his authorization, he might have done.

At the Casablanca airport, enplaning for Algiers on the eleventh, Murphy encountered Lemaigre Dubreuil, who was returning from Dakar. Murphy was able to give him some hints on the magnitude of the American intervention, but with Germans also aboard the plane, there was no time for serious talk. That came when the plane touched down at Algiers.[3]

Algiers, October 1942
Murphy, Darlan, and Juin

Murphy had now been absent for two months. In that critical period TORCH had been adopted, the command structure established, troops allotted and trained, and equipment stocked on wharves ready at the moment for loading.

In Algiers underground units had continued to meet and train, preparing for action, but for what sort of action no one could really be sure. Henri d'Astier's charismatic personality had engendered in hundreds of young men a patriotic enthusiasm to bring France back into the war.

In France, Darlan and Giraud had worked on parallel but sepaate plans, waiting for news that their agents had made some sort of meaningful contact with the Americans.

By 14 October, after three days of secret meetings, Murphy had conferred at length with Colonel Chrétien, representing Admiral Darlan; with Major Dorange, representing General Juin; and with General Mast, representing General Giraud. To comprehend Murphy's dilemma and to understand the course of action which followed, one must look at these clandestine conferences with some attention. In his memoirs, Murphy provides no details about these meetings.

The first encounter was organized by Col. Jean Chrétien, who since 1941 had run the army's G-2 (Deuxieme Bureau) in North Africa.[4] He was convinced Germany would ultimately lose and that France must cooperate in one way or another with the Allies. During Murphy's absence from Algiers, one of Chrétien's agents, a Vichyite named Bègue, had uncovered most of the details regarding The Five's secret operations, especially those involving d'Astier and Van Hecke. When Chrétien received Bègue's analysis he found himself embroiled in an agonizing dilemma—whether or not to conceal the report from his superiors. If he did, he had to allow for the possibility that Bègue might forward a duplicate report via other channels; in which case Vichy authorities, unidentifiable by Chrétien, would possess devastating information and his own usefulness would be jeopardized. Chrétien decided to forward a watered-down version and continued, through other agents, to track down intelligence about the conspirators and about Allied operations. He wondered, when he was in Vichy in August, whether he should report his conjectures to General Revers, then chief of Darlan's military cabinet. He was dissuaded by his own immediate superior from doing so.

During his next visit to Vichy, however, on 20 September (when Murphy was in London conferring with Eisenhower) Chrétien unburdened himself to General Revers and revealed his conviction that an Allied landing could be expected before 15 November. He argued that Admiral Darlan should make some sort of contact with Robert Murphy. (Chrétien had never met the American representative and did not know about the overtures of Admiral Fenard and Alain Darlan.) Revers agreed to discuss the problem with Darlan, who authorized Chrétien to sound out Murphy and to promise French cooperation provided assurance was forthcoming from the Americans that they had specific operational plans and were coming in force. Darlan reasserted the point he had consistently made: let the Allies land with enough men and equipment to assure success and the French would support them; but at all costs avoid commando raids which would cause the certain occupation of France and possibly North Africa.

Back in Algiers by 26 September, Chrétien soon learned that Murphy had not returned. He had to wait for two weeks when, through d'Astier and Saint-Hardouin, he arranged a secret meeting. It is ironic indeed that Murphy's return had been delayed so long by insignificant bickering about commercial arrangements in North Africa. If he had flown back immediately after his conference with Eisenhower, Murphy would have had more leisure to explore the exciting avenues now open to him.

As it was, Chrétien met Murphy for the first time on the evening of 12 October, the day after the diplomat's return. They talked at Guyotsville, a few miles west of Algiers. Chrétien prefixed his remarks by observing that French intelligence had good reason to believe Germany would soon be making some move against North Africa. He then hinted that Darlan might change his base of operations to North Africa and could bring the fleet with him, provided the United States were willing and able to bring assistance. Chrétien spent considerable time explaining the French military weakness in Africa, making the inescapable point that the French, namely Darlan, could not resist German pressures but that they were ready to work with the Allies if German penetration into North Africa could be prevented. This was essentially the message that Darlan had already conveyed to Leahy when he left Vichy six months earlier.

But six months ago no operation in North Africa had been contemplated. Now the landings were less than a month away. If Darlan could be brought into the fold, Murphy reasoned, his authority would certainly exceed Giraud's, and the value to the Allies of his collaboration would be incalculable. Could he be trusted? Murphy correctly placed reliance in Chrétien's integrity, but he could hardly judge Darlan's. In any case he did not possess enough military information to satisfy Darlan. If Darlan were to be dealt with, Murphy would need authorization. He cabled a summary of his talk with Chrétien and then asked:

> Please inform me how far I may go in replying to Darlan's Representative who in effect asks: (1) would we be willing to cooperate with Darlan and (2) if so, are we able to do so quickly on a large scale here and/or Europe. I urge that we encourage Darlan and believe this would be reconcilable with eventual cooperation with Giraud.[5]

Before Murphy could obtain a reply from Washington he was immersed in another discussion, the following day, with Major André Dorange, Juin's aide. Handsome, dashing, conscientious, Dorange embodied all characteristics of the correct French officer, conservative, authoritarian, and steadfast in his loyalty to Juin, Darlan, and Pétain.

Dorange went to some length in assuring Murphy that Juin would hold to the Vichy policy of defending North Africa against all invaders. The United States should think seriously before occupying Africa.[6]

"But I assure you," Murphy replied, "the Government of the United States has never had such an intention. We will not set foot on French territory without invitation."

The discussion moved to the question of Axis versus Allied material superiority, and Murphy did his best to impress Dorange with the great potential in production, manpower, and shipping which, he insisted, the United States was already prepared to commit. He deprecated Dorange's fears that Russia or Britain would capitulate.

"But," he added, "all this is far afield from General Juin. I should like to be sure he understands that I haven't gone to see him simply because I didn't want to make his job any more complicated than it already is."

Murphy could remember one of the reasons given for Weygand's recall. Weygand had been accused of maintaining too close association with the Americans.

"General Juin is grateful," Dorange replied. "However he has authorized me to tell you that in case of absolute need he is ready to receive you. I think this should not be too frequently, but you may contact me when you consider it useful. . . ."

Murphy then came to the point, authorizing Dorange to inform Juin that as President Roosevelt's special representative, he had authority to embark on conversations with the French. In speaking to Dorange he reiterated public formulations of American policy, such as Sumner Welles's published statement of 13 April 1942, to the effect that "the Government of the United States recognizes the sovereign jurisdiction of the people of France over the territory of France and over French possessions overseas. . . . The Government of the United States fervently hopes that it may see the reestablishment of the independence of France and of the integrity of French territory."[7]

In Welles's statement the phrase "people of France" quite clearly neither recognized nor repudiated the Vichy government. A basic section of the document affirmed that until the French people had regained "control of their own destinies," the United States, with regard to French territories in Africa, "will continue . . . to maintain, or to enter into relations with those French citizens who are in actual control of such territories." In the light of this official policy, it is not likely that Murphy pledged the United States to deal only with Vichy. However, when Dorange wrote up his notes (which Murphy later approved), he recorded Murphy's policy statement as:

> (1) The government of the United States, will deal only with the French Government, or with anyone to whom, officially or secretly it has delegated its power. The Government of the United States will not deal with dissident groups [i.e., de Gaulle] which set themselves up as Governments.
>
> (2) The Government of the United States will not make any hostile gesture in regard to French territory. It will come only at the request of France and under conditions fixed by it: rumors about an American attack are without foundation.
>
> (3) If you appeal to us, we are ready to bring you not only the material which you need but the collaboration of our armed forces.[8]

Such statements stretched the actuality of the situation. It is understandable that under the exigencies of wartime diplomacy Murphy might exaggerate American promises in order to line up French support or to lull French suspicions. Murphy walked a hazardous chalk line, for if at this late date he had begun serious negotiations with Darlan or Juin, he might jeopardize the benefits potentially accruing from the conspiracy so long developed with Giraud, The Five, and with General Mast. If Murphy had bluntly told Dorange that the United States planned to occupy North Africa whether the French liked it or not, he risked triggering some adverse reaction in Vichy, with unknown repercussions in Berlin.

Dorange asked whether he might forward Murphy's information to Darlan and to Pétain. At this Murphy demurred. His own embassy at Vichy knew neither that the invasion was planned or that he, Murphy, had become the president's personal representative. He preferred that his information go only to Juin, who might pass it on to Darlan should he feel it appropriate. He suggested that Darlan be reminded of the overture Darlan had made to Ambassador Leahy, in which he had intimated that if the Americans came with half-a-million men he would join them. Murphy carefully insisted that it was not he who had initiated the present discussions. He did not want to get involved with Darlan unless he had full backing from his superiors.

In making his report, Dorange did his utmost to make sure he read Murphy correctly. Two days after the interview, on the morning of 15 October, he brought his summary to Murphy, at Juin's request, for checking over and for approval. He ended his report with an interpretation he felt caught at Murphy's intentions. What Murphy was trying to say, he believed, was this:

> The offers which we are making you are unconditional; don't feel that they contain a sort of hidden ultimatum imploring you to create immediately a second front in French North Africa. We are simply letting you know that the size of our aid will not be same.[9]

Every day Murphy's problems became more and more difficult. He realized that in Darlan he stalked bigger game than Giraud, and he had to acknowledge that Juin loomed larger than Mast; yet at this final moment it would be virtually impossible to work out some sort of deal that would bring all Frenchmen cooperatively into the picture. But it could just possibly be accomplished if Mast, The Five, and Giraud would do the negotiating.

Murphy decided on a policy of wait and see. Before following through on the Dorange contact, he would confer at length with Mast and The Five. A full-scale discussion could not be held before the fourteenth, because Rigault and Van Hecke had gone to France, where they had seen General Giraud.

Algiers, 15 October 1942
Murphy and The Five

Rigault and Van Hecke had passed several days at Lyons and had received from General Giraud his latest thinking about the Grand Design. Significantly, Giraud continued to play down the strategic value of North Africa. Although his plan fundamentally featured a bridgehead on the French Riviera, he envisaged some six months of secret staff work with the British and Americans to coordinate a series of simultaneous landings south of the Garonne, between the Garonne and the Loire, in Brittany, in Normandy, and at other points. He thought in terms of a build-up of material at Gibraltar and (assuming some sort of deal with Franco) in Spain.

Although Giraud lacked enthusiasm for a North African operation, he was willing, as he told Rigault on 7 October, to cooperate with it. He continued vehemently to argue for the bridgehead operation, but he was becoming apprehensive, because of growing rumors of Axis and Allied intentions regarding North Africa, that his own plans might be jeopardized by precipitous German or American action. Against these eventualities he gave Rigault instructions for Mast on the line to be taken: resist intervention. If the Americans came in without prior agreement, they should be repelled. If such an operation was already planned, they should be asked to postpone. If they still insisted, Mast must ascertain the reasons for such a decision. Giraud could understand that reasons unknown to him could exist and that, isolated in his hideaway, he might be poorly informed about many relevant factors.[10]

Rigault and Van Hecke arrived back in Algiers on the thirteenth, and they immediately learned that Murphy had returned with plans for a 500,000-man operation. A full-fledged conference, to include The Five and General Mast, was arranged.[11] Mast had already seen Murphy and had emphasized the urgent, immediate need for military staff talks.

When the conference took place, on the fifteenth, Murphy explained how the overall situation now stood in the light of the president's 22 September directive. He verified that an operation, involving half-a-million men, 2,000 planes, with supporting naval forces of eight battleships, seven aircraft carriers, and 100 destroyers, was aimed at North Africa. Although he gave neither the place nor the date, Murphy implied that the equipment had been assembled and shipping had been organized. General Mast had already conjectured that this operation must be coming earlier than next spring, and in accordance with Giraud's request, he pressed Murphy to explain why the assault had to be scheduled at this time. Murphy reiterated the widespread rumors to the effect that the Axis soon intended to move in on North Africa and added as well that the operation would support the Russians—then hard-pressed at Stalingrad—and would coordinate with a British Eighth Army offensive at El Alamein.

Appreciating the imminence of the enterprise and realizing how little Murphy knew about military details, Mast pushed hard for a military staff meeting. This could be arranged at a house near Cherchell, on the coast about seventy-five miles west of Algiers. If five American officers—a senior officer familiar with the entire operation and representatives from operations, supply, and landings, together with a naval officer—would come, Mast would undertake to bring them in touch with key officers on his own staff. Murphy promised to wire Washington immediately to try to arrange it.

Murphy broached the question of Darlan. It was imperative that he should explore this new development with Mast. None of the plotters—The Five, the Algiers resistance, Giraud, Mast—had any meaningful contacts with Darlan or with the navy. Yet the navy, badly mauled as it may have been, not only operated ships and submarines in the Mediterranean, but controlled the most deadly shore batteries. Murphy did have contacts with naval personnel. Through his long personal friendships with Admiral Fenard, through his not infrequent meetings with Darlan's son, Alain (struck with an as yet undiagnosed illness in Tunisia on the thirteenth), and now through the special secret encounter with Colonel Chrétien, Murphy possessed extraordinary contacts with important navy officers. And Admiral Darlan represented not only naval power; in his person resided the absolutely supreme French military authority, which could give orders directly to the top ground, air, and sea officers in North and West Africa.

But Mast would have none of it. He told Murphy that Darlan was double-faced and could not be trusted. Murphy tried to argue, pointing out that if the French remained split they would only weaken any effort to bring France back into the war.

"The Army is loyal to General Giraud," Mast declared, "and it will follow him, not Darlan. The Navy will fall in line with the Army."[12]

Mast's adamant defense of this position, which ruled out feelers in Darlan's direction, now became a central feature of the conspiracy. Mast was, as events would show, dead wrong. Let us not at this point ask whether the Allies should have dealt at all with any Vichy official. Washington's Vichy policy, still in effect, assumed that France remained a friend and ally. Under these circumstances, one can readily defend the position, as Murphy did, that Darlan was *the* man. General Mast refused to see this and preferred to gamble on becoming Giraud's Number 2 once Giraud had been named commander in chief by the Allies. If in fact Mast was influenced by personal ambition, he took a great deal upon himself in leading the relatively uninformed and naive Americans to believe that French military discipline had so utterly collapsed that a public hero, with no official connections, could brush aside the established military hierarchy.

Murphy may have questioned Mast's overconfident pretensions, but he could scarcely disregard the group with which he had been working for a year simply to grasp at the uncertain straw Darlan temptingly proffered. Murphy possessed an exceptional grasp of French politics and attitudes, but even he could not probe all the interwoven circles of Gallic deviousness, and he had to rely on the advice of Lemaigre Dubreuil, Rigault, Saint-Hardouin, d'Astier, and Van Hecke. They, like Mast, were committed, each for his own reasons, to a Giraud coup d'état, and they did not incline to last-minute gestures toward the Admiralty.

As we have seen, Murphy had already asked Washington how far he might go with Darlan, and he had volunteered the belief that Darlan might cooperate with Giraud. Now, after discussion with Giraud's representative, he was forced in a second message to state:

> Mast also told me bluntly that Giraud contemplates that we deal with him and not with Darlan.[13]

At this same conference, Rigault, who had brought with him the latest version of the Giraud strategic plan, urged that the United States bring Giraud the aid which he would need. Mast lent his arguments to those of Rigault pointing out how hard Giraud had been working on the idea of a bridgehead in southern France. Mast was beginning to suspect that the American operation, coming too soon, would strangle French efforts to exploit their unoccupied zone; but out of loyalty to Giraud he had to argue for the plan so close to his chief's heart.

Mast then broached the question of command.[14] It will be recalled that Giraud believed he had received approval direct from President Roosevelt for the proposition that if he cooperated with the United States he would be named commander in chief. He saw himself as another Foch, fighting on French soil, willing to accept American material (the Americans are good at turning out equipment) and in return willing to provide experienced leadership (no American general had ever led troops in combat). Certainly Giraud was thinking of his personal prestige, his professional stature, his "honneur," but he also believed sincerely, if somewhat arrogantly, that his gesture was required in the interests of Allied victory. It could not occur to him that Americans might look at his record in the campaign of 1940 and develop doubts as to his capacity (or the capacity of any French general) to assume the high responsibility of supreme command.

Murphy could not touch this problem. Knowing the complex relationship of Allied commander to the Combined Chiefs, to Marshall and Brooke, to Roosevelt and Churchill, Murphy realized how difficult any last-minute change in the command set-up would be. He thought it possible, however, that Eisenhower could command the Anglo-American forces and Giraud the French once the landings had been achieved. Murphy insisted that his authorization covered only political, not technical matters.

"But this *is* political," insisted Mast. "It is political and it should be settled in advance." He was, of course, correct; but Murphy could not settle it. He would have to refer it back to Washington. At the end of his message describing the conference, he cabled:

> Are you able to suggest a happy formula for this delicate point which would leave the command effectively with Eisenhower but permit the French to regard the operation as theirs and require them to lend us their maximum aid? Mast asserts that Giraud's command will give us entry practically without firing a shot.[15]

Optimistic Mast. Around this central issue the whole political structure of the invasion would revolve.

If Murphy lacked qualifications for deciding the command issue, he could, however, as President Roosevelt's representative, negotiate on some of the political understandings. The Five considered themselves potentially a political group which might serve as a successor to Pétain's government. They could claim political authority with as much validity as de Gaulle could claim it for his National Committee in London. Those with political ambitions, especially Lemaigre Dubreuil and Henri d'Astier, pictured themselves as forming a cabinet around Giraud, who might just possibly relegate de Gaulle to a secondary spot and become himself the head of a provisional government recognized and supported by the Allies. Consequently they were very concerned not to be exploited simply as instruments in Allied policy, but to be recognized as the nucleus of a government replacing Vichy—equal partners, representing sovereign France with a temporary capital in Algiers. They claimed exactly the same status which de Gaulle had been demanding, and they believed they possessed greater validity in making such a claim. That de Gaulle was an extremely masterful politician and that he would ultimately magnetize world and French opinion could not be appreciated then as clearly as it would be in 1943 and 1944.

Out of the deliberations emerged the draft of an agreement which if honored would give The Five what they wanted. This was couched in the form of a letter from Murphy to Giraud:

My dear General:

Referring to the declarations made on several occasions by President Roosevelt; and the obligations already undertaken by the American Government as well as by the British Government I am able to assure you that the restoration of France to full independence, in all the greatness and vastness which it possessed before the war in Europe as well as overseas, is one of the war aims of the United Nations.

It is thoroughly understood that French sovereignty will be reestablished as soon as possible throughout all the territory, metropolitan and colonial, over which flew the French flag in 1939.

The Government of the United States considers the French nation as an ally and will treat it as such.

May I add further that in case of military operations in French territory (whether in Metropolitan France or in the

Colonies) in all instances where French collaboration may be found, the American authorities will not intervene in any way in those affairs which are solely within the province of the national administration or which have to do with the exercise of French sovereignty.[16]

In approving such a formulation Murphy believed he was remaining within official dicta on American policy. The Atlantic Charter affirmed that the United Nations "wish to see sovereign rights and self-government restored to those who have been forcibly deprived of them" and also that "they desire to see no territorial changes that do not accord with the freely expressed wishes of the people concerned."[17] In April, Sumner Welles had given the French ambassador a policy statement already referred to. The president himself, in a fireside chat on 28 April, 1942, had said: "The overwhelming majority of the French people understand that the fight of the United Nations is fundamentally their fight, that our victory means the restoration of a free and independent France."[18] And Murphy's directive from President Roosevelt had stated: "No change in the existing French Civil Administration is contemplated by the United States."

These statements seemed to cover Murphy in guaranteeing France's prewar boundaries and possessions and in asserting that the United States would refrain from imposing a military government in French areas. In any case, this letter of Murphy's, drawn up on 15 October, constituted no more than a preliminary draft which Giraud would have to approve and, as it concerned policies to be followed by the American government in the area, would have to be, in accordance with Murphy's directive, submitted to the president also for approval.

Yet the political parts of the letter did not exactly coincide with Roosevelt's thinking. In a message to Eisenhower, received in London on 14 October, Marshall pointed out that "the only statement of American policy desired by the President regarding TORCH is the defeat of the Axis powers and the preservation of French administration in the colonies."[19] Did Murphy not receive a copy? Later Roosevelt would repudiate the Murphy letter. Reporting a meeting of the Joint Chiefs of Staff, on 7 January, 1943, the minutes state:

> The President said that Mr. Murphy had given certain written pledges to Giraud to restore France and the colonial

possessions of France after the war. He said that in doing this Mr. Murphy had exceeded his authority and that he as President was not prepared to make any promises. There are some of the colonial possessions which he was certain would not be returned to France, and he had grave doubts whether Indo-China should be. He thought that the Chiefs of Staff in their discussions in North Africa should make this plain to both Mr. Murphy and to General Eisenhower.[20]

Normally a statement of policy such as Murphy set forth in the draft formulation would have been debated and ultimately approved, disapproved, or altered by the State Department. But because he was the president's special representative, Murphy bypassed State and sent his dispatches directly to the War Department. Copies for the president would presumably pass through Admiral Leahy's hands. The Murphy draft letter became available to General Clark at the Cherchell meeting on 22 October, and he brought a copy with him back to London. The text was included in his report to Marshall dated 30 October. There was time for someone to question the political concessions if he had wished to.

The original draft letter included one more paragraph, dealing with the command question. This final paragraph read:

> In the event of military collaboration, it would be understood that after the debarkation of American forces, if the Allies are obliged to face an enemy intervention on French territory in North or West Africa, the general direction of operations would be exercised by you [i.e., Giraud]—the command of French and American armies being assured by their respective general staffs. The United States Government furthermore is ready to aid by the abundant supply of all material necessary for the rapid renaissance of a French Army under French command.[21]

Regarding the last sentence, Murphy stood on safe ground: the president's directive had authorized the provision of equipment "as rapidly as possible for those French troops who join in denying access to French North Africa to our common enemies." But the matter of "general direction" Murphy knew would be questioned. The text he and Mast had drafted provided no more than a balloon for others to shoot at.

Such was the situation in Algiers on 15 October, when Murphy filed his dispatches. They were to provoke a great deal of discussion and action in Washington and London.

London, October 1942
Reaction to Murphy's proposals

By Friday, 16 October, Murphy's messages had been relayed to London.

Next morning Eisenhower went to his office at 20 Grosvenor Square. He immediately phoned Clark who had just read the dispatches at Norfolk House.

"Come up," Eisenhower said, "Come up right away."

At Grosvenor Square the two officers, together with Bedell Smith, bit into the hard issues: Should Mast's request be met? If so, who should go? What means of reaching the rendezvous were available? How did the odds against leakage or capture stand? They phoned Churchill—he was weekending at Chequers with Eden, Smuts, and Ismay. Annoyed that his holiday was disrupted but impressed with the urgent tone of Eisenhower's voice, the prime minister agreed to convoke a strategy meeting at 10 Downing Street late that Saturday afternoon.[22]

A certain irony overlaid the excited response in London.

The information so urgently wired by Murphy covered almost precisely the same ground as that embodied in the "Protocols of June 15" brought to Washington early in July by Colonel Solborg. In both communications could be found the same leader, General Giraud; the same representative, General Mast; the same proposals, drawn up by Colonel Jousse and Saint-Hardouin, for a military and political accord.

But in early July TORCH had not yet been approved. The Solborg memos had nowhere to go except in the file of contingency plans; and Solborg himself, having lost credibility with his superiors, had no way of pressing the significance of his information.

With the proposal for French-American military talks arriving only three weeks before the operation, Eisenhower had to move at emergency speed to make the discussions useful.

Before the afternoon meeting with the British, Eisenhower, Clark, and Smith reached some preliminary decisions. They agreed that they should accept Mast's invitation and that Clark should lead a delegation of senior officers. They discussed the command formula to see if Giraud could be somehow worked in, but they balked at granting a meaningful operational command to an officer who had not participated in the planning and build-up. They could hardly tell Giraud that because of the debacle of May 1940 they could see little reason to put faith in the command abilities of any French general. The most useful function Giraud could perform initially, as Eisenhower saw it, would be to *not* fight—that is, to keep the French army from opposing his landing and then, once the troops came ashore, to administer the territory as governor general. Later, when the French troops had been rearmed, Giraud (or Darlan) might take over a military command, possibly as Eisenhower's deputy. Clark would by then have taken command of the Fifth Army, to be formed in North Africa. Clark expressed his willingness to step down as deputy commander to permit a Frenchman to take his place.[23]

Such was Eisenhower's thinking as he, Clark, and Bedell Smith drove over to 10 Downing Street late in the afternoon. Churchill had convoked most of his war cabinet—Smuts, Attlee, Eden, Sir Dudley Pound, General Brooke, Lord Mountbatten—as Clark put it later: "about as dazzling an array of Britain's diplomatic, military and naval brains as had yet been seen." Churchill bubbled with excitement, as he frequently did when a new adventure loomed up. The prospect of Clark's secret rendezvous on the Algerian coast appealed to his sense of adventure. "This is great," he kept repeating.[24]

In spite of the prime minister's outward and momentary exuberance, the British as a whole nevertheless guarded serious reservations about the enterprise, which was possibly too "American" for their liking. Neither Churchill nor Brooke mentions this meeting in his memoirs. They had, to be sure, the British aspects of the North African campaign on their minds. Montgomery was about to launch his offensive at El Alamein and British attention was focused more keenly on this crucial operation than on the American adventure. The British were also a bit touchy about the Algerian landings. These would be carried out mostly by British ships and men, yet the Americans insisted on playing a preponderate role in the arrangements. The Americans argued that no publicity could be given British participation because of the known antipathy of Vichy-oriented officers to their allies of 1940. Neither did the idea of a last-minute communion with Darlan sit too well with the British. Not only did they rankle at Darlan's notorious Anglophobia, but they considered him responsible for augmenting Rommel's strength. Furthermore, the British were linked to de Gaulle—whether they liked it or not—

and they could foresee problems in bringing Vichy Frenchmen to the Allied fold.

Anthony Eden registered strong suspicions about Darlan's offer. Later he wrote: "it seemed too much like the way Germans would play their hand if they wanted to know our plans and delay them."[25]

After some discussion, Americans and British agreed that Giraud should be recognized as the principal collaborator and should be appointed governor general in North Africa. Eisenhower suggested that Darlan might be reached through Giraud, and if a useful military role could be mutually agreed on, such a purely French agreement would be acceptable to him. The group approved of this but the British pointed out that Giraud could hardly serve both as governor general and as Eisenhower's deputy; therefore Darlan would fit better as deputy. (No one seemed to realize that Giraud's and Darlan's capacities would require a reversal of the roles: Giraud as military commander and Darlan as governor.)

The Giraud plan for Allied landings or assistance in southern France was discussed. Everyone agreed that facilities did not exist to make such aid practicable. Giraud had better give up this plan and come to North Africa, where equipment could be landed more readily.

So far as the Americans were concerned, the meeting at 10 Downing Street had been essentially consultative. The Clark mission to Mast would be a military mission; it therefore came under Eisenhower, as Allied commander, and would be authorized under his basic directive. Eisenhower immediately forwarded the gist of the discussions to Washington.[26] Before a reply was made, President Roosevelt was consulted. After that, two sets of instructions went forth from Washington: one to Clark and one to Murphy.

Clark was told that on the matter of overall command he should limit himself to the position already affirmed in September when Eisenhower had talked with Murphy: that the expedition is American and under American command. The only command to be held by a Frenchman would be over French troops, and this was a matter to be handled by Frenchmen themselves. Darlan was not to be mentioned.

Inasmuch as Roosevelt had been consulted on this matter, the president must have recalled no previous commitment, such as general Giraud maintained he had received regarding the overall com-

141

mand. Otherwise he would certainly have referred to it in the communication to Clark.

The message to Murphy came to him from the War Department (Handy), signed Leahy:

> Inform your contact we also have information that Germany comtemplates occupation of African colonies and it is our opinion that Darlan should resist aggression by Axis with Army and Navy in which event America will provide at once large scale military, material, and economic aid in the colonies. . . .[27]

Murphy must have puzzled over this phraseology. He had asked "how far may I go in replying to Darlan's representative?" The reply clearly enough indicated that once the Axis *had* attacked, and once Darlan *had* resisted, the United States would bring assistance. Yet Darlan had consistently implied that Vichy was helpless, and unless some definite assistance was guaranteed, he could not resist. Murphy presumably could say: if the Axis attacks, and you resist, we will help you. But Darlan had no intention of resisting. Therefore, Murphy did not have authorization to proceed further with Darlan, but the message did seem to imply that, once hostilities had started and Darlan had revealed anti-Axis tendencies, Murphy could deal with him. Certainly Murphy had no instructions suggesting that he take positive steps on his own initiative to work Darlan into the American scheme of operations. Murphy later wrote that he interpreted Leahy's instructions as "authorizing me to initiate any arrangement with Darlan which, in my judgment, might assist the military operations."[28] What is most important is this: *nothing in any message received by Murphy hinted that Darlan, being untrustworthy, a shifty turncoat, a skunk, or a collaborator, should be avoided at all costs for political reasons.*

The Leahy message continued with instructions regarding the command situation. Murphy had asked whether Leahy could come up with a "happy formula" which might satisfy Giraud. The text read:

> Inform Giraud's contact that question of command of French Army and Navy should be settled by Frenchmen and that America will undertake a large scale operation upon resistance by French to Axis invasion of the colonies.[29]

This was no answer at all, and, although Murphy had made it clear enough in his cable, did not even seem to comprehend the issue.

Murphy may have been tempted to repeat his request for a formula, but before he could do so he learned that Eisenhower was sending General Clark to the rendezvous with General Mast. It would be more appropriate for the two generals to straighten out this essentially military dilemma. Clark would have to examine very carefully the final paragraph of Murphy's draft letter.

Once Clark received authorization from Washington, he moved rapidly. While Eisenhower went off to observe maneuvers in Scotland, his deputy worked out the details for the Mediterranean venture. No American submarine was available, but out of Gibraltar the British operated a number of submarines whose commanders had considerable experience landing and picking up personnel and supplies. The British agreed to assign the P-219 (later named H.M.S. *Seraph*), commanded by Lt. N. L. A. Jewell, for Clark's mission. At Gibraltar the SBS (Special Boat Section), a unit trained in the use of folbots for secret landings, had the equipment and experience to take the American officers into shore. Three commandos, Capt. G. B. Courtney, Capt. R. P. Livingstone, and Lt. J. P. Foot, were ordered to make the necessary preparations.

In London, General Clark had selected his companions to represent diverse responsibilities—for operations: Brig. Gen. Lyman L. Lemnitzer, assistant chief of staff, G-3; for supply: Col. Archelaus L. Hamblen, assistant chief of staff, G-4; for the navy, Capt. Jerauld Wright; and for landings, Col. Julius Holmes of the Civil Affairs Section. Holmes was bilingual.

Clark and his party spent most of Sunday, 18 October, in final preparations. They obtained about $1,000 in gold pieces and some Algerian francs for emergency use, and they worked out communication arrangements. The takeoff of two B-17s, which would take the group to Gibraltar, was unfortunately delayed until dawn of the nineteenth, and the group did not reach the Rock until late afternoon. They held a quick conference with Lt. Gen. Mason MacFarlane, the governor of Gibraltar, together with naval, air, OSS, and SOE experts, and then embarked on the submarine at 9:00 P.M.

Having started a little later than expected, they were not certain of making the rendezvous on time. But before leaving, Clark sent Murphy a message, via Tangier, stating that he would meet Mast on the night of 21/22 October. Murphy had meanwhile wired that the French group would expect Clark the night of the twentieth, and if the rendezvous was missed, they could meet him two nights later. Because of the late departure, Lieutenant Jewell ran the P-219 on the surface but even then did not arrive at Cherchell until just before dawn on the twenty-first. Practice exercises with the folbots, absolutely essential to their safe employment in the dark, had somewhat delayed the trip.[30]

Algiers, October 1942
Murphy's further negotiations with The Five[31]

While Clark traveled toward Cherchell, Murphy and The Five continued their negotiations. Having drawn up a preliminary draft on political and military questions, they now turned their attention to rather complex economic and financial matters. North and West Africa were knit to metropolitan France, and if the economic threads were cut, the colonial area would become quickly depleted of manufactured goods. Foodstuffs would not move, and considerable hardships would result. What The Five wanted, basically, were guarantees that the United States would support the North African economy during the abnormal period of occupation and take measures to prevent speculation and inflation. They were extremely anxious that the North African franc should have the same strength that the franc maintained, thanks to British support, in areas controlled by the Free French.

All the important points had been listed four months earlier in the ten-point questionnaire which Solborg had taken to Washington. This was dusted off and placed on the table before Murphy. Point number three had already been answered: in the 15 June document the Frenchmen had asked that an American representative be authorized to negotiate political and economic agreements.

With his powers as the president's representative, Murphy could go a certain distance without referring to Washington. He could assume, for example, that the general terms of the Murphy-Weygand Agreement would remain in effect and could be expanded. His directive mentioned that money "will be made available for additional expenses incurred through cooperation with American forces," and he was specifically instructed to prepare, for the president's approval, recommendations on policies, "including economic supply and financial support."[32] Murphy could thus commit the United States in general terms, although some specific matters would have to be referred to Washington.

On the French side, Tarbé de Saint-Hardouin, representing The Five, and Goetz, inspector of finances, carried on most of the negotiations.

They went down the items on the protocol of June 15:

What is the present state of French government investments made in the United States for war production? This complicated question ranged beyond Murphy's competence, but he undertook, through the consulate in Algiers, to recommend that $5,098,000 held by the Franco-American Banking Corporation be unblocked and transferred to the State Bank of Morocco. In Washington, steps were initiated to get the Treasury to take action.

Will Lend-Lease be applied to North Africa? Murphy was within his authority in guaranteeing that Lend-Lease, especially to give the French army a chance to fight, could be negotiated.

Will the United States establish an exchange rate of 43.80 francs to the dollar, comparable to the British-Free French Agreement placing the franc at 176.625 to the pound? The exchange-rate problem was complicated. The open exchange rate fluctuated around 125 francs to the dollar, and a sudden modification might upset the economy and introduce speculation. Murphy could offer no guarantees, as any such alteration would require British consent. He did, however, forward a recommendation that a rate of 50 francs to the dollar be established. Washington agreed in principle that the rate should be altered, and discussions were begun. But nothing was settled until D-Day. On 7 November, Washington agreed to set the rate at 75 to the dollar. Further changes had to await high-level decisions at the Casablanca Conference, in January 1943, where the 50-to-1 rate was finally accepted.

Will the United States restrain its nationals from bringing dollars into North Africa? This question lay beyond Murphy's competence, and he could give no assurances. The American government had already printed "invasion currency," bills with a yellow seal which would circulate only in North Africa. Presumably, once the exchange rate had been established, this device would minimize speculation and inflation. But Murphy could give no basic guarantee on this matter.

Several questions in the 15 June protocol asked essentially

whether the United States, considering the enormous disruption in North Africa's economic life, would be willing to stabilize the markets by bringing in consumer goods and by purchasing African products. These matters, basically similar to those in the Murphy-Weygand Agreement, fell into Murphy's purview, and he provided favorable answers. He knew that the State Department was attempting to accelerate the departure of two ships, held up by the BEW, and on this knowledge he could specifically give guarantees. In some instances he fell back on diplomatic hedges—for example, if exchanges did not balance out, the means of payment would be "re-examined by mutual agreement." Although some of the economic problems could only be solved by time and hard work, Lemaigre Dubreuil and Saint-Hardouin placed great store on basic agreements concerning them, because they realized that the strength of a new French regime in North Africa would depend heavily on the political and economic foundations established by the United States.

As a result of strenuous discussions on 18 and 19 October, the economic and financial questions were partially resolved. What Murphy could not answer he referred to Washington; what he could was drawn up into a draft letter which would be sent to General Giraud.

Meanwhile, preparations were being made to receive General Clark and his party. The location seventy-five miles west of Algiers had been chosen because of the risk involved in a rendezvous closer to the city.

The head of the Cherchell underground movement, Jean Queyrat, an associate of Henri d'Astier, knew an ideal spot, a house directly on the sea, isolated, half-hidden in pine trees. The house, situated on a lonely beach at Messelmoun, about twelve miles west of Cherchell, belonged to the father-in-law of Jacques Teissier, a staunch member of the Cherchell Resistance. Teissier would persuade the occupants and the servants to vacate the house, while Queyrat would establish security lookouts around the property.

Murphy and Mast agreed. Murphy wired the exact locality to London, setting the date for the night of 20/21 October, and indicating that a white light facing the sea would reveal to a submarine offshore that the party of officers was expected.

Mast made the final arrangements for his party, which consisted entirely of military personnel. D'Astier and Van Hecke would have general responsibility for arrangements, but of the Five only Jean

Rigault would actually attend the conference—in the role of reporter, not negotiator. Mast's immediate staff included Lieutenant Colonel Jousse (army), Captain Barjot (navy), and Major Dartois (air). Jousse had for a long time worked on plans to cooperate with an Allied landing; he would be prepared to present those plans personally to the American officers.

To assist in security arrangements, Bernard Karsenty (a resourceful officer who took care of the food) and Capt. Lindsay Watson, of the Chantiers de la Juenesse, participated, as well as two officers from the local anti-smuggling coast guard (les douaïrs garde-côtes), Lieutenant Le Nen and Aspirant Michel.

On the night of the twentieth, Murphy and the Frenchmen waited, but no submarine appeared. Already Clark had suggested a second rendezvous the following night, if contact was not made.

Fortunately, the shore group was able to return the following night, although getting all the participants together for a second time had not been easy. During the evening of the twenty-first Murphy and Ridgway Knight, together with d'Astier, Rigault, Teissier, Captain Watson, and Karsenty, took over the house and had the light beamed toward the sea shortly before midnight. The servants had been aroused and, grumbling, they left the villa for a second time, somewhat unhappy that their normal rest had been abruptly interrupted.

Within a few hours the party had come ashore. Murphy was able to greet his guests and with vast relief introduce them to his French companions. The folbots were stored, and the group settled down for a short nap until General Mast should arrive.

7

General Clark's Secret Mission

Cherchell, 21–22 October 1942
Clark meets Mast

Serious discussions began soon after dawn when General Mast and his party arrived. Mast had to leave at noon, and he spent the intervening time almost entirely with Clark. Mast spoke adequate English, but Murphy was present to interpret when necessary. Rigault also remained in the room, taking notes.

Much has been written on these Cherchell deliberations, and a great many misunderstandings have developed around them.[1] Some of the anecdotes associated with the meeting give the impression that the Americans considered the expedition quite a lark. The operation was, in fact, a dangerous and unorthodox one, which appealed enormously to newsmen once the basic facts had been made public. In his news conferences Clark was asked again and again by reporters for stories about his odyssey. For reasons of security, he could not reveal much about the intelligence or operational aspects of the meeting, and he made up for this, with encouragement from the chief of staff,[2] by recounting dramatic details of the folbot operation and of surveillance by French police. This lightness and banter, although quite characteristic of Americans and possibly overstressed in an American press hard put for war news, seemed overjocular to Frenchmen who felt sensitive about their own defeats and personal risks.

More to the point, the American deception at Cherchell, once it was understood as a deception, added rankling injury to French sensitivities, for it increased French officers' awareness that they had not been considered, in spite of professions to the contrary, as equal partners. When the French came to see that they had been duped, they felt injured in several ways: first, that the Americans, reputed to be open, honest, and frank, had revealed themselves as callously Machiavellian; but also, that the Americans held the French in such low esteem that an "honorable" relationship—in the sense that it controlled relations with the British and the Russians—did not have to be developed with those whom the Allies considered second-class partners.

In a sense, American deception had been imposed by Frenchmen, although not by the French with whom they were now deliberating. A widespread feeling existed among the British and Americans that French security could not be trusted. Ironically, a good deal of this feeling originated in the abortive Anglo-Gaullist operation against Dakar in 1940. It was unfair to hold Armistice Army officers as unreliable when the presumed leak came from Free French personnel, for whom the Armistice Army had little use. It was unfortunate though true that an attitude toward all Frenchmen had been engendered by the untrustworthiness of a few. It was unfortunate as well that the French, not occupying a position of strength, were unable to argue their own case with the Allies. The Russians also were considered unreliable from a security standpoint (Anthony Eden had exchanged some harsh words with Ambassador Maisky on this issue prior to the African landings);[3] but the Russians had equal status. The French, as de Gaulle sadly and continuously observed, did not.

As a matter of fact, American security was equally suspect. Many Frenchmen felt that Weygand might have held his own if American newspapers had not publicized aspects of Murphy's relationship with him. Be all this as it may, the Allies made the decisions, and the French were in no position to make an effective argument that their security matched that of the British and Americans. The conviction regarding French untrustworthiness was held at the highest level; as Churchill cabled Roosevelt on 3 September, 1942: "Free French have got inkling and are leaky."[4]

Consequently, the orders for Clark and Murphy to conceal vital military information from the French originated at the top Allied command, not at the level of the Allied force commander. The experience at Dakar had shaken Churchill and the British staff; they did not dare rely too heavily on anyone in the French ranks. Frenchmen like Mast, Jousse, Beaufre, and others, who decry Clark's deception at Cherchell, must look for the causes in the entirety of Franco-Allied relations after 1940. Both Clark and Murphy have testified that personally they deplored their Machiavellianism; but wartime exigencies blanket the moral rectitude of the best of men.

Another aspect of the deception also stemmed from French sources. When asked the scope of the American intervention, Clark blandly raised the effectives by five, affirming that 500,000 men together with appropriate air and sea supporting forces would participate. The figure 500,000 goes back to conversations Ambassador Leahy had with Darlan. According to Leahy, Darlan

> told me somewhat sarcastically, as I recall, that if the Americans showed up with 500,000 men his attitude would be entirely different, and if we came with enough force to give the French a reasonable prospect of holding their colonies against an Axis invasion he would join with us.[5]

Whether Darlan spoke sarcastically or not, the figure of half-a-million men, used by both sides, approaches so close to the ridiculous that neither side could take the other seriously. The sum total of Rommel's North African forces numbered fewer than 100,000. Clearly 500,000 troops, with modern equipment, could dominate North Africa and, landed in France, could make a creditable showing against the Axis. But Darlan knew full well that to recruit, train, equip, and ship a contingent that size remained an absolute impossibility for 1942. If he meant his comments with any sincerity at all, he was talking about 1943 at the earliest; and he was hinting that he might be able to keep France unoccupied until then. For Murphy and Clark to have picked up this figure and to have exploited it served no purpose, for anyone experienced with logistics must have realized how exaggerated the numbers were. What the French really wanted to know related to effectiveness: they wanted assurance that the contemplated operation would loom larger than a commando raid, larger, to be specific, than the abortive 4,000-man assault against Dieppe two months earlier. This satisfaction they never received, and the consequence—a certain skepticism about American capabilities—existed just as if no figure had been mentioned. Mast and Giraud were accepting an American pig in a poke, trusting in

Yankee reliability; Darlan remained where he stood, convinced that in 1942 the Allies could not field a team which could prevent German occupation of France and North Africa. Between Giraud and Darlan, Darlan was the more realistic.

So much for deception. Clark and Murphy were restricted by specific orders from honestly sharing information with the French. And these orders emanated from the highest authority.

Throughout the morning of Thursday, 22 October, Clark and Mast exchanged views.

Mast was obligated, as Giraud's representative, to obtain certain information: what would the United States do if French resistance forces seized the initiative in France? What if the Axis attacked France or North Africa? Did this appear imminent? Did the United States plan to seize the initiative? When? If earlier than 1943, why? Would the Americans act alone?

Under close restrictions regarding what he could tell, and yet anxious to enlist Mast's cooperation and support, Clark produced guarded answers. The question of giving support to French insurgents in southern France had already been examined briefly in London on 17 October and had been ruled out because of shipping shortages. Clark did not wish to give a completely negative answer, however, and he promised to look into the question further. Not realizing the imminence of TORCH, Giraud had not yet transmitted a full version of his plan to his representative in North Africa.

On American aid if the Axis made an aggressive move, Clark could make a firm pronouncement because official policy affirmed that the United States would bring immediate and effective assistance to French forces which resisted. Both Mast and Clark agreed that their intelligence reports warned of an early German assault, and Clark left the impression with the French that the United States intended to anticipate an Axis move. The Frenchmen wanted to know how long it would take, if they resisted the Germans, for American assistance to reach them. Clark replied that ships from England would take about two weeks, from the United States about three.

Except for a statement that he wanted to attack the Axis "as soon as possible," Clark did not indicate that the TORCH operation had already been mounted and that convoys even then were inexorably moving toward Africa; but Mast and Rigault drew certain conclusions. They correctly assumed that Clark and his group would not have reached Cherchell so quickly and been so willing to get into specifics unless a landing was scheduled for the immediate future, not 1943. But amphibious operations would become increasingly risky with winter weather, especially after 1 December. The French, therefore, guessed that the Americans would be coming in about a month.

There followed a bit of sparring. As it was clear that Clark would not reveal details about American plans, the discussion took the shape of a hypothetical operation: if the Americans planned to come in, how would they do it? Clark replied with a mixture of fact and fancy—that they would consider landing in the regions of Casablanca, Oran, and possibly Algiers, but not farther east than Algiers. Mast insisted that unless Algiers was included, his personal assistance would be almost useless.

How large an operation? Mast inquired. Clark replied that they would think of using around 500,000 men (fifteen divisions, two or three of them armored), approximately 2,000 planes, together with appropriate supporting naval units.

Mast was impressed but somewhat skeptical. "Do you have sufficient shipping to bring in a force of this size?" he asked.

Clark assured the French general that he did.

Mast wondered whether the Americans could mount such an operation by themselves. Clark admitted that with American commitments in the Pacific, they would have to rely on British sea and air support. Remembering the Anglo-Gaullist attacks on Dakar and in Syria, and the British shellfire at Mers-el-Kebir, Mast expressed the hope that British participation would be minimal and Free French absolutely excluded. He pointed out that British naval units offshore would inflame French admirals to all-out defense, and revelation of British troops ashore would make Mast's job doubly difficult and risky, if not impossible. He strongly urged Clark to make the landings an entirely American operation.

Sensing that he could learn no more specifics about American intentions, Mast brought the discussion around to General Giraud. He believed Giraud would continue to cooperate but that it would be necessary to get his approval and also to bring him to North Africa before D-Day. Mast recommended that a submarine pick Giraud up at D minus four.

How essential was Giraud? Clark wondered. Mast did his persuasive best to convince Clark that Giraud would provide the magic appeal necessary to rally the French army. He was absolutely certain that Giraud could produce, and that to bring Darlan into the picture would endanger the entire operation. Mast's sincerity and personal conviction assuaged whatever doubts Clark and Murphy may have had, and they left the conference with the sense of assurance that in Giraud they held the certain key to an unopposed landing.

In this they were wrong. If Mast to some extent was deceived by American bluff, on his own part he led the Americans astray in his overenthusiastic insistence that Giraud's prestige could conjure up support which in fact it could not. Mast's error coupled his own ambition and desire to exploit the American intervention with his blindness to the real apathy of his fellow officers. He was perhaps, like Giraud, a victim of his long internment in Germany, during which he idealized French honor and anti-Nazi feeling and lost touch with the defeatism of Vichy. Also, his obvious distrust, even dislike, of Darlan and Juin caused him to magnify his own position and influence at the expense of theirs. When Clark returned to London, Butcher asked him what motivated the Frenchmen he met. "Well," Clark replied, "until the police came, all I heard was *l'honneur, l'honneur, l'honneur.*"[6]

But suppose, Clark wondered, Giraud did not reach North Africa, either because he refused the Allied terms or because he could not get out of France. What then?

Mast insisted he had the answer. "I will assume command."

"But will the troops rally to you?" Clark queried.

Mast assured Clark that they would. When Clark asked about Juin, and whether the troops might not retain their loyalty to him, Mast was emphatic in his insistence that he could take care of Juin.

This strong assurance on the part of General Mast would loom large at the time of the invasion.[7] It was not that Eisenhower counted on French cooperation as absolutely necessary for TORCH's success; he had always believed that he should be strong enough to take North Africa with or without French assistance. But if Mast had not emphasized so strongly that Giraud would be obeyed, or had not insisted so adamantly that Darlan should be bypassed, or that he, Mast, could control Algiers in Giraud's absence, the Americans might have maneuvered more freely among French alternatives. It would work out that Giraud could *not* rally the troops, that Mast could *not* dominate Juin, that Darlan *could* prevail. Without denigrating General Mast's great services in collaborating with the Allies, it must be pointed out that, whether through misjudgment or over-ambition, he did not correctly assess conditions in Algiers.

Mast then brought up the question of small arms: if 2,000 Bren guns could reach d'Astier's and Van Hecke's young men, replacing the antique guns they were relying on, the group could become a formidable underground army, a force to be reckoned with. Clark saw no difficulty here and promised to make arrangements.

To push ahead for a moment, it might be mentioned that when he arrived back at Gibraltar, Clark sought out the SOE representative, Col. Brien Clarke, and arranged with him to supply the weapons from British stocks. Colonel Lemnitzer turned over 16,500 Algerian francs to Clarke to cover expenses. As Murphy now had general authority over both Eddy and Clarke, in OSS and SOE, the practical plans for delivery were to be worked out with him. On 1 November, back in London, General Clark checked with Colonel Mockler-Ferryman, G-2, to ascertain whether the shipments were being made. By D-Day, however, the small arms had not been delivered. Their absence may have influenced, to some extent, the attitude and actions of General Mast on 8 November.[8]

Talk of the small arms led to discussion of their distribution and of communication with the resistance. Granted the Allies were unwilling to reveal the date of their operation, would they give the French time enough to make contact with all the underground elements, some of which, in Morocco, were hundreds of miles from Algiers? Mast said that he needed at least ten days' preliminary notice, with positive confirmation at D minus four and D minus one. When Clark expressed his concern about information leaking out, Mast insisted that no more than eight persons would have to know. Clark felt that ten days' notice could not be given, but that four or five was perhaps not unreasonable. He gave no promise at Cherchell but undertook to discuss the question with the Allied authorities on his return to London.

Mast requested that liaison officers be sent, and this was promised. It should be mentioned that three vice-consuls, Knox, Culbert, and Rounds, had been transferred to the assault forces and would land with them. But these men could not be considered as liaison officers. Unfortunately, too little time now remained; the planners should have anticipated this reasonable requirement of Mast's.

The conversation now broached the delicate question of French command. Mast may have felt it was presumptuous of Giraud to make a claim to supreme command of an operation he had not planned (so Mast affirms in his memoirs), but as Giraud's representative he held himself obligated to get Clark's reaction.[9] Mast brought out the letter, drafted by Murphy, The Five, and himself, which stated that "the general direction of operations would be exercised by you [Giraud]." This question had already been explored in London, and Clark knew that such a commitment could not possibly be made, although an alternative, naming a French general to become Eisenhower's deputy, had not been ruled out.

Clark and Mast debated the issue at some length and finally, with Lemnitzer's and Murphy's help, compromised on a new draft which postponed French supreme command to some indefinite future when the French army had become entirely rearmed. Realizing that the process of equipping the French would take many months, Clark could believe that the transfer of command would thus take place only after the Axis had been expelled from Africa. The new draft read:

> Insofar as command is concerned the United States has no other thought or desire but that military command in the area be placed in French hands at the earliest practicable date. However, during the initial phase of the operation—that is, the landing and the establishment of necessary bases—it is considered essential that the command be not changed while the operation is in progress. During this period we shall lend every effort to provide French Forces with modern arms and equipment. While French Forces are being thus equipped and organized, the command machinery can be perfected so as to permit French assumption of the supreme command at the appropriate time. Immediately following the landing it would facilitate direction of the operation if a French General officer was appointed as a Deputy to the Commander-in-Chief.[10]

This text conformed closely to the compromise formula Eisenhower had recommended when he met the British on 17 October with one exception: when Eisenhower spoke of French command he meant military command of North Africa, not operational command of Allied forces.[11] The expression "supreme command," as used by Clark, was somewhat ambiguous and might require further clarification. But as the document would have to be referred to both Giraud and Eisenhower for approval, both sides could assume that this clarification, if required, would come in a few days.

Mast and Clark had now covered the major general points. Shortly before noon Mast excused himself, pointing out that he had official responsibilities which would not brook further absence from Algiers. He and Rigault drove back to the city.

After lunch the discussions resumed on more technical levels. Major Jousse explained his plan for cooperation with the Allies.[12] This was essentially the same program he had worked out in the spring of 1942 and which Colonel Solborg had taken to Washington in July. The plan may therefore have languished in a file drawer, but it was quite new to Clark, Lemnitzer, and Hamblen, the people who should have known about it. The Americans were astonished how closely the French concept approximated their own; it contained some details which could be usefully applied to TORCH. Most important from the Allied point of view was the French revelation that certain strategic points—the airfield at Oran, the airfield at Blida near Algiers, and the airfield at Bône—might be made immediately available to the Allies by Mast's fellow conspirators. If planes could be brought into Oran during the night, for example, it would be easy to deny the airport to the Axis. The Americans wanted to know how they would get lights. Major Dartois, then stationed at Oran, was confident it could be done. "I'll turn on the lights myself," he insisted.[13]

The airfield at Bône fell under the control of Colonel Lorber, a trusted associate of General Mast's. The TORCH plan did not envisage a landing at Bône, almost 300 miles east of Algiers and less than 100 miles from the Tunisian border. Yet, if by such cooperation Bône could become available, it would provide a key base for a quick assault on Bizerte and Tunis. This intelligence was worth considering.

The French plan assumed that landings would be made east of Algiers, at Pointe Pescade, and at Sidi Ferruch. TORCH was already scheduled to land at approximately these points. The French concept so closely approximated the Allied one that, as General Lemnitzer later put it, "it looks as though they might have read a copy of the TORCH outline plan."[14]

Together with their plan for an Allied landing, the French officers brought to the conference a mass of specific intelligence material. This included the location of shore batteries, amounts of ammunition available, and the location of arsenals. They gave the numbers and dispositions of ground forces and of naval units. They had naval defense plans, together with details on methods of blocking harbors, and information about harbor defenses. They gave Clark the location of fuel storage depots, as well as capacities and defenses. They enumerated the airfields in North Africa and told the American general which fields could be used by paratroops, which became unusable in rain, and what air units were stationed at the various bases.

General Clark has testified that the information given proved to be absolutely correct. Immediately after his return to London, Clark had the material translated, duplicated, and distributed to the appropriate units. On 26 October, he personally briefed air force officers on the air information and Admiral Cunningham on the harbor defenses. Cunningham was especially interested in the devices planned for blocking harbors. According to officers at headquarters, "The completeness and terrific value of the information were astounding."[15] On the following day a full-scale planning session examined the question of moving on to Bône, which General Anderson wanted urgently to obtain.

In *Our Vichy Gamble,* Professor Langer lists some of the intelligence data, which are also briefly enumerated in a contemporary article by Frederick Painton. Langer believed Painton exaggerated somewhat the importance of the intelligence obtained. During the war, Professor Langer directed the Research and Analysis Section of OSS, and was consequently in a position to assess information coming in from North Africa. Possibly because Langer knew how much information had already become available, from air surveys and from Murphy's vice-consuls, he could assess how much of the new material duplicated what was already available. But the freshness of the intelligence, the dramatic way in which it was procured, and its very special relevance, brought it unusual attention at Norfolk House.

At Cherchell talks continued throughout the afternoon of 22 October, not only on technical military matters, but on the political and civil questions which had been incorporated in Murphy's two draft letters. No significant alterations were made.

Cherchell, 22 October 1942
End of the Cherchell conference

About 6:00 P.M. the discussion came suddenly to an end. What happened between six o'clock that evening and five o'clock the following morning provided most of the anecdotal material which later made the Cherchell conference so newsworthy.

The coast guard officers, Lieutenant Le Nen and Aspirant Michel, learned by chance that the local commissioner of police planned to take a look around the Teissier place. He had been notified by one of the Arab servants that something unusual, possibly smuggling, was going on. A phone call warned the people at the house that the policeman was on his way.

What happened after that is best described in the words of the participants. These accounts contain the bulk of the stories which, while unimportant in relation to overall objectives, provided most of the color, drama, and sense of adventure associated with the operation.

Mark Clark (telegram to Eisenhower):

Detailed conferences continued throughout day until afternoon when local police intervened in rendezvous area. This event brought conference to abrupt conclusion. While Frenchmen flew in all directions our party hid in empty repeat empty wine cellar of the house while argument ensued with police.[16]

Robert Murphy:

Ridgway Knight and I received the police who were polite but firm, while Teissier explained to them that I was an American diplomat, Counselor of Embassy at Vichy, temporarily in Algiers, his guest for a pleasant party which included some imaginary ladies upstairs. He skillfully persuaded them that the smuggling story was ridiculous while Ridgway and I made appropriate noises.[17]

Richard Livingstone:

The trap door was lowered upon us, barrels were rolled on top, and some artist scattered dust over the boards, which percolated through and caused someone to sneeze devastatingly at intervals for some time, in spite of his efforts to control himself and the muttered exhortations of the others to make less noise. We sat silently in that pestilential cellar in pitch darkness, getting more and more cramped, for two hours listening to the carefree whistling and cheerful shouts of the people upstairs, who were giving a fine performance as honest citizens with nothing to conceal, certainly not a cargo of contraband generals in the wine cellar.[18]

Mark Clark:

Poor Courtney . . . was seized with a coughing fit. He choked and sputtered in the darkness and finally whispered to me, "General, I'm afraid I'll choke."

I answered, "I'm afraid you won't!"

I slipped him a wad of chewing gum on which I already had worked for a while. This quieted him, but he later expressed surprise that "your American chewing gum" had so little taste, and I had to tell him I'd chewed all the taste out of that piece.[19]

Some time after 8:00 P.M., once the police had left, everyone pitched in to carry the folbots down to the beach. All of the French had now driven back to Algiers except Teissier and Bernard Karsenty. The wind had whipped the sea into white-capped waves, and forbidding rollers pounded the beach. Clark and Livingstone attempted to launch one of the boats.

Richard Livingstone:

We floated the boat, waist deep, waited for the lull with the undertow tearing at our legs, and at a favourable moment made a dash for it—but just as we were almost clear an extra large wave turned up. The boat reared up almost vertically, the crest of the wave crashed down on top of us, she rolled over, and in an instant we were struggling to free ourselves in a boiling turmoil of foam. As the water receded I managed to get a grip on the bottom, trying to avoid being drawn back by the powerful undertow and at the same time to rescue the floating paddles and the waterlogged boat. . . . The general swears he heard someone say "Never mind the general, for heaven's sake get the paddles!" It had been impressed on the generals that on no account must the paddles be lost, and at one time, it seems, all that could be seen of General Clark was an arm holding a paddle firmly aloft above the swirling water.[20]

Mark Clark:

I knew I was going to be soaked, so I stripped to shorts and my o.d. shirt. It was cold paddling around in the water. We tried one spot and immediately were overturned by a wave. I had put my money belt—containing several hundred dollars in gold

—in my rolled-up trousers, not wishing to be weighted down by the gold in a turbulent surf and heavy undertow. My pants and the money—later described as a large sum in news displatches—were lost at that time.[21]

Next day Murphy found the pants, together with other odds and ends, had them cleaned, and returned them to Clark after the invasion. Unfortunately they had shrunk too much to be wearable, but they provided anecdotal wealth to Clark's many retellings of the episode. After the war General Clark presented the celebrated trousers to the Citadel Museum in Charleston, S.C.

The sea showed no signs of abating. Cold and wet, not daring to return to the house, the shivering group discussed alternatives—buying, renting, or stealing a fishing boat at Cherchell, driving to Spanish Morocco, returning to Algiers—but all possibilities contained unacceptable risks. They decided to wait. Around four o'clock in the morning, with the sea slightly lower, they decided to try again. Courtney recalled how Gold Coast natives launched their canoes in a surf by carrying them out beyond the breakers and then climbing in. The shore group—Murphy, Knight, Teissier, and Karsenty, reinforced now by the coast guardsmen Le Nen and Michel—stripped off their clothes, waded into the frigid water with the folbot above their heads. This time the launch was successful and, although two of the boats capsized and had to be righted, they all made it safely back to the submarine. As the last boat, carrying Livingstone and Holmes, came alongside, it was swamped by a rush of water and had to be abandoned. Holmes's musette bag, containing letters Murphy had written and more gold coins, was lost. In order to lighten the folbot as much as possible, General Clark had given his carbine to Karsenty.

Mark Clark:

> I wanted to stay and look around a little, but the sky already was glowing with approaching day, and Lieutenant Jewell said we must submerge. We reluctantly went below and started back toward Gibraltar.
>
> We were all soaked and exhausted. I asked Lieutenant Jewell, "Haven't I heard somewhere about the British Navy having a rum ration, even on submarines?"
>
> "Yes, sir," answered the lieutenant, "but on submarines only in emergencies."

"Well," I said, "I think this is an emergency. What about a double rum ration?"

"O.K., sir," said Lieutenant Jewell. "If an officer of sufficient rank will sign the order."

"Will I do?" I asked.

It seemed that I was a satisfactory signer and I actually put my name to a formal written order for a double rum ration to crew and passengers of the P-219.[22]

Clark and his party were picked up next day by a flying boat. After a short sojourn at Gibraltar, they returned to London, greeted by a jubilant Eisenhower on Sunday evening, 25 October.

Murphy and his friends next day diligently searched the beach for telltale remnants and then drove wearily back to Algiers. Murphy had not slept for three days, but he was back at work on Saturday, with an enormous number of decisions ahead of him.[23]

From many points of view, one can argue that the dangerous and melodramatic meeting at Cherchell accomplished nothing and could have been foregone.

On the Allied side, preparations had been made to occupy North Africa whether or not the French cooperated. If there existed possibilities of French cooperation, could not all the contacts have been handled by Murphy? Or, if a military liaison was required, could not an officer have been flown in as consular attaché, or even disguised as a businessman or journalist? Even if Clark had not come to Cherchell, would not Mast have cooperated?

While these questions can possibly all be answered in the affirmative, certain conditions that existed at the time have to be taken into account.

When Jean Rigault returned from Lyons on 13 October, he was not at all certain that Giraud would continue in the Algerian plot. Rigault knew that the Allies planned to move on North Africa, and he conjectured that it would be soon. He knew equally that Giraud was thinking in completely different terms—of an operation which was basically French, would take place in France, assisted by the Allies, and would be scheduled for 1943. If Giraud were to have been abruptly notified of the true facts, undoubtedly he would have refused to associate himself with the Allied venture. What if he dropped out? Rigault and Lemaigre Dubreuil foresaw that in such a case the Allies would land anyway and would then negotiate with, or install, any Frenchman who they felt could bring North Africa into their orbit. If the Allies dealt with Darlan or Juin or Noguès—or even de Gaulle—the entire work of The Five would have gone for nothing. The Americans *must* be persuaded that Giraud was their man, and Giraud must be persuaded that the Allied venture could not be ignored.

How else could this be accomplished except by a direct, high-level confrontation of military experts? However much authority Murphy possessed as presidential representative, he alone could not convince Giraud about the seriousness of American intentions. This sort of persuasion had been tried over a year earlier, when Murphy told Weygand that the United States would bring him military support. Well and good, but in time enough to counter an Axis occupation of France and North Africa? Only a high-ranking American officer, actually involved in planning, could convincingly make such an assurance. It was for this reason that General Mast and The Five so forcefully pressured Murphy to bypass Darlan and Juin and to bring Giraud and the Allied command, through their representatives, face to face.

Thus, even if the French were treated as junior participants and kept in the dark about Allied intentions, they accomplished their major goals, of obtaining facts which enabled them to persuade Giraud that an important American operation was projected and of persuading the Americans that Giraud was the only individual who could guarantee success. Later, disillusioned with the Darlan deal, angry at American deception, and dismayed when many conspirators were jailed, French writers became critical of the Cherchell meeting. André Beaufre wrote that the French had believed it to be a working conference and only later realized it was no more than a "psychological contact to prove to each other the reality of the participants. . . . Clark paraded, bluffed with the innocent duplicity which most of our American friends deploy under such circumstances. It was not a matter of informing the French, but of taking them in. . . . It was a frightful comedy which the prodigious General Clark played before Frenchmen who risked not only their honor and lives, but French interests as well."[24]

Tarbé de Saint-Hardouin feared that the confrontation had done more harm than good. He found in one of General Clark's post-conference utterances a symbol of the entire relationship. Referring to his temporary interment in the wine cellar, Clark had said (according to Saint-Hardouin), "I had my carbine in one hand and fifteen thousand francs in the other, without knowing which arm I might use if someone showed up." To Saint-Hardouin this remark conjured up a vision only too symptomatic of the American attitude—that cooperation could be obtained only through threats or bribes. Saint-Hardouin deplored the comic-opera dramatics which terminated the conference; he wondered at the impression made on Clark by a situation "where the general commanding an Algerian division did not have sufficient authority to offset that of a petty police official."

"In my opinion," Saint-Hardouin stated, "far from being useful the Cherchell meeting created an impression of too great confidence on the French side and too much distrust on the American. It was actually harmful to collaboration between the two countries."[25]

Did the Americans obtain any real benefits from having come face to face with French officers? It must be remembered that the planners of Torch had grave reservations about their operation, at one time giving it 50 percent chance of success. They were extremely aware of their problems: the lack of training, the shortage of equipment, and above all, the absolute novelty of an amphibious assault across the Atlantic, never before attempted. Any opportunity which could change the odds slightly was worth pursuing. Murphy's dispatch had read: "Mast asserts that Giraud's command will give us entry practically without firing a shot."

To enter North Africa by invitation had been, after all, the ultimate goal of President Roosevelt's long-standing liaison with General Weygand. Now it appeared that Giraud might be able to bring off what Weygand's dismissal and reluctance had rendered impossible. There was no time to assign a military attaché to the Algiers consulate. (This might have been done, as General Clark later admitted, if the planners had thought of it in time; but they did not.[26]) From the Allied point of view there was a risk, but the possibility of an unopposed landing far outweighed the danger of General Clark being captured. And to have entrusted the mission to a lower-ranking officer, thus admitting a certain lack of faith, might have proved the difference between Giraud's acceptance or refusal. Who can blame Eisenhower or Clark if they overestimated Giraud's influence? Who could have given accurate advice?

Algiers and Lyons, 23–27 October 1942
Aftermath of Cherchell

After the morning session at Cherchell, Mast, Van Hecke, and Rigault had driven back to Algiers. Lemaigre Dubreuil held reservations on the Air France plane leaving at 8:00 A.M. on the twenty-third, and he hoped to be able to carry to Giraud the conclusions reached. Although Rigault was prepared to draft a statement, he could not do so until Murphy returned to conform the document from the American side. But Murphy was still policing the beach at the Teissier villa. Thus Dubreuil flew to Lyons with the draft letters prepared *before* Cherchell and with only a verbal summary of the recent discussions, given him by Mast and Rigault. Reservations on the flights between Algiers and the mainland could not be too easily obtained, and Dubreuil did not dare cancel. At least the industrialist could prepare Giraud for accepting a North African operation in November, even though all of the general's planning pointed in a different direction.

Lemaigre Dubreuil spent two whole days—the twenty-fourth and twenty-fifth—in the Lyons-Vichy area and had several long conversations with General Giraud both in Lyons and at Giraud's villa, La Fromente, several miles outside the town.[27]

The draft letters posed no problem at all. The paragraph on command had been deleted from the political letter, as the exact text would have to be approved by Clark's superior. Giraud cared little about economics, and he was perfectly prepared to subscribe to the financial provisions drawn up by Saint-Hardouin and Murphy.

The important parts for Giraud related to the commitment by the Allies to his southern France operation, and agreement that he should command it. Yet Lemaigre Dubreuil was now telling him that the Allies planned to land in Morocco and Algeria, probably before the end of November 1942. Giraud could see that they obviously wanted him to cooperate with them, but they had not yet offered him a clear-cut, unambigious command. The general could comprehend well enough that responsibility for the difficult landings, largely a naval affair, should rest with the planners, but he still saw no reason why the Americans should wish to retain the supreme command once the initial stages had passed. Giraud remained dubious, as well he might, about the value of an operation in North Africa. This area, of minor strategic importance, would rally automatically once the offensive had started on the mainland.

On the other hand, the possibility that the Allies might move unilaterally into North Africa without invitation had to be reckoned with. If they did this without a simultaneous thrust into southern France, then Giraud's concept of Armistice Army resistance became utterly meaningless. Giraud's plan may have been unrealistic, but the general was not such a fool as to believe it had any chance of success without air support and reinforcements from the Allies. His dilemma then was simply this: to join the Allies in a premature operation of which he did not approve or to remain aloof and lose all opportunity of fighting the Axis.

Giraud was not a complicated man and he wanted to fight Germans. He had no real choice; he would go to Africa.

But Giraud's entourage *was* complicated. Lemaigre Dubreuil had not been working with Murphy for a year simply to put Giraud on a white horse so he could attack Germans.

With considerable obstinacy, Lemaigre Dubreuil and the rest of The Five had resurrected the June 15 protocol and had obtained from Murphy tentative guarantees of political autonomy and economic support. After the invasion, cut off from Vichy, North Africa would become a headless creature requiring a strong political leash. To permit Vichy officials like Châtel, the governor of Algeria, or Noguès to establish themselves as viceroys would completely negate The Five's ambitions. Lemaigre Dubreuil saw the possibility of bringing Pierre Laval to North Africa to head a civil government in the truncated colony, but he could not brook the thought of Darlan, or worse, of de Gaulle.

Giraud had promised Lemaigre Dubreuil on 25 October that he would sleep on the American proposition and let him know in the morning. Next day he had made up his mind: he would cooperate with the Americans under certain provisos: that the official Cherchell report, as approved by Murphy, proved satisfactory, especially in regard to supreme command, and that the Allies would give serious consideration to the southern France operation. Lemaigre Dubreuil immediately coded this reaction and sent it off to Algiers. Later the same day Murphy cabled Eisenhower:

> Messenger sent to France after Flagpole's [Mast's] meeting with Clark reports that Kingpin [Giraud] agrees in principle to our proposition. He asks that we continue study of his idea of establishing a bridgehead in Southern France. I am also informed under promise that it is for my personal information only and

not as yet for communication to you that Kingpin will be willing to come to Africa for the operation. . . .²⁸

This message was received at Eisenhower's headquarters on the twenty-seventh.

In London, steps had already been taken to make sure that Giraud would get to North Africa in time. Although the general might simply fly directly from Lyons to Algiers (secret arrangements with an Air France official had already been made), Eisenhower felt it would be advisable to have a submarine waiting just in case. Giraud had already indicated, through Mast, that this should be an American vessel. No American submarine, however, could readily be assigned to such a mission, whereas the P-219, having returned to Gibraltar after the Cherchell adventure, was available. It was decided that Captain Jerauld Wright, who already knew Lieutenant Jewell, the 219's skipper, should return to Gibraltar, ostensibly take the 219 under command—thus making it "American"—and proceed to the French Riviera. The operation was given the code name MINERVA.²⁹

With Colonel Bradford Gaylord, who would serve as interpreter, Wright flew into Gibraltar early in the afternoon of October 27 and after conferences with British officers at the Rock, embarked on the P-219 that evening. His orders: proceed 42° north latitude and 6° east longitude [about fifty miles south of Toulon] and stand by for further instructions. By 1 November the 219 was on station.

Lyons, 27–31 October 1942
Giraud's reaction to Cherchell

As soon as possible Jean Rigault drew up a memorandum covering the understandings reached at Cherchell, a long document which he had not completed in time for Lemaigre Dubreuil's departure. The memorandum was finished soon afterward and sent off by another messenger, but *without Murphy's having had an opportunity to correct it*. In general, the document summarized accurately what had transpired, including the Allied deceptions about the date of the operation, its size, and the exclusion of the British. It stated quite accurately that no invasion of southern France was anticipated but that the problem would be studied. On one important issue, however—the supreme command—the report was completely misleading. The key passage stated (italics added):

> Operations placed under French command. Our colleagues accept this position in principle except for the landing phase, including:
> —getting ashore
> —taking possession of a certain number of beachheads (they feel that as they have organized this landing operation it should be directed by them).
> On the other hand, in this first phase, a French representative (for example, the deputy of the commander in chief) would be attached to the American commander in chief to facilitate relations and to present observations of the French commander on the conduct of operations during this first phase, in principle very short.
> Once this phase is completed, *the American army, with all its resources, would pass, as was mentioned above, under French command.*
> On this basis, General Mast gives his approval, subject to approval of General Giraud.[30]

Giraud obtained the memorandum on 27 October, and immediately reviewed it together with Captain Beaufre and others on his staff. He was forced to agree with the American plan, but he believed firmly that the operation would be unprofitable if the landings "will bring about the occupation by the Germans of that part of France still free." Nor was he pleased with the assumption, reflecting Mast's educated guesswork, that the Americans intended to move in about a month. In response to the section covering command he wrote:

> It is quite normal and it is understood, that all the landing operations will be regulated by the General Staff of the American Army.
> The Inter-Allied Command [i.e., Giraud as supreme allied commander] will begin to function after the landing, that is to say, for each point of debarkation, forty-eight hours after the hour set for the beginning of the initial landing operations of the first convoy. With respect to subsequent operations, the American troops will come under the Inter-Allied Command as soon as they are landed.

And he concluded:

> To sum up, the Inter-Allied Commander-in-Chief in North Africa accepts the propositions of the American General Staff for the debarkation in Algiers and Morocco, provided that he himself set the date for the landing, following American advices that preparations are completed.
>
> He desires that this African operation coincide with the landing on the French coasts of the Mediterranean of American personnel coming from Ireland—50,000 men in principle—and of material coming from Gibraltar—140,000 tons in principle—upon radioed request from the French command.[31]

In addition to his principal memorandum, Giraud drew up several annexes giving specific data on his strategic Grand Design. He also approved the draft letters which Lemaigre Dubreuil had brought, covering the political and economic issues discussed with The Five in mid-October. He also requested 10,000,000 francs to be used in organizing the Resistance in southern France.

The Giraud reply was drawn up in great haste so that Lemaigre Dubreuil could take it back with him to Algiers on the twenty-eighth. However, because of an Allied convoy in the Mediterranean, all flights from France to North Africa were cancelled on that date, and Lemaigre Dubreuil could not depart until three days later, on the thirty-first. Giraud, harassed by Vichy, decided to leave the Lyons area at this time and drove south for a visit to his brother in Aix-en-Provence. Captain Beaufre lived twenty miles away, in Marseilles, a place from which he could communicate by code with Algiers and also, through his friend Léon Faye's underground network, with London. (It will be recalled that Faye and Beaufre had held secret discussions with Colonel Solborg in 1941.) A safe hiding place was available for General Giraud in Marseilles, in case departure by sea would suddenly become necessary.

8

Last Minute Preparations

Algiers, 1942
The resistance plot[1]

In 1942 military leaders were just beginning to explore what is now considered a central feature of military operations: guerrilla warfare—a welding together of hard-core resisters who can play on the apathy, lack of preparedness, and sympathy of their fellow citizens to gain control, even for a short time, of an urban complex. In 1942 Maoism had not become an expression that evoked a response among military thinkers; and even though eighteenth-century rebels in America, or anti-Napoleonic Spanish peasants in 1808, had staked their hope of victory on underground resistance, few of the French officer elite, crammed with 1914 military lore at St. Cyr or perfected in horsemanship at Saumur, had speculated very much on ways to paralyze a city with a handful of irregular, poorly armed volunteers.

But in Algiers this happened. In Algiers a new form of warfare was practically invented, engineered out of the imagination and will of a few French officers, to make possible France's reentry into the war.

The objective was extremely simple. Algiers, metropolitan hub and communication center for North Africa, must be made available to the Allies. It had to be presumed that the ranking ground-officer, General Juin, would consider himself obliged to follow his standing orders, to fire on any troops whatsoever, Axis or Allied, that tried to land on the Algerian mainland. So, assuming that Juin could not be persuaded to cooperate, the guerrilla command had to fix upon tactics which would keep pro-Vichy officers from their men, would sever the fibers of telephonic communication, and would keep guns from being fired.

What were the means? A handful of officers in the regular army: General Mast, General de Monsabert, Colonel Jousse, Colonel Baril, and a few others who might be able for a short period to persuade some companies or battalions to follow their orders; a few hundred young Frenchmen in the Vichy youth movement, of uncertain reliability; some professional officers on inactive duty who were passionately anxious to fight Germans; a hodgepodge of young people, students, refugees from France or old-time colonial residents, especially those of Jewish ancestry whose antifascist, anti-Vichy alignment was solidly anchored in a dread of anti-Semitic persecution. Of the civilians there were possibly 800 all together, mostly youngsters united in emotional enthusiasm for Charles de Gaulle but untrained in war.

Against them, in Algiers alone, could be ranged elements of the Armistice Army: the XIX Corps headquarters, the Algiers division, the Gardes Mobiles—some 11,000 troops in all. This Armistice Army, seamed with the defeatism of Vichy and deficient in modern weaponry, may not have been entirely up-to-date, but it sufficed for maintaining order. Nor should it be overlooked that Vichy also had its paramilitary reserves, a militia, known as the Service d'Ordre Legionnaire (the SOL), whose history of betrayal and brutality during the war gave it a reputation for repression of patriots, and especially of Gaullists and Jews, that made its name more despicable to many Frenchmen than that of the German occupation army. The SOL could be mobilized in short order to supplement the police, and armbands to give it a measure of authority, initialed "VP" (*Volontaires de Place*, that is, "Volunteers of the Stronghold," comparable to civil defense), had already been prepared by the army.

What about the police force? With determined leadership, could the local police have put down an insurrection without army or SOL interference? It would largely depend on who gave the orders. The Algerian police in general lacked the Vichy orientation that permeated the army and navy officer corps and, dependent on local direction rather than on a hierarchy emanating from metropolitan France, gave vent for the most part to a sentiment both anti-German and anti-Vichy. Some police officers, like Achiary and former Director of Security Bringard, clearly and openly favored the conspirators; while the ranks, whose principal job was simply to keep order, were inclined not to get involved in political affairs but to do as they were told.

Long before any definite possibility of an Allied landing existed, a few Resistance leaders, particularly Pierre Alexandre, Colonel Jousse, and Henri d'Astier de la Vigerie, had nursed the embryo of a plan designed to paralyze Algiers and the military forces located there. In the early days of World War II, no one really knew that a handful of students could take possession of a building and defy civil authorities for hours, days, or weeks; no one appreciated the staggering potential for confusion that control of a central administrative complex could give. But new situations and problems give birth to new solutions, and the insurgent command group imaginatively proposed an operation whereby the civilian resistance would literally take over Algiers.

Their strategy set forth five objectives:

1. Control of telephone and wireless communications
2. Possession of the principal military barracks and command posts
3. Prevention of naval forces from operating
4. Custody of principal military and civilian leaders
5. Possession of major public buildings: police headquarters, post office, radio station.

To carry out these missions the strategists planned to form twelve task groups, each with a leader and deputy (presumably reserve officers to the extent available), together with sixty to seventy armed men, to be transported by five or six cars, gasoline for which would be provided by the American consulate. In order to maintain security, no group leader would be notified as to his objective until immediately before D-Day, and the men would learn only on the day itself.

If the plans worked, every vital nerve center would be paralyzed, except possibly one. The planners had to admit that they could think of no way to satisfactorily neutralize the navy. Admiralty offices were located on a quay, access to which required passing gates and guards; the buildings could be neither assaulted nor surrounded. On the other hand, naval headquarters, then located in the Hotel St.-Georges, might possibly be isolated. The conspirators did not realize (as they had few co-plotters among naval personnel) that a secret wire connected the admiralty with naval headquarters in the St-Georges. Nor did they know that the navy maintained a direct, secret teletype line to naval headquarters in Vichy.

One of the most determined of the resistance movements in Algiers had been organized by some young Jewish men, the brothers Raphael and Stéphane Aboulker, André Témime, and others, who used a physical culture program as cover for their activities. The physical education work, under the direction of a non-Jewish professional, Géo Gras, achieved widespread acceptability in Algiers, and in time the Salle Géo Gras, with its variety of programs and equipment, attracted a considerable membership. Many of the members, and the director himself, remained ignorant of the club's clandestine interests.

By 1942 over 200 Jewish members had organized themselves into an underground substructure of five-man cells. The members of each cell knew only the others and their chief, who in turn was alone acquainted with his group leader, coordinator of five cells. Thus, when the invasion was being prepared, the Géo Gras organization could count some eleven groups. About 100 young men out of these made up the hard core of shock troops, organized into four sections by young Jewish reserve officers: Lt. Fernand Fredj, Lt. Jean Dreyfus, Sub-Lt. Roger Jaïs, and Aspirant Jacques Zermati.

The overall command of the Géo Gras force had been given to a tough professional soldier, Captain Alfred Pillafort. A storybook character out of "What Price Glory," Pillafort (who was not Jewish) had bragged, sworn, fought, and made love all over the French Empire. Always ready for a scrap, he could become sentimental as a schoolgirl when moved. He had won the Legion of Honor for bravery in single-handed combat in 1932. At the beginning of 1942, when the units with which he had served in Syria were transferred to North Africa, Pillafort came to Algiers on armistice leave. He sought out old pals and soon came into contact with members of the anti-German, pro–de Gaulle resistance. These contacts then led to association with the Géo Gras organizers. Some among his colleagues considered "Pill" too truculent and loud-mouthed for effective underground leadership, but no one denied his courage, his dedication, or his professional ability.

Another clandestine group had been gradually built up by a twenty-one-year-old Jewish medical student, José Aboulker, who had passed on his enthusiasm to some of his friends and fellow students.

He communicated frequently with his cousin Roger Carcassonne in Oran, who in turn had been working with Henri d'Astier. It was only natural that d'Astier, after his transfer to Algiers in the spring of 1942, should have begun to discuss resistance matters with him. Aboulker had become acquainted with Commissioner of Police Achiary through a common friend Guy Calvet (actually Guy Cohen), who as a one-time member of the Deuxième Bureau continued to carry out espionage assignments. It was in the Calvet clothing shop, Elysée Couture, that the underground plotters frequently met. Bernard Karsenty, the young reserve officer who retrieved Clark's carbine at Cherchell, also became associated with Aboulker and served essentially as his second in command.

By the time Robert Murphy left Algiers early in August, some 350 young men, besides the Géo Gras group, had affiliated loosely in a resistance movement compartmentalized into cells of ten or twelve persons each. The individuals represented a cross section of French youth: some were reserve officers whose military training had been curtailed by the war; many, possibly 85 percent, were Jewish, strongly republican and anti-Pétain, but they cooperated with royalists like Henri d'Astier and Jean Rigault. Some cells developed along special lines, bringing together refugees from occupied areas: Alsace-Lorraine, Brittany, and even Poland.

It is difficult to assess the size of this organized resistance, and even more difficult to assess its overall political orientation. Probably as many as 800 were affiliated in one way or another, although on the night of the landings only about 350 showed up at the rendezvous points. When guns were passed out, many of the young resisters drifted away, leaving a hard core of perhaps 200 who actually carried out the Algiers *Putsch*. To these can be added the young men in the Chantiers de la Jeunesse, especially Unit 103, which was quartered at the Blida airport outside Algiers. But the Chantiers force as a whole did not take an active part in the conspiracy, and in the absence of Colonel Van Hecke a contingent of 100 even refused to take orders from insurgent headquarters.

So diverse was the ideology which motivated the individuals banded together in the Resistance that they themselves decided to eschew political action until after the landings. José Aboulker came to an agreement with d'Astier and Rigault that they would work together for a common end—to fight against the Axis with the help of the Americans—but that they would "have no political activity...." Each will regain his liberty of action after the occupation."[2]

Undoubtedly the rank and file of young men were mostly Gaullists. But the rank and file had no real contact with the sophisticated political thinking of The Five, and there was no ideology which unified all the members. The lack of political orientation would, indeed, prove a drawback. Having no plans beyond assistance for the landings, the resistance group fell apart once the Americans came into Algiers. Thus, when the American commanders began to negotiate with Darlan and his Vichy-appointed administrators, the republican elements in the underground had no way of effectively expressing their opposition and dismay.

Algiers, 25 October–2 November 1942
Last minute discussions

When Robert Murphy finally returned to Algiers after retrieving General Clark's trousers but searching in vain for the missing briefcase, he was exhausted from several arduous days without sleep. But he still had a great many tasks to perform before the invasion took place. He was very much concerned about the command issue. Clearly Rigault's memorandum to Giraud contained a faulty interpretation, but Murphy could not very well correct it: the version he and Clark had worked out required Eisenhower's approval. There was no point in sending off the draft version until he heard from the supreme commander, and in any case, with Lemaigre Dubreuil still in France he possessed no easy means of communicating with Giraud.

Murphy also chafed under the restriction of informing his French allies only four days before the landings. General Mast had specifically stated that to make adequate preparations he needed to know the date at least ten days in advance with confirmation four days ahead. Preparations had to be arranged not only in Algiers, but in Oran and Casablanca, where it was hoped that General Béthouart could keep Noguès from ordering resistance. But telegraphic communication was out of the question: someone would have to drive to Casablanca in order to alert the conspirators there.

The problem of getting Giraud to Algiers had by no means been solved. On 26 October, all Murphy knew was that Giraud, presumably still at Lyons, had agreed in principle to participate in the invasion provided that the operation would conform with his own plans for southern France. If Murphy waited until 4 November, at which time he would have to acknowledge that no plans for the French coast existed, he might not have time to reach Giraud, persuade him to come, and get him to Algiers.

On 27 October, Murphy received a cable from Eisenhower giving his opinion on matters raised at the Cherchell conference. The cable informed Murphy that a British submarine, under American command, would be standing by to pick up Giraud. Then it stated: "You are authorized to notify Kingpin [Giraud] or Flagpole [Mast] on November 4 of the assault date and of the name of the Commander-in-Chief." On the command question, Eisenhower was quite specific:

> . . . during those phases of the operation that involve the landing, establishing the security of French North Africa, and providing the necessary bases, it is considered essential that the American Command and organization which has been set up with so much effort and difficulty for this special operation, should remain unchanged. By the time this has been accomplished it is to be assumed that the French forces, reinforced by the material support provided by the United Nations will be sufficiently strong to insure the complete security of French territory. Thereafter the primary interest of the American Commander lies in the use of the area as a base of further operations against the Axis, and the defense of French North Africa will be turned over to French Command.[3]

The statement on command seemed straightforward and unambiguous: the French would *not* be given any supreme command at all, but would be responsible only for defense of French territory. Murphy might have forwarded this statement to Giraud and ended the matter except for one small item: instructions in the message said that the new wording should replace *only one sentence* in the final paragraph of the Cherchell text, while "the rest of the letter remains unchanged." Now, in "the rest of the letter" stood the sentence: "While French forces are being thus equipped and organized, the command machinery can be perfected so as to permit French assumption of the supreme command at the appropriate time." Obviously Gruenther, who drafted the cable for Eisenhower, had made a mistake; he must have meant the new text to replace the *entire paragraph*, not a single sentence. But Murphy was placed in a dilemma, whether to follow instructions exactly and preserve a ridiculous ambiguity or take responsibility for the correction, which might be unacceptable to Giraud. He decided to hold the cable until such time as Lemaigre Dubreuil returned. Meanwhile he dispatched a message to Eisenhower requesting five days' notification time instead of four.[4]

Eisenhower appreciated the need to give Giraud ample notice and returned a guarded approval in his reply of 28 October, for Murphy to notify Giraud at once that the operation was "set for early November" and that a submarine was already on the way.[5] On the twenty-ninth, Murphy called on General Mast and relayed this information. Mast was furious that so little time was left—he assumed that he had received his ten days' notice—and came close to withdrawing his cooperation. Calming himself somewhat, he made two points clear to Murphy: that the submarine should move on toward southern France and that confirmation regarding landing points suggested at Cherchell should be given. Murphy still remained in an anguished dilemma: while Mast was able to conclude by adroit questioning that the landings were indeed scheduled for 8 November, Murphy was still not authorized officially to impart specific information until four days before D-Day; nor could he give information (which he did not have) about precise debarkation points. In any case, General Mast acted on the assumption that the invasion would take place on the eighth, and he so informed Colonel Jousse and Henri d'Astier. Lemaigre Dubreuil had not yet returned from France and did not learn the date until 31 October.[6]

A complication developed during the days after Cherchell when Admiral Darlan came to Africa for a tour of inspection. Three weeks previously, on 5 October, he had tried to resign from the Pétain cabinet, but his letter had been rejected.[7] Instead, the marshal had insisted that Darlan take his place in a projected tour of Africa, to inspect French defenses. Darlan had agreed, and he left for Rabat, in Morocco, on 23 October. Meanwhile, Colonel Chrétien had seen Murphy again, right after the Cherchell conference, and had received an assurance that 500,000 Americans would be coming. "You can tell Admiral Darlan," Murphy told Chrétien, "that now you have them."[8] Chrétien, unaware that Murphy was in touch with Juin via Dorange, felt it imperative that he get this information to Darlan. He knew that after visiting Morocco, Darlan would be coming back to France by way of Algiers.

Darlan did not, however, reveal by any hint whatsoever that he was interested in making contact with the Americans. On the contrary, he gave every evidence of being more pro-Axis than ever. One must conclude, therefore, that his probings in the direction of the Americans were only serving two purposes: first, to obtain some inkling of Allied plans; and second, to make certain he could have contact with them in 1943 or later, when they might possibly reach Europe in force. At the moment Darlan harbored few doubts that the Germans were invincible and that continued close cooperation with them best served French interests. Most of September had been filled with Franco-German negotiations to permit stronger defenses in North Africa, and agreement had been reached late in the month permitting the Armistice Army to supplement its forces by 50,000. While in Morocco, Darlan was seen publicly in the company of General Vogl, chairman of the German Armistice Commission at Weisbaden, and he impressed the Germans by his relaxed acceptance of them and by his apparent will to collaborate.[9] In his contacts with French officers during his African tour, Darlan underscored the standing order to defend French territory against all attacks. He was especially concerned about Dakar, which according to rumor was to be the objective of imminent Allied assault.

After completing inspections in Casablanca, Fez, and Oran, Darlan flew into Algiers on the twenty-eighth. He discussed defense matters with General Juin, and he read Dorange's summary of the Murphy conversations. The admiral did not find it necessary to see Chrétien, who by this time had made a full report to General Juin, with whom Darlan was observed deep in conversation during a dinner that night at the Villa des Oliviers. Seeing no reason to alter the basic Vichy policy, Darlan instructed Juin to keep in touch with the Americans via Chrétien but to think in terms of 1943. He accepted the Admiralty estimates that the United States could not be prepared to embark on a major undertaking in the immediate future, and he undoubtedly felt reassured by Murphy's promise, inherent in the Dorange report, that the Americans would land only after an invitation to do so. But, while he did not believe an attack to be an immediate danger, he ordered that defenses should be improved and that every effort should be made to repel premature commando raids which might invite German occupation of France and North Africa.[10]

At that moment no one, French, German, or British, knew which way the battle of El Alamein, which had begun 23 October, would go. If Rommel had to retreat, pressures would be placed on France to relinquish additional supply facilities in Tunisia; if the Germans broke through Montgomery's defenses and seized Cairo, it would make the Axis more invincible than ever. Either way, the Vichy French needed to play a careful game and to avoid alienating the Germans.

Before he left Algiers Darlan inspected the Algiers division which, led on horseback by General Mast, paraded before him on 29 October. On the same day, he and Madame Darlan spent some time at the Hospital Maillot where their son, Alain, lay stricken with polio. The young man had become ill while traveling in Tunisia and had been brought to Algiers, where his case had finally been diagnosed. When the admiral returned to Vichy early on the morning of the thirtieth, leaving his wife in Algiers, he planned to have Alain brought to France as soon as he could make adequate arrangements. He had made no contacts, open or secret, with the Americans.

On 31 October, around noon, Lemaigre Dubreuil finally returned to Algiers via Air France from Marseilles. He brought with him General Giraud's agreement, military plans, and approval of the draft letters. Almost immediately he learned from Mast that the landings would take place in exactly one week. If Mast had become furious, Lemaigre Dubreuil became almost apoplectic at the news. He more than anyone else knew how little enthusiasm Giraud had for the North African venture and how important to the general was an operation in France itself. The imminence of the attack not only constituted a virtual double cross by the Americans, but it endangered everything The Five had worked for; it terminated all chances of obtaining a bridgehead in southern France, and it destroyed the possibility of obtaining real French cooperation under a unified Resistance. As Lemaigre Dubreuil put it in a letter to Murphy:

> The impossibility of making adequate preparations . . . is going to place me in a frightful dilemma . . . :
> To continue to help you in an operation I consider compromised by intemperate haste . . . or:
> To end my cooperation and admit that the Germans will collaborate with French African troops which have received the order—as you know—to defend themselves against any invader whoever he may be.
> I believe that rarely have men been forced into a crisis of

conscience as tragic as ours. It is the future of our country which is at stake. Your move compromises the fierce hope of redressing our wrongs for which we have worked silently during two years with the risks you well know.[11]

Lemaigre Dubreuil not only deplored the American lack of faith, but he pointed out that it would be physically impossible for Giraud to make the necessary arrangements for an immediate departure. He insisted that more time be granted and that the submarine be canceled.

No one could have been more sympathetic with the French position than Robert Murphy, who felt uncomfortable about the inevitable deceptions of war and who realized how time-consuming last minute arrangements would be. Overwrought from lack of sleep, Murphy grasped at the possibility of postponing the invasion without letting his imagination range sufficiently over the complex monster which TORCH had become: its 100-odd ships and 107,000 men then steaming relentlessly toward Gibraltar—already seven days at sea. In a telegram to Leahy, to be referred to the president, Murphy on 31 October outlined the developments thus far and then said:

> Mast proposes that we demonstrate some confidence in Giraud if we wish him as a partner and at least be willing to give him a reasonable number of days to organize what he considers the more important part of the operation, that is, France. . . .
>
> I am convinced that without French Army cooperation and the danger of its active opposition if we do not have French command with us that TORCH may fail. I urgently recommend that it is not unreasonable that Giraud be given three weeks interval to perfect his metropolitan organization and arrange his departure with maximum advantage to us. . . . No one here doubts that TORCH will lead to separation of Europe from Africa and total occupation of France.[12]

As Murphy himself later realized, his request could not be taken seriously; it was received in Washington and London with amazement and some little dismay at the diplomat's naiveté. No one at TORCH headquarters had put as much store on French cooperation as Murphy had; in fact, Eisenhower only two weeks previously had expressed to Marshall his opinion that "with a decent break in the weather, we should get on shore firmly and quickly and, at the very least, should find divided councils among the French, which should prevent them offering really effective resistance."[13] Mark Clark, drafting a reply, was tempted "to tell Mast that we are coming as planned; that all hell and the North African Army can't stop us; that if he uses the information . . . by regrouping . . . or otherwise betraying our cause, we'll hang him higher than a kite when we get ashore."[14] Ultimately a more temperate though just as stern message reached Murphy on 2 November, telling him that the operation could not be postponed and that he must do his utmost to secure French cooperation. TORCH, said the message,

> represents the only hope in the predictable future for the redemption of France and it involves a tremendous naval, shipping, air, and troop concentration. It cannot be delayed. It must be executed. Therefore there can be no change in the plan as recommended by you.
>
> You will not divulge the date or location of landings to anybody until Eisenhower authorizes you to do so.[15]

By this time Mast and Lemaigre Dubreuil had calmed down somewhat and had committed themselves to do what they could in the few days remaining. Using his secret code, Lemaigre Dubreuil had alerted Beaufre in Marseilles that the landings were scheduled for 8 November, and that Giraud must be ready to leave by the fourth.[16] Lemaigre Dubreuil himself decided to return at once to Marseilles; he was fortunate to obtain a place on an official Vichy seaplane which was taking Algerian Governor Yves Châtel to France for consultation. Meanwhile Murphy had been able to review the letters, drafted by The Five earlier in October, which Giraud had approved. Murphy signed the ones relating to political and economic matters, as well as a personal note of good will. He also signed a note guaranteeing that the Free French would not participate and the British ("non-American Allied formations") forces would not enter French territory except after an understanding between French and American authorities. Knowing full well that British troops would land in Algiers, Murphy felt uneasy at this deception but rationalized it as part of military necessity.

Finally Murphy had to face up to the command problem. It was now too late to obtain clarification from London, and it made no sense to disabuse General Giraud at this late date. With a certain ingenuity Murphy decided to forward part of Eisenhower's correction, but to leave out the part which said the French would have responsibility only for the ultimate defense of North Africa. Then he repeated Giraud's formula about the command reverting to the French forty-eight hours after the landings and added: "I am communicating your suggestion to the General Staff of the American Army and I am certain that an agreeable solution will be found." The section drafted at Cherchell, mentioning that "the French will be in a position to take over the Supreme Command at the proper time," thus remained in the letter. As this accorded with Eisenhower's specific instructions, Murphy was technically correct in including it; but it meant passing on a palpable error. It meant that Giraud, receiving the letter on 3 November, believed that the command issue was still open for discussion of details, but not of principle.[17]

With the letters all signed, Lemaigre Dubreuil took plane for Marseilles. He chatted with the governor on the way, and learned that Châtel planned to return on Saturday or Monday. Lemaigre Dubreuil urged him to stay in Vichy until Monday: "one less person," he thought to himself, "to have to arrest on Saturday."[18]

Algiers and Marseilles, 2–6 November 1942
Final Arrangements of Murphy, Giraud, and Mast

Although Murphy had officially informed Mast on 28 October only that the landings would be in "early November" and that Giraud must be prepared to leave, the date 7/8 November had been arrived at by Mast's shrewd guessing and further interrogation. Knowledge about an American operation had seeped into several circles at Vichy, but accurate intelligence was lacking. The Italian Armistice Commission removed its dependents from North Africa, and the French, expecting another thrust at Dakar, took special precautions in West Africa.

With rumors on all sides, it was not unreasonable that General Juin should have attempted to extract further information from the Americans. After Darlan had returned to France, on 30 October, Juin had conferred further with Colonel Chrétien and had approved the idea of bringing in to Algiers some American military experts disguised as diplomatic couriers. He authorized Chrétien to continue his negotiations, and on the thirty-first the colonel told Murphy about this sympathetic move on Juin's part. Chrétien furthermore let it be known that French intelligence estimated a landing to be imminent and that, if the cooperation of Juin and Darlan was to be obtained, serious negotiations had to begin. But it was too late: the convoys would soon be coming through Gibraltar; the arrangements with General Giraud had gone too far. Nevertheless, during the evening of 2 November, the same day that Lemaigre Dubreuil left for Marseilles, Juin did have a secret talk with Robert Murphy. He told the diplomat that if the Germans attacked he would request American aid, but that if the Americans tried to land, he would fire. Juin's manner struck Murphy as more sympathetic than that of Noguès, but not so friendly and pro-Allied that Murphy dare entrust him with guarded information about TORCH. On the contrary, Murphy assured Juin that the Americans would not land without an invitation. (He did not hint that the request might come from a Frenchman outside the official hierarchy.) Next morning, Colonel Chrétien came to see Murphy and told him that Juin would be prepared to discuss Franco-American cooperation with a high-ranking American officer.[19]

Murphy now held in his hands a heaven-sent opportunity to obtain Juin's cooperation, but having moved so far down the Mast-Giraud-Dubreuil road he hesitated to place confidence in Juin. Without revealing that he was in personal touch with the French commander, Murphy talked the problem over with General Mast, who emphatically advised against telling his superior anything. It is possible that Mast saw himself on the threshold of superseding his three seniors: General Juin, General Koeltz, commanding the XIX Corps, and General Boisboissel, Koeltz's deputy. Once Giraud had established himself with American tanks and guns, Mast could count on becoming at least chief of staff, while high-ranking Vichy officers would be set aside. Mast's stubborn refusal to explore resistance possibilities with a great patriot like Juin is difficult to explain except in terms of Mast's personal ambition. To be sure, in November 1942, no one knew how strenuously Juin would fight in 1944 for the Allied cause; but his high authority in North Africa demanded that every effort should have been made to cue him into the secret.[20]

Meanwhile, in France, General Giraud faced up to the question of cooperation. As soon as Beaufre learned the date from Lemaigre Dubreuil's message, he had driven from Marseilles to Aix, where the general was spending the weekend. Giraud's first reaction had been "When do we leave?," and he had immediately moved down to Marseilles. Lemaigre Dubreuil, arriving on 2 November, brought complications. He reported his own indignant response to the American action, showed Giraud his letter to Murphy, and told Giraud's entourage what he had done to get the operation postponed. He explained that he had ordered the submarine cancelled.[21]

Giraud began to have second thoughts, especially when he read Murphy's ambiguous letter regarding the command. The general also had to realize that planning for operations in southern France would not be adequate. For a while he hesitated in the face of Lemaigre Dubreuil's persuasive arguments but finally decided to leave France if it were possible. For Giraud there was really no alternative: if the Americans seized North Africa, the Germans would occupy France and operations in the south would be hopeless. If he cooperated, there was just a chance he could persuade the Americans to send immediate reinforcements into the French Riviera. It was worth the risk, and he agreed to go. During 3 and 4 November, he drew up new plans and orders for a resistance against a German move into the Unoccupied Zone. Some of these he sent to the Ministry of War in Vichy, and the others he gave to Lemaigre Dubreuil. When Lemaigre Dubreuil returned to North Africa on the fourth, he carried with him the text of a proclamation and also Giraud's Order No. 1, which authorized French officers and men to cooperate with the Allies.

One problem still remained: how to get Giraud out of France. A plan to fly him out foundered when the Germans, learning of the convoy at Gibraltar, placed special restrictions on French planes. There was still the possibility of escaping by submarine. Beaufre had already requested, via the French underground, that the British send a submarine to stand by off the coast of Nice. But if Lemaigre Dubreuil had canceled the submarine, it might not be available.

Actually two submarines were waiting, the P-217 (Captain Turner), requested via the underground, and the P-219 (Captain Jewell, with the American Captain Wright in temporary command), ordered by Eisenhower to stand by fifty miles south of Toulon. Beaufre at once asked his friend Faye, heading the ALLIANCE underground group in Marseilles, to radio London to see if a submarine could be made available at once. Faye recommended an embarkation point closer to Marseilles. By the afternoon of 3 November, Faye had made contact with London and later confirmed a rendezvous for the following night at Le Lavandou, about seventy-five miles east of Marseilles. But when Giraud and his party reached the point, they found no submarine.

Through a difficulty of transmission, the P-219 had not received the order to proceed until 9:00 P.M. on 4 November, when Giraud was already waiting at Le Lavandou. The rendezvous was postponed then for the following night, and this time, although hampered by rough seas, General Giraud, his son Bernard, Captain Beaufre, and the general's aide de camp embarked during the small hours of the sixth. The submarine ran submerged during the day but surfaced during the night. Unable to transmit because of a breakdown in the radio, the P-219 had no way of informing Eisenhower that Giraud had been picked up. Lacking any other orders, the submarine set a course for Gibraltar.

London and Gibraltar, 26 October–7 November 1942
TORCH headquarters

General Clark completed his mission to Algeria at the same time that the last convoys sailed from the United States and England. Very little could now be done at Norfolk House except to make last-minute adjustments and to examine the information which Clark brought back with him.

Eisenhower's staff was impressed by the intelligence which Clark had obtained from Mast and especially by advice that a rapid stab at Bône might bring the airfield and port, on the eastern edge of Algeria, into Allied hands. It was too late, however, to alter the basic landing pattern. The TORCH strategists were less impressed by Giraud's recommendations for a landing in southern France, but they still deliberated over the ramifications of such an operation for several days before they abandoned it. On 29 October, Eisenhower wrote Marshall:

> I would like very much to be able to send a half dozen ships loaded with 75's, machine-guns and ammunition into southern France if the French Armistice Army actually fights the Germans. But we *cannot* do it simultaneously with TORCH.[22]

In the same letter, Eisenhower anticipated trouble with Giraud over the command issue; he foresaw that he would "have to ride a rather slippery rail," but believed he could "manage it without giving serious offense."

The TORCH commander planned to transfer his advance headquarters to Gibraltar on 2 November. This was several days ahead of the time he really needed to establish himself there, but he wished to allow plenty of time in case of bad weather. Indeed, the airports around London were closed in most of the week, and it was not until the evening of 5 November that Eisenhower, Clark, and a number of staff officers, including Matthews, Mack, and Holmes of the Civil Affairs Section, finally reached Gibraltar. The headquarters offices were located 500 yards underground, in solid rock.

At this moment the Western Task Force was steaming north of the Azores toward Casablanca, while the convoys for Oran and Algiers, almost due south of Portugal, were headed for Gibraltar. The first group of ships would pass through that night. From now on there would be increasing danger of air and submarine attack.

Operation TORCH had thus far been blessed with an inordinate amount of luck. Back in September, General Clark had written a letter to the commander of Gibraltar, giving him details of the operation and the requirements of Eisenhower's staff when it moved to the Rock. This letter had been carried by a plane lost in Spanish waters; the courier's body had been washed ashore, retrieved by Spanish authorities, and ultimately returned to the British, who found the letter intact in the officer's pocket. Eisenhower had to assume that no one had opened the letter, and he continued his planning on this assumption. Nevertheless, important information *had* been retrieved from the plane: three days after the crash an entry in the German naval war diary noted that important documents had been recovered and sent to Madrid. One in French, dated 22 September, referred to an "English attack against French Morocco, Tunisia and other places in French North Africa." This information and the date, both different from General Clark's letter, indicates that another letter contained highly classified information and could have revealed to the Germans, had they heeded it, some of the landing sites.[23] Fortunately for TORCH, however, Hitler remained convinced that the Allies would attack further east, possibly Crete or Corsica; and no special counteroffensive measures were planned by the Axis for North Africa.[24]

The convoys had fantastic luck in avoiding German submarines. A U-boat wolf pack, Group STREITAXT, was in fact patrolling the Atlantic 500 miles west of Gibraltar in late October when it made contact with a slow British convoy steaming northward from Cape

Town toward England. A week of submarine attacks wreaked disaster on the convoy, but it drew the wolf pack toward Spain with depleted torpedo supplies just at the time the Western and Central Task Forces moved into the regular U-boat patrol area. Even after the passage through Gibraltar, when visual sightings gave the Axis, as well as Vichy, precise information about the fleet, only one ship of the immense armada was knocked out of action before the landings actually began.[25]

Once established at Gibraltar, Eisenhower could do little but wait. The problem of General Giraud held a high priority, but with the P-219 unable to transmit, Eisenhower did not even know if the French general had been picked up. There was considerable discussion on how to get Giraud to Algiers. The best plan seemed to be to bring him to Gibraltar and then fly him, either in a French plane or in an Allied plane with French markings, directly to Algiers. For a while Eisenhower believed his policy should be not to see Giraud himself but to give him a letter requesting him to issue a proclamation. Giraud would then be recognized as head of all French civil and military affairs in French North Africa. In the letter (which he drafted on 6 November) Eisenhower sanguinely wrote:

> Under the stimulus of your leadership, it seems probable that, with inconsequential exceptions, all French Army and Air Forces, from Casablanca to Tunis, will promptly rally to the task of freeing the French Empire of foreign domination, and will gladly welcome the American Army to assist in this great task.[26]

If Eisenhower really meant this as more than political smooth talk, he was quite wrong in his estimate of Giraud's influence. He and Murphy would later express dismay at the "legality" of the French officers who failed immediately to switch their loyalty from their legally constituted superiors to a dissident leader who had no more authority (if somewhat greater seniority) than Charles de Gaulle. In any case, Eisenhower decided to follow the advice of his civil affairs officers, Matthews and Mack, to hold the letter and see Giraud in person. Having reviewed copies of the Eisenhower-Murphy and Murphy-Giraud correspondence, they believed a confrontation on the command issue to be imperative. Interestingly enough, Captain Beaufre, advising the French general, had reached exactly the same conclusion.

During the morning of 7 November, Eisenhower held a staff conference at the Rock. By this time the convoys were pushing on in broad daylight, passing Algiers as if their destination lay farther east, under surveillance of hostile planes. The luck of TORCH still held: only one ship, the *Thomas Stone*, had so far been disabled. There had been no transmission during the night from the P-219; but in midmorning a PBY seaplane, sent out to survey the submarine's assumed track, had reported back an ambiguous message: "Task gone. P-219 transmitter out." ("Gone" turned out to be a deciphering error for "done.") By four o'clock in the afternoon, General Giraud, somewhat gaunt in his rumpled civilian clothes, unshaven, but emanating a sense of authority, was landed by the PBY at Gibraltar. Almost immediately he was ushered to a conference with Eisenhower and Clark.[27]

Eisenhower later considered the interview with Giraud one of the most painful he had ever been subjected to. Unquestionably, if he had realized how little influence Giraud would carry, the TORCH commander would not have spent hours of argument, at a critical moment, with a Frenchman who would be shunted aside by Darlan and, later, by de Gaulle. But on 7 November 1942, with his first operation minutes away, uncertain about what he confronted in North Africa, Eisenhower was willing to make, on Murphy's recommendation, concessions he did not need to make. What transpired during the discussion, which continued almost until midnight, is best described in a message Eisenhower sent to the Combined Chiefs directly afterward, dictated while the first troops were wading ashore at Algiers.

> At end of conference KINGPIN [Giraud] flatly declined to participate in operation except as Allied supreme commander in a position in which he could be completely independent to carry out his own strategic and tactical conceptions. Moreover he insisted that this position must be given to him at once. He stated categorically that by November 10 all forces then ashore must come under his control and that thereafter all forces landing in North Africa would have to come under his command upon debarkation. He stated that the present Allied Commander in Chief could retain control of base and administrative arrangements near the ports and take care of arrival of reinforcements, including supplies, but that he (KINGPIN) would make all decisions respecting the tactical and strategical employment of the

troops. . . . He is obsessed with the idea of moving immediately into France and implied that if he were made commander, he would promptly use the entire air force coming into North Africa in neutralizing Sardinia and transporting troops into southern France and transfer the fighter and bomber units to airfields in southern France. Both the EAGLE [Clark] and I urged him to go along with us temporarily on the basis previously outlined and under all the assurances that the President has made respecting French sovereignty and territorial integrity. We pointed out that eventual command has already been promised him but that as a soldier he would realize that the establishment of secure bases and development of land and sea communications would require several weeks at least. To all of this he was completely deaf; nothing matters to him except personal command and he could not repeat not accept any promises of close collaboration and consultation in the ordering of tactical and strategical enterprises. He even indicated that as Commander in Chief he could not repeat not be responsible to the Combined Chiefs of Staff but that it would be my responsibility to deal with them, particularly in obtaining necessary reinforcements and supplies from the Allied governments, after which he alone would direct their employment—whether in North Africa, in Sardinia, in Sicily or in France. . . .

. . . During an hour's recess in the conference, I conferred with principal subordinates, particularly Cunningham, concerning KINGPIN's demands. Admiral Cunningham labelled them as preposterous and unreasonable in current circumstances. In my anxiety to keep KINGPIN with us, even though it is too late for him to assist us in the role in which we especially desired him, I conceded every point he made except only that I must remain directly responsible to the Combined Chiefs of Staff for operation of the Allied force until different arrangements could be made with the consent of the two governments. I even went so far as to state that I would support his ambition to command the forces here as quickly as he had completed the great civil and military organizational task in North Africa and he could place in the field an organized French force of any respectable size. He replied that his organizational task would be completed in two days repeat two days during which time he would devote himself to the civil and military population and local leaders. He would, therefore, assume command at that time as he had already planned. . . .

My impression, shared by the EAGLE and Cunningham, is

that KINGPIN is playing for time and that he is determined, knowing that there will be some French resistance, not to lay himself open to the charge of being in any way responsible for the shedding of French blood. He realizes that he can do nothing with respect to the landing itself and can gain no credit from it, no matter how successful. Consequently he is choosing to wait to see what happens. His method of gaining time is to insist upon a point which as a soldier he is well aware the Allies cannot accept at this moment. If we are generally successful tonight, we will not be surprised to find him more conciliatory tomorrow morning since it must be obvious to him that in every way we are trying to make him the big man of the region and give him a definite personal influence and leadership in winning the war. . . .[28]

With no conclusion having been reached, no plans to fly Giraud to Algiers were developed. The *Putsch* would have to go on without him. This was the situation when the first report, at 3:38 A.M., was received at Gibraltar that troops were ashore on three beaches around Algiers.

Algiers, 4–7 November 1942
General Mast's final plans

Lemaigre Dubreuil had flown out of Marseilles on 4 November, before Giraud had rendezvoused with the P-219. With him on the plane he found General de la Porte du Theil, head of the Chantiers de la Jeunesse, en route to North Africa for a tour of inspection. Because of the general's untimely visit, Van Hecke, forced to accompany him, would be absent from Algiers on the night of the *Putsch*. No one, incidentally, had revealed to him the D-Day date.[29]

By 4 November, Murphy had learned that Giraud would definitely come. Now, according to the instructions that permitted him to reveal the date and name of the TORCH commander four days in advance, Murphy requested Mast to send a trusted messenger to the villa of Consul General Cole. Having no one available more trustworthy than his wife, the general sent Mme. Mast, to whom Murphy after some hesitation gave a slip of paper on which was written the exact hour of the landing, 2:00 A.M. (local time), 8 November.

Now that Mast possessed the precise time, he tried, in the few remaining days, to do what he could. He still did not know the exact places of landing, only that one would be in Morocco, where he hoped that General Béthouart, commanding the Casablanca division, would cooperate; and that one would be in the Mediterranean, presumably at Algiers. Mast now had two possible lines of action: one, arresting his three superiors in Algiers, leaving himself officially in command; or two, going in person to a point of Allied landings (ideally to the west of Algiers) and doing what he could to facilitate the assault. In the event, Mast followed the second alternative, but he never made his decision entirely clear to Colonel Jousse and The Five, who were mystified at Mast's disappearance after midnight on D-Day.

Mast left the Algiers *Putsch* entirely to Colonel Jousse, Henri d'Astier, and José Aboulker. By appointing Jousse *Commandant de la Place*, Mast had given him authority for maintaining order in Algiers. Jousse could act as a military commander who in emergencies had under his orders forces which would correspond in the United States to the National Guard and Civil Defense. It was Jousse, however, not Mast, who worked out a detailed plan for paralyzing the city. Mast secretly prepared orders which on the night of D-Day would go to various military contingents in the Algiers district, instructing them to cooperate with the American forces; but Jousse made out the orders for the resistance task groups which were to occupy key points in the city.[30]

Although General Mast commanded the Algiers division and could temporarily limit its actions, he had no illusions about his officers, most of whom, unsympathetic with republicanism, obeyed Marshal Pétain out of conviction. Mast knew that the navy remained entirely outside his influence and control, yet it was the navy which manned the coastal defenses. If the Americans arrived without adequate sea and air cover, the naval batteries could maul them badly before they even reached the shore.

There were two officers in the Algiers area on whom Mast could rely: Gen. A. J. de Monsabert and Col. Louis Baril. Monsabert, who would later distinguish himself during the reconquest of France, commanded the Blida subdivision of the XIX Military District. Allied control of Blida, the important airport twenty-five miles southwest of Algiers, could permit land-based planes to fly in from Gibraltar for support of the landing forces. Monsabert did not, however, command the air base nor the gun emplacements which protected it. Nevertheless he could exert influence and possibly persuade the Air Force officers to cooperate. Neither Mast nor Monsabert realized that a secret Air Force telephone line ran from Algiers to Blida; this circuit, like those of the navy, remained in service.

Colonel Baril had long held pro-American sentiments. As director of Vichy's Deuxieme Bureau he had facilitated the work of American intelligence officers at Vichy, and early in 1942 he had issued a secret report affirming that with Russia and the United States entering the war, Germany would ultimately lose.[31] Darlan read the report and, unwilling to brook such anticollaborationist sentiments (even though they may have influenced his thinking), he had Baril transferred to a minor command near Algiers. Mast knew that he could rely on Baril and on his regiment of *Tirailleurs*; he therefore fixed upon a plan which could take advantage of the pro-Allied convictions of Monsabert and Baril. Shortly before the landings he ordered the garrison at Fort Sidi Ferruch to be reinforced by elements of Baril's regiment; then on the night of the landings Baril was ordered to move with another company from his post at Kolea (about halfway between Sidi Ferruch and Blida) to the fort. If the Americans landed in the area, which Mast had strongly advocated at Cherchell, Baril could neutralize the navy gunners, help troops ashore, and provide transport which would enable the Americans to reinforce Monsabert.

General Mast also insisted that a strong force should land in the small bay at Pointe Pescade, just north of Algiers. From here a quick five-mile march could gain possession of the Admiralty.

Following Mast's recommendations, Murphy continued to send Eisenhower messages about Giraud's plans and about landing places in North Africa. Fortunately the TORCH directive already included Sidi Ferruch and Pointe Pescade as debarkation points; otherwise it would have been too late to alter the complex arrangements. In any case, Murphy's radio contact with TORCH headquarters was too unreliable for tactical use.[32]

Other plans which Mast had formulated and discussed with Murphy ran into serious trouble. There was simply no time to communicate with Morocco, where General Béthouart waited for instructions. Only on 2 November, a Monday, had Murphy's vice-consul, Kenneth Pendar, found out by intensive questioning that the landings would take place the following Saturday. Yet he and Jean Rigault, who, having been away from Algiers did not know the date, were supposed to prepare the Moroccan underground for the imminent invasion. On 3 November, after agonizing indecision, Pendar told Rigault the D-Day date while the two of them were driving to Marrakech. Next day, back in Casablanca, Rigault alerted Béthouart by informing him that the convoys had already sailed; but Béthouart did not receive the exact D-Day information until the evening of 6 November. This did not permit Béthouart to make adequate preparations in a situation which, because of General Noguès's unsympathetic attitude, posed fundamentally more problems than Algiers.[33]

In Oran the situation had also become less promising. Major Dartois, the air officer who had assured Clark at Cherchell that he would turn on the airport lights, had been transferred to Maison Blanche airport near Algiers, where he held a lower position in the military hierarchy. Many of the reliable Oran resistance people (for example, Henri d'Astier, Abbé Cordier, Pierre Alexandre) had joined the Algiers underground. This left Colonel Tostain virtually alone in Oran, and he was unwilling, under the circumstances, to take extreme measures.[34]

While last-minute preparations were being made, an event occurred which would have enormous political ramifications: Admiral Darlan suddenly and unexpectedly, on 5 November, returned to Algiers. He had been notified that his son, Alain, still suffering from polio at the Hospital Maillot, would probably not long survive. The admiral had immediately made special plane arrangements and hastened to be with his wife and son at the hospital. While in Algiers, he stayed with Admiral Fenard.

Darlan's presence in Algiers, one of the most unusual coincidences of history, has long been a matter of speculation. Did he go there, not merely because of his son's illness, but because he knew of the invasion? No one questions that Darlan possessed information about Allied plans: he had reports on The Five from Colonel Chrétien, he knew about the massing of convoys at Gibraltar, and he suspected an attack at Dakar. He had discussed all these possibilities with Juin during his tour of inspection; but there is no evidence that he had new information or that he believed an attack was either imminent or directed specifically at Algiers.[35]

Although Darlan did not return to Algiers for military reasons, this does not mean that French authorities in North Africa were unaware of the invasion threat. They, like the Germans, had accurate intelligence about the fleet build-up at Gibraltar, and they knew a major operation was developing. On 3 November, Admiral Moreau, in charge of the IV Maritime District (the Mediterranean coast from Morocco to Tunisia) had placed Condition MENACE, a partial alert, in effect for the Oran area. He himself, believing the task force would head for Sardinia, Sicily, or the Libyan coast, flew from his Algiers headquarters on 5 November to Tunisia, where he could better observe the convoy's passage. Thus Moreau was absent from Algiers when Darlan arrived, and he was unable to consult with the Admiral of the Fleet until his return on the seventh. The previous day Condition DANGER, requiring that coastal batteries be manned, had been imposed at Oran.[36]

Meanwhile other information about the Allied threat had become available to the French—more particularly to General Bergeret, inspector general of territorial air defense, with headquarters at Vichy. One of his subordinates, Major de Beaufort, worked with the Alliance network which had contacts with Giraud in Lyons, with Beaufre in Marseilles, and with Lemaigre Dubreuil in Algiers. Through this chain, de Beaufort (who was Giraud's financial agent) learned of the invasion date on 5 November.[37] He transmitted this intelligence to Bergeret. But by this time Darlan, the only one with authority enough to act, had abandoned Vichy for Algiers. Bergeret, therefore, flew at once to North Africa, sought out Darlan (who was maintaining a vigil at his son's bedside), and reported, on the evening of the sixth, everything he knew.[38]

But Darlan simply would not believe him. Darlan knew, and Bergeret did not, that his agents had been in close touch with Robert Murphy, who had assured them that the Americans would not come without an invitation. This simple faith on the part of the French admiral, notorious for his own wily and calculated negotiations with the Nazis, caused him to misjudge the American use of mendacity. Darlan went so far as to twit Bergeret for transmitting fairy stories and told him not to listen to rumors. He, Admiral Darlan, had the inside track. His reliance on Murphy's word would mean that no army alert would be placed in effect—even though the convoy could be seen from Algiers, steaming eastward across the horizon.

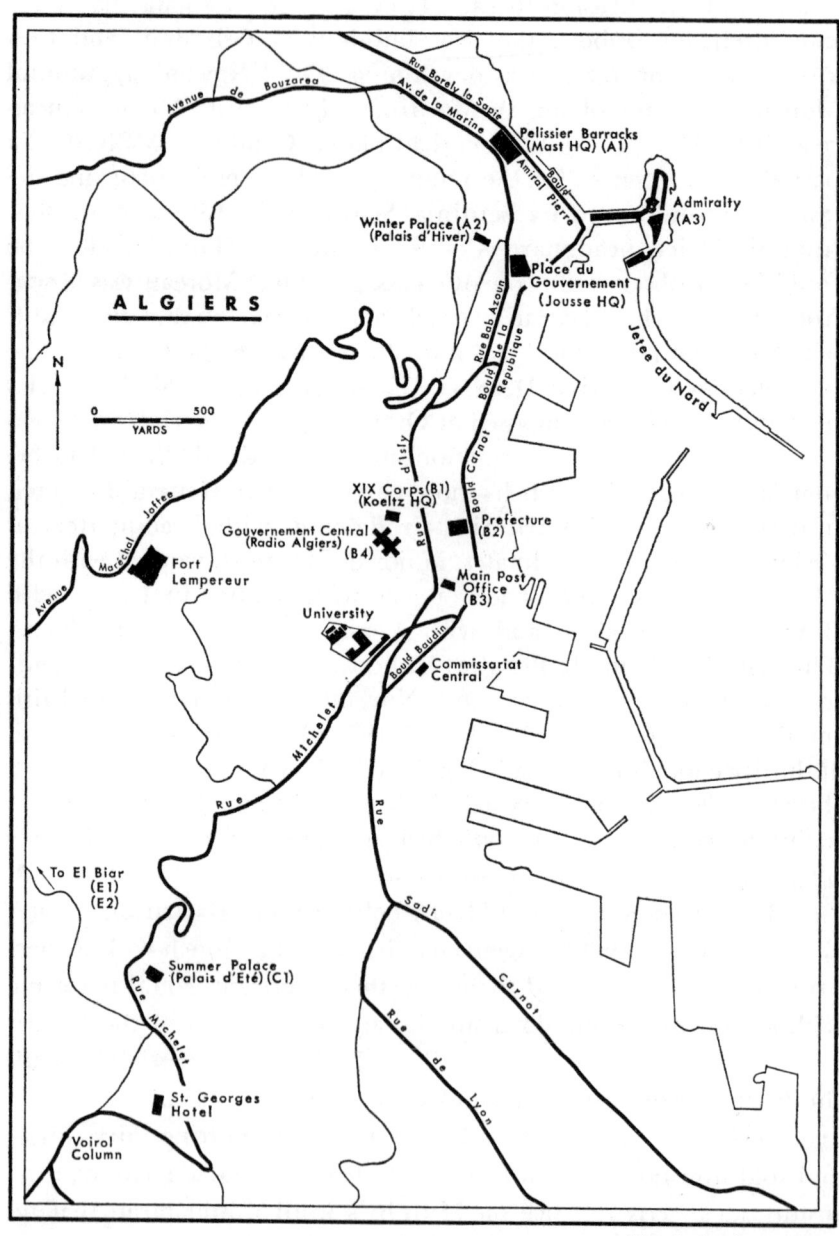

Map by Lewis Armstrong

Algiers, 4–7 November 1942
Arrangements for the Putsch[39]

Until 4 November, the date on which Murphy was authorized to reveal the exact moment of D-Day, the insurgency plans had existed on a theoretical, contingent basis. Colonel Jousse and other leaders could now count on four days to build a workable structure from their blueprints.

Headquarters had been established at 26 rue Michelet, home of José Aboulker's father, the distinguished Jewish leader and eye specialist, Dr. Henri Aboulker. Previously, the insurgents had been meeting at Henri d'Astier's apartment, which was too small. José Aboulker had gone to his father.

"What we need," he pointed out, "is a fairly large place, a place where lots of people regularly go in and out, so that what we are doing won't attract attention."

The eminent physician recognized that his son was describing his own residence, and after some troubled reflection, he agreed that headquarters could be established there. One of the radios Murphy had brought back in the diplomatic pouch was installed in a bathroom. José's sister Colette permitted her room to be used as a center for strategy discussions.

The Aboulker residence was ideally situated. The rue Michelet (now the rue Didouche Mourad), one of the city's principal arteries, connected downtown Algiers with the western heights where the Palais d'Eté (governor's residence) and Hotel St.-Georges (Admiralty headquarters) were located. Dr. Aboulker's office stood only a few blocks from the American consulate. The Garage Laveysse, where the insurgents stored their vehicles and arms, could be reached by a short walk.

On Thursday, 5 November, Colonel Jousse met with José Aboulker to work out the mechanics for Saturday night. With them in their deliberations sat a relatively new recruit to the conspiracy, an air force officer, Colonel Anselme. The plans had long since been drawn up; it only remained to make the assignments for each of the twelve task groups and to verify that the cars and weapons were ready.

Colonel Jousse would act as coordinator between the military operations and the civil *Putsch*. General Mast had been careful not to get involved with the civilians, and during the landings he would concern himself only with military phases of the operation. The Five would remain apart from specific insurgent tactics, acting more or less as "chiefs of staff," giving advice on overall strategy and maintaining liaison with Robert Murphy. One of The Five, Colonel Van Hecke, had been unavoidably called out of town and would not be available during the landings. Colonel Jousse would draw up the specific orders for the task groups, and Colonel Anselme, with José Aboulker as deputy, would remain at headquarters in charge of operations. As soon as possible, through prior secret arrangement with the chief of police, the command post would move to police headquarters: the Commissariat Central.

The operation was laid out by Colonel Jousse with military care and precision. Each of the twelve task groups was given a specific mission and place in the organizational hierarchy.

Dr. Morali-Daninos was designated as officer in charge of Task Group A, and at H-Hour, set at 1:00 A.M. on the morning of 8 November, would establish headquarters at the administrative offices of the First Arrondissement, located in the northern part of Algiers. Task Group A would neutralize several key establishments in the area of the Place du Gouvernement (now the Place des Martyrs), located in the old part of Algiers between the Casbah and the Jeteé du Nord, where the Admiralty was located. On the northern side of this area, across the street from Algiers's largest lycée, stood the Pélissier barracks, in which General Mast's offices were housed. Nearby, on the edge of the Casbah, stood the Winter Palace (now the Dar Mustapha Pasha Palace) in which General Juin's headquarters were located. One section from Group A would report to Mast; the second would occupy the Winter Palace; and the third would set up a roadblock at the foot of the quay so that no one could enter or leave the Admiralty offices.

The Second Task Group, B, under the orders of Dr. Raphael Aboulker, was principally made up of insurgents from the Géo Gras organization. Captain Pillafort, leading Section B-1, would move on XIX Army Corps Headquarters and with good fortune would take its commander, General Koeltz, into custody. Colonel Jousse would accompany Pillafort and would try to persuade Koeltz to throw in his lot with the Allies. B-1 would also obtain control of the military telephone exchange. A second section, B-2, had the Prefecture, located next to the Hotel de Ville, about two blocks from the XIX Corps building, as its objective. Under Jacques Zermati, B-2 would endeavor to rally whatever officers were there and if necessary hold the prefect in custody. The third section, led by Jean Dreyfus, would move into the main post office, thus controlling telegraph lines; and the final group, B-4, made up of Felix Tilly and a formidable gang of Bretons, would occupy the radio broadcasting station. According to plan, General Giraud would be arriving during the night and would broadcast a message urging all anti-German elements to support him.

Task Group C had a single objective: to occupy the Summer Palace (now the Palais du Peuple) in which Governor General Châtel resided. Group D, under Lieutenant Ruff, would move into the interurban telephone exchange in Belcourt, on the southern side of the city. Finally, Group E, made up of three sections, would occupy key points in El Biar, a suburb on the heights above Algiers. The first, E-1, under Bernard Pauphilet, would occupy General Juin's residence; the second, the home of General Mendigal, commander of the air force; and the third would take over the Air Force Transmission Center.

The overall plan assumed that the insurgents could also obtain control of Blida airport through General Monsabert. Control of the airport would facilitate the arrival of General Giraud, who according to plan would be greeted by an appropriate reception committee, headed by Lemaigre Dubreuil.

If everything worked out, the conspirators would have gained control of the principal military officers, Generals Juin, Mendigal, and Koeltz; the principal headquarters, including those of the police; both the military and civil telephone exchanges; and the radio station. With their small numbers they could not consider attacking barracks or forts; they could only hope that with key officers and communications not functioning, they could paralyze the city at least until dawn, by which time the Allies would have arrived. They could think of no way to neutralize the navy and naval defenses. Located on a guarded quay, the Admiralty, where Admiral Leclerc resided, stood impregnable, and the guns on the Jeteé du Nord guarded all entrances to the harbor.

On Friday, 6 November, with only one full day to go, the leaders called a meeting of all section heads and deputies. At 5:00 P.M. the twenty-odd chiefs, excited that something important seemed to be in the air, filed into Dr. Aboulker's house. With maps of the city in front of him, Colonel Jousse brought the group to order. Colonel Anselme and José Aboulker stood by.

Jousse announced that the convoy, already sighted offshore and presumed to be heading toward Malta, was destined for Algiers—and would land tomorrow night. The news brought startled responses from the group, which until this moment had received no inkling that an Allied action loomed so near.

Jousse then told the group that General Giraud was assuming command in North Africa and had designated General Mast as his deputy. It will be recalled that Lemaigre Dubreuil had flown into Algiers on 4 November bearing Giraud's Special Order which stated in part:

> VII. All civil transport services, air, rail, sea, will cease to function after D-Day, at midnight.
> VIII. The command post of the commander of French North African forces is activated at Algiers.[40]

These orders, however vague, gave sanction to the conspirators' actions. They permitted General Mast to bypass Juin and Koeltz, and they authorized Colonel Jousse, as *Commandant de la Place* responsible for the city's security, to take over strategic areas, to bring the police under his orders, and to hold certain Vichy officers in custody. It should not be thought that the young men who seized Algiers considered themselves revolutionaries or outlaws. On the contrary, in their minds the mandate derived from a chain of command legitimately stemming from General Giraud. It is not impossible that many of the insurgents even thought Giraud and de Gaulle were cooperating in the operation.

Under Mast's general orders, Jousse explained, Colonel Anselme would take over police headquarters; Jean Brunel (Jousse's brother-in-law) would organize transport; Henri d'Astier would go to Juin's villa and take the general into custody; Lemaigre Dubreuil and Pierre Alexandre would go to the Blida airport to receive Giraud; he, Jousse, with Captain Pillafort, would go to XIX Corps Headquarters to arrest Koeltz.

Pillafort protested. He had already planned, with Henri d'Astier, to move against the German and Italian Armistice Commissions. Jousse explained that the strategy had changed. The captain grumbled that no one told him anything (he was right; they feared his quick temper and loquacious truculence), but he consented to carry out the assignment.

Sectors and objectives were then assigned to section leaders, who were to report back next day at the same time for specific orders and final instructions. Meanwhile they were to alert their men to stand by for the big operation.

After the meeting Captain Pillafort and the other section leaders began to send out their instructions.

For this operation Pillafort would count on some fifty young men from the Géo Gras organization—the sections led by Roger Jaïs and Fernand Frédj. He would be personally seconded by Lieutenant Daridan and Mario Faivre. During the day of 7 November, the group leaders hustled all over Algiers, passing the word along through their deputies for a 5:00 P.M. rendezvous at the Salle Géo Gras. There the nervous youths stood by while Pillafort and Faivre went over to headquarters for final instructions.

Dr. Aboulker's apartment was soon crowded as the various section chiefs reported in. A sort of restrained gaiety, as if pent-up emotions were finally released, pervaded the atmosphere. As deputy operations officer, José Aboulker busily checked in the groups, gave instructions, typed out last-minute orders. Colonel Anselme, who possessed most of the written materials, had failed to appear.

At six o'clock Colonel Jousse began his briefing. Each group, already designated by symbol, received its orders: A-1 to the Pélissier barracks, A-2 to Juin's headquarters, A-3 to the Admiralty, B-1 (Pillafort's group) to XIX Corps Headquarters, and so on down to group E-3. The orders were mostly signed by Jousse, as General Mast's instructions would go not to the underground groups but only to regular army units. Each leader picked up a quota of armbands, with the initials "VP". These were the brassards originally manufactured for the pro-Vichy SOL, but now made available by Jousse to the insurgents. Some of the section leaders, being reserve officers, would wear their own uniforms, but the armbands would provide a semblance of military authority to the ranks.

Jousse continued with his instructions. At ten o'clock each group leader with his deputies would report to Jean Brunel, at the Garage Laveysse not far from headquarters, to pick up cars and guns. Jousse had to explain apologetically that the cars would be few, although well enough fueled by courtesy of the American consulate; and that the expected supply of Bren guns had not arrived. For arms the insurgents would have to rely on long-barreled Lebel rifles, of a vintage antedating World War I.

Following the briefing, Pillafort, Faivre, and the other section leaders returned to their rendezvous points. Most of them gave their men leave, instructing them to muster at points near their objectives in two hours. Those leaders who were reserve officers then went home to change into uniform and around ten o'clock the twelve task group leaders picked up cars and weapons at the garage. They settled down to wait for the final order to proceed.

9

The Algiers Landings 8 November 1942

Algiers, 7–8 November 1942
The landings: Murphy, Juin, and Darlan

As midnight, 7 November, drew near, apprehension that the elaborate plans would miscarry descended on The Five (technically The Four, as Van Hecke was away) and on their American associates. No one among the leaders had slept properly for the last two nights, and they all nervously amplified their nagging dread that this unorthodox adventure, to which their lives were forfeit, might fail. As reports from mustering task groups began to come in to headquarters, Dr. Aboulker's house, at 26 rue Michelet, they had to recognize that only a fraction of the young men they had relied on would show up. With Van Hecke gone, they could place no faith on the Chantiers de la Jeunesse. Because of the delivery failures, they had no modern weapons; but worse, the group was plagued by an uneasy suspicion that the Allies had failed them on purpose or because of incompetence. If arrangements for putting a few sten guns ashore could go awry, what might happen to the organization of a full-scale landing? Had the plans been changed? Had word failed to reach Algiers? Were the ships behind schedule? Would General Giraud arrive on time? Where was Colonel Anselme?

With the uncertainties that piled on each other through the waning hours of 7 November, the four leaders anxiously deliberated on alternatives. Ideally, Giraud should have been in Algiers, and Darlan should not have been there. Ideally, over a thousand young men, armed with the most modern guerrilla weapons, led by a regular colonel, were to take over the city. All of the senior officers would be taken into custody, leaving General Mast, as chief of staff, XIX Region, in effective control under the direct command of General Giraud. By 2:30 A.M., or at the latest by dawn, the Allied forces would have marched into the paralyzed city, and the Vichy commanders, General Juin, General Koeltz, Admiral Moreau, and Admiral Leclerc, would face the alternatives of imprisonment or cooperation. Even though Giraud possessed no mandate from Vichy, his seniority would, it was assumed, make his leadership palatable.

But by 11:30 it looked as if these eventualities would not develop. General Giraud had not arrived. Messages had come in stating that he was at Gibraltar, but no message indicated when he would reach Algiers. Murphy and The Four had conferred with General Mast until about 11:00 P.M. Mast had then proceeded to the Pélissier barracks, headquarters of the Algiers division, where he made final arrangements for his orders to be disseminated. The others went back to rue Michelet to wait anxiously for the code message revealing that the invasion had in fact begun.

But they then lost contact with Mast. Although the plans had appointed a liaison officer, Paul Driguez, to maintain contact between Mast and 26 rue Michelet, the arrangement misfired. The Four had understood that Mast would remain at his headquarters, where task group A-1 would report, and would throughout the night be coordinating the actions of the regular military forces with the "Volontaires de Place" under Colonel Jousse. Mast had convinced himself, however, that he should stay close to the landing sites, and about 1:00 A.M., with Squadron Chief Lecoq, he left Algiers for Staoueli.[1] No one at division headquarters knew where he had gone, and no means of communication connected him with 26 rue Michelet or the Commissariat Central.

At Dr. Aboulker's apartment, now a turbulent vortex of comings and goings, of last-minute instructions, of misgivings and hopes, the four leaders debated whether, with Giraud's nonappearance, they should make an appeal to General Juin. This could readily be done through Colonel Chrétien who had seen d'Astier that afternoon and had insisted that Juin be informed if, in fact (as Chrétien's agents reported) an Allied landing was scheduled. The risks seemed about equally divided: if General Juin could be persuaded to cooperate, he could order all the North African ground forces to offer no resistance—there would be no casualties on either side and France would have solidly reentered the war; if he refused to cooperate, he could do no more than hold to Vichy's standing orders of resisting anyone whatsoever. But Juin's capability of resistance, to be hamstrung by Mast's orders and the simultaneous *Putsch*, would not increase appreciably, they believed, whether he was told about the landings or not.

The Four agreed that on balance the odds favored Juin's being informed.

Murphy accepted the awkward and unpalatable charge of telling the general that the Yanks were coming. The delicacy of Murphy's position can hardly be overemphasized: he was on record as having stated there would be no landing without invitation, and he would have to emphasize that the Americans were arriving in force when he could not be certain they would get to the beaches at all. He would have to admit he had used his diplomatic status as cover for a military and civil conspiracy against a legally constituted government recognized by his own country. All of Murphy's very considerable charm would be taxed in persuading Juin to stomach a revolt brewed up in his own bailiwick.

Vice-consul Pendar drove Tarbé de Saint-Hardouin to Colonel Chrétien's home. Apprised of the urgent situation, Chrétien agreed to accompany them to headquarters, where the desirability of informing Juin was vigorously debated. Finally it was agreed that Chrétien should go up to Juin's residence in El Biar, a five-minute drive from downtown Algiers, to find out if the general would receive Murphy. Juin agreed, and Chrétien returned to pick up the American diplomat.[2]

Shortly before twelve o'clock the radio at 26 rue Michelet had received the go-ahead message: "Allo Robert. Franklin arrive."

With Murphy's assent, Henri d'Astier gave the order at midnight which placed the task forces in motion. Then, in Chrétien's car, Robert Murphy was driven to the Villa des Oliviers. Pendar followed in Murphy's Buick. A Senegalese sentry permitted them to enter, and after a short wait General Juin, now in uniform, came to the door in person to receive the American. Juin was well aware of reports that a large Allied convoy was steaming eastward; he had conferred earlier that evening with Admiral Moreau on fleet dispositions, but he was not prepared for Murphy's message.

When he learned that landings would shortly take place, General Juin was, in Murphy's words, "startled and shocked." His mind tried to sort out the elements involved in Murphy's explanation: Giraud would be coming to Algiers (which was something like telling Eisenhower that General Pershing, on his own initiative, had decided to lead Operation TORCH); 500,000 American troops would soon land on the North African littoral. (This number surpassed the combined totals of the French Armistice Army, the British Eighth Army, and the German Afrika Korps.) If what Murphy indicated was correct, one would be a fool not to cooperate. But suppose, and this was more likely, Murphy was misrepresenting what in reality must be described as a commando raid—such as the British had launched at St. Nazaire and Dieppe. In this case the French navy, over which Juin held no authority, might easily repel the invaders, and Juin would end his career with a court martial. What steps should he take? The dilemma was eased somewhat for Juin because, with Admiral Darlan physically present in Algiers, there was someone to whom he could, in timeworn military phraseology and continual practice, "pass the buck."

"If the matter were entirely in my hands I would be with you," Juin told Murphy. "But, as you know, Darlan is in Algiers. He outranks me and no matter what decision I would make, Darlan could immediately overrule it."

"Very well, let us talk to Darlan."

Juin immediately rang up the residence of Admiral Fenard, where Darlan was staying, and soon had Darlan's aide, Admiral Battet, on the phone. Battet was reluctant to awaken his chief, who was exhausted from the anguish and sleeplessness resulting from his son's illness; but the urgency in Juin's voice left no alternative. Darlan agreed to come over to Juin's. Pendar was dispatched to pick up the admiral. Juin also summoned his chef de cabinet, General Sevez, to meet with him at the Villa des Oliviers.

While Pendar was gone, Task Group E-1 closed in on General Juin's residence.

Bernard Pauphilet, a twenty-two-year-old cadet (aspirant of the 65th R.A.A.) had received his orders earlier that evening.

    19th Region
    Territorial Division of Algiers
       "Place d'Alger"
       No. 808.   Algiers, 7 November 1942

> *Orders of Mission*
>
> In application of the Plan of Protection of the "Place d'Alger," volunteer group E-1 will take over custody of the villa "des Oliviers," residence of the General Commander in Chief of the Forces in French North Africa.
>
> It will relieve the guard, which will immediately return to barracks.
>
> Le Général Commandant d'Armes délégué
> de la Place d'Alger
> P.O. le Major de Garnison
> JOUSSE[3]

Pauphilet picked up a car from the Garage Laveysse, loaded it with antique 1889–1900 type long-barreled rifles, and with two friends drove to the rendezvous where he expected to pick up the remaining sixty volunteers of his group. He found three. The six young men, of whom only the leader wore a uniform, then drove up to the Villa des Oliviers. Chrétien's car was parked outside the gate, which was guarded by a Senegalese sentry. Pauphilet ordered the sentry to summon the captain of the guard, who, acknowledging the Orders of Mission, placed his men under the aspirant's charge. A Senegalese was reposted at the gate. When Pendar returned a few minutes later with Admiral Darlan and Admiral Battet, they did not know that the guard had come under insurgent control. Nor, for that matter, did Robert Murphy.

When he heard Murphy's news, Darlan exploded with indignation and dismay. He was taken completely off balance. He had anticipated long, secret negotiations with Murphy during which he could have judged whether the time was ripe to cooperate with the Allies. Anyone could see that action now was premature. He burst out angrily: "I have known for a long time that the British are stupid, but I always believed Americans were more intelligent. Apparently you have the same genius as the British for making massive blunders!"[4]

Darlan has been scourged as a fascist collaborator, but in this particular judgment he could easily have been right. What he had in mind, of course, was the primary Pétain strategy, however defeatist or misguided it may have been, of preserving some modicum of French autonomy, some fraction of independent French territory, some hopes of safeguarding the fleet, some chance of keeping the Empire. If these could be preserved by ruse, by minimal collaboration, by restraint, there might have been some chance, especially if Hitler became mired in the Russian Steppes, of cooperating with the Allies, especially for a foothold in France. No one will know how seriously Darlan held to these views, and it seems likely that if Russia surrendered he would have become more collaborationist than ever. But the evidence is clear that both the American and British chiefs of staff also favored holding off a major operation until 1943. If Darlan considered the Americans and British stupid, he was in reality agreeing with American and British military thinking, and directing his wrath, even as Marshall and Brooke frequently vented theirs, at Churchill's restless insistence on premature attacks and against Roosevelt's requirement that something be done in 1942. It is no wonder that Eisenhower and Clark, when they later became colleagues of Darlan, developed admiration for the "little fellow's" intelligence.

Before Darlan had time to recover from his emotional outburst, General Sevez showed up at the villa and revealed that the guard had been taken over by irregulars, who would let pass only Colonel Chrétien and the Americans. Juin stormed out, followed by the others. He was stopped alongside Murphy's Buick.

"Who are you? What are you doing here?" Juin demanded.

"I am Aspirant Pauphilet and I have orders to let no one leave or enter."

"I am General Juin. Who gave you these orders?"

"I do not have to report to you, General," Pauphilet replied. His career, to say nothing of his life, was on the block.[5]

So were the careers, and even the lives, of Darlan, Juin, and Murphy. Attempting to phone for outside assistance, Juin learned that the service had been cut. The Frenchmen angrily accused Murphy of leading them into an ambush, of holding them incommunicado while his countrymen came ashore. Murphy disclaimed responsibility for the takeover, and instructed Pendar to verify at 26 rue Michelet whether the guard was deemed necessary. A previous decision had exempted Fenard's residence from custody, and now that the conspirators had control of communications, it might have been argued that Juin could do little with a broken chain of command. Pendar returned around 2:00 A.M. with Jean Rigault, who categorically insisted that Darlan stay at Juin's villa and that the guard remain in place.

Murphy kept on trying to persuade Darlan that he should throw in his lot with the Americans, and by ordering a cease-fire, save countless French and American lives. Together they paced the floor, the stumpy, diffident-looking admiral alongside the tall, balding American, who reminded him of his promise to Ambassador Leahy that he would cooperate if the Allies came with 500,000 men.

"That moment has now arrived!" Murphy exclaimed.[6]

Indeed, for Darlan, this was exactly the point. Were 500,000 men landing on the beaches? Were any men landing on the beaches? On this latter point, Murphy found himself as uninformed as Darlan. When Pendar came in at two o'clock, there was no hopeful news, although in fact the first units had already landed at Sidi Ferruch, ten miles west of Algiers. Unknown to Darlan, Admiral Moreau had sent a messenger to him, but this sailor, when he finally reached the Villa des Oliviers, had been kept in custody by Pauphilet.

Both Murphy and Darlan now sparred for time, waiting for some authentic information that would swing the balance one way or another. Murphy told Pendar to return to headquarters, but to take his time, pending definite intelligence about the troops' arrival.

Algiers, 8 November 1942
Takeover by urban guerrillas

At Dr. Aboulker's house, reports began to come in from some of the task groups. As Colonel Anselme had not reported, twenty-one-year-old José Aboulker took it upon himself to coordinate the entire operation, relying upon advice from Colonel Jousse, Jean Rigault, and Henri d'Astier, all of whom were coming and going throughout the night.

Some problems had developed in the A sector. Lieutenant Imbert, heading A-1, had proceeded to the Pélissier barracks in order to report to General Mast. But he found that Mast had gone and had left no one with instructions. The only officer at the barracks turned out to be Colonel Dorange, who had been acting as go-between for General Juin and Murphy. Imbert had no instructions except to put himself at the orders of General Mast. When Dorange, the highest ranking officer at the barracks, insisted that Imbert and his contingent should come under *his* orders, Imbert saw no alternative but to comply.

Dorange left Imbert at the barracks and went immediately to

Juin's headquarters at the Winter Palace, about four blocks away. There he found that sixteen young men with "VP" armbands had replaced the regular guard. This was section A-2 which, after a mix-up with the police, had finally reached its objective. The Winter Palace guard had made no difficulty and had retired in favor of the emergency group. Dorange now realized that something very strange was developing. Not permitted to enter the Winter Palace, and having no way of communicating with General Juin, Dorange decided that the Admiralty offices, on the quay about four blocks distant, would best serve his purposes. At the entrance, however, he found the street cut off by Lt. André Cohen's A-3 section. Unable to get through by land, Dorange crept along the basin to the fishing docks, found a small boat, and rowed out to the Admiralty. It was now about 2:00 A.M.[7]

Meanwhile José Aboulker had learned that the Commissariat Central, the large police administrative building on the Boulevard Baudin, about halfway between Dr. Aboulker's residence and the Prefecture, had been made secure for the conspirators by police chiefs Muscatelli, Bringard, and Achiary. Armed with a sten gun (which Murphy had brought in by diplomatic pouch), accompanied by twenty of the conspirators, José Aboulker moved down to the new headquarters. By about 2:00 A.M. he had installed himself at the police switchboard, where he could communicate with the various arrondissement stations. At once he made contact with the tenth arrondissement headquarters of Group B, and learned that B-2, under Jacques Zermati, had successfully and without incident taken over the Prefecture.

A report then came in that B-1, under the redoubtable Captain Pillafort, had obtained control of XIX Army Corps headquarters. There had been no problem at all. "Pill" made an imposing figure in uniform, with his shining silver helmet providing an additional touch of authority. He had shown the captain of the guard his orders, signed by Colonel Jousse, instructing him to relieve the guard. There was no question of authenticity; the guards mustered in the courtyard and marched off to their barracks in military formation.

Pillafort quickly deployed his men throughout the building, surrounded General Koeltz's apartment, and took control of the military telephone exchange, the current for which was cut off by an engineering officer.

Colonel Jousse came over from headquarters and tried to persuade the indignant Koeltz that he should cooperate with the Allies. Koeltz, however anti-Axis he may have been, refused to take action without orders and chose to remain in custody. He tried in vain to phone and to smuggle a note out the window. Koeltz was like a college president whose office had been invaded by student rioters. He underwent the agonizing travail of established authority standing impotent before cigarette-smoking, disrespectful youth. The young men made the most of it: as Jews, they found it difficult to act courteously before a symbol of authority which had implemented so many anti-Semitic decrees.

Another who fell into Pillafort's custody was General Roubertie, General Mast's deputy, who entered the building to find out why the telephone had ceased functioning.[8]

B-3 and B-4 had run into no difficulties, although they both had to carry out their missions with depleted contingents. The experience of Group B-4, under command of a young man from Brittany, Félix Tilly, was typical.

On the morning of 7 November, Tilly learned that his group was to occupy the large building near XIX Corps headquarters, the Governement Général, which housed not only many administrative offices but also the central telephone exchange and Radio-Algiers. All day long he tried to reach members of his group but, as the one person who kept the complete list was out of town, he could not locate everyone. By 10:30 that night he and his deputy had rounded up about fifty. At midnight a truck from the Garage Laveysse brought them the Lebel guns, the sight of which so dampened the enthusiasm of some twenty amateur insurgents that they drifted away.

Arriving at the Governement Général, Tilly broke a window to get in, then tripped and accidentally discharged his gun. This discouraged a few more. When his men had finally entered the building, Tilly took another muster and found his group had diminished to twelve. With some pride he noted that those who stuck with him were all from Brittany. As the building was virtually unoccupied, Tilly's group easily took over the telephone exchange and the vacant radio station. One young man, installing himself at the switchboard, proceeded to give explanations of pure fantasy when queries started coming in over the official lines.[9]

By 2:30 A.M. all sections had reported that their missions had been accomplished.

The interurban telephone exchange had been closed down by Group D, leaving no communications in all Algiers except the military, administrative, and police circuits now controlled by the insurgents. (The Admiralty telephone lines, connecting the Admiralty and navy headquarters at the Hotel St.-Georges and the line to Vichy had not, however, been cut; nor was the air force line to Blida airport.)

Henri d'Astier had made rounds and knew that Darlan had gone to Juin's villa. On returning to the Commissariat Central, d'Astier told Aboulker that it would be impractical to move Darlan or Juin to some safer place because Murphy was at that moment engaging them in serious discussions. Colonel Jousse returned from XIX Corps headquarters and notified the group that Koeltz had been arrested. Achiary joined them, having seen to the arrest of key members of the pro-Vichy SOL. Representatives of the Gaullist movement "Combat" reported to Aboulker, inquiring if they could be of any service; and interestingly enough, the missing Colonel Anselme finally showed up but decided against throwing in his lot with the conspirators; he looked around and left.

At three in the morning, a moment in time that no one living then in Algiers soon forgot, the sound of heavy guns and the whine of a siren broke across the quiet city. The policemen at the Commissariat looked in surprise at José Aboulker, who explained to them that the Americans were landing. One of them expressed what may have been the stupefied reaction of them all: "You mean then that this isn't just a civil defense drill?"

Algiers, 8 November 1942, 1:00 A.M. to 4:00 A.M.
The Allied landings[10]

By dawn of 8 November, the American and British forces had come ashore at all the points, east and west of the city, that had been designated. From one point of view, the feat was remarkable: soldiers and sailors who had never embarked on an amphibious operation before and who had practiced very little did land by the thousands and did install themselves in key positions. As Dr. Johnson said about dogs walking on their hind legs, it is noteworthy that it is done at all; so it was with the landings. But from the point of view of military professionalism, the landings succeeded as well as they did only out of courtesy of the French who, partly from General Mast's and The Five's preparations, and partly from disinclination to fight Americans, produced minimum opposition.

The experience in TORCH made possible the later development of amphibious doctrine and equipment, so that by 1944 the techniques used on Normandy beachheads had become enormously superior to those employed in Algeria and Morocco. The widely used LST (Landing Ship Tank), with its shallow draft and lowered ramp enabling men and vehicles to strike beaches simultaneously, had not yet been perfected. And later doctrine usually called for landings at dawn, not in the darkness which while it conceals the operation also hampers the navigation of small craft. At Algiers landing vessels became lost, hit the wrong beaches, stopped in water too deep, and instead of coming in well-organized waves, moved toward shore in helter-skelter disarray. The soldiers, once on land, were frequently mustered together in open places which would have been critically vulnerable to enemy fire; and many officers, during that frantic night, could not find their scattered troops. Because of the primitive amphibious methods used, very few vehicles and guns came ashore during the night, and the men were forced to march toward objectives with unnecessarily heavy packs and critically inadequate fire power.

Nevertheless, from Surcouf on the east to Castiglione on the west, on scattered beaches extending over twenty miles on each side of the city, the Eastern Assault Force landed elements of its troops, somewhat behind schedule, but without opposition. On the eastern end a British commando and the American 39th Combat Team moved onto the broad beaches, well known as resorts to surf-minded Algerian residents, lying beyond the little town of Jean Bart. These beaches can be swept by guns of the Lazeret battery, located on the point of Cap Matifou, and when dawn arrived, permitting accurate aim, a contingent of French navy gunners prevented an advance toward Algiers. On the other hand, those forces of the 39th Combat Team whose objective was Maison Blanche airport, about ten miles inland, were able to move on during the darkness toward the field, which they reached just before dawn. The only resistance they encountered were a few bursts of machine-gun fire, after which they surrounded the field. A short parley with the officers in charge, one of whom, it will be recalled, was the Major Dartois whom Clark had met at Cherchell, brought the airport over to the Allied side.[11]

Least effective of all the landings was the one scheduled for Pointe Pescade, lying northwest of the city. If the British commandos had landed on time, they might have filtered past Fort Duperré in the darkness and occupied northern Algiers, including the Admiralty, which lay only five miles from the debarkation points. But the method of loading the landing craft was so involved, and the pilots so inexperienced, that long after the French were alerted, the troops had not come ashore in sufficient force to move. By dawn they were still landing and still blocked by the fort from entering the city.

Ten miles farther to the west lay the beaches close to Sidi Ferruch, swept by the batteries which General Mast and Colonel Baril had undertaken to silence. It was indeed fortunate that the French did not fire, as the pilot vessel guiding the 168th Combat Team to shore missed its bearings and led most of the landing craft south instead of north of the peninsula. The bad navigation and unfavorable currents scattered the 168th along beaches three to ten miles from their designated landing points and into the shallow water where the British 11th Brigade Group was landing. One ignominious result of all this confusion was that the first group to reach Fort Sidi Ferruch was not American, but a British commando under Lt. Col. T. H. Trevor. He and Colonel Baril were discussing the security of the fort, about 3:00 A.M., when they were joined by General Mast.[12]

It will be recalled that around one o'clock General Mast, with another officer, had left his office in the Pélissier barracks and had proceeded to Staoueli, a small town about ten miles west of Algiers and about a mile from the beaches where the Allies presumably would land. He was only two miles from the fort at Sidi Ferruch, where Baril, at midnight, had entered with his company and imposed his authority over the naval gun crews. Mast had located himself strategically to intercept any units moving from the beaches toward Algiers, but having no means of communication he decided to move on to the fort. That Mast, in his early encounters with the landing forces, should discover British forces in the area, did nothing to relieve his concern. Even Baril's troops, many of whom had fought the British in Syria, questioned the wisdom of what they were doing. Unfortunately for Mast and Baril, they had come into contact right at the beginning with a British commando, and learned forcefully about the deceitfulness imposed on the Americans by the strategy of their leaders. Nevertheless they cooperated and did what they could to assist both the British and American troops.

Until three o'clock, the landings had taken place in relative secrecy and had been unopposed; but no Allied force had moved closer than five miles of the city. It was at this moment that French naval batteries identified the two British destroyers, H.M.S. *Malcolm* and H.M.S. *Broke*, which were trying to ram the barrier guarding the port. At once searchlights illuminated the vessels, and guns from Algiers and on the northern jetty raked the ships in deadly close-range fire. The *Malcolm* was badly hit and withdrew, but the *Broke* finally tore through the barrier and, as dawn began to break, started to unload its assault force (3rd Battalion, 135th Infantry, of the U.S. 34th Division) on the docks.[18]

Algiers, 8 November 1942
Darlan and Murphy

At General Juin's villa, when the firing started, Murphy was still trying to persuade Admiral Darlan that he should throw in his lot with the Allies. Darlan kept insisting that he could take no unilateral action and that he would have to obtain Pétain's approval. This argument could produce more delay, because even if Pétain could be reached he would certainly wish to know, even as his commander in chief did, whether the landings were being made in force. What the Vichy Frenchmen feared, with the impotent anguish of defeated soldiers, was another fiasco, like de Gaulle's effort at Dakar, or a hit-and-run affair like Dieppe. If this were to be the Allied gesture, then it would mean the end of France. A gambling analogy haunted the Vichy mind: the fleet and North Africa comprised the single trump that Vichy had to play, and neither Pétain nor Laval nor Darlan wanted someone else to play it for them—without their knowledge and without their permission.

Shortly after 3:00 A.M. Pendar returned again, this time bringing Admiral Fenard with him. The vice-consul had taken Rigault back to 26 rue Michelet, where he and Tarbé de Saint-Hardouin concluded it might be worthwhile to induce Fenard, whose pro-Ally sympathies were well known, to help Murphy reason with Darlan.[14]

Even though no one doubted anymore that some sort of action

was under way, Darlan still refused to do anything without Pétain's authorization. Would he act if Pétain approved? Murphy posed the question, and after some moments Darlan agreed to shift the burden of decision to the marshal. He sat down, and with Fenard's and Battet's help, drafted a telegram:

> Admiral Darlan to Marshal Pétain:
>
> I was called at 0115 by General Juin and I found at his house Mr. Murphy who told me that quote on the request of a Frenchman, General Giraud, President Roosevelt had decided to occupy North Africa with important forces this very morning; that the United States had only one objective: to destroy Germany and to save France whose integrity they desire to maintain. End quote
>
> I told him that France had signed an armistice agreement with Germany and that I could only conform to the Marshal's order to defend our territory.[15]

The wording and dispatch of this telegram has evoked a certain amount of commentary and criticism. Murphy has been accused of naiveté in permitting Darlan to seal the envelope without verifying its contents; Darlan has been attacked for not requesting authorization to resist but, in fact, giving veiled support to Admiral Leclerc that standing orders should be carried out.

A good deal of the criticism is actually irrelevant. Because the telephone was cut and because Darlan depended on either Murphy or the insurgents (whose identity could not have been clear to him) for transmittal, the text had been carefully worded to go uncoded. As anyone might have read it, including German monitors, Darlan judiciously affirmed that standing orders remain in effect, but he gave Pétain the option, without recommendation, of changing them. Some have argued that the telegram might have tipped off pro-Vichy officers to prepare for the invasion; but the landings had already begun, and cannon were already firing when Pendar left the Villa des Oliviers around 4:00 A.M. with the dispatch. Murphy knew that President Roosevelt's message to Marshal Pétain would be delivered during the night and that propaganda broadcasts and leaflets had been prepared. From a tactical point of view it would make little difference whether Vichy learned the news from Roosevelt, from Darlan, or from the Admiralty. Unknown to the conspirators, the Admiralty had already alerted Vichy that something was amiss, and had reported the attack on the harbor at 3:36 A.M.[16]

As it worked out, Darlan's draft telegram was never delivered to the Admiralty. Pendar and Saint-Hardouin decided they had better check out its contents and the desirability of its transmittal at headquarters. There the message was opened, and a decision was made that it should not be sent. Pendar then drove back to the Villa des Oliviers by himself, arriving about 4:30 A.M. Admiral Fenard may have suspected that the first telegram had been waylaid, possibly by Pendar's evasive answers to his questions about the way in which it had been dispatched. He urged the vice-consul to make sure it was sent and pressed on him another copy. As Pendar was about to leave, Robert Murphy also dictated a telegram:

> Western Task Force Commander from Murphy. It is urgently necessary that some Allied troops arrive in the city of Algiers as quickly as possible. Situation well in hand but unwise to let this endure too long.[17]

Before Pendar could leave, Major Dorange arrived on the scene. It will be recalled that Dorange had learned about the insurrection and had rowed out in a small boat to the Admiralty, where he finally was able to arouse Admiral Leclerc. Leclerc had no idea what was happening, but from Lieutenant Cohen, the insurgent officer whose young men were blocking the road to the Admiralty, he began to obtain a few insights. He read General Mast's order, which Cohen showed him, but from it he could not comprehend whether the navy was involved or not. One sentence, "By reason of the secret kept until the last moment in order not to reveal the anticipated aid, it is possible that some French units have not been reached by the order fixing the conduct to follow," suggested that Mast's order simply implemented for the Algiers division a decision at higher levels. It did not seem possible that Leclerc's seniors—Admiral Moreau and Admiral Darlan—would have overlooked him, but he could not be sure.

Unable to reach Darlan or Juin, Major Dorange placed Cohen and his car under his orders and raced to the barracks of the Gardes Mobiles des Tagarens. He explained the situation to Colonel Zwilling, the officer in charge, who provided him with a detachment of men. To the men it was pointed out that the Americans were landing but that General Juin may have been taken into custody by German agents. The detachment, with Dorange at their head, set off for the Villa des Oliviers. It was now about 4:30 A.M.

Dorange and the Gardes Mobiles arrived at Juin's residence just at the moment Pendar was turning his car around to deliver the messages he had been given.[18]

A captain of the Gardes approached Bernard Pauphilet, the insurgent officer in charge, and told him (just as Pauphilet had told the sentry four hours earlier) he had come to relieve the guard. On Pauphilet's refusal to be relieved, the captain left. But a moment later the armed Gardes returned with Dorange, who, revolver in hand, took the insurgents into custody together with Murphy and Pendar.[19] The prisoners were herded into the porter's lodge.

Pendar later described the scene:

> Serious as the whole business was, it had an *opéra bouffe* quality, and reminded me irresistibly of the "Pirates of Penzance." I knew, however, that both sides in North Africa had itching trigger fingers and few scruples, and I had an authentic chill up my spine as they lined up in front of the fireplace and told us to keep our hands up. We were thoroughly searched and stripped of our papers. One soldier said a few words in German to us, and I was so tired by this time that I thought wildly that they might be German troops in French uniforms. All of us, however, behaved with great dignity, I thought. Mr. Murphy was extremely pale, and he assured me that I was. He told me later that as he had been taken into the porter's lodge after me he had heard the order given to take us both out and shoot us. Luckily, that item had escaped me or I couldn't have answered for my dignity.
>
> In a moment, the Commandant d'Orange [sic], Juin's aide, rushed into the room, dressed oddly in a civilian brown tweed suit, wildly waving a huge revolver and crying: "What have you done? What have you done?" Some of the soldiers tried to arrest him, and he turned on them in a fury, crying: "I am the Commandant d'Orange, and you are under my orders." Then he turned back to Murphy and me, and said: "You know my sentiments; what made you do this idiotic thing?" Neither of us said anything: the man was so excited that he wouldn't give us time to answer, and wouldn't have listened if we had. In the midst of this Gallic scene, Juin, Fenard and Crétien [sic] appeared at the door, and said that Murphy must be brought back to the villa at once. Murphy and d'Orange asked them to include me, and Juin agreed.[20]

A few minutes later Pendar was released, in the custody of three

Gardes Mobiles, to take Darlan's message to the Admiralty. The vice-consul gave the message directly to Admiral Leclerc, who felt however that he must authenticate the text before transmitting it. This took over an hour, and the message did not go out until 6:15 A.M.

Meanwhile, at the Villa des Oliviers, Darlan and Juin prepared to go down to Fort Lempereur. Before leaving they dashed off a telegram:

> Admiral Darlan to Marshal Pétain:
> According to information reaching me, the landings seem to be general and in progress from the Tunisian coast to southern Morocco.
> In Morocco and in Algeria, there appear to be American troops. In Tunisia, it is probable there may be British troops. Frequent intelligence to the interior of the country.
> Telegram drawn up jointly with General Juin.[21]

This telegram went directly to the Admiralty and was actually transmitted before the controversial one carried by Pendar.

Darlan also sent a message to Admiral Moreau by the sailor whom Pauphilet had captured earlier in the morning:

> If you can communicate with Bizerte and Casablanca, try to find out what is happening.
> I am at General Juin's villa. According to Murphy, the landings seem to be general, from southern Morocco to Tunisia. I have reported to the Marshal by Baudot [teletype].
> Until new orders from me, do our best to execute the Marshal's orders.[22]

By six o'clock Darlan and Juin had reached Fort Lempereur and started to try to make sense of the reports coming in.

Robert Murphy, tired and rather dejected, was required to remain out of touch at Juin's villa, consoled by Admiral Fenard. Later in the morning Pendar and Harry Woodruff, another vice-consul, brought him some shaving things and a bottle of Scotch.[23]

At 7:00 A.M. Vichy time (8:00 A.M. in Algiers) Pétain was informed of what had happened in North Africa. He read Roosevelt's message and approved Laval's draft reply: ". . . We are attacked. We shall defend ourselves. This is the order we are giving." To Darlan he wired:

> I have received your messages via the Admiralty and am

happy you are on the spot. Stop. You can thus act and keep me informed. Stop. You know you have my entire confidence.[24]

As dawn spread over the white hills of Algiers, a crucial day was beginning.

Algiers, 8 November 1942, 4:00 A.M. to noon
Actions on D-Day

While Darlan and Juin attempted to interpret reports and organize resistance, Major Dorange moved down to XIX Corps headquarters, still held by Pillafort. Between 6:00 and 7:00 A.M. Dorange confronted the few remaining insurgents and ordered them to evacuate the building. Pillafort argued back, insisting that Dorange join Giraud and the Allies. The discussion continued for over an hour until Dorange had the best of it when armored trucks of the Fifth Chasseurs lumbered onto the scene. But there was no violence. Actually both sides joined together singing the *Marseillaise*. By eight o'clock the insurgents had stacked their weapons and abandoned the building.

General Koeltz, now released, immediately appointed General Roubertie to command of the Algiers division. Roubertie's first order, hurriedly scribbled in longhand, countermanded Mast's instructions of the previous evening.

Gradually, as the morning wore on, French resistance became organized, although it was badly hampered from poor communications and the difficulty of officers getting to their units. General Juin was not at all certain what his policy should be: he did not want to engage in an all-out defense against Americans, but he felt obliged to carry out Vichy's orders and to follow Darlan's lead. Juin's order to the forces defending Algiers was to maintain "elastic contact without aggressivity" until the French command could obtain a clearer picture.[25]

Darlan had meanwhile moved to the Hotel St.-Georges, where the principal Admiralty offices were located. Because the insurgents had no knowledge of the navy communications network, the system remained intact and Darlan possessed direct lines to the Admiralty and to Vichy. He immediately informed Vichy that the situation was bad and that the city's defenses would soon be overrun. He tried to cope with certain contingencies which his astute imagination envisaged: what countermeasures would the Axis take? What would happen if he surrendered without Pétain's approval? What sort of situation would develop if the Americans took him prisoner? Whatever one may think of Darlan's devious politics, one cannot charge the admiral with lack of preparation for future situations.

Darlan first had to convince himself that the assault possessed power enough to withstand an Axis counterattack. On the morning of 8 November, he could not yet assess whether, as Murphy assured him, 500,000 men would be disembarked; but he could gauge from the warships and transports offshore that he was confronted with more than a minor commando raid. He knew that attacks were being made in Morocco and at Oran; he did not yet know what was happening in Tunisia. Darlan had to anticipate possible German reactions: Would Hitler give the order to occupy southern France? Would he attack the fleet at Toulon? In Darlan's judgment an occupation of France would be the worst catastrophe to befall the country; the admiral stood firm with Pètain and Laval that every effort should be made to forestall German action. If Darlan's subsequent negotiations with the Allies appear stubborn and devious, it was because first in the admiral's mind stood a determination to keep the Germans from crossing into southern France.

Almost at once Darlan faced a decision when he read a Vichy telegram: "OKW proposes air support from Sicily/Sardinia. How would you welcome this support?"[26] If he refused and the Allies occupied Algiers, his message could be interpreted as anti-German; if he invited planes to operate from airfields in Algiers he would face the possibility of a German rather than an Allied occupation. He hedged and, referring to the Vichy message, replied: "Support on transports at sea off Algiers."[27] As he had approved neither French bases nor permission to operate in French territorial waters, Darlan acquiesced only to what the Germans could legally do in any case: attack enemy vessels from their own bases in the open sea. Darlan could now do nothing but wait—to assess how the attack was developing and to learn what Pétain and Laval intended to do.

By noon of 8 November, the military situation had reached a critical point. On the eastern side, the city was in no danger of immediate attack as the battery at Lazeret continued to hold down the Allied troops trying to move along the shore. The battery was being bombarded from the sea, however, and could not hold out indefinitely. Maison Blanche airfield was held by the Americans, and eighteen British Hurricane fighters had already landed.

In the city itself was confusion and disorder, but only a few scattered remnants of the insurgent takeover remained. José Aboulker continued at the Commissariat Central; Jean Dreyfus still held the Post Office; and Tilly at the broadcasting station had even got the transmitter into operation. The XIX Corps headquarters had been retaken by Dorange, but Pillafort and six of his men still stood by.

Not quite certain what to do, Pillafort's group finally decided to leave the center of town for the suburbs. Later in the morning they agreed to go back toward Algiers. When they reached the Colonne Voirol, at a point on the Rue Michelet overlooking the city, they ran into a military roadblock. As they tried to drive through it, a soldier fired, putting one of their three cars out of commission. Pillafort and his colleagues jumped out to find themselves threatened with arrest. The insurgents showed their guns, and in short order the tables were reversed. Pillafort, right in his element, took charge.

The military instinct in Pillafort grasped immediately what the roadblock signified: if it could keep the insurgents from helping the Americans, it could equally hinder the Vichy command from organizing against it. The road, one of the main arteries out of Algiers, leads to the Blida airport. While waiting for reinforcements from the Commissariat Central, to which he had sent a messenger, Pillafort began to stop any vehicle that carried military personnel. By noon, when José Aboulker and some cooperative policemen took Pillafort's prisoners into custody, he had held up about twenty cars.

If he could get away with a roadblock at the Colonne Voirol, Pillafort thought, perhaps he could set one up at a more important intersection, on the Boulevard Baudin, directly in front of the Commissariat Central, now the only building still held by the insurgents.

With his cars, prisoners, and men, Pillafort moved his operation down to the center of Algiers. By 2:00 P.M. he had 100 men under his orders and had arrested all officers who tried to pass through his net. Into the trap, among others, fell Admiral Battet, Darlan's aide, who was attempting to obtain an appropriate uniform for his chief. Pillafort's group also stopped two antiaircraft trucks, the 75 mm. guns from which were promptly mounted in the Commissariat.

Around three o'clock a military car filled with French officers approached the roadblock. As Pillafort sauntered over, a gun from within the automobile was fired. Pillafort staggered, mortally wounded, clutching his abdomen. His men, quickly recovering from the shock of seeing the intrepid Pillafort cut down, sent a volley of bullets smashing into the car. Pillafort's assailant, a Colonel Jacquin, was instantly killed but, miraculously, all the other occupants emerged untouched.

José Aboulker ran out of the Commissariat to Pillafort's assistance and had him taken to the nearest hospital. In the stifling Algerian heat, with the operating room temperatures near 100°, Aboulker —then an intern—and other doctors tried to patch the captain's shattered intestine and liver. For several days Pillafort unsuccessfully fought for his life. He died, one of the two insurgent casualties in this most strange, most unnecessary internecine conflict of Frenchman against Frenchman.[28]

The other casualty was Lt. Jean Dreyfus, whose B-3 group had occupied the main Post Office. For a while in the morning of November 8 the fifteen members of the team had repulsed an assault by the military. Dreyfus had gone out to parley with the attackers and, as he turned back to his friends, had been shot down.

By noon, all of the buildings occupied during the night had been retrieved by the authorities. The insurgents had been arrested or, unidentified, had dispersed and drifted back to their homes.

The Vichy forces had also repulsed the battalion which, having landed from H.M.S. *Broke*, had tried to take possession of the port. For a few brief moments it looked as if the landing party would succeed, but the *Broke* could not shield itself from the shore batteries and, having taken twenty-two direct hits, had to withdraw. (Next day the destroyer sank.) This left the battalion surrounded, cut off from reinforcement, and short of ammunition. Around 11:00 A.M. several French tanks grouped for an attack. Rather than prolong a needless conflict, the Americans surrendered.

Of all the unnecessary and erroneously planned operations in TORCH, the frontal assaults of the harbors at Oran and Algiers take first place in violating fundamental concepts of military tactics. It was very well to *hope* that the flanking attacks on Algiers would reach the city in a few hours, but to *base* a port landing on the assumption that British commandos would silence the batteries and join up with the forces on the docks, revealed how poor was G-2's assessment of French resistance capability. To be sure, the plan had been advocated by the British, and its principal supporter, Admiral Ramsey, had since been superseded by the appointment of Admiral Andrew Cunningham as Eisenhower's naval commander in chief; but it was an American battalion which suffered most heavily from the operation's faults. Even then, casualties at Algiers were lighter than those at Oran, where both attacking ships were sunk and 300 men were killed.

The landing battalion at Algiers lost fifteen men killed; the two British destroyers lost nine, and the French suffered about seventy. These needless casualties were far higher than any sustained elsewhere in the Algiers operation. One of the American survivors has written:

> The mission . . . was, by its very nature, ill conceived, foolhardy, and well nigh impossible of accomplishment. In its adherence to the correct principles of warfare, it should be placed in the same category as Pickett's Charge at Gettysburg, and the Charge of the Light Brigade in the Crimean War. . . . Instead of being a calculated risk it was a wild gamble against almost impossible odds. It resulted in the 3rd Battalion's having to make an unsupported frontal assault against an enemy who possessed great fire superiority. Such an attack was in direct violation of the fire and maneuver principles as taught for many years at The Infantry School.[29]

By noon, it was clear that no more commando raids on the port would take place. But it was equally clear, because Albacore bombers had knocked out two French batteries during the *Broke*'s withdrawal, that Allied air superiority could ultimately make a shambles of prolonged Vichy efforts to hold the city.

Algiers, 8 November 1942, noon to 8:00 P.M.
Situation to the west of the city

On the western side of Algiers, by noon the Allied forces were approaching the suburbs. Mast and Baril had succeeded in persuading Colonel Trevor to send some men to Blida in the trucks they had provided, and by early morning the airport had been neutralized: an agreement was reached that the Allies would not use it, but neither would the French. Elements of the British 11th Brigade group, which had landed in the Castiglione area ten miles southwest of Sidi

Ferruch, reinforced the commandos at Blida and also pushed eastward in order to encircle the city.

As soon as it was light, General Mast tried to locate Gen. Charles Ryder, commanding the assault force, in order to advise him on action to take. Notified that Ryder was aboard the command ship *Bulolo*, Mast spent a good part of the morning getting out to the vessel, only to find that Ryder had gone ashore and was setting up a command post about three miles west of El Biar—the suburb in which Juin's villa, where Murphy still nervously waited, was located.

By this time three battalions of the 168th Combat Team had moved across the ten miles separating the landing beaches and El Biar, on the western heights of Algiers. Some of the confusion of the night's landing had given way to a semblance of order, and trucks, half-tracks, mortars, and mobile guns had come ashore, giving the green American troops some muscle which they had lacked during the earlier part of the day. The troops had moved toward Algiers without serious opposition. Natives lined the roads to watch the soldiers; some French citizens cheered them as they passed; and a general sense of "maneuvers" rather than of real fighting pervaded many of the heavily packed and underarmed troops. Some of the landing forces were being guided by young men from the Chantiers de la Jeunesse, and a few scattered elements were already filtering into the city. One small group, guided by Captain Lindsay Watson, the Chantiers officer in charge of security at Cherchell, pushed so far ahead of its main unit that, finding too many French soldiers in the city, it had to seek refuge at 26 rue Michelet, the insurgent headquarters in Dr. Aboulker's apartment.

As American reconnaissance elements moved into El Biar they were met by sniper fire. One group under Col. Edward J. Doyle reached the Summer Palace (*Palais d'Eté*), residence of the absent Governor General Châtel, and occupied it at the cost of several casualties. Doyle himself was killed.

As the afternoon wore on, the fire fight in the city streets became confusing, and some of the inexperienced soldiers found that they were shooting not at the enemy but at each other. The bulk of the Allied forces remained outside the city, however, waiting for mortars and howitzers with which to attack Fort Lempereur, Juin's command post and the principal defense of western Algiers.[30]

Around noon, Juin and Darlan held a conference to decide on the course to follow. There was no question but that the French could put up a stronger resistance: they had thus far committed no tanks (except in the port), nor had they made any firm effort to counterattack the Allied forces. But, granted that the green American troops could be held up for some time, the French commanders had to concede that except for the bombardment of Fort Lazeret, still going on, the Allies had not unleashed the potential destruction inherent in their air and sea power. Ultimately, Darlan and Juin concluded, the Anglo-American force would prevail: why prolong an unnecessary conflict which could result only in American, British, and French soldiers being killed and in the city's destruction?

Darlan, putting his subtle mind to work, began to analyze the consequences of surrender. Darlan held a position at Vichy comparable to that of Marshall in Washington or General Sir Alan Brooke in London: an action by him would commit the government. He could no more act on major issues without Pétain's approval than Mashall could act without Roosevelt's or Brooke without Churchill's. His position was quite different from that of Juin or Noguès, who had specific responsibilities in specific areas. If, for example, Noguès surrendered in Morocco, the capitulation could be interpreted by Hitler as a local move, not as an act emanating from the Vichy government. But if Juin surrendered in Algiers, with Darlan there, it would be assumed that the French commander acted with Vichy approval. In an effort to dissociate his actions with those of Vichy, Darlan undertook to alter the North African command structure: he himself accepted authority only for the Algiers area, while General Noguès would exert authority in Morocco and the Oran district, and General Barré, ground commander in Tunisia, would control not only Tunisia but the Constantine military district of eastern Algeria as well. Noguès and Barré were to take orders only directly from Vichy. This reorganization move of Darlan's must be understood in order to appreciate his actions when the Allies pressured him to announce a cease-fire for all North Africa. Darlan could say, quite accurately, that he no longer held authority over any area other than Algiers. If he had retained his authority as commander in chief, he knew that a surrender would certainly be repudiated by Pétain; and that most likely the Germans would march into the unoccupied zone. Darlan grasped at a straw to prevent a German occupation. He wired Vichy that Algiers would be taken and that it was impossible to reinforce the garrison.[31]

Having made their decision early in the afternoon, Darlan and

Juin asked Murphy, who still remained at the Villa des Oliviers, to arrange a parley with the American commander. By the time Murphy had located General Ryder's command post and conducted him back to Fort Lempereur, Darlan had notified Vichy that he was surrendering—in the Algiers area only. Although Axis bombers were then attacking the fleet offshore, Darlan had received no instructions regarding military action. He could imagine easily enough, however, that Pierre Laval would be desperately seeking some way to prevent a German occupation; Pétain's basic orders, resist anyone whatsoever, still remained in force.

About 6:00 P.M. Ryder and Murphy arrived at the fort and quickly arranged for a cease-fire. Cars immediately started going around the city with loudspeakers or bugles announcing to both French and Allied combattants that firing was to stop. By this time night was falling, and some units did not receive the word until nine or ten o'clock. Juin agreed to turn over the city to the Americans that evening and to open the port to Allied ships the following day. Formal discussion of armistice terms was to start at ten o'clock the next morning. Ryder did not believe he had authority to go further and having made these brief arrangements, excused himself so that he could return to the *Bulolo* to radio Eisenhower a report: he wished to request authorization to impose the "soft" armistice terms. Meanwhile he left Murphy to work out details.[32]

Gibraltar, 8 November 1942
Eisenhower and Giraud[33]

Throughout the early morning hours of 8 November, spasmodic reports kept coming into Eisenhower's headquarters. By dawn he knew that his assault forces had landed at all points, but he could not tell very accurately what was happening. At one point he jotted down in his own handwriting some notes which he titled "Worries of a Commander":

    1. Spain is so ominously quiet that Gov. of Gib. reports himself uneasy. No word from any agent or Ambassador.

    2. No news from Task Forces. Reports few and unsatisfactory.

    3. Defensive fighting, which seemed halfhearted and spiritless this morning, has blazed up, and in many places resistance is stubborn.

4. No Frenchman immediately available, no matter how friendly toward us, seems able to stop the fighting. (Mast, et al.)

5. Giraud is in Gibraltar, manifestly unwilling to enter the theater so long as fighting is going on.

6. Giraud is difficult to deal with—wants much in power, equipment, etc., but seems little disposed to do his part to stop fighting.

7. Giraud wants planes, radios.

8. We are slowed up in eastern sector when we should be getting toward Bône-Bizerte at once.

9. We don't know whereabouts or conditions of airborne force.

10. We cannot find out anything.[34]

Later in the morning another meeting between Eisenhower and Giraud was arranged. Giraud, having reflected on Eisenhower's arguments, concluded that if he did not agree he would have no opportunity at all to fight against Germany. During the previous evening's arrangements Clark had been overheard telling the interpreter to render into French: "Old gentleman, I hope you know that from now on your ass is out in the snow."[35] The record does not say how this was translated, but the message must have come through. It is unreasonable to believe, as Eisenhower did at the time, that Giraud procrastinated with the idea of seeing whether the landings would succeed. In a letter to Marshall, Eisenhower had insinuated as much:

> The Kingpin proved most difficult. Even so, I could have forgiven him if he would have stepped out vigorously to stop the French resistance. Actually he is doing everything possible to kill time until the French have quit of their own accord. After that he wants to step in and become the knight in shining armor that rallies all North Africa and becomes finally the Saviour of France.[36]

Giraud had never viewed his role except as commander in chief forty-eight hours after the landings; he had admitted that the Americans would supervise the first phase of the operation; nothing in his communications suggests that he anticipated a dramatic arrival in Algiers with the first wave of invaders.

In any case, Giraud concluded that further argument was useless and that to be commander of French troops within an Allied command was better than no command at all. He was, therefore, prepared to accept Eisenhower's offer when the two met late in the morning of 8 November.

Eisenhower's decision to keep his offer open after it had been flatly rejected the night before is more difficult to explain. By the morning of D-Day the TORCH commander realized that there would be continuing French resistance at all points but that Giraud could not possibly reach Algiers before 9 November. Could not Eisenhower have waited until he had a clearer picture of the situation before offering Giraud, in complete defiance of his own civil affairs directive, the governorship of French North Africa? Undoubtedly Eisenhower had been impressed by Giraud and, agonizing over the lives and time wasted, accepted the French general as the man for the job. Whatever his shortcomings may have been, Giraud did impress those he met. Darryl Zanuck (then at Gibraltar with the Signal Corps) assessed Giraud:

> His is a grim, determined face. He rarely smiles. . . . You feel the presence of great strength behind the slender frame. He is at all times tense. . . . He is not a man with whom I would like to argue. Yet, when he speaks, his voice is soft and full. I am sure that if I were not aware of his identity, I would become conscious of his importance even in a crowded room.[37]

By noon Eisenhower had concluded with Giraud a "gentleman's agreement" which gave command over all French forces in North Africa to the French general, made him supreme civil administrator over the region, and gave him membership in a small inter-Allied staff to consider plans for the Tunisian campaign. At one stroke, even though the president's directive to Murphy insisted that friendly French administrators should remain at their posts, Eisenhower had granted Giraud authority over General Noguès (who outranked him), General Juin, Governor General Châtel, and scores of other Vichy appointees. With no authority other than his own presence, Giraud had negotiated more power in a few minutes than de Gaulle had extracted from the Allies in two years. Captain Beaufre, who was at the general's side during the Gibraltar discussions, later wrote of Giraud:

> If it is true that the man often took quick, insufficiently ripe decisions in political affairs which required profound reflection, he had also an exceptional insight and surprising intuitions. In his short passage in the first rank of History, he committed er-

rors which justified his fall. But here at Gibraltar was the best Giraud who fought, not for himself as has been maliciously stated, but for the prestige of the defeated French Army; and he obtained what no person after him was able to obtain.[38]

There is irony in the fact that at the moment Eisenhower reached his agreement, Darlan had decided to negotiate with General Ryder. Murphy learned of the deal with Giraud late in the afternoon of 8 November, and Eisenhower received Ryder's message, reporting that Darlan was prepared to negotiate, that evening. As Butcher described it:

> . . . in came Admiral Cunningham with a message he thought possibly the C-in-C would want to see. Said DARLAN WANTS TO NEGOTIATE. And wants to know where they can meet. Ike spluttered. Then, what to do with Giraud? Will they work together now?
>
> Cunningham said to remember what the Prime Minister had said: "Kiss Darlan's stern if you have to, but get the French Navy."
>
> Now Ike has one hell of a headache, and Darlan in his message refuses to deal with any other Frenchman.[39]

The availability of Darlan, commander in chief of all French sea, air, and ground forces, already holding legally and officially the powers Eisenhower had so readily accorded to Giraud, introduced a complication which would plague Eisenhower, Clark, and Murphy for another week. Yet, although tempted many times, Eisenhower never accepted, as a way out of the impasse, repudiation of his "gentleman's agreement" with Giraud.

The cease-fire in Algiers, reported to Gibraltar in the evening, meant that Eisenhower could now send in his deputy, General Clark, to establish an advance command post. Eisenhower authorized Ryder to accept Darlan's cease-fire and notified him that Clark would be flying to the city next morning, 9 November. He also approved plans for General Giraud to fly to Algiers at the same time. Eisenhower still hoped that Giraud would be instrumental in ending the conflict at Oran and in Morocco and asked him to report to Clark the "steps you are taking to stop French resistance."[40] The TORCH commander had not yet completely grasped the fact that Darlan's intrusion would completely negate any action Giraud might take.

10

Negotiating with Darlan

Algiers, 8–9 November 1942
Murphy and Darlan

Murphy had spent a busy and difficult twenty-four hours. Arguing with Darlan, chafing at his helplessness while held in temporary custody, finally, acting as intermediary and interpreter between Ryder and the French, he badly needed rest. Nevertheless, the crucial negotiations were just beginning. At the end of D-Day, the situation had developed in ways not entirely anticipated:

First, Giraud had still not arrived, and the time of his usefulness in effecting a peaceful landing had passed. A proclamation in Giraud's name, largely ignored, revealed that the general carried little influence either with civilians or with the military.

Second, General Juin had revealed himself as genuinely pro-Ally, and although he had ordered resistance, he seemed anxious to end hostilities as soon as possible. Darlan also had not ordered a last-ditch defense and, although obviously delaying and playing the Vichy game until he obtained accurate reports, seemed disposed to negotiate and cooperate.

Third, Darlan was in charge. True, General Mast and the underground groups had during the night minimized opposition to the landings and had paralyzed the city. But by noon Vichy regular forces had regained the principal strongpoints. Mast dared not show his face. Darlan and under him, General Juin, held undisputed control.

Fourth, negotiating with Darlan would mean imposition of the "soft" armistice, which Murphy now saw for the first time. These terms, which left administrators at their posts, would be immediately advantageous to military operations and seemed at the time to suggest few dangers of political entanglement. A Giraud imposed as governor, with the Group of Five as cabinet claiming the sovereign powers of a French government and equal status as an ally, constituted an arrangement which would have rough going. There would probably be more problems from an administration of Giraud and The Five than from an administration of Darlan under the "soft" armistice terms.

Fifth, an arrangement with Darlan could bring certain benefits which Giraud could not produce. Darlan might possibly rally the fleet. Darlan in charge would bring a smooth transition of French administrative machinery to the Allied cause. He would probably bring the Armistice Army into line more quickly, and this in turn would safeguard internal security. He might be able to persuade Governor General Boisson at Dakar to join the Allies.

Sixth, from an ideological point of view, one could scarcely choose between Darlan and Giraud. Neither of them was a Charles de Gaulle. Giraud's reputation had been made fighting the enemy, not fighting for causes. Giraud's attitude—toward Pétain, toward Vichy, toward democracy, toward anti-Semitism—did not differ distinguishably from Darlan's. If ideology was a consideration it should have been introduced in Washington. In the field, at Algiers on 8 November 1942, it was too late. Murphy's choice was effectively limited to two: favorable armistice terms with Vichy officials, or an imposed Giraud whose supporters would demand an equal and allied status.

On the other side of the table, Darlan also had problems to work out. By the evening of 8 November, his orders releasing himself from the Moroccan, Oran, and Tunisian commands had gone out. These orders also implied that the French fleet, lying at Toulon, should act only on orders from Vichy. Later, when Darlan told Clark that he had no authority over the French fleet, he was telling the truth; he consistently maintained, beginning with a refusal given to Murphy on the eighth, that he could not rally the immobilized navy. Darlan did not exactly know what the Americans considered his status to be, and he asked Murphy whether by dealing with him the United States in effect recognized Vichy sovereignty in North

Africa. If the answer was yes, then Murphy palpably repudiated his own letter to Giraud. Both of them tired and perplexed, Murphy and Darlan agreed to postpone an attempt to answer this haunting question until they could obtain clarification from their respective superiors.[1]

Next morning, 9 November, Darlan received a message from Vichy notifying him that, as Laval was absent, he should not negotiate with the Americans until the prime minister's return. In response to another query from Vichy, Darlan analyzed the current situation in a report which goes far in explaining the position he consistently held during the next few days:

> 1. East of Algiers, no action to date. American intentions seem to be move toward Tunisia by land, then attack Italy.
> 2. Algiers and vicinity solidly held by Americans.
> 3. Oran seems to be weakening.
> 4. Morocco cannot continue long magnificent resistance.
> 5. Possession all airfields makes possible from now on large increase in American air power.
> 6. From general point of view, we must hold our positions. Therefore it is difficult to accept a cease-fire in areas not yet attacked for fear of seeing Germans repudiate Armistice and occupy free zone.
> 7. However if Germans don't move soon into Tunisia, we can only anticipate complete American occupation of North Africa. In this case we must try to preserve sovereignty of legal French government by negotiating with Americans and excluding British and dissidents. These negotiations will become more difficult with time because of resistance encountered.
> 8. On the other hand, it does not seem desirable to seek foreign assistance in Tunisia because we would turn North Africa into a battlefield and cut it into two pieces that we won't be able to put back together.
> 9. Solution very complicated and it would be necessary to know intentions and means of Germans.
> 10. If Germany helps us, it is essential that she modify Armistice terms and replace them by another political formula which would let us recover our possibilities.[2]

Nothing in this message suggests either support of the Allies or a pro-German stance. Like so many of Darlan's analyses, it tries to eke out for France maximum benefits from a complex situation, by playing off the Axis against the Americans. Meanwhile Darlan intended to play for time as long as he could, while waiting specific instructions from Pétain and Laval.

Murphy also had to put off any decisions until Clark, who was expected around noon on 9 November, should land in Algiers. Murphy drove out to Blida airport to meet him, but the plane from Gibraltar which landed carried not the American general, but General Giraud. Clark's plane had been held up by weather and had not yet taken off from the Rock.

Murphy, tired and distraught, was in no mood to involve himself with the heroic French general. Anticipating the possibility of wrapping up the whole North African political problem in an agreement with Darlan, Murphy had no thought but to confer with Clark before he did anything else. He placed a car at Giraud's disposal and, thinking he may have driven to the wrong airport, hurried off toward Maison Blanche.[3]

General Giraud was thunderstruck. He had imagined an impressive reception, a military guard of honor, a triumphal procession into the city. Instead, there was nothing. He and Beaufre, who accompanied him, did not even know what was expected of them, where they should go, what they should do. Finally they drove to the Villa Dar Mahieddine, Beaufre's former home which he had turned over to Lemaigre Dubreuil. There, during the afternoon they encountered General Mast and the other conspirators: Lemaigre Dubreuil, d'Astier, Rigault, Saint-Hardouin, and Van Hecke. (Van Hecke was outraged at not having been given the date of D-Day. On tour with General de la Porte du Theil, he had learned of the landings while at Constantine and only reached Algiers in the small hours of 9 November—twenty-four hours too late.)

The insurgents were angry and depressed. They blamed Giraud for not arriving in time, and they reproached the Americans for negotiating with Darlan. Briefly they considered an attempt to kidnap Darlan and proclaim Giraud governor through a coup d'etat. But they had to acknowledge how hopeless such a move would be: Darlan and Juin completely controlled the army, which was already cooperating with the Allies on security measures; Mast, de Monsabert, and Baril had been relieved of their commands and might soon be subjected to courts-martial; the young insurgents who had implemented the *Putsch* were dispersed or still held in custody. Worst of all, General Giraud, overwhelmed by events, sank into an unaccustomed despondency which left him apathetic before talks of coups and uprisings. There seemed to be no way to break through to Murphy and hold him responsible for the agreements he had signed.[4]

No progress could be made on French-American relations until Clark arrived, and the afternoon had worn away before word came in that the TORCH deputy's plane would arrive about 6:00 P.M. Meanwhile Tunisia had been lost. Vichy, in a vain effort to stall off an occupation of southern France, had conceded that Germany could fly its troops into Tunisian airfields. During the afternoon these forces began to land and jeopardized Eisenhower's last hopes of seizing Bizerte before the Axis did.

The negotiations at Algiers must be viewed against the backdrop of Tunisia, ultimate objective of all TORCH planning. Eisenhower saw everything keyed to an imperative effort to get on with the campaign eastward. Darlan, on the other hand, only wished to align his actions with what he interpreted as Vichy policy. The release of Tunisian airports clearly revealed Pétain's intentions: to collaborate with Germany and resist the Americans. If he were to continue to represent Pétain, Darlan must be the instrument of this policy.

In Clark's absence, General Ryder did not wish to negotiate, but he felt that some basic decisions regarding the status of French troops must be made. Although he had cancelled the morning meeting, Ryder by noon had received Eisenhower's approval to impose the "soft" armistice, and he felt that some preliminary steps could be taken before Clark arrived. Ryder and Murphy, therefore, sat down with Darlan, Juin, and Koeltz, during the afternoon of 9 November, and they all concluded that French arms should temporarily be stockpiled. Darlan agreed to examine the armistice terms but indicated he would have to send them to Vichy for approval.[5]

Algiers, 9–10 November 1942
Negotiations of Clark and Darlan

The meeting broke up when Murphy and Ryder left for the airport to meet Clark, whose arrival, almost symbolically, coincided with a German bomber attack. Briefed by Murphy during the half-hour drive to Algiers, Clark was then introduced to Darlan and the French officers, but agreed to postpone formal discussions until the following morning. Both Americans and French felt that a delay would enable them to comprehend more accurately their mutual positions. Clark required further briefing from Murphy, and Murphy needed to know how firmly Eisenhower had committed himself to Giraud.

By this time the French had examined the "soft" armistice terms and had agreed that they were acceptable. Later Admiral Moreau noticed that the Americans had left an envelope on the table. In it were copies of the "hard" armistice. Darlan and he concluded that this was no more than an example of American gamesmanship ("une tentative de bluff").

That evening Clark and Murphy called on General Giraud, finding him lethargic and depressed, unwilling to take the sort of vigorous action Clark expected of him. Clark guaranteed that the United States would continue to back him, and this support, even though for the moment Giraud's baraka seemed to have deserted him, helped momentarily to bring the Frenchman to life. With his courtesy calls completed, Clark retired from the arena; but Murphy and Darlan stayed up most of the night. They had preparations to make.

Darlan transmitted the armistice terms to Vichy, adding that he would not negotiate, only transmit. In his judgment, backed by that of Juin, Koeltz, Mendigal, and Moreau, the terms if accepted would precipitate a rapid Axis occupation of southern France; but from the local Algerian point of view the armistice would have the advantage of stifling Giraud and the dissident movement. But Darlan did not advise: he affirmed once more that he would do no more than carry out Pétain's orders.

Pétain's orders would surely be whatever Laval and the Council of Ministers decided, but the cabinet could or would reach no decision until Laval had seen Hitler. A rendezvous had been tentatively set for 10 November. Darlan consequently must temporize and make no commitment until Laval advised regarding the success or failure of his mission.

Because of the navy teletype line directly to the Admiralty at Vichy, Darlan was better informed on French policy than might have been expected. Not only did Darlan receive and send official messages, but by a secret personal code he maintained a private exchange with his friend Admiral Auphan, who as secretary of state for navy was in a position to make informal commentaries on aspects of Vichy thinking. While waiting for word from Germany, Auphan transmitted his personal opinion that Pétain saw eye to eye with Darlan ("le Maréchal est en accord intime avec vous"), but that he would have to hold off an official statement until he had consulted with Laval.[6]

At Algiers, during the night of 9–10 November, Darlan and Murphy kept in touch, trying to reach some sort of solution which could be confirmed at an official conference next morning. Having sensed from General Clark the strength of Eisenhower's commitment to Giraud, Murphy had to concede that the only practical solution would be a compromise in which Giraud could exercise a military command under Darlan as civil administrator. At the moment, however, Darlan would not speak to Giraud and was even seeking authority to take judicial action against Mast, Béthouart, and the other dissident officers for treason. It would also be necessary to persuade Giraud to relinquish the claims to the civil authority which Eisenhower had conferred on him.

Convincing Giraud to limit his talents to military spheres was probably the easiest of the various tasks which lay ahead. Interestingly enough, it was now General Juin who took an initiative in finding a way through the impasse. Late that night of 9 November, Juin requested Giraud to come see him. Escorted by Juin's messenger, the omnipresent Colonel Dorange, and accompanied by Lemaigre Dubreuil, the general drove to the Villa des Oliviers, where Juin frankly and convincingly argued that only Darlan possessed the authority to hold North Africa together. By this time Juin had reached the conclusion that regardless of consequences the French must support the Allies. Giraud was greatly struck and influenced by Juin's arguments. Next day he shocked his adherents by telling them he was now interested only in a military command. He imparted this new line of thinking to Clark and Murphy when they drove over to his villa early in the morning prior to the scheduled meeting with Darlan.[7]

General Clark approached the pending conference with one overriding military requirement on his mind: hostilities must be ended. The question of Giraud could wait. Fighting still continued at Oran, and Patton was still confronted with vigorous resistance in Morocco. Plans for rapid thrusts toward Tunisia all depended on French cooperation; no large-scale campaign to the east could be mounted unless it was clear that troops could be released from occupation duties. Clark was grimly determined to extract a cease-fire order from Darlan, and he intended to use all the means at his disposal.[8] During the early morning hours American artillery and mortar units on the outskirts of Algiers received orders to be prepared to shell French installations at 9:30 A.M.—if an armistice was not signed.

The plenary meeting began at nine o'clock on the morning of 10 November, in a small room off the foyer of the St.-Georges Hotel. Darlan appeared with ceremonial guard, flanked by Admirals Moreau, Fenard, and Battet, by Air Force General Mendigal, and by Generals Juin and Koeltz. Clark's entourage presented a somewhat less imposing front (a protocolic drawback which Clark quickly corrected in future negotiations), but its small size was compensated for by the general's forceful and abrupt demands. Clark later admitted that he may have "thrown his weight around" somewhat, but he felt the occasion demanded it; reflecting Eisenhower's impatience, he was tired of French shuffling and he wanted action. Clark had two principal cards in his hand: the threat of a bombardment and the possible imposition of Giraud together with a military occupation. Darlan wanted neither. But much as he pleaded that a cease-fire order for all North Africa would mean his repudiation by Pétain, the American commander would not listen. Had Clark possessed more up-to-date intelligence about Oran, which was on the verge of surrendering, he might not have pressed quite so hard. In that case Darlan might not have been disavowed, and negotiations might have been shortened by several days.

Faced with Clark's unnegotiable demands, Darlan finally yielded. At one point the Americans had left the Frenchmen together, and during this interval General Juin had so eloquently analyzed the alternatives that Darlan had come around.[9] The admiral now felt that if he issued a cease-fire "in the name of the Marshal" he could still preserve American recognition of French sovereignty. If he could do this he could place a barrier against de Gaulle, Giraud, or any other dissident French organization which sought to usurp the authority Pétain had established. The cease-fire thus affirmed that Darlan "for the present" should assume authority over North Africa "in the name of the Marshal. The present senior officers retain their commands and the political and administrative organizations remain in force." Thus Darlan and Clark essentially agreed to the terms of the "soft" armistice, just as anticipated back in October. To Clark and Murphy this was successful negotiation in accordance with written instructions. Neither of them anticipated that the "deal with Darlan" would soon be excoriated in the press and that they both would be charged with naiveté and profascist sympathies.[10]

Darlan's cease-fire order was instantly transmitted to Oran, Tunisia, and Morocco. By the time it reached Oran, that city had already capitulated. In Morocco, Noguès refused to accept the order until validated, and the situation in Tunisia had deteriorated too far for the order to have any effect.

After the plenary session, in a private conversation, Clark placed pressure on Darlan to bring the fleet over to the Allies. The admiral countered by explaining that he had already issued orders for the navy to be prepared to move on short notice in case the Germans violated the unoccupied zone. Clark could not get Darlan to move further on the fleet issue, but he did extract from the admiral an agreement to confer with Giraud that afternoon.[11]

Before the Darlan-Giraud discussion could take place, however, the Vichy government repudiated Darlan. Pétain released an announcement: "I issued the order to defend North Africa. I maintain that order." Shortly afterward Auphan dispatched a secret commentary to Darlan: "You realize that this order was necessary for the negotiations in progress."[12] Much was made of this message at the Pétain trial as indicating that the marshal, acting under constraint, secretly supported Darlan's resistance. Such an interpretation stretches the facts: the message simply provided Darlan with a reminder that Laval had not concluded his discussions in Germany (he had not yet even seen Hitler). At no time did Darlan receive a message suggesting that Pétain privately supported the Allies' moves in North Africa.

Around 7:30 that evening of 10 November, Clark reported to Eisenhower in a long cable what had occurred in Algiers during the afternoon:

> Since my last cable the diplomatic jockeying for position has changed many times. Conferences with KINGPIN [Giraud] and gang this afternoon indicated his great displeasure in permitting Darlan to order cessation of hostilities. KINGPIN insisted that he be set up immediately and announced as Comman-

der-in-Chief of all French forces in North Africa or any place in the French Empire.

If this were done at this time it probably would have caused Darlan to revoke his order. Went with KINGPIN and Murphy to Darlan's residence to attempt to adjust their claims to power. Darlan has just received word that he had been fired by Pétain. He was greatly dejected and told me that he would have to revoke his order for cessation of hostilities. Juin was present. I replied to Darlan that I would not permit him to issue such an order. He then stated that under those conditions he must become a prisoner. I told him that was highly acceptable to me and immediately took steps to place a guard around the house to prevent him leaving. He also gave his word of honor that he would remain there and would not revoke the order. This changed situation brought new life to KINGPIN who immediately started asking Juin if he would play along with him. I pled with Darlan to order the French fleet here.

He replied that his order would no longer have effect. I therefore asked him to make a plea to the French fleet. He replied that he could not. I left the meeting with Juin and KINGPIN attempting to work out their situation. About an hour later Admiral Fenard, friend of Darlan, called Murphy to state that word had just been received that the Germans were about to occupy France. Darlan stated that if this were true, and he received verification, he would ignore Marshal Pétain's order firing him and would feel relieved of further moral responsibility.[13]

If at this time Giraud had come forth with that dash and impetuosity which normally characterized him and through his personal magnetism had shown that he could command the allegiance of French officers and administrators, he might have influenced a dubious Clark to abandon Darlan and throw all his support to Giraud. Had the Americans then used their prestige and control of Algiers radio on Giraud's behalf, they might have kept the "Darlan deal" from becoming an international issue.

But the swing to Giraud did not take place. The general could not rouse himself from the despondent mood which had engulfed him ever since he landed in Algiers, and although he revived momentarily at talk of action against Germans, he had entirely lost interest in the governorship which Eisenhower had offered him. He embarrassed the Americans by now insisting that he wanted an immediate military command and nothing else. Giraud's entourage went so far as to engineer a "coup d'état" which involved the general's taking up residence in the governor's mansion and making a public announcement that he had assumed governing powers. But no one paid any attention. Giraud himself did not have the heart for it. He convinced no one, neither the Americans who refused to give him publicity, nor the Algerians who saw no evidence that French power resided elsewhere than in the hands of Marshal Pétain and his representatives. However reluctant he may have been to do so, Clark turned back to Darlan; he could see the Darlan-Giraud compromise as the only way out, especially as Darlan was now intimating that he was prepared to accept Giraud as commander in chief.[14]

Clark's decision to keep playing along with Darlan, in spite of all the difficulties and rebuffs, developed not strictly out of logic but out of a "feel" for the situation. Clark found Giraud consistently in an apathetic funk, unable to act decisively and unwilling to exert leadership. It should be emphasized that Clark, never having known General Giraud, could hardly estimate how atypical was his present behavior. Darlan on the other hand was always the center of attention and venerated by other officers. Although the admiral was tired, nervous, and upset by the turn of events, he never lost his sense of the historical situation and played masterfully for power and time. He made sure that the trappings of authority always surrounded him, and Clark could not help but be impressed by the aura of command that emanated from Darlan's headquarters.

Algiers, 11 November 1942
Continued negotiations

The morning of 11 November brought a significant change to the political problem of North Africa and the Vichy government. Hitler had given the order that Operation ANTON, an occupation of the southern zone, should begin at 7:00 A.M. Laval, still in Germany, had phoned Vichy to take no action until he could get back; but unwilling to wait, Pétain called a cabinet meeting to determine policy. Weygand, who had been invited to participate, urged Pétain to protest the occupation and to support Darlan. But no one in Vichy knew whether Darlan was acting as a free agent or under constraint, and the final decision, which reached Algiers in mid-morning, repudiated Darlan by naming General Noguès as commander in chief. Orders went out to Juin, Koeltz, Moreau, and Mendigal that they should accept instructions only from Noguès, not from Darlan. Auphan then sent a private message to Darlan, saying, "Only because you are believed to be prisoner that you were not named representative."[15]

It was ironic that at the moment he was named military commander in North Africa, General Noguès had already decided that further resistance in Morocco would be useless. Since the late afternoon of 10 November, convinced that the Americans would bombard Casablanca the next day, Noguès had been negotiating with Patton. Already some 500 Americans and 700 French had been killed. Whether or not Noguès had been influenced by Darlan's cease-fire order, or would have capitulated without it, is impossible to determine. If the former is true, then Clark's hard line with Darlan was justified; if not, his insistence that Darlan send out the cease-fire order, bringing about the admiral's disavowal, must be considered rash because it only complicated an already confused situation.

The argument is frequently made that Darlan's cease-fire order "saved lives." Actually Oran had surrendered by the time the order came; and in Morocco, most of the casualties had already occurred. The question of additional casualties revolves around the planned attack on Casablanca, scheduled for the morning of 11 November. If Noguès had not given in, the city would have been subjected to severe bombing; there would have been heavy French losses and certainly some American casualties. Noguès's acceptance of the "illegal" Darlan order suggests he was ready to find some face-saving way of ending hostilities. His message to Pétain (sent early in the morning of 11 November), reporting that he was executing Darlan's instructions, described the position of Casablanca as desperate.[16]

With the total occupation of France and imminent threat of the fleet, no Frenchman in North Africa could any longer pattern his actions on the hope of saving his country from an Axis invasion. Darlan had lost both his objectives—a relatively free country and an independent navy—and could, if he wished, retire from the political arena. That he did not do so, that he judiciously leaked Auphan's message, suggesting that he, not Noguès, still represented Vichy, reveals that the possession of power, whether based on Germany,

France, or America, basically governed the Fleet Admiral's actions. He could not bear the thought that he be shunted to one side, especially by generals—whether Giraud *or* Noguès. After lunch on 11 November, Darlan notified Clark that Operation ANTON had altered his perspectives, that he might be willing to cooperate, that he might (sure bait to an anxious Clark!) be able to rally the French fleet.[17]

Throughout the long afternoon Clark conferred once more with Admiral Darlan, who finally sent a message to Toulon, "inviting" Admiral de Laborde to direct his ships toward North Africa.[18] That evening Clark cabled the text of Darlan's appeal to Eisenhower and added:

> I am not optimistic that it will be obeyed. If French Fleet sails it will be given later instructions to move to Mers-el-Kebir or other ports, except British, as determined by you for refueling and thence to an American port where subsequent negotiations will determine its future use. This step by Darlan came after a hectic day of rapidly changing situation. Final conference attended by Darlan, Giraud and heads of air, ground and navy of North Africa.
>
> Agreement reached that Darlan will head up political end while Giraud will be accepted as military commander of all French forces in North Africa. Marshal Pétain has designated General Noguès as his Supreme Commander and representative in North Africa because, as he stated, Darlan was not available being a prisoner of war. This complicated the picture so I am requesting, and French are arranging, that Noguès come here for a conference tomorrow. I have removed the guard from Darlan's house. Hope to make public announcement tomorrow emphasizing unity of all factions in common effort to support us in our operation. Hope you agree. If not, advise immediately.
>
> Darlan phoned Esteva and Juin phoned other commanders in Tunisia directing resistance to Germans and support for us. Commanders indicated to him that they would resist where means were available. Giraud is following up with similar orders.[19]

Eisenhower was gratified to learn that Clark seemed to be making progress, but he fretted that the campaign to the east had not gotten under way more rapidly. Some progress, however, was being made. General Anderson was beginning to move against Tunisia and had successfully landed at Bougie; attacks on Bône and other localities would be carried out in the course of 12 November. Eisenhower had hoped to fly in to Algiers on that day but was restrained by weather and postponed his trip to the thirteenth. He wrote Clark:

> Naturally, I approve of everything you have done. My only purpose in coming down was to bring up the last piece of ammunition we had and simply lay down the law with a bit of table pounding. Unfortunately, since I don't speak French, any such attempt would have lost much of its force, but I had actually prepared my little speech in my own mind and was determined to refuse to listen to any more argument. It was my idea simply to say that you had explained the whole situation, that their objections and reasons were perfectly futile and largely personal, and that they would now get together and come with us and be the future Marshals of a greater France, or they would go into oblivion as far as I was concerned. Of course, all this was made up in my own mind on meager information and possibly you would have convinced me I was wrong. In any event, you may be sure that I will back you up to the limit and am ready to come rushing down there if you think it necessary.
>
> I applaud Anderson's initiative and energy in getting into the East. If the French will only turn in and help him now, we will really go somewhere! Welch is doing everything possible to push fighter strength into that direction and all we need is a few fields.[20]

Algiers, 12–13 November 1942
The final settlement

It seemed now that Clark had resolved his political problems and that a conference with Noguès would place the final stamp of approval on the compromise he had reached. But other complications stood in the way. The delicate arrangement was jeopardized on 12 November by the refusal of some subordinate French officers to accept Juin's orders as taking precedence over Vichy's.[21] Once more Clark found himself on the verge of switching to Giraud. After a frenetic early-morning conference, Clark summed up the situation as he then saw it in a telegram to Eisenhower:

> Another stormy session just concluded with Darlan, Juin, Murphy, and myself. I demanded that they revoke orders issued

last night which would permit Germans to enter Tunisia unopposed. This has been done. Noguès arrives about 1400Z this afternoon. Conference with Darlan may bring all factions together. The appointment of Noguès as Supreme Commander here by Marshal Pétain has complicated matters. Hope to get it settled this afternoon with Darlan the politico; Noguès, Governor of French Morocco, and Kingpin [Giraud] as military commander. If this is agreed to will make public announcement. . . . If your PRU [photographic reconnaissance] shows fleet still in Toulon, and if no agreement can be reached by Darlan, Noguès and Kingpin this evening, must take a chance on repercussions and set up Kingpin as the supreme authority. In that event I will arrest Darlan. . . . It is absolutely essential that we get an established leadership here without delay. I have played along in hope of getting the fleet and knowing that Darlan could issue the orders. Darlan just told me that the fleet had acknowledged receipt of his message but he did not know of their contemplated action, if any.[22]

Clark received strong encouragement from Eisenhower, who instructed him to use eloquence and threats to prod the French into action. "They must move now and fast," cabled the TORCH commander:

> Time is running out on them and if we have to do it all ourselves, or with other Frenchmen that we will have to seek out and raise up, then these men will merely disappear. Am I to believe that these men with demonstrated capacity for leadership would rather be spectators than participants in the great drama now unfolding and in which the whole future of France is involved? You are on the ground and must decide upon the best means of jarring these people to their senses. If, in your opinion, the reading of this telegram to them, either as now written or as you may alter, as an expression of my convictions will be of any help, by all means have it translated and have your best orator read it to them. Moreover, the composition of the group may have to be determined by you. It will rest with you to decide whether all now negotiating are to be included or whether one or more may have to be excluded.[23]

But there was nothing to do until Noguès arrived. Meanwhile Darlan received a reply from Admiral de Laborde regarding the French fleet at Toulon. The message was short and succinct—*"merde"*—saying in effect "go fly a kite" but much more bluntly to the point. The reply bore special significance emanating from the aristocratic de Laborde, and Darlan wired Auphan: "We really appreciated the reply of Count Jean." But Darlan was merely playing for time, as he also admitted to Auphan, and he even played further in the afternoon, about half an hour before Noguès flew in, by broadcasting an appeal over the radio, that the fleet should sail to join the United Nations. Darlan knew well enough that his messages would have no effect, but he calculated that they might soothe an ever more irritated Clark by giving the appearance of a pro-Allied stance. Yet even Darlan could not have foreseen the tragic denouement two weeks in the future when the fleet would be scuttled rather than be captured by the Germans.[24]

Finally, late in the afternoon of 12 November, Noguès arrived in Algiers. Almost at once he went into conference with Admiral Darlan. Noguès was quite willing to accept Darlan as chief in North Africa, but he could not countenance the dissident General Giraud as military commander, nor did he harbor any enthusiasm for France's reentry into the war. He preferred that North Africa should remain neutral.

At nine o'clock that evening, at the Hotel St.-Georges, another major conference took place. Darlan, Noguès, and other French officers represented the Vichy contingent, while Giraud and Mast, somewhat apart from the others, represented the dissidents. Clark not only had Murphy by his side but had arranged for a large retinue to be present, making sure that the American group would not be overshadowed in rank and elegance by the vanquished French. Clark and Murphy conferred privately with Darlan and Noguès for an hour and then called in Giraud. Clark insisted that all the Frenchmen shake hands, and they once again tried to hammer out an acceptable formula. Finally Clark left the room, having testily instructed the French to compose their differences or face a military government.

Noguès remained adamant so far as Giraud was concerned: he could not accept Giraud as a commander of the French army and even went so far as to accuse Giraud of treachery for having ordered French officers to disobey their superiors. At Giraud's denial, Noguès bellowed at him: "Vous êtes un lache et un menteur!" (You are a coward and a liar). Strong and bitter words; but out of the tension gradually emerged a compromise: that Giraud should command a force of volunteers—a Corps Franc—which would be recruited from various elements in North Africa. Incredibly Giraud, sensing that from utter exclusion he would emerge at last as commander of a fighting unit, grasped at the idea. It appeared that the way out had been found. Clark agreed to a final conference for next morning but insisted that agreement be reached by noon, when Eisenhower was expected. Clark instructed Ryder to alert his forces for possible imposition of martial law.[25]

The meeting broke up about midnight. The French officers went off to General Juin's villa, where they debated the issues and finally concluded that Giraud might well have a command, but not immediately. Noguès reported developments in a long cable to Pétain, glossing over the Giraud arrangement, but urging that the marshal once more consider Darlan, "who has complete freedom," as his representative in Africa.[26]

Next morning, 13 November, the Americans and the French went to it again. Although the essence of the agreement had been worked out during the night, it was not publicly clinched until General Juin, in a masterful harangue, destroyed the Noguès neutrality stance and persuaded the French officers to reenter the war alongside the Allies. Juin deplored the fact that so eminent a general as Giraud should command only volunteers when he stood out as the obvious and qualified officer to head the regular army. Juin's eloquence persuaded the rest, and although the announcement of Giraud as commander in chief was to be temporarily delayed, the French reached agreement, as Clark had insisted, by noon.

General Clark meanwhile had left the conference in order to greet Eisenhower at Maison Blanche airport. While he and the TORCH commander were having lunch, Murphy came in with the text of what the French had agreed to. Later, in introducing Eisenhower, Clark summed up the accord—the notorious "deal with Darlan"—in the following words:

> Admiral Darlan will head up the political and civil end of the Government of North Africa. This will bring complete cooperation and accord with the Allied forces. Through General Giraud, you [the French North African officials] will assist us militarily in our North African campaign. Admiral Darlan will cooperate so that French forces will defend French North Africa. He will use his influence to assemble all available means for helping us.
>   The two territorial governors at present installed will re-

main at their posts. At an appropriate time, General Giraud will be announced as head of all French armed forces in North Africa. Certain other general questions will be taken up later. This concerns equipping, organizing and coordinating French units that will fight at our side. To facilitate our operations, French troops in strategic positions will vacate their facilities to make room for us. I look to Admiral Darlan for signature of the permanent armistice terms. We will work up the details of this armistice later. I propose now to bring in the Commander-in-Chief, General Eisenhower.[27]

Eisenhower was thus able to congratulate the French commanders on schedule, and he returned to Gibraltar, taking Murphy with him, believing that the political problems in North Africa were well on their way toward solution.

Far from being solved, the North African confusion was just beginning. That afternoon a further development, which bound the Darlan deal even closer to Vichy, capped this first phase of the negotiations. In Vichy, on 13 November, the cabinet gave approval to Noguès's recommendation that Darlan be reinstated but decided to check its decision with the Germans. A private telegram went to Darlan: "Marshal and President Laval in secret agreement [*accord intime*] but official decision submitted to the occupying authorities." The message could not have been more timely. Although it had nothing to do with the agreement reported to Eisenhower, Darlan permitted the impression to leak out that it confirmed the arrangement. Clark told Allied correspondents: "a few minutes ago I was informed Pétain gives our accord his blessing." And the evening newspapers announced that Darlan assumed responsibility in North Africa "in the name of the Marshal and in agreement with him."[28]

A myth had been started. It would provide a defense for Pétain at his trial, and it enabled Vichyite officers in North Africa to obey with a free conscience the orders of Giraud and Juin. But it seemed to tie the Allies closer to Vichy than was actually the case.

11

The Clark-Darlan Agreement

London and Washington, 14–30 November 1942
Repercussions of the Darlan deal

Almost immediately the press began to criticize an arrangement which meant giving support and encouragement to the most notorious collaborator in France. De Gaulle was furious, and he accused the United States of buying the treachery of traitors. Churchill was embarrassed that negotiations over which he had no control should have set off a storm in the newspapers.[1]

Eisenhower on 14 November set forth a justification for Clark's action which still stands as a masterpiece of reasoning based on military expediency. (Murphy cooperated in framing the original draft.) It was addressed to the Combined Chiefs of Staff:

> Can well understand some bewilderment in London and Washington with the turn that negotiations . . . have taken. . . . The following salient facts are pertinent. . . .
>
> Foremost is the fact that the name of Marshal Petain is something to conjure with here. Everyone from highest to lowest attempts to create the impression that he lives and acts under the shadow of the Marshal's figure. The civil governors, military leaders and naval commanders will agree on only one man as having an obvious right to assume the Marshal's mantle in North Africa. That man is Darlan. Even Gen. Giraud, who has been our most trusted adviser and staunchest friend since early conferences succeeded in bringing him down to earth, clearly

249

recognizes this overpowering consideration and has drastically modified his own ambitions and intentions accordingly. . . .

. . . The KINGPIN is honest and will watch Darlan. Moreover, Murphy, who has done a grand job, will as head of my Civil Affairs Section, practically live in Darlan's pocket. Mack and other capable men will cooperate with him. I realize that there may be a feeling at home that we have been sold a bill of goods, but I assure you that these agreements have been arrived at only after incessant examination of the important factors and with the determination to get on with military objectives against the Axis and to advance the interests of the Allies in winning this war. . . .

. . . It must be remembered that hostilities in Morocco ceased by order of Darlan and not repeat not by full military conquest. French military position in that area is still such as to be capable of causing us additional trouble particularly if Nogues, who will obey no one but Darlan, chooses to influence tribes. The certain and deleterious results on Spanish Moroccan situation are obvious.

Finally, it must be clearly appreciated that if Darlan is repudiated and we attempt from the outside to dictate the personnel of the coalition to run this section of the world, the following will be the consequences: (*a*) Our hope of securing organized cooperation in this region will be gone, at great cost to us in additional troops and in stagnation of operations. (*b*) All French Armed Forces in this region will resist us passively and in certain instances actively. (*c*) Our hope of getting Tunisia quickly will not repeat not be attainable because Esteva will not repeat not cooperate. He may already be helpless to do so but there is still a good chance. (*d*) The opportunity for gaining some military assistance from remaining French naval, air and military units in North Africa will disappear. (*e*) The last glimmer of hope with respect to the Toulon fleet will be gone.

Assisted by General Clark and Admiral Cunningham and our full staff, I have made what we consider to be the only possible workable arrangement for securing advantages and avoiding disadvantages I have outlined in this telegram. I am certain that anyone who is not repeat not on the ground can have no clear appreciation of the complex currents of feeling and of prejudice that influence the situation. Also it should be clear that the KINGPIN's earnest participation in this arrangement gives indication of the necessity for the argreements we have made.²

The British and American military advisers believed that Eisenhower should have complete support, but in both London and Washington voices began to protest the arrangement. All of the groups supporting de Gaulle—British sympathizers and the press, statesmen and agents of the Resistance—viewed the Darlan agreement with horror, as completely incompatible with everything for which they had worked since 1940. The deal threatened British contacts with the underground. In the War Cabinet on 16 November, Eden pressed the prime minister so hard that Churchill cabled the president:

> I ought to let you know that very deep currents of feeling are stirred [here] by the arrangement with Darlan. The more I reflect upon it the more convinced I become that it can only be a temporary expedient, justifiable solely by the stress of battle. We must not overlook the serious political injury which may be done to our cause, not only in France but throughout Europe, by the feeling that we are ready to make terms with the local Quislings. . . . A permanent arrangement with Darlan or the formation of a Darlan Government in French North Africa would not be understood by the great masses of ordinary people, whose simple loyalties are our strength.³

In Washington, Roosevelt soon felt the repercussions from pro-Gaullist and anti-Vichy sentiment. Secretary of the Treasury Morgenthau voiced his indignation to the president on 17 November. Later he wrote in his diary:

> You can't tell me the whole campaign was set up with the expectation of using Darlan because the President told me that that wasn't so. . . . If [the working men and women] get the idea that we are going to sit back and favor these Fascists, . . . these people are going to have sit-down strikes; they're going to slow up production, and they're going to say, what's the use of fighting just to put that kind of people back in power.⁴

Secretary of State Hull also pressured the president into making a statement and sent him a note to that effect. Taking sections from both Hull's note and Churchill's cable, Roosevelt put together a statement and announced during a press conference on 17 November that the "present temporary arrangement in North and West Africa is only a temporary expedient, justified solely by the stress of battle." He tried to render his renunciation of Atlantic Charter idealism somewhat more palatable by citing a Bulgarian proverb to the effect that it was permissible to take the Devil's hand while crossing the bridge.[5]

Whether or not one approves of the Darlan deal depends on whether one views it from a military or political point of view. No one has seriously proposed that Eisenhower could have found a more effective way of obtaining French support for the attack on Tunisia. Eisenhower's arguments at the time, although they seemed to reverse Clausewitz in insisting that military achievement be sought at the expense of diplomatic disaster, convinced the policy makers on both sides of the Atlantic. The military case was a strong one. It would have been even stronger if Eisenhower had immediately captured Tunisia and if the French fleet had rallied to Darlan. As neither occurred there is a temptation to argue that without Darlan the French in North Africa—under Juin or Giraud or Noguès—would sooner or later have abandoned their neutrality and joined the Allies: therefore Darlan was unnecessary. But such reasoning is unfair to Eisenhower and Clark, as well as to Darlan. They did not know that the Tunisian campaign would bog down; the Americans had every hope and intention of moving out of North Africa in a few months. The urgency of getting started against Tunisia took precedence over everything else, and Eisenhower was convinced by evidence available to him that Darlan alone possessed the power and the will to bring North Africa into line with this objective.[6]

A more difficult question to answer is whether the deal was a political error. Obviously, for those leaning to the Left, for idealists, for Jews, and for Gaullists, the American North African policy was sheer disaster—and the fact that Darlan, rather than Giraud, fell into the protagonist role gave dramatic emphasis to the pro-Vichy orientation of American policy. But Darlan after all was simply an episode—he was assassinated forty days after the landings—and the brevity of his appearance on center stage diminishes the need to assess his personal, long-range political impact. More to the point is President Roosevelt's overall French policy, which influenced events against the interests of the Gaullists and continued to influence them after Darlan's death and even after the middle of 1943, when all logic pointed to support of de Gaulle.

Roosevelt favored North Africa in 1942, against cross-channel in 1943, for at least three basic reasons: to extract advantage from and to justify the Vichy policy; to fulfill his promise to Molotov for a second front before the end of the year; and to boost flagging war enthusiasm at home. Given these fundamentals, and given Roosevelt's basic conviction, grounded on an analysis of Wilson's errors, that the United States should support or recognize no new regimes until the voice of the people could be heard, the anti–de Gaulle policy becomes inevitable. Roosevelt believed this policy to be a "moral duty" that transcended the "easy way" of supporting the Gaullists. "Self-determination," he later wrote Marshall, "is not a word of expediency. It carries with it a very deep principle in human affairs."[7] Such a policy did indeed lead to a weak postwar France, as Gabriel Kolko maintains;[8] but the policy of self-determination was with Roosevelt one of principle, not one of deliberately seeking to break the French empire for the sake of American economic ambitions. Certainly the president wished to avoid the predicament of Wilson, who had voiced high principles but had committed himself to unfortunate secret arrangements.

To be sure, the dangerous implications of the deal—that the Allies might at any time engage in unilateral peace feelers—were blunted by the famous pronouncement, a month after Darlan's death, that unconditional surrender alone reflected the Allied position. This policy, announced by Roosevelt at the Casablanca conference and strongly seconded by Churchill, could have communicated to Stalin the idea that the Darlan Deal would not reoccur, that it was an accidental and unpremeditated arrangement, and that the western leaders did not intend to play any more political games while the war's active phase continued. Whether the stated lofty objectives of the unconditional surrender policy completely cancelled out the actual day-to-day negotiations with Vichyites and Badoglios can be questioned; but nevertheless the shaky alliance persevered throughout the war, and "unconditional surrender" undoubtedly softened the impact of the Darlan episode.

In *Our Vichy Gamble,* drafted during the war and published two years after the war ended, Professor Langer tried to justify the Vichy policy by emphasizing the short-range advantages, such as the availability of intelligence and the almost bloodless occupation of North Africa. Neither of these could offset some long-range consequences that Langer did not emphasize, partly because in 1947 his vision was limited to the immediate postwar years.⁹ The most important result, especially significant in the 1960s, came from the hostility engendered in Charles de Gaulle and many of his followers. The Vichy policy dismayed and frustrated Leftist Resistance movements which saw their sacrifices and visions of a new world negated by a possible continued influence of the prewar establishment. The policy alienated de Gaulle personally, and he never forgot nor forgave the Americans who rejected him in 1942 and 1943.¹⁰

In practical terms, the Darlan decision did not have the tremendous adverse effects which many commentators feared. Material support of Resistance movements in 1943 lay in British, not in American, hands; only the British possessed the Bren guns, the containers, and the planes with which to deliver weapons to the continent. British *operations* thus had a much greater practical effect on the underground than American *policy*.¹¹ While the Darlan deal certainly provided inspiration for Rightist anti-Mussolini action in Italy, it probably did not much affect or influence what was happening in Yugoslavia.¹² Stalin, with characteristic bluntness and possibly savoring the embarrassment of his western Allies, approved. On 14 December he wrote Roosevelt that Eisenhower's policy was absolutely sound. "I consider it an important achievement," he said, "that you have succeeded in winning Darlan and others to the Allied side against Hitler."¹³

Stalin undoubtedly sensed an advantage for the Soviet Union that had nothing to do with ideology: the occupation of North Africa by the Americans established a precedent for unilateral control of a liberated area. Stalin and Molotov followed developments in North Africa with concentrated interest, and their efforts to send a representative to Algiers continued to be frustrated long after Darlan had passed from the scene. But the policy of excluding Russians was unrelated to Darlan—it was a policy which would have prevailed whether the deal had been made with Giraud, de Gaulle, or even with Maurice Thorez.

Nor do the long-range implications of the North African policy have much to do with Robert Murphy or General Clark, whose instructions gave them little leeway in their negotiations. Murphy had pleaded earnestly for guidance, and, although he recommended looking into Darlan's initial proposals, he correctly assumed that authorization to negotiate at government level remained a Washington prerogative. When he had requested instructions, he could have been told that for political reasons he should have no relations with Admiral Darlan. But his superiors gave him no such orders.

That they did not should surprise no one. American and British citizens have long been fond of voicing elaborate phrases to justify, to cover, and to divert attention from actions and arrangements pursued by reason of the coldest calculations of self-interest. They attempt with intensity to maintain somehow that their own banal policy statements are more honest and based on more fundamental truths than those of other political persuasions. Stalin made a deal with Hitler in 1939; in so doing he baffled many naive and earnest Communists, but he did not deceive experienced observers who perceived, with whatever misgivings and despair, that the interests of states dominate the relationships of states. Many Americans were still, in 1942, wallowing comfortably in a Wilsonian delusion that wars are fought to preserve the world for those on the side of right; they had ahead of them the agony of the endless liaison with Diem and Thieu, which ultimately revealed to Americans that they had come of age, that they could not expect homely morality in high places, and that only heavy and dedicated popular pressure, itself motivated by strong self-interest, can slowly force a government to swerve from practical, self-serving, and short-range apparent benefits. The Darlan deal was the precursor, the eyeopener for those who chose to see; it was the first step in the scenario to be followed thereafter as the United States, stumbling out of isolation, whetting its appetite on the fruits of realpolitik, blundered toward the excitement and existential despair of the postwar world.

Algiers, Washington, London, November–December 1942
The forty days of Admiral Darlan

The aftermath of the Darlan deal continued to plague Eisenhower long after he had turned his attention primarily to the Tunisian campaign. His problems, and the ways in which de Gaulle ultimately achieved power in North Africa, have been chronicled in some detail by this writer in his *Charles de Gaulle: The Crucial Years, 1943–1944*, to which the reader is referred for coverage and analysis of events after the landings.

As I pointed out in that volume, Eisenhower

> exposed himself to devastating criticism on the part of Allied correspondents, who, chafing under censorship and not too oc-

cupied with news from the front, peered inquiringly at every aspect of French and Allied administration in North Africa. They saw a vast population of underprivileged Arab natives with no political rights; Jews persecuted under Vichy laws which remained in effect; prisons and concentration camps filled with Communists, Jews, anti-Vichy political prisoners, and Spanish Republicans; fascist organizations—*the Légion des Anciens Combattants* and the SOL effectively bullying the population and carrying on their petty graft through the *groupements*; and all of the French officials, civil and military, who for two years under Vichy had permitted these conditions to flourish, still in office. All this the American and British correspondents observed and, in spite of censorship, managed to report in their newspapers until the liberal press in both countries, and the Gaullists in London, became livid in their denunciation of Anglo-American follies.[14]

Typical of press attacks in the United States were those of Walter Lippmann, who relentlessly belabored in his column the theme that American policy had been naive and short-sighted (italics in original):

> It is now necessary to examine candidly the cause of this political muddle in North Africa. *It is due to bad judgment based on incorrect information received from our agents in France and North Africa before the expedition landed.* According to their information, General Giraud was held to be capable of rallying the French authorities to our cause and therefore of leaving General Eisenhower free to devote his attention to the military campaign against the Axis. The whole political plan based on this information broke down at the outset.
>
> Thus it was not foreseen that in addition to commanding the United Nations forces, General Eisenhower would have to deal with the subtle and explosive complications of French imperial politics.... That is the kind of burden we have placed on this brilliantly promising young American commander.
>
> *It was placed there because our political agents misjudged the situation and the men with whom we were preparing to deal.* Yet when General Eisenhower was confronted with a political problem which no one had prepared him for, his chief American adviser was the political agent, Mr. Robert Murphy, *who had misjudged the situation.*[15]

For better or worse, Admiral Darlan remained in American

official good graces and was ultimately given the title of French high commissioner for North Africa.[16] His position had been officially confirmed on 22 November, when formal signing of a somewhat modified "soft" armistice, to be known as the Clark-Darlan Agreement, provided a basic constitution for Allied-French relations. The final signatures had been delayed because Eisenhower had forwarded the draft for clearance to the Combined Chiefs of Staff. The chiefs had already approved the "soft" armistice terms, and the present agreement contained only minor changes; but Eisenhower was persuaded that to avoid misunderstandings, especially because of the protest over Darlan, he had better resubmit it. No objections were raised although the British were clearly unhappy that the roles of Darlan and Giraud had been reversed since the London meeting of 17 October. President Roosevelt also examined it and, with the stricture that no political recognition of Darlan should be implied, gave it his immediate approval. The president, under pressure of adverse public opinion, had already admitted that he supported the admiral only as a provisional measure; but he never repudiated the agreement to which Darlan gave his name. As for the promises Murphy had made to Giraud in his letter of 2 November, although not forgotten by The Five, they became virtually obsolete.[17]

With Darlan in power, the underground organization which had backed Giraud became completely altered. So virulent had been the antagonism of French military personnel against Mast, Béthouart, Monsabert, and Baril, that these officers, who had played such an important part in the landings, could not return to their ordinary duties. For a while Mast acted as a liaison officer between Giraud and Anderson's First Army, while Baril established an intelligence operation in Constantine. Later, in 1943, when Tunisia was finally conquered, Mast became governor general of Tunisia. He had narrowly escaped death, shortly before, in an airplane accident which, tragically ending the career of a brilliant officer, killed his friend Baril.[18]

General Béthouart, unable to find useful employment in North Africa, was sent by Giraud early in December to the United States to begin arrangements for the rearmament program promised by the Americans. With him went Lemaigre Dubreuil, who continued with Giraud as adviser on Lend-Lease matters and supplies. Later Lemaigre Dubreuil would be shunted aside when Jean Monnet eclipsed his influence with Giraud. Three members of The Five, d'Astier, Rigault, and Saint-Hardouin became members of Darlan's (and later Giraud's) civil cabinet, but they did not retain these positions of influence after 1943. Rigault resigned in March, 1943, and after the war became editor of *Le Bulletin de Paris*.[19]

General de Monsabert succeeded Giraud as commander of the Corps Franc when Giraud became officially recognized as commander in chief of French forces. Many of the young men of the Resistance joined the volunteer corps, which also recruited from the regular army and from the Chantiers de la Jeunesse. Colonel Van Hecke was able to transform one of his Chantiers groups into the 7th Regiment de Chasseurs d'Afrique, a unit which later served with distinction under General Juin in Italy.[20]

The smaller conspirators did not fare well under the new regime, which inherited so much of the autocratic, anti-Semitic authoritarianism of Vichy. An American correspondent, A. J. Liebling, met José Aboulker, his father, and some of the conspirators seven weeks after the landings. His report conjures up the mood of that time:

> "It is now almost impossible for one of us to see Mr. Murphy," the old doctor said. "He shuns us like a case of an extremely contagious disease."
>
> "The army brass hats and the people of the Prefecture whom we arrested hate us," one of the younger men said. "They hate us because we know what cowards they are. You should have seen how miserably they acted when they saw the tommy guns, the brave Jew-baiters. The chief of the secret police, who has been of course restored to his position, kneeled on the floor and wept, begging one of my friends to spare his life. Imagine his feelings toward the man who spared him! Another friend, a doctor, is to be mobilized—in a labor camp, of course—under the military jurisdiction of a general whom *he* arrested."[21]

Later in December, after Darlan had been assassinated, the Algiers police, then reporting to Giraud, arrested Muscatelli, Achiary, Dr. Aboulker, José Aboulker, Bernard Karsenty, Pierre Alexandre, Dr. Morali, André Temime, and nine others on suspicion of conspiracy. In time the prisoners were released and, when de Gaulle came in, honored; but the insurgents' post-landing rewards were in general hardly commensurate with their services to the Allied cause.[22]

Darlan in power rapidly gained not only acceptance but support from Eisenhower and Murphy. Somewhat disturbed to be referred to as a "temporary expedient," Darlan addressed himself to the Allies on 21 November:

> Information from various sources tends to substantiate the view that I am "only a lemon which the Americans will drop after they have squeezed it dry."
>
> In the line of conduct which I have adopted out of pure French patriotic feeling, in spite of the serious disadvantages which it entails for me, at a moment when it was extremely easy for me to let events take their course without my intervention, my own personal position does not come into consideration.
>
> I acted only because the American Government has solemnly undertaken to restore the integrity of French sovereignty as it existed in 1939, and because the armistice between the Axis and France was broken by the total occupation of Metropolitan France, against which the Marshal has solemnly protested.
>
> I did not act through pride, ambition, or calculation, but because the position which I occupied in my country made it my duty to act.
>
> When the integrity of France's sovereignty is an accomplished fact—and I hope that it will be in the least possible time—it is my firm intention to return to private life and to end my days, in the course of which I have ardently served my country, in retirement.[23]

Even though the pressure against Darlan mounted, Eisenhower came more and more to rely on him. Darlan was able to get the French administration in gear; Darlan had a grasp of economic needs; Darlan had been able to persuade Governor General Boisson that French West Africa should ally itself with the American cause. Boisson's agreement, engineered early in December, meant that Dakar, so long a bugaboo to President Roosevelt, would now become available to the Allies. Eisenhower sang Darlan's praises in a long dispatch to Churchill on 5 December (italics added):

> At every meeting with Darlan, I tell him that so far as this headquarters is concerned, he is the head of a local *defacto* organization through which we are enabled to secure the cooperation, both military and civil, that we need in the prosecution of this campaign. He knows that I am not empowered to go farther than this. I assure you again that we are not entering a cabal designed to make Darlan the head of anything except the local organization. Here *he is absolutely necessary, for he and he alone is the source of every bit of practical help we have*

received. If you will picture the situation existing along our line of communications, which extend 500 miles from here through mountainous country to Tunisia, you can understand that the local French could, without fear of detection, so damage us that we would have to retreat hastily back on to ports from which we could supply ourselves by sea. The KINGPIN quickly gave up in trying to help us and it was only through Darlan's help that we are fighting the Boche in Tunisia instead of somewhere in the vicinity of Bone or even west of that. It appears to us that both Boisson and Darlan have committed themselves irrevocably to an Allied victory; and my conversations with them this morning, in which Cunningham participated, dealt with their desire to get French naval forces at Dakar quickly into the fight against the enemy.[24]

But the British were not persuaded. A motion in the House of Commons on 26 November had protested that the Darlan deal was "inconsistent with the ideals for which we entered and are fighting this war." Twelve days later, at about the same time that Eisenhower's dispatch reached London, Clement Attlee expressed the strong disapproval of the Labour party. Labour leaders, he wrote Churchill,

ask whether, if some Fascist overthrew Mussolini, the United States of America and Great Britain would accept peace overtures which would leave the Fascist regime intact. If so, where is this to stop? I am certain that it would be unwise to disregard these anxieties which, if not allayed, may have a serious effect on morale. I think that the majority of the people of the country regard the war as a crusade for ideals.[25]

These pressures forced the prime minister to convoke the House of Commons in secret session, on 10 December, to explain the situation to its members. He brilliantly implied that the blame, because they had authority in North Africa, lay with the Americans. Churchill glossed over the fact that he had acquiesced in allocating that authority and had been consulted at every step; but he managed to convince Commons that for the sake of the present military necessity, it would be better to go along with the French admiral. Already Churchill had received assurances that a British representative, equal in rank to Murphy (now graced with the title of minister) would be welcomed at Eisenhower's headquarters. The person designated was

Harold Macmillan, who was scheduled to get to North Africa early in the following year.[26]

But before Macmillan arrived, only two weeks after Churchill's secret speech, Darlan was dead, toppled by an assassin's bullet. The murderer was a young man, recently converted to the cause of French royalism, Fernand Bonnier de la Chapelle. He had served in the Chantiers de la Jeunesse, and at the time of the assassination was a member of de Monsabert's Corps Franc. Since Darlan's appointment there had been agitation among royalists to request the admiral to resign in favor of the French pretender, the Count of Paris, then living in Spanish Morocco. When this effort failed, some young men, all of whom had been close to Henri d'Astier in the Algiers *Putsch*, decided to take matters into their own hands and bring about by violence what negotiation had failed to accomplish. Bonnier de la Chapelle, who was executed almost immediately afterward, had volunteered himself as the willing instrument of the young men's decision.[27]

With Darlan's death, the North African story entered a new phase: the office of high commissioner fell into the inept hands of General Giraud; and Charles de Gaulle, who had disdained to soil *his* hands on Darlan, now found in charge a Frenchman with whom he could at least communicate. While Roosevelt and Churchill formulated new policies in anticipation of the conference scheduled for Casablanca, de Gaulle began to explore ways in which he might reach North Africa and have his say regarding the future of France.[28] The following year, 1943, would bring a long-delayed victory in Tunisia and the expulsion of the Axis from all Africa. Eisenhower, with Murphy continuing as his political adviser—"diplomat among warriors"—would focus his eyes on Sicily and Italy, and in 1944, on more distant and more alluring prospects: the Normandy landings and the invasion of the German heartland.

Appendices
Notes
Bibliography
Index

Appendix A

Text of the "Soft" Armistice Terms and the Final Version of the Clark-Darlan Agreement

Draft Armistice of 12 Oct. 1942 (CCS 381, Sec. 1A, National Archives)	Final Agreement of 22 Nov. 1942 (FRUS[1942], 2:453-57)
	PREAMBLE The forces of the United States and their Supporting Allies have landed in French North Africa for the purpose of preventing the domination of this territory by German and Italian forces and their Allies and for carrying on the war for the defeat of the Axis powers. By a common agreement among leading French officials in French North Africa, a High Commissioner in French Africa has been established in the person of Admiral of the Fleet François Darlan. It has been agreed by all French elements concerned and United States military authorities that French forces will aid and support the forces of the United States and their allies to expel from the soil of Africa the common enemy, to liberate France and to restore integrally the French Empire. In order that this high purpose may be accomplished, and to make appropriate arrangements for the presence in

1. There shall be no further opposition to the landing and operations of land, sea and air forces under the command of the Commanding General, United States Army and supporting forces, the presence of such forces being for the purpose of preventing the subjugation of this territory by the German and Italian forces and their Allies, and for carrying on the war against the Axis powers for their defeat.

The (sovereignty [or] rights) of France in (ALGERIA, FRENCH ZONE OF MORROCO, [and/or] TUNISIA) remain (s) unimpaired.

No undertaking requiring allegiance to any non-French authority will be required.

2. Except as herein otherwise provided there shall be no change in the status, command, functions, employment rights, privileges, emoluments and pensions of French land, sea and air forces, the honor of which will be respected. Such forces will continue in the service of internal security and in the performances of their military duties in their normal stations. No military or air forces will be moved from their normal stations without prior consultation and agreement with the Commanding General, U.S. Army.

3. There shall be no changes in the status, functions, employment, rights, privileges, emolu-

North Africa of large forces of the United States and its allies, the following agreement is entered into at Algiers this 22nd day of November 1942.

1. There shall be the closest cooperation between the Commander-in-Chief of the French Land, Sea and Air forces and the Commanding General, United States Army and supporting forces to accomplish the purpose set forth above.

2. The status, command, functions, employment, rights and privileges of French land, sea and air forces will remain under French direction. Such forces will continue in the service of internal security and will be employed, in cooperation with the forces of the United States and its allies, in driving Axis forces from French African territory and in protecting it from further violation by them. All movements of French military, naval or air forces from their normal stations will be notified to the Commanding General of the United States Army by the French command.

3. French governmental personnel will continue in the performance of their functions with loy-

ments and pensions of government personnel who continue in the performance of their functions without disloyalty to the purposes of the forces under the command of the Commanding General, U.S. Army and supporting forces. Such government personnel will take such measures as, in the opinion of the Commanding General, U.S. Army, after consultation with the French authorities, are necessary for the maintenance of order and of public and administrative services throughout the territory.

4. The control and command of all landing facilities for aircraft, harbor and port facilities, defenses, fortifications and arsenals will be placed at the disposal of the Commanding General, U.S. Army, for the purpose set forth in paragraph 1, above. The control of these facilities shall not involve the use of French personnel without the consent of French authorities.

5. Full information will be given as to the location of all facilities, installations, equipment and devices (such as airfields, anti-aircraft batteries, observation posts, radio-location and other technical observing stations, minefields, tank-traps, military, naval and air forces stores, fuel, supplies and equipment, etc.) which may be a hindrance or useful to the purpose of the forces under the command of the Commanding General, U.S. Army and supporting forces.

6. All telecommunication services essential to the maintenance of law and order and the preservation of human life will be maintained

alty to the purpose of the forces under the command of the Commanding General, United States Army and supporting forces. Such government personnel will take such measures as are necessary for the maintenance of order and public administrative services throughout the territory in consultation with the Commanding General of the United States Army.

4. The control and command of all landing and other facilities for aircraft, harbor and port facilities, defenses, fortifications and arsenals will be available to the Commanding General of the United States Army, and supporting forces, for the purpose set forth in the preamble hereof. The control of these facilities will not involve the use of French personnel without the consent of the French authorities.

5. Full information will be given as to the location of all facilities, installations, equipment and devices (such as airfields, anti-aircraft batteries, observation posts, radio-location and other technical observing stations, minefields, tank-traps, military, naval and air forces stores, fuel, supplies and equipment, etc.) which may be a hindrance or useful to the purpose of the forces under the command of the Commanding General, United States Army and supporting forces.

6. All telecommunication services will be operated and maintained normally by the French authorities. The United States mil-

unaltered. For the purpose set forth in paragraph 1, above, all other communication services whether civil, military, naval or air will be temporarily closed down and maintained in good order. The resumption of these services will be subject to the consent of the Commanding General, U.S. Army, and any services resumed will be operated under such control as he may direct.

All telecommunications installations, civil, military, naval and air, with all connected plant and records, will be placed at the disposal of the Commanding General, U.S. Army, and any necessary repairs will be carried out by the French authorities concerned with such assistance as the Commanding General may be able to afford.

7. French warships will continue to fly the French colours and will retain and be provided with sufficient fuel to provide light, power, and the upkeep of machinery. All torpedo warheads, torpedo pistols, explosives, fuses, cordite and fixed ammunition will be landed together with such parts of guns as will render the guns inoperative. Such parts of machinery as will prevent ships putting to sea in less than 12 hours will be landed and wireless offices will be sealed and the transmitting and receiving gear rendered inoperative.

In order to maintain the ships in good order 33 per cent of each ship's company will remain on board, the balance of the crews being disembarked and accommodated ashore.

It is the intention, the hazards of war permitting, that all warships

itary forces and supporting Allies will have the unrestricted use of the telecommunication services insofar as may be required for military purpose.

7. French warships shall operate in close cooperation with the Commanding General, United States Army or allied representatives acting with his approval for the accomplishment of the purpose set forth in the preamble hereof. Such warships will continue to fly the French flag and be placed under French command, and will retain such personnel and equipment, and will be provided with fuel and all necessary supplies to enable them to become effective fighting units.

shall be maintained, both on board and in regard to stores and armament landed, so that warships can be returned intact and efficient to FRANCE when the Axis Powers have been defeated.

Warships will proceed when so instructed to such suitable port on which the United States may decide.

8. The officers and crews of all French merchant vessels now in the harbors of (ALGERIA, FRENCH ZONE OF MORROCCO [and/or] TUNISIA), will disembark as may be required by the Commanding General, U.S. Army. They can then make free choice whether to work for the United Nations; in case of volunteering, pay and pensions will be guaranteed from the date of volunteering.

Merchant vessels will be employed in the service of the United Nations to take part in the war effort against the Axis and, subject to the hazards of war, will be held in trust for FRANCE and returned to her after the defeat of the Axis Powers.

9. All port facilities, harbor and naval installations, and establishments together with their records, will be placed intact at the disposal of the Commanding General, U.S. Army, and such assistance as he may require will be rendered to allow proper maintenance and operating of all machinery and fittings.

As may be required, personnel will withdraw temporarily in accommodation provided and may then volunteer to continue their duties, in which case pay and pensions will be guaranteed from the date of volunteering.

8. All French merchant vessels in the harbors of French North Africa or those which in the future may enter those harbors will be operated by crews, preferably French, under the French flag in cooperation with the Commanding General, United States Army or allied representatives acting with his approval. Such operations shall be by charter with the public or private owners. Such chartered vessels will be employed in the service of the United Nations to take part in the war effort against the Axis.

9. All port facilities, harbor and naval installations and establishments in French North Africa, together with their records, will be placed intact at the disposal of the Commanding General, United States Army, or allied representatives acting with his approval, all remaining under French Command, subject to the provisions of Par. 4 above, and such assistance as he may require will be rendered to allow proper maintenance and operation of all machinery and fittings.

10. Requisitioning of billets, supplies, lands, buildings, transportation and services for the military needs of the forces under command of the Commanding General, U.S. Army, is authorized, if not procurable by agreement promptly, in sufficient quantities and at fair prices. Requisitions will be made only by authority of the Commanding Officer of the troops in the locality and upon the Mayor or other appropriate civil authorities, but may be upon individuals in cases of necessity. Payment will be made at once in cash or in voucher payable in cash by the disbursing officer of the Army to which the officer belongs upon whose authority the requisition is issued. Prices will be the fair market value to be fixed by agreement if possible, otherwise by the appropriate military authorities.

11. The authorities in (ALGERIA, FRENCH ZONE OF MORROCO, [and/or] TUNISIA) will furnish the Commanding General, U.S. Army, with a list of all persons of whatsoever nationality who have been placed under restriction, detention or sentence (including persons sentenced "in absentia") on account of their dealings or sympathies with the United Nations. Those still under restriction or detention will be released when the Commanding General so directs.

12. All service personnel and merchant seamen of any of the United Nations who are interned in (ALGERIA, FRENCH ZONE OF MOROCCO [and/or] TUNISIA) will be released forthwith and transferred

10. In North Africa, requisitioning of billets, supplies, lands, buildings, transportation and services for the military needs of the forces under command of the Commanding General, United States Army is authorized, if not procurable by agreement promptly, in sufficient quantities and fair prices. Requisitions will be made only by authorization of the Commanding Officer of the troops in the locality and upon the Mayor or other appropriate civil authorities, but may be upon individuals in cases of necessity. Payment will be made at once in cash or in voucher payable in cash by the disbursing Officer of the Army to which the officer belongs and upon whose authority the requisition is issued. Prices will be the fair market value to be fixed by agreement if possible, otherwise by the requisitioning military authority.

11. The authorities in French North Africa will furnish the Commanding General, United States Army with a list of all persons of whatsoever nationality who have been placed under restriction, detention or sentence (including persons sentenced in absentia) on account of their dealings or sympathies with the United Nations. Those still under restriction or detention will be released when the Commanding General, United States Army, so directs.

12. All service personnel and merchant seamen of any of the United Nations who are interned in French North Africa will be released forthwith and transferred as the Commanding General, United

as the Commanding General, U.S. Army, may direct.

13. The authorities in (ALGERIA, FRENCH ZONE OF MOROCCO [and/or] TUNISIA) will take such measures as the Commanding General, U.S. Army, may deem appropriate with regard to the control of foreign property of foreign nationals, neutral consular officers and such other persons as the Commanding General, U.S. Army may direct.

14. No tax, direct or indirect, will be collected upon the property of the United States, its Allied Governments, their representatives and civilian employees, governmental agencies or authorized welfare organizations; nor will any tax be collected upon any purchase from, sale to, or any transaction of any kind with the United States, its Allied Governments, their representatives, civilian employees, agencies or organizations.

15. The Commanding General, U.S. Army, the forces under its command and supporting forces and their governments, the representatives of their governments and civilian employees of these governments shall enjoy extraterritorial privileges and be exempt from the jurisdiction and immune to the process of the courts, civil and criminal, of the territory.

16. Areas deemed by the Commanding General, U.S. Army, to be of importance or useful to the purpose set forth in paragraph 1 above, from time to time, may be declared by him to be military areas under his control, whereupon the mainte-

States Army may direct.

13. The authorities in French North Africa will take such measures as the Commanding General, United States Army, may deem appropriate with regard to the control of foreign property and of the persons and property of foreign nationals, neutral consular officers and such other persons as the Commanding General, United States Army, may direct.

14. In North Africa no tax, direct or indirect, will be collected upon the property of the United States, the Allied Governments, their representatives and civilian employees, governmental agencies or authorized welfare organizations; nor will any tax be collected upon any purchase from, sale to, or any transaction of any kind with the United States Government, its Allied Governments, their representatives, civilian employees, agencies or organizations.

15. The Commanding General, United States Army, the forces under his command and supporting forces and their legal Governments, the representatives of their governments and civilian employees of these governments shall enjoy extraterritorial privileges and be exempt from the jurisdiction and immune to the process of the courts, civil and criminal, of the territory.

16. In North Africa areas deemed by the Commanding General, United States Army, to be of importance or useful to the purpose set forth in the preamble hereof, from time to time, may be declared by him to be military

nance of order and administrative and public services in such areas shall come under direct control of such Commanding General.

17. If the internal situation at any time be such as in his opinion to endanger his line of communication or threaten disorder, the Commanding General, U.S. Army, will inform the French authorities of such danger and the French authorities will undertake, in concert with the Commanding General, such administrative and other measures as may be necessary for the protection of military interests of the forces under his command and supporting forces.

18. The Commanding General, U.S. Army will appoint such military, naval, air and economic missions and branch missions as he may deem requisite to administer the provisions of these arrangements in liaison with such agency or agencies as the local authorities may employ in cooperation.

areas under his control whereupon the maintenance of order and administrative and public services in such areas shall come under the direct control of such Commanding General. The French authorities will be promptly notified in the event that such a step becomes necessary.

17. If the internal situation at any time be such as in his opinion to endanger his lines of communication or threaten disorder the Commanding General, United States Army will inform the French authorities of such danger and the French authorities will undertake, in concert with him, such administrative and other measures as may be necessary for the protection of the military interests of the forces under his command and supporting forces.

18. The Commanding General, United States Army, will appoint such military, naval, air and economic and branch Missions as he may deem requisite to regulate, in liaison with such agency or agencies, as the local authorities will institute for this purpose, the application of the present accord.

19. There shall be immediately appointed a Joint Economic Commission which will be charged with the study of the economic needs of French North Africa. The Commission will suggest such measures as may seem appropriate to it regarding exportation and importation, as well as for the increase of agricultural production, as well as for the establishment of economic stability, and the creation of prosperity in French North African territories.

19. The foregoing arrangements will be drawn up in the English and French languages. The English text is authoritative.

20. A Joint censorship commission shall be established. It will extend its action to the press, radio broadcasts, telecommunications, postal services and all public means for the dissemination of information and shall operate in full conformity with the common purpose set forth in the preamble hereof. The French members of the Commission will be appointed by the High Commissioner.

21. The foregoing arrangements will be drawn up in the English and French languages. The English text is authoritative.

Appendix B

Note on the Assassination of Admiral Darlan

Although most of the details regarding Darlan's assassination were known shortly after the event, it has not so far been possible to determine the extent to which the murderer was subject to outside influences. The assassination is covered in Kammerer, Richard and Sérigny, and in great detail by Ordioni and by Chamine, *La querelle des généraux* (Paris, 1952), vol. 2 of *La conjuration d'Alger*. The only extensive coverage in English is to be found in Peter Tompkins's *The Murder of Admiral Darlan* (New York, 1965), which arrays all of the information known for twenty years but which adds nothing new.

Darlan was assassinated on Christmas Eve, 1942, by a young man named Fernand Bonnier de la Chapelle, who had close ties with Henri d'Astier de la Vigerie, one of the original Five, and his young associate, the Abbé Cordier. It has been acknowledged that d'Astier, a royalist, had tried to replace Darlan with the French pretender, Henri, Comte de Paris, and also that d'Astier had received a large sum of money, in dollars, from his brother, General François d'Astier, a Gaullist, who had come to Algiers shortly before the assassination. The assassin confessed that he knew both Henri d'Astier and Cordier and that he had received a gun from Cordier. Later, d'Astier and Cordier were put on trial for implication in the murder, but after de Gaulle assumed power in North Africa the charges were dropped. As Bonnier de la Chappelle was executed within forty-eight hours of the murder, the brief statements which he made could not be verified later by intensive inquiry.

Because of the unusual political climate of wartime North Africa, a full-scale trial was never completed, and no court, civil or military, ever reached a verdict. Of the two individuals who had been charged, one, Henri d'Astier died shortly after the war; the other, the Abbé Cordier, returned to his priestly duties but, never free of the assassination's shadow, he did not rise in the ecclesiastical hierarchy. Thirty years later he was *chanoine* in a small community north of Paris. Cordier has consistently denied that he provided the murder weapon and has refused to comment on one of the assassin's statements: "I affirm having killed Admiral Darlan, after having referred to it during confession with the Abbé Cordier."

The unanswerable questions do not so much concern the relationship of Bonnier de la Chapelle to d'Astier and the Abbé Cordier but rather to larger matters: was the assassination part of a royalist plot? was it related to de Gaulle in London? was British or American intelligence involved? or did Bonnier act virtually alone, with the help of only three or four young men?

None of these questions has been satisfactorily answered. In his *French Royalism in the Third and Fourth French Republics* (1960), Samuel Osgood concluded that the Comte de Paris was not personally involved. Indeed, one can make a good argument for the case that the only way in which the count could play a political role would be for Darlan to voluntarily relinquish his position. No evidence has come forth to invalidate Osgood's conclusion.

The case against the Gaullists is strong. Coming from London to Algiers, the Gaullist General François d'Astier de la Vigerie did bring $38,000 to his brother Henri. Some of this money was found on the assassin. Even then, it would be difficult to implicate de Gaulle personally. An article in the French newspaper *L'Aurore* (7 Nov. 1972) implied that de Gaulle had in fact approved, and it attested that this information had been derived from an interview with the Abbé Cordier. But Cordier had simply referred to a conversation, after the war, in which he had overheard General François d'Astier tell his nephew that de Gaulle had "given the green light." This is suggestive, but scarcely proof. I have interviewed both General d'Astier and the Abbé Cordier but can only attest to their denials.

From the beginning there have been rumors that British Intelligence was involved, but these have not been proved. (See Paul Bret, *Au feu des événements* [Paris, 1968]).

If it cannot be conclusively demonstrated that Bonnier de la Chappelle acted on orders from royalists or Gaullists, it is nevertheless quite clear that he had accomplices—at least two young men, Jean-Bernard d'Astier (son of Henri d'Astier) and Mario Faivre (who had fought with Pillafort during the *Putsch*), drove him to Darlan's headquarters. Reports indicate that a third young man, sometimes identified as Gilbert Sabatier, also was in the car. This is disputed by a French journalist, Roger Rosfelder, who maintains that he was the third person and that Sabatier did not exist. Under the pen name of Roger Curel, Rosfelder published in 1969 a novel, *Brancula*, which describes the assassination in fictional terms, spelling out what the historian cannot be sure of. From Rosfelder's account it would seem that the young men had been planning the assassination for some time, filled with zeal implanted in them by the charismatic Henri d'Astier. Rosfelder affirms that the murder weapon, an Eibar 7.65, belonged to Mario Faivre and was used because the dueling pistols given to Bonnier by the Abbé Cordier proved unserviceable. Rosfelder's testimony can be found in the newspaper story mentioned above (*L'Aurore*, 7 Nov. 1972) and in *Today in France* (the newsletter of the Society for French-American Affairs, in New York), nos. 99 and 100 (Jan.-Feb. and Mar.-Apr. 1972). Mario Faivre and Jean-Bernard d'Astier have never released their own versions of the assassination.

Clearly the young men knew that both royalists and Gaullists saw Darlan as a hindrance to their ambitions. In many places, but especially in London and in Algiers, Frenchmen were saying, "We must get rid of Darlan." The day before he was murdered Darlan told Robert Murphy that he knew of four plots in existence to assassinate him (Murphy, p. 143). It did not require a direct order from the Comte de Paris or from Charles de Gaulle to motivate ardent young patriots who yearned for involvement and action. One report has it that some time before the actual assassination a group of young men drew straws to determine who would be the instrument to liberate Algiers from the Darlan tyranny. Bonnier de la Chappelle accepted the responsibility of becoming this instrument and thereafter dedicated his life with impassioned zeal to one aim: to carry out a deed for which he believed himself to be the chosen agent.

Notes

The notes give citations for the published and unpublished materials used in this volume. A considerable amount of information and atmosphere has been provided by interviews and correspondence. In this area the major sources have been:

José Aboulker: Medical student and leader of Resistance elements in Algiers; after the war residing in Paris; interviewed 1 April 1969.

Admiral Paul Auphan: secretary of state for navy at Vichy in 1942; interviewed 15 November 1972.

General André Beaufre: captain in 1942, on staff of General Giraud; interviewed 22 October 1972.

General Jean Chrétien: in charge of military intelligence in North Africa in 1942; correspondence (18 December 1972, 14 January 1973) and loan of unpublished memoirs.

General Mark W. Clark: deputy commander of Operation TORCH; interviewed 3 November 1969.

Canon Pierre-Marie Cordier: member of the Algiers Resistance; close supporter of Henri d'Astier; interviewed 14 November 1972.

Donald Coster: vice-consul at Casablanca in early 1943; interviewed 13 November 1972.

Alain Darlan: son of Admiral Darlan; stricken with polio shortly before the landings; interviewed 28 September 1972.

General Charles de Gaulle: leader of the Fighting French in London in 1942; interviewed 12 January 1955.

General Dwight D. Eisenhower: commander of Operation TORCH in 1942; interviewed 31 July 1968.

Admiral R. Fenard: secretary of the French delegation in Algiers; close friend of Admiral Darlan; interviewed 18 December 1954.

Bernard Karsenty: leader of Resistance elements in Algiers; after the war residing in Paris; interviewed 14 November 1972.

Jacques Lemaigre Dubreuil: one of The Five, leaders of the pro-Ally movement in North Africa; interviewed 15 April 1951.

General Charles Mast: pro-Ally commander of the Algiers division in 1942; interviewed 31 March 1969.

H. Freeman Matthews: American diplomat at Vichy; later of Eisenhower's civil affairs staff; interviews 4 January 1955 and 12 June

1971, and loan of commentary made on pre-publication text of Langer's *Our Vichy Gamble*, dated 17 January 1945.

Robert D. Murphy: counsellor of embassy at Vichy; chief negotiator between French and Americans in North Africa in 1942; interviewed 17 January 1955 and 2 October 1972, with considerable correspondence in intervening years.

Bernard Pauphilet: leader of Resistance elements in Algiers; after the war residing in Paris; interviewed 15 March 1969; 13 November 1972.

Robert Solborg: representative of OSS in Lisbon; negotiator with Resistance groups in North Africa; interview 28 August 1970 and loan of personal papers.

1. *Before Pearl Harbor*

1. For U.S. Government attitudes toward North Africa prior to Pearl Harbor, see Langer and Gleason, pp. 58–75, 85–95, 360–90, 580–89, 761–86.
2. Murphy, p. 66.
3. Hytier, pp. 301 ff. On Weygand, see Maxime Weygand, *Recalled to Service* (Garden City, N.Y., 1952); P. C. Bankwitz, *Maxime Weygand and Civil-Military Relations in Modern France* (Cambridge, Mass., 1967).
4. Esquer, p. 84; Dick Cooper, *The Adventures of a Secret Agent* (London, 1957), pp. 35–55.
5. Based on Murphy's own account, in Murphy, pp. 70–81.
6. Pendar, pp. 18–19. A German intelligence report on Murphy characterized him as "cultured, fond of social life, an excellent conversationalist, easy-mannered, able to deal with any situation." Cited in Smith, p. 390.
7. Murphy, p. 70.
8. *Ibid.*
9. Langer, pp. 128–35.
10. Most information derived from interview with Mr. Solborg (August, 1970), who gave the writer access to his personal papers. For background, see Francis de Guingand, *Generals at War* (London, 1964), which describes Solborg's activities in 1940 but does not identify him by name. See also the Halifax (Nova Scotia) *Chronicle Herald*, 25, 28 May 1964; FRUS (1941); 2: 343, 361; Smith, pp. 27, 41: Langer, p. 232. Murphy does not mention Solborg in his memoirs.
11. Beaufre, pp. 30–61; Jousse, pp. 194–95; FRUS (1941), 2: pp. 343–44. Beaufre later served in the Italian campaign, and after the war in Indochina, in Suez, SHAPE, and NATO. Retired in 1961, he has written a variety of books on military strategy.
12. Information derived largely from the doctoral dissertation of William A. Hoisington, Jr., "A Businessman in Politics in France: The Career of Jacques Lemaigre Dubreuil" (Stanford University, 1968).

See also Hoisington, "The Struggle for Economic Influence in Southeastern Europe: The French Failure in Romania, 1940," *Journal of Modern History* (Sept. 1971). Ordioni, pp. 177–83 and *passim*, sets forth interesting recollections.
13. Murphy, pp. 116–17; Crusoe, pp. 7–18; Murphy to State, 5 Dec. 1941, FRUS (1941), 2: 494–96.
14. Beaufre, pp. 59–61.
15. Charles Burdick, *Germany's Military Strategy and Spain in World War II* (Syracuse, 1968); Donald S. Detwiler, *Hitler, Franco und Gibraltar* (Wiesbaden, 1963); M. A. Hillgruber, *Hitlers Strategie: Politik und Kriegführung 1940–41* (Frankfort, 1965).
16. Beaufre, pp. 30–61; Jousse, p. 195; Paul Stehlin, *Témoignages pour l'histoire* (Paris, 1964), pp. 312–14; Paillat, pp. 247–49; Georges Loustaunau-Lacau, *Mémoires d'un français rébelle* (Paris, 1948); Marie-Madeleine Fourcade, *L'Arche de Noé* (Paris, 1968), pp. 99–100; Ordioni, pp. 187–96.
17. Murphy, pp. 84–90.
18. Memorandum of 29 Sept. 1941 on his mission (Solborg Papers).
19. Murphy, pp. 84–85; FRUS (1941), 2: 394–98. On the code: FRUS (1941), 2: 466 n.14; David Kahn, *The Codebreakers* (New York, 1967), p. 497.
20. Murphy, pp. 90–92; FRUS (1941), 2: 318–20, 485; FRUS (1942), 2: 308. Pendar is the only one to have written memoirs. Bartlett and Canfield were transferred before the landings. Donald Coster, who had represented Donovan's OSS in Morocco, may also be considered an agent, but his tour had begun before the Murphy-Weygand assignment of vice-consuls. See Donald Coster, "We Were Expecting You at Dakar," *Reader's Digest* (Aug. 1946).
21. Beaufre, pp. 30–61; Jousse, pp. 195–96; FRUS (1941), 2: 343–44. See also Danan, pp. 5–67; Van Hecke, pp. 87–111; Ordioni, pp. 175–360.
22. For a good characterization of Henri d'Astier, see Edmond Taylor, *Awakening from History* (London, 1971), pp. 257–68.
23. Information about Darlan based on Darlan; Paxton, *Parades*; Paxton, *Vichy*; Hytier; Kammerer; Mordal; Vulliez; together with Jules T. Docteur, *La grande énigme de la guerre: Darlan, Amiral de la Flotte* (Paris, 1949); Jacques Mordal, "Qui était Darlan?" *La revue de Paris* 62 (Aug. 1955): pp. 99–111; Russell Brooks, "The Unknown Darlan," *U.S. Naval Institute Proceedings* 81 (Aug. 1955): pp. 879–92; unpublished doctoral dissertation of George E. Melton, "Admiral Darlan and the Diplomacy of Vichy 1940–1942" (University of North Carolina, 1966); Henri Michel, *Pétain, Laval, Darlan, trois politiques* (Paris, 1972).
24. On Darlan's overall policies and his involvement in the celebrated Protocols of Paris, see Paxton, *Vichy*, pp. 109–31; Robert L. Melka, "Darlan between Britain and Germany, 1940–41," *Journal of Contemporary History* (April 1973), pp. 57–80.

25. Darlan, p. 20.
26. FRUS (1941), 2: p. 189; Leahy, p. 133. Darlan's comment about 500,000 men was not casual, although Leahy may have considered it so; it was repeated many times. See Darlan, p. 161; P. J. Stead, *Second Bureau* (London, 1959), p. 97; FRUS (1942), 2: 440–41. Statement of Freeman Matthews (then in U.S. Embassy at Vichy) to author in interview (June 1971) confirmed this view.
27. Murphy to State, 3 Oct. 1941, FRUS (1941), 2: 440–41; *Washington/Casablanca*, p. 186.
28. Hytier, pp. 300–8; DGFP, Ser. D, 13: 671–72, 770; FRUS (1941), 2: 457–63, 466–68, 496–502; FRUS (1942), 2: 500–1.

2. After Pearl Harbor: The Rise and Fall of GYMNAST

1. Winston S. Churchill, *The Second World War*, vol. 3, *The Grand Alliance* (Boston, 1950), pp. 479–89.
2. For detailed coverage of the First Washington Conference, see Gwyer and Butler, pp. 349–401; Matloff and Snell, pp. 97–146; Churchill, *The Grand Alliance*, pp. 604–711; Pogue, pp. 261–88; Sherwood, pp. 439–78; *Washington/Casablanca*, pp. 3–415; Steele, pp. 53–73.
3. Churchill, *Grand Alliance*, p. 656.
4. *Ibid.*, pp. 648–50.
5. During November and December, 1941, former Ambassador to France William C. Bullitt was traveling in North Africa and the Middle East as the president's personal representative. His reports, some of which came in during the Washington conference, emphasized the advantages of a North African occupation. *Washington/Casablanca*, pp. 47–50; *For the President, Personal and Secret: Correspondence Between Franklin D. Roosevelt and William C. Bullitt*, ed. Orville H. Bullitt (Boston, 1972), pp. 529–45.
6. Maxime Weygand, *Recalled to Service* (Garden City, N.Y.) pp. 538–40; *Washington/Casablanca*, pp. 68, 185–91, 234–37.
7. Smith, pp. 1–44; Langer, pp. 232–33, 274–77; Corey Ford, *Donovan of OSS* (Boston, 1970); interviews with Colonel Solborg.
8. FRUS (1942), 2: 278, 284.
9. Murphy to Dunn, *ibid.*, p. 227.
10. Jousse, pp. 196–97. Murphy reported a long conversation with Lemaigre Dubreuil on 5 Dec. 1941 (FRUS [1941], 2: 494–96), and forwarded the Jousse plan to Washington on 12 Jan. 1942 (FRUS [1942], 2: 229–36). The plan was rejected by Eisenhower, as head of the War Plans Division, on 25 Feb. (*ibid.*, pp. 258–59).
11. In his memoirs, Colonel Van Hecke argues that he was considered the leader (Van Hecke, pp. 116–17). It is true that he had facilities to travel throughout North Africa, but his leadership was not confirmed by others. He was later not even told the date of the landings.

12. FRUS (1941), 2: 496–98; FRUS (1942), 2: 236–37, 248–49, 257–58, 283–84. Darlan, pp. 157–59, 164–65. See also Alain Darlan's long statement published in Paillat, pp. 382–84; and Murphy, pp. 131–33. Interviews with Alain Darlan, Admiral Fenard, and Robert Murphy by the author. The Murphy reports in the National Archives (not all of which have been published) indicate that Murphy thereafter conferred with Fenard on 1, 6, 11 April; 15 May; 21, 26 June; and 2, 8 July.
13. FRUS (1942), 2: 313, 345; Leahy, pp. 86–94; Warner, pp. 285–301.
14. Murphy to State, 6 May 1942, FRUS (1942), 2: 298. Lemaigre Dubreuil, a friend of Laval's, deplored the possible influence of Darlan on Murphy (*France during the Occupation*, 3: 1114–15); FRUS (1942), 2: 286.
15. As late as July, Murphy is still asking for advice and counsel. FRUS (1942), 2: 332.
16. The best biography of Juin has been written by his close friend, René Chambe: *Le Maréchal Juin, "Duc du Garigliano"* (Paris, 1968). Regarding Juin's contacts with the Allies, see especially pp. 117–44 in Chambe. On 15 May 1942 Murphy wrote State that Juin was friendly and anti-Axis but reportedly could not "be depended upon for independent initiative" (FRUS [1942], 2: 300–1). See also Darlan, pp. 299–300; and Juin. Parts of Juin's memoirs must be read with care, as General Schmitt warns in his "Le général Juin et le débarquement en A.F.N." *Revue d'histoire de la 2ᵉ guerre mondiale* (Oct. 1961), pp. 57–59.
17. Danan, pp. 36–39; Soustelle, pp. 421–32.
18. Langer, pp. 382–98, defends the Vichy policy; but note the contrary argument, comparable to the position here expressed, in Louis Gottschalk, "Our Vichy Fumble," *Journal of Modern History* (March 1948), pp. 47–56. See also Paxton, *Vichy, passim*.
19. Matloff and Snell, pp. 174–97; Steele, pp. 100–14.
20. FRUS (1942), 2: 259–72; Jousse, pp. 198–201; Langer, pp. 239–44; Solborg Papers.
21. FRUS (1942), 2: 265.

3. The French

1. General Giraud's two books (*Evasions* and *Un seul but*) contain useful but sometimes confused information. Accurate and detailed are the articles by René Chambe, who was closely associated with Giraud (see bibliography). On Giraud, see also Robert Aron, *Le piège où nous a pris l'histoire* (Paris, 1950); Price; Beaufre, pp. 85 ff.
2. According to Richard and Sérigny, p. 47n.
3. De Gaulle, pp. 315–17.
4. *Hitler's Table Talk*, ed. H. R. Trevor-Roper (London, 1953), pp. 441–42.

5. Warner, pp. 297–99; Giraud, *Evasions*, pp. 142–44.
6. Kammerer, p. 106.
7. *Ibid.*
8. Giraud, *Evasions*, pp. 144–45.
9. René Chambe, "Weygand à l'heure d'Alger," *La revue des deux mondes*, 15 August 1965, p. 499.
10. FRUS (1942), 2: 293–94.
11. Based on Solborg Papers. See also Langer, pp. 277–80; Smith, pp. 47–48; Goodfellow Papers.
12. Crusoe, pp. 25–26; Girard, *Evasions*, pp. 147–58; Van Hecke, pp. 131–33.
13. The following account of Mast's activities is based mostly on Mast, pp. 20–34; see also Murphy, pp. 117–18.
14. Mast, pp. 29, 33.
15. Discussion of the Solborg mission is based on Crusoe; Chamine; Ordioni; Mast; Esquer; Langer; Van Hecke; but mostly on Solborg Papers. See also Murphy to Atherton, 6 July 1942, FRUS (1942), 2: 331–33.
16. Crusoe, p. 29. A copy of the original agreement is in the archives of the Comité d' histoire de la 2e guerre mondiale, Paris.
17. Text of the protocol in Chamine, pp. 416–19. Many aspects of the document were later confirmed by Murphy, FRUS (1942), 2: 414–17.
18. Solborg Papers.
19. *Ibid.* See also Langer, pp. 305–07; Smith, pp. 48–52. Solborg remained in military intelligence, later becoming military attaché at Lisbon.
20. Chambe, "Weygand à l'heure ... ," pp. 499–500.
21. Giraud, *Évasions*, pp. 148–151; Paxton, *Parades*, p. 295; Guy Salisbury-Jones, *So Full a Glory: A Life of Marshal de Lattre de Tassigny* (London, 1954), p. 105.
22. Giraud, *Evasions*, p. 150.
23. For American thinking about important Frenchmen, see *Washington/Casablanca*, p. 404 (Herriot), p. 816 (Léger, Monnet, Cambon), p. 819 (Le Brun); Langer, p. 165 (de la Laurencie), pp. 260–61 (Chautemps, Léger, Cot, Maritain); *France during the Occupation*, 2: 691 (Flandin); FRUS (1941), 2: 468 (General Georges). Former Ambassador William C. Bullitt was interested in rallying Herriot or Jeanneney: Bullitt to Roosevelt, 15 October 1942, in Orville H. Bullitt (ed.), *For the President, Personal and Secret* (Boston, 1972), pp. 563–64.
24. For Giraud's contacts, see Giraud, *Évasions*, p. 152; Chambe, "Weygand à l'heure ... ," pp. 500–1.
25. Giraud, *Evasions*, pp. 152–53.
26. Beaufre, p. 87.
27. For the response to Giraud's proposal, see Giraud, *Evasions*, p. 153; text of the proposal in Giraud, *Un seul but*, p. 335. MacArthur and

Cassady testimony in letters to the author (2 Sept., 19 Aug. 1969). Freeman Mathews, then in the American Embassy at Vichy, and Arthur Roseborough, the key officer in OSS, have written the writer they knew nothing of it. For a writer who asserts MacArthur brought the message, see Paillat, p. 336. The question remains unanswered. Perhaps Vichy or German intelligence invented a trap to ascertain Giraud's plans. See also, Arthur L. Funk, "Eisenhower, Giraud, and the Command of TORCH," *Military Affairs* (Oct. 1971), p. 104.

28. On Giraud's Grand Design, see Giraud, *Évasions*, p. 154; Beaufre, pp. 84–88; Marie-Madeleine Fourcade, *L'Arche de Noé* (Paris, 1968), pp. 274–78. De Gaulle was very critical of the Giraud plan: de Gaulle, pp. 316–17.

4. *The TORCH Decision*

1. Sherwood, pp. 554–79. See also Burns, pp. 231–38; Steele, pp. 115–42.
2. Sherwood, p. 562.
3. *Ibid.*, p. 569.
4. Churchill, p. 342 (italics in original).
5. Churchill to Roosevelt, 28 May 1942, Churchill, p. 340.
6. Detailed accounts can be found in Sherwood, pp. 580–614; Meyer, pp. 135–53; Matloff and Snell, pp. 217–93; Gwyer and Butler, pp. 601–38; Pogue, pp. 302–49; Churchill, pp. 326–51; *Washington/Casablanca*, pp. 419–83; Stimson, pp. 417–38; Steele, pp. 143–66.
7. *Washington/Casablanca*, p. 420.
8. Langer, pp. 275–76.
9. Stimson, p. 419.
10. Combined Chiefs of Staff, 19–21 June 1942, in *Washington/Casablanca*, p. 427.
11. *Ibid.*, p. 428.
12. Churchill, p. 382.
13. Sherwood, pp. 586–88 (italics added).
14. Churchill, p. 381.
15. *Ibid.*, p. 433. See also *The Memoirs of General Lord Ismay* (New York, 1960), p. 281: "Churchill not only conceived the idea, but pressed it so persistently that President Roosevelt overruled his advisers and agreed to its adoption."
16. Stimson, p. 425.
17. Bryant, pp. 407–8.
18. *Washington/Casablanca*, p. 435, 478–79.
19. *Ibid.*, p. 479.
20. *Ibid.*, p. 478.
21. Churchill, pp. 433–34; Sherwood, pp. 599–602; Gwyer and Butler, pp. 630–31; Bryant, pp. 418–21.
22. Clark, pp. 26–29.

23. Churchill, pp. 434–35.
24. Sherwood, pp. 602–6; Stimson, p. 425; Pogue, p. 341.
25. For detailed treatment, see Steele, pp. 167–79; Meyer, pp. 139–44; Pogue, pp. 341–49; Matloff and Snell, pp. 275–82; Howard, pp. xv-xxv.
26. Butcher, p. 29.
27. Eisenhower, p. 71.
28. Sherwood, pp. 610–11. See also Churchill, pp. 447–48; Butcher, pp. 29–30.
29. Pogue, pp. 344–46.
30. On de Gaulle's approach, see Clark, p. 29; Pogue, pp. 413–14; de Gaulle, p. 317; Smith, pp. 53–55.
31. De Gaulle, p. 317.
32. Sherwood, p. 611.
33. Matloff and Snell, p. 283.
34. Sherwood, pp. 611–12.
35. Butcher, p. 32
36. Churchill, pp. 447–51; Meyer, p. 143; Pogue, pp. 347–49.

5. *The Planners: Washington and London*

1. Smith, p. 51; Langer, pp. 307–08; Solborg Papers; Richard and Sérigny, pp. 50–51; S. Alsop and T. Braden, *Sub Rosa* (New York, 1964), p. 57.
2. FRUS (1942), 2: 343, 345, 349.
3. On the activities of The Five, see Crusoe, pp. 22–23; Van Hecke, p. 137; Mast, pp. 55–64.
4. These negotiations are covered in detail in Howard, pp. 111–39. A graphic account of planning evolution can be followed in Butcher, pp. 42–86, and in Eisenhower Papers, 1: 433–538.
5. Pogue, pp. 400–1. See also Lucien K. Truscott, *Command Missions: A Personal Story* (New York, 1954), pp. 25–48.
6. The place of Spain in allied maneuvers is a fascinating topic, but beyond the scope of this study. For a brief but competent summary, see Howard, pp. 159–67. See also Sir Samuel Hoare (Viscount Templewood), *Complacent Dictator* (New York, 1947), pp. 162–74; Carleton J. H. Hayes, *Wartime Mission in Spain* (New York, 1945), pp. 86–92; Sir Llewellyn Woodward, *British Foreign Policy in the Second World War*, 2: 354–55; Charles Burdick, *Germany's Military Strategy and Spain in World War II* (Syracuse, N.Y., 1968), pp. 155–66; Eisenhower Papers, 1: 433, 606, 619.
7. Eisenhower to Marshall, 15 Aug. 1942, Eisenhower Papers, 1: 470–71.
8. For Churchill in Moscow, see Churchill, pp. 477–99; A. H. Birse, *Memoirs of an Interpreter* (London, 1967), pp. 97–104; Eden, pp. 336–38; Lord Tedder, *With Prejudice* (London, 1966), pp. 318–39.

9. Eisenhower Papers, 1: 504.
10. Butcher, p. 97.
11. Although Roosevelt hoped the operation could develop before the 3 November congressional elections, he did not make an issue of it when 8 November was designated as D-Day (Pogue, p. 402; Clark p. 51).
12. *Public Opinion Quarterly* (Fall 1965): 400–410.
13. Lord Ismay received a copy of the Eddy report, which he sent on to Churchill on 27 August. The prime minister had seen it by 1 September (Premier 3/442. Public Record Office). Leahy, p. 112.
14. Handy to AGWAR, No. 1417, President's Map Room File, Roosevelt Library, Hyde Park.
15. Leahy, pp. 111–12.
16. Clark, pp. 46–47; Eisenhower Papers, 1: 499–500.
17. Churchill, pp. 530–31.
18. Marshall to Eisenhower, Map Room File, R 166, Roosevelt Library, Hyde Park. Parts published in Eisenhower Papers, 1: 513.
19. Churchill, pp. 531–43.
20. On 25 August, Eisenhower expressed this view to Captain Butcher (Eisenhower Papers, 1: 494, n.5). Cf. Butcher, p. 83.
21. Murphy, p. 102. On 4 September, Murphy drafted a memorandum summarizing the position of The Five (Langer, pp. 311–12). It is improbable that this memorandum influenced the president, as Langer believed (*ibid.*, p. 312 n.), to insist on American leadership. Roosevelt had arrived at this position at least a week earlier.
22. Langer, p. 310; Butcher, pp. 98–99.
23. Assisting in the draft was Edmond Taylor, who later headed the Psychological Warfare Section in Algiers. See Edmond Taylor, *Awakening from History* (London, 1971), pp. 253–54. Text in FRUS (1942), 2: 379–81.
24. Eisenhower Papers, 1: 563, n.1.
25. Murphy, p. 104.
26. Sir Llewellyn Woodward, *British Foreign Policy in the Second World War*, 2 (London, 1971): 351–52; Eisenhower Papers, 1: 444–47, 485, 582–83; Howe, pp. 54–55.
27. Eisenhower Papers, 1: 485.
28. Howard, pp. 144–46; Eden, pp. 392–99.
29. Langer, pp. 313–17; Smith, pp. 56–59. The authoritative British study of SOE (Special Operations Executive), M. R. D. Foot, *SOE in France* (London: H.M.S.O., 1966), does not, unfortunately, deal with the North African landings. British advocacy of Juin is referred to in a memo from Mark Clark to Eisenhower, 17 September 1942 (Clark Papers, The Citadel).
30. Eden, p. 398.
31. Howard, pp. 145–46.
32. Woodward, *British Foreign Policy*, 2: 353–56.

33. Eisenhower Papers, 2: 521–22, 554; Matthews Papers; interviews and correspondence of Matthews with the writer.
34. Letter of Matthews to author, 10 July 1971.
35. Eisenhower, pp. 85–88; Butcher, pp. 103–10; Murphy, pp. 103–5.
36. Murphy was recognized at Prestwick, Scotland, by one of the vice-consuls, Donald Coster, who, according to Murphy (p. 103) was arrested and "kept incommunicado until after the landings." This is not correct. Coster was being transferred to the air force and thereafter helped plan Operation TORCH in General Doolittle's headquarters in London. (Information from Mr. Coster's unpublished memoirs loaned to the writer.)
37. Murphy, p. 121. In September 1972 Mr. Murphy told the writer he believed Tunisia was to have been included in the landings.
38. Text in FRUS (1942), 2: 379–81. On military control and relationship with OSS, see Eisenhower Papers, 1: 562, 573–74. See also Robert Murphy, "Operation TORCH," *Foreign Service Journal* (November, 1967), p. 29.
39. Butcher, p. 106.
40. Eisenhower to Marshall, 19 September 1942. Eisenhower Papers, 1: 562–63.
41. Murphy, p. 104.
42. A detailed description of the planning, fascinating though it is, lies beyond the scope of this study. For details, see especially the day-by-day record in Butcher and the Eisenhower Papers; see also Howe; Pogue; Clark. General Clark's Diary (loaned to the writer) has much information. See also the special study by Frierson.
43. Frierson, p. 2.
44. On Patton's participation in TORCH, see Ladislas Farago, *Patton: Ordeal and Triumph* (New York, 1964); Truscott, *Command Missions*; Morison.
45. Butcher (entry for 15 October), pp. 143–44. See also Howe, pp. 54–55.
46. Directive of 11 October, 381 TORCH, Sec. 1, OPD Files (National Archives). Excerpt in Coles and Weinberg, p. 33.
47. A proclamation, to be broadcast and disseminated in North Africa, was being drafted in TORCH headquarters. Memo, Clark to Eisenhower, 28 September 1942 (Clark Papers); Eden, p. 398; Eisenhower Papers, 1: 615–16; James M. Erdmann, *Leaflet Operations in the Second World War* (privately printed, 1969), pp. 82–84.
48. Woodward, *British Foreign Policy in the Second World War*, 2: 357–58.
49. 381 TORCH, Sec. 1, OPD Files (National Archives). Excerpt in Coles and Weinberg, pp. 33–34.
50. The complete text is printed as an appendix to this volume. A French as well as an English text was produced. In the French version, Article 11 is quite different: it states that the French authorities

will do everything in their power to maintain law and order and to safeguard the security of Allied forces. A summary of the terms in Kammerer (p. 374) gives the reading of the French version. This was apparently the summary sent by Darlan to Vichy; it is not completely accurate. On 18 October, Eisenhower's headquarters issued Operations Memorandum No. 23, "Explanatory Notes on Armistice Terms," giving the assault commander leeway regarding the use of the documents. CCS 381, Sec. 1A (National Archives).
51. On 13 October, Marshall wrote Eisenhower: "The only statement of American policy desired by the President is the defeat of the Axis Powers and the preservation of French administration in the colonies. The President does not want to make any statement of policy which would involve an attitude, either favorable or unfavorable, towards the Vichy government. He wants the Axis kicked out of the area and wishes to insure that the colonies be administered by the French." A copy of this letter is among Churchill's personal papers. It was sent to the Prime Minister by Ismay on 18 October (PM 3, 442, PRO). See Butcher, p. 142.
52. Eisenhower to Marshall, 15 August 1942, Eisenhower Papers, 1: 471. The same feeling is voiced again on 12 October (*ibid.*, p. 544).

6. *The Planners: France and Algiers*

1. Darlan, p. 161.
2. Murphy to the writer, 24 February 1970. See also Murphy, p. 112; Pendar, p. 90.
3. Crusoe, p. 32; FRUS (1942), 2: 390. Murphy brought back with him five radio transmitters and a sten gun (Murphy, pp. 107–8). Murphy arrived in Algiers on 11 October, not 16 October as he states in his memoirs (p. 118). He treats the crucial period 11–21 October with great brevity.
4. The following account is based largely on General Chrétien's unpublished memoirs, loaned to the writer. See also Van Hecke, pp. 135–41; Kammerer, pp. 208–9.
5. FRUS (1942), 2: 392–93. Michael Howard goes too far in suggesting that Darlan was prepared to come to North Africa with the French fleet (Howard, pp. 153–55). There was no clear-cut proposal. See Murphy's commentary in Paillat, p. 384, n. 16. Darlan simply wished to maintain contact in view of some future Allied action which he did not believe could develop before 1943.
6. Details of the Murphy-Dorange meeting are from Dorange's report, printed in Kammerer, pp. 641–45. (See also Paillat, pp. 387–91.) The writer has verified the printed text against a photostat of the handwritten copy. For Murphy's report of this encounter, see FRUS (1942), 2: 398–400. Further verification is available in the film of Roger Stéphane, "Une certaine idée de la France," made for French

television in 1967. This documentary includes many interviews with wartime resistance leaders and is an invaluable historical record.

7. Department of State *Bulletin* (18 April 1942), pp. 335–36. Roosevelt had already promised Weygand he would respect the integrity of France and her empire (*Washington/Casablanca*, pp. 235–36).
8. Paillat publishes (p. 391, n. 17) a letter from Murphy in which the diplomat doubted he would have said that the United States would treat only with the French government. Looking back, Dorange in 1967 wrote: "I am astonished at the confidence I myself demonstrated toward Murphy, whose loyalty I did not doubt one single instant" (letter to Messrs. Calvet and Montaigne, 16 November 1967, copy in possession of author).
9. Kammerer, pp. 645.
10. Beaufre, pp. 91–93; Marie-Madeleine Fourcade, *L'Arche de Noé* (Paris, 1968), pp. 274–77; Kammerer, pp. 210–15, 645–47; Van Hecke, pp. 138–42; Mast, pp. 63–66.
11. Mast, pp. 67–69; Crusoe, pp. 115–16. Plans published as appendix in Mast, pp. 369–71.
12. FRUS (1942), 2: 394.
13. *Ibid.*
14. See A. L. Funk, "Eisenhower, Giraud, and the Command of TORCH," *Military Affairs* (October 1971), pp. 103–8.
15. FRUS (1942), 2: 395–96.
16. FRUS (1942), 2: 416. See also Crusoe, p. 116; Van Hecke, p. 143.
17. Burns, p. 130.
18. Samuel I. Rosenman, ed., *The Public Papers and Addresses of Franklin D. Roosevelt, 1942* (New York, 1950), pp. 228–29.
19. Butcher, p. 142.
20. *Washington/Casablanca*, p. 514.
21. Crusoe, p. 116. See also Van Hecke, p. 143. A version was transmitted in Clark's report to Marshall, 30 October 1942 (Clark Papers).
22. Clark, pp. 66–68; Clark Diary.
23. Eisenhower to Marshall, 17 October 1942, Eisenhower Papers, 1: 622–24.
24. Clark, p. 71.
25. Eden, pp. 344–45.
26. Eisenhower Papers, 1: 625–26. In spite of the importance of this conference, there is no mention of it in Churchill's memoirs; nor, in spite of diligent searching by archivists in charge of the Premier records, could minutes be found at 10 Downing Street.
27. FRUS (1942), 2: 397.
28. Murphy, p. 118.
29. FRUS (1942), 2: 397.
30. Clark, pp. 68–79; Clark Diary; Jewell, pp. 1–23.

31. FRUS (1942), 2: 380, 414–17; *Washington/Casablanca*, p. 820; Crusoe, pp. 29–34.
32. FRUS (1942), 2: 380.

7. *General Clark's Secret Mission*

1. The conference has been very well documented. Clark's first report to Eisenhower and Clark's later recollections are available (Clark, pp. 67–89), together with his official dispatch of 30 October (Clark Papers). What Clark told Eisenhower is recorded in Butcher, pp. 152–56. See also Murphy, pp. 118–20, as well as his "Operation TORCH," written for the *Foreign Service Journal* (November 1967). Julius Holmes has some brief references in "Eisenhower's African Gamble," *Collier's* (12 January 1946).

The official French account, drawn up by Rigault and sent to Giraud, is in Kammerer, pp. 650–54. General Mast gives his reactions in an article, "L'entrevue de Cherchell," *Miroir de l'histoire* (May 1954) and in Mast, pp. 70–88. (An abbreviated version of this account came out in *Historia*, No. 43, 12 September 1968.) Jousse gives some comments in "La libération de l'Afrique du Nord." Another participant, Captain Barjot, has written memoirs (see Barjot). Other accounts with information from participants can be found in Chamine, pp. 205–30; Crusoe, pp. 35–40.

A number of those who participated in the rendezvous, but not in the negotiations, have given accounts of the adventure aspect; Jewell, pp. 1–47; G. B. Courtney, "General Clark's Secret Mission," *Life* (28 December 1942), with interesting sketches; Richard Livingstone, "Mark Clark's Secret Landing," *History of the Second World War* (periodical), vol. 3, no. 11 (n.d.); Ridgway Knight, "General Clark's Secret Mission to Algeria," *Foreign Service Journal* (March 1943); Jacques Queyrat and Bernard Karsenty wrote up accounts for *Les cahiers français*, no. 47, published in London, August 1943.

Several journalists have written about Cherchell, using material from Clark and other participants: Demaree Bess, "The Backstage Story of Our African Adventure," *Saturday Evening Post* (3 July 1943); Wes Gallagher, *Back Door to Berlin* (N.Y., 1943); Gosset; John MacVane, *Journey into War* (New York, 1943); Frederick Painton, "Secret Mission to North Africa," *Reader's Digest* (May 1943); Melvin K. Whiteleather, *Main Street's New Neighbors* (New York, 1945) pp. 136–44.

Except as indicated, my account is based on these materials together with impressions gathered from interviewing General Clark, General Mast, Robert Murphy, Julius Holmes, Ridgway Knight, Lemaigre Dubreuil, and Bernard Karsenty.

2. Pogue, p. 418. Marshall later considered that the levity had been overdone (*ibid.*, p. 483, n. 37).
3. Eden, p. 398.
4. Churchill, p. 538.
5. Leahy, p. 133. See also FRUS (1942), 2: 189. Darlan refers to his comments in a letter to Leahy dated 27 November 1942: Leahy, p. 485. See also Darlan, p. 161, in which the date of the conversation is given as April 1942.
6. Butcher, p. 155.
7. The emphasis Mast placed on Giraud's leadership does not come out in his own memoirs (see Mast, p. 78), but it does in Clark's dispatch to Marshall and in Clark's diary.
8. Details in Clark Papers. Murphy has written (Murphy, p. 126): "Eddy and I were later convinced that British SOE let us down because they had no confidence in our judgment or our French underground." John Knox (one of the vice-consuls sent to London to help with planning) told the writer in November 1972 that Mockler-Ferryman admitted as much. On the other hand, Bernard Karsenty and José Aboulker have told the writer, also in November 1972, that they learned, after the war, that the shipments had been sent, but to the wrong rendezvous.
9. Mast, pp. 83–84.
10. Clark to Commander in Chief, 30 October 1942 (Clark Papers).
11. Eisenhower Papers, 1: 625–26. See chap. 6, n. 23.
12. FRUS (1942), 2: 266–271. The plan submitted at the Cherchell conference, somewhat modified, is in Kammerer, pp. 647–50.
13. Dartois's comments from Clark Diary.
14. Clark Diary.
15. Clark Diary. See also Langer, p. 330; Painton, "Secret Mission."
16. Clark, p. 88.
17. Murphy, "Operation TORCH," p. 31.
18. Livingstone, "Mark Clark's Secret Landing."
19. Clark, pp. 83–84.
20. Livingstone, "Mark Clark's Secret Landing."
21. Clark, p. 84.
22. *Ibid.*, pp. 86–87.
23. An interesting exhibit on General Clark's mission can be seen at the Citadel Museum in Charleston, S.C. After the war, when General Clark learned that the *Seraph* (P-219) was to be scrapped, he salvaged from it the conning tower and main hatch. These have now been made into a monument on The Citadel grounds.
24. Beaufre, p. 94.
25. Richard and Sérigny, pp. 56–57.
26. Interview with Clark, October, 1971.
27. Lemaigre Dubreuil, *La rentrée en guerre de la France africaine* (privately printed June 1943), pp. 26–32; Beaufre, pp. 95–96; Giraud,

Un seul but, p. 17; Marie-Madeleine Fourcade, *L'Arche de Noé* (Paris, 1968), pp. 282–84.
28. FRUS (1942), 2: 405.
29. For Operation MINERVA, on the Allied side: Jewell, pp. 48–83, and Capt. Jerauld Wright's report, 7 December 1942 (Clark Papers); on the French side, Fourcade, *L'Arche de Noé,* pp. 274–90; Beaufre, pp. 95–117.
30. Kammerer, p. 652.
31. FRUS (1942), 2: 420, 422. French version in Kammerer, pp. 654–56.

8. Last Minute Preparations

1. The best sources for the resistance plot are Aboulker, Jousse, and Van Hecke. Some details from participants can be found in Barjot, Crusoe, Mast, Murphy, and Pendar. Secondary works whose authors received information from participants include Chamine, Esquer, Gosset, Kammerer, Price, Richard and Sérigny. Of later accounts, those of Danan and Paillat are useful. The author has interviewed or corresponded with several of the participants: José Aboulker, Colonel Chrétien, Abbé Cordier, Bernard Karsenty, Jacques Lemaigre Dubreuil, General Mast, Bernard Pauphilet.
2. Esquer, pp. 98–99.
3. Eisenhower to Murphy, 27 October 1942, FRUS (1942) 2: 406.
4. Murphy to Eisenhower, 27 October 1942, President's Map Room Papers, Franklin D. Roosevelt Library, Hyde Park, New York.
5. Eisenhower to AGWAR, 28 October 1942, No. 4181, OPD Exec 1, Item 9, Rec. Group 165, National Archives, Washington, D.C.
6. According to Mast (p. 106), Murphy told him, on 28 October, "I am authorized to tell you that the operation will take place on November 8." As he was only authorized to reveal the date four days in advance, Murphy probably was not so explicit. Murphy recalls: "I really don't remember the exact date of my first visit to Mast on this subject. It seems to me that I used the 'quelques jours' formula. Maybe I added 'early in November'" (letter to writer, 11 December 1969). On 31 October, Murphy cabled Eisenhower: "In accordance with your authorization Flagpole [Mast] has been informed that operation is imminent and set for early November. He has also been informed regarding submarine under Capt. Wright's command. . . . I urged that Kingpin [Giraud] arrange to depart November 4 at latest. Flagpole said he thought this would be possible. I realize that this is rather close indication of date but at this stage in view of the delicate business of getting Kingpin over here there seemed no other course" (President's Map Room Papers, Roosevelt Library, Hyde Park, N.Y.).
7. Henri Ballande, *De l'amirauté à Bikini* (Paris, 1972), p. 165.

8. Unpublished memoirs of General Chrétien.
9. Report of conversation at Rabat, 24 October 1942, German captured records, T-77, Roll 851 (National Archives). See Walter Warlimont, "The Decision in the Mediterranean 1942," *Decisive Battles of World War II*, edited by H. A. Jacobsen and J. Rohwer (New York, 1965), pp. 205–6.
10. Vulliez, pp. 78–81; Ballande, *De l'amirauté à Bikini*, pp. 162–68; Darlan, pp. 169–70; FRUS (1942), 2: 426–29.
11. Lemaigre Dubreuil to Murphy, 2 November 1942, in Crusoe, pp. 121–23; Robert Murphy, "Operation TORCH," *Foreign Service Journal* (November 1967), p. 31.
12. FRUS (1942), 2: 409–10; Murphy, p. 121.
13. Eisenhower to Marshall, 12 October 1942, Eisenhower Papers, 1: 544.
14. Clark, p. 92.
15. Leahy to Murphy, 2 November 1942, FRUS (1942), 2: 423.
16. Kammerer, p. 226.
17. FRUS (1942), 2: 412–19.
18. Richard and Sérigny, p. 71.
19. Unpublished memoirs of General Chrétien.
20. FRUS (1942), 2: 425. In his memoirs Murphy says that Juin "had been ruled out because he had given his word of honor . . . not to fight against Germans" (Murphy, p. 127). Churchill apparently confuses Juin and Mast (Churchill, p. 611). For Mast's reasoning in advising Murphy to avoid Juin, see Mast, pp. 113–14.
21. For French versions of Giraud's escape from France, see Giraud, *Un seul but*, pp. 18–22; Beaufre, pp. 100–05; Beaufre's version is given in English as "General Giraud's Escape," in *History of the Second World War*, vol. 3, no. 11 (1967). On the Allied side, basic is Captain Gerauld Wright's report on Operation MINERVA (Clark Papers, The Citadel), and the account in Jewell, pp. 48–68; also FRUS (1942), 2: 426.
22. Eisenhower to Marshall, 29 October, 1942, Eisenhower Papers, 1: 643; Clark Diary; Butcher, pp. 157–58.
23. Detailed report of the "Catalina Incident" in Premier 3/439/17, PRO. German record in *Kriegstagebuch der Seekriegsleitung*, 1 Abt., Teil A, Heft 37, 565:28.9.42 (microfilm, Captured German Documents, National Archives, Washington, D.C.). See also Bryant, pp. 508–9; Clark, p. 52; Butcher, p. 104. This incident was the prototype of the deception identified as Operation MINCEMEAT, described in Ewen S. Montagu, *The Man Who Never Was* (London, 1953). See also A. L. Funk, "TORCH: Les opérations de diversion alliées et les renseignements de l'Axe," *Revue historique de l'Armée* (no. 4, 1973), pp. 78–87.
24. Walter Warlimont, "The Decision in the Mediterranean, 1942," *Decisive Battles of World War II* (New York, 1965); A Hillgruber, "La politique et la stratégie de Hitler dans le bassin méditerréen," *La*

guerre en Méditerrannée, 1939-1945 (Paris, 1971); Walter Ansel, *Hitler and the Middle Sea* (Durham, N.C., 1972); *Kriegstagebuch des Oberkommandos der Wehrmacht,* edited by A. Hillgruber (Frankfort-am-Main, 1963): 901, 902, 912, 916, 918.
25. S. W. Roskill, *The War at Sea, 1939-1945,* 2 (London, H. M. Stationery Office, 1956): 320; Warlimont, "The Decision . . ." p. 208.
26. Eisenhower Papers, 1: 656–57. See also pp. 654–55 and notes, p. 658.
27. Murphy, pp. 125–26; Beaufre, pp. 115–24; Eisenhower, p. 99; Jewell, pp. 80–83; Clark, pp. 95–97; Butcher, pp. 163–71.
28. Eisenhower to Combined Chiefs, 8 November 1942, Eisenhower Papers, 2: 670–72.
29. Van Hecke, pp. 162–74. General de la Porte du Theil had information about the Algiers Conspiracy (Ordioni, p. 386).
30. Mast, pp. 116–29.
31. The intelligence report has been published: "La situation militaire à la fin de 1941," in *Bulletin de l'Amicale des Anciens Membres de Services Spéciaux de la Défense Nationale,* no. 16 (October-November 1957), pp. 16–25. Mast, pp. 21–24. Interview of author with Mme. Baril.
32. Butcher, p. 165; Clark Diary; Murphy file, National Archives, Washington, D.C.
33. Pendar, pp. 97–100; General Béthouart, *Cinq années d'éspérance: Mémoires de guerre, 1939-1945* (Paris, 1968), pp. 128–33.
34. Kammerer, pp. 118, 195–96.
35. The conclusions of Henri Michel, in his "Darlan et le débarquement allié en A.F.N.," *Cahiers d'histoire de la guerre* (January 1949), that Darlan's trip was only to see his son, are still valid. Peter Tompkins, in *The Murder of Admiral Darlan* (New York, 1965), pp. 57–66, tires to invoke a conspiracy theory, but he has no evidence unknown to Michel.
36. Kammerer, pp. 192–94; Moreau Papers.
37. De Beaufort was to receive ten million francs from the American Embassy, but the money arrived too late. Eisenhower Papers, 2: 672, 673 n. 5.
38. Bergeret's personal testimony in Chambe, *Le Maréchal Juin . . .* (Paris, 1968), pp. 282–83. See also Marie-Madeleine Fourcade, *L'Arche de Noé* (Paris, 1968), pp. 282–83.
39. Details in this chapter and in chapter nine mostly from Aboulker, Barjot, Chamine, Esquer, and Jousse.
40. Giraud, *Un seul but,* p. 347.

9. *The Algiers Landing—8 November 1942*

1. Mast, pp. 115–35.
2. Concerning this visit Murphy has provided several accounts: Langer, pp. 345–48; Murphy, pp. 127–31; Robert Murphy, "Operation

TORCH," *Foreign Service Journal* (November 1967), p. 53. Juin glosses over the event in his memoirs (Juin, pp. 75–88); see Schmitt's review of this book in *Revue d'histoire de la 2ᵉ guerre mondiale* (October 1961), pp. 60–61. Darlan made some brief notes (Darlan, pp. 188–94). Bernard Pauphilet, who took over the guard, has made available to the writer a twenty-page account he wrote in 1945. The author has also used Colonel Chrétien's unpublished account. See also José Aboulker, "Nous, qui avons arrêté le général Juin, *La Nef* (April 1959), pp. 14–19; Pendar, pp. 104–11; Chamine, pp. 288–346; Kammerer, pp. 257–68; Mast, pp. 134–35. Mast's allegation (p. 149) that Murphy acted imprudently must be judged against the fact that Murphy accepted the advice of The Five and that Mast was not available.
3. Personal papers of Bernard Pauphilet.
4. Murphy, p. 129.
5. Unpublished account of Bernard Pauphilet.
6. Murphy, p. 129.
7. Kammerer, pp. 264–65; Moreau Papers. The insurgents were not able to enter the Winter Palace, and the duty officer there had alerted both the Admiralty and Admiral Moreau's headquarters at the Hotel St.-Georges around 1:30 A.M. As the insurgents had not been able to cut the navy's telephone lines, communication was maintained between the St.-Georges, the Winter Palace, the Admiralty, and with Vichy. By 2:00 A.M. Vichy had been alerted and gun crews of coastal batteries were at their posts.
8. Esquer, pp. 104–6; "Rapport du Sous-Lieutenant M. H. Faivre (MARIO), adjoint au capitaine Pillafort, dans la préparation et l'exécution du putsch des 7 et 8 novembre 1942," *Afrique*, no. 201 (March 1945), pp. 34–39.
9. "L'action du groupe des Bretons à Alger," *Revue de la France Libre* (June 1956), pp. 45–49.
10. Based principally on Howe, pp. 229–49; Playfair, pp. 137–46.
11. Report on Landing Operations, Third Battalion, 39th Infantry, 16 Nov. 1942 (18 pp., typed); Critique of Landing Operation, First Battalion, Combat Team 39, 16 Dec. 1942 (12 pp., typed); Regimental History, 39th Infantry Regiment, 23 Oct. 1943 (9 pp., typed). Washington (D.C.) National Records Center.
12. Mast, pp. 135–46. On 31 October Murphy had wired Eisenhower: "Friendly reception at Sidi-Ferruch. Battery with Mast. Don't start firing there" (RC 36, President's Map Room Papers, Roosevelt Library, Hyde Park, N.Y.). See also Company reports, 168th Infantry Regiment, 17 Nov.–23 Dec. 1942 (27 pp., typed), Washington National Records Center; testimony of French legionnaire Capt. Lindsay Watson in Price, pp. 127–29. The correspondent, William H. Stoneman, recalled thirty years later his efforts, as "front man" for Colonel Trevor, to persuade the French that there were indeed Americans

who were landing (featured story of *Chicago Daily News* service, 8 November 1972).
13. Playfair, pp. 143–44.
14. Pendar, p. 106.
15. Darlan, p. 193. Other texts of this message, with slight variations, in Chamine, p. 341; Kammerer, p. 262.
16. Moreau Papers.
17. Pendar, p. 108.
18. Kammerer, pp. 266–67.
19. Pauphilet account, made available to writer.
20. Pendar, pp. 108–9.
21. Darlan, p. 194.
22. Paillat, p. 45.
23. Pendar, p. 112; Murphy, pp. 131–32.
24. FRUS (1942), 2: 430–41; Kammerer, p. 267.
25. Aboulker, pp. 26–28; "Rapport du Sous-Lieutenant M. H. Faivre . . . ," *Afrique* (March 1945), pp. 36–37; Juin, pp. 78–82.
26. Kammerer, p. 269.
27. *Ibid*. Kammerer and most anti-Darlan writers consider Darlan's message as pro-Axis and not as a judicious attempt (this writer's interpretation) to straddle a difficult issue. For German suspicions of French actions, see Warner, p. 326.
28. "Rapport du Sous-Lieutenant M. H. Faivre . . . ," *Afrique* (March 1945), pp. 34–37.
29. Maj. L. W. Bailey, "The Operations of the 3rd Battalion, 135th Infantry, at Algiers," Typewritten report prepared in 1948 at the Infantry School, Fort Benning, Ga. (in Infantry School Library, Fort Benning). See also Morison, pp. 207–8; Playfair, pp. 143–44; Howe, pp. 241–44.
30. Howe, pp. 238–41; Juin, pp. 83–84; Mast, pp. 148–49; Price, pp. 125–32; Gen. Charles Ryder, "Brief Report of Operations of Eastern Assault Force, 19 November 1942," National Archives.
31. Kammerer, pp. 273–74.
32. Murphy, pp. 132–33; Kammerer, pp. 275–79; Pendar, pp. 112–16; Juin, pp. 85–86; Howe, p. 252.
33. Based on Eisenhower, pp. 99–103; Clark, pp. 96–102; Eisenhower Papers, 2: 669–80; Beaufre, pp. 118–30; Giraud, *Un seul but*, pp. 22–27.
34. Eisenhower Papers, 2: 675.
35. Butcher, p. 171.
36. Eisenhower to Marshall, 9 November 1942, Eisenhower Papers, 2: 680.
37. Darryl F. Zanuck, *Tunis Expedition* (New York, 1943), pp. 32–33.
38. Beaufre, p. 130.
39. Butcher, p. 178a.
40. Eisenhower to Giraud, 9 November 1942, Eisenhower Papers, 2: 682.

10. *Negotiating with Darlan*

1. Kammerer, pp. 280–82; Murphy, pp. 133–34.
2. Darlan, p. 196; Kammerer, pp. 370–72.
3. Beaufre, pp. 131–35. Murphy's description of his first encounter with Giraud (Murphy, p. 136) presumably refers to a later, calmer, meeting.
4. Giraud, *Un seul but*, pp. 33–37; Beaufre, pp. 135–43; Mast, p. 283; Van Hecke, p. 172.
5. Darlan, pp. 302–15; Clark, p. 104; Daryl F. Zanuck, *Tunis Expedition* (New York, 1943), pp. 38–42; Murphy, p. 136.
6. Darlan, p. 197; Kammerer, pp. 374–76; Schmitt, p. 173; Dhers, pp. 123, 141–51; Warner, pp. 329–30; Moreau Papers. The personal code was extremely simple, consisting of duplicate dictionaries in which the page and line were indicated. (Information from interviews of Alain Darlan and Admiral Auphan.)
7. Beaufre, pp. 136–52; Mast, p. 284; Juin, p. 90; Murphy, p. 158; Clark telegram of 10 November, quoted in Clark, *Events*, p. 13.
8. At this time fewer than 4,000 men were ashore, and few tanks. Clark had to bluff (Julius C. Holmes, "Eisenhower's African Gamble," *Collier's*, 12 January 1946), but he could if necessary call in an aerial and naval bombardment which would have destroyed Algiers. Mast's arguments (Mast, pp. 261–76) that without French cooperation the operation would have failed overlooks the overwhelming superiority of the Allied navy and air forces.
9. Juin felt strongly about his role in the negotiations. In reviewing Clark's memoirs, *Calculated Risk*, he wrote to Clark in 1948: "Dans cet épisode il ne faut pas oublier de mentionner que c'est moi, Général Juin, qui à un moment donné vous ai prie de sortir avec Murphy, pour faire une scène à Darlan, et le déterminer à donner des ordres de cessation du feu, ce que j'obtiens du reste" (Clark Papers, The Citadel, Charleston, S.C.). See also Juin, pp. 92–94.
10. Verbatim text in Clark, *Events*, pp. 8–12 (part of which is duplicated in Clark, pp. 109–12) and in Darlan, pp. 201–13. See also Juin, p. 95; Murphy, p. 137; Kammerer, pp. 390–94.
11. Admiral de Laborde, commander of the French High Seas Fleet at Toulon, was senior in grade to Darlan, and more anti-Gaullist and anti-British even than Darlan. Immediately prior to the TORCH landings, de Laborde had been conferring in Paris with German authorities about an anti-Gaullist expedition. The day de Laborde returned to Toulon, on 7 November, the Admiralty at Vichy imposed an alert because of the Allied fleet sailing eastward from Gibraltar. When de Laborde learned that the Allies were landing, he immediately phoned Vichy for permission to attack the Allied convoy; when his request was refused he became furious at having to put up with the aggressions of the Anglo-Saxons "who for two years have inflicted bloody humiliations on our flag" (Vulliez, p. 101). De

Laborde received news of Darlan's cease-fire order over the radio, and also of Pétain's "resist all aggressors" order. In the afternoon of 10 November the Vichy Admiralty ordered de Laborde to disregard any orders emanating from Algiers, "neutralized by the Americans." The Toulon fleet episode is a complex story. See Vulliez; Albert Kammerer, *La passion de la flotte française* (Paris, 1951); Henri Noguères, *Le suicide de la flotte française à Toulon* (Paris, 1963); Jacques Mordal, *La marine à l'epreuve* (Paris, 1961), chap. 9.

12. Darlan, pp. 203–5. See also discussion in Warner, pp. 330–32.
13. Clark to Eisenhower, 10 November 1942, in Clarks, *Events*, pp. 15–16. This cable, not heretofore published, clarifies events at this point. See also Kammerer, pp. 415–16; Clark, pp. 113–14.
14. Beaufre, pp. 151–55; Crusoe, p. 59; Juin, pp. 96–97; Kammerer, p. 440; Mast, pp. 285–87. Eisenhower sent Clark a strong telegram on 10 November urging Giraud to "move speedily and effectively" (Eisenhower Papers, 2: 683–84).
15. Warner, pp. 334–38; Kammerer, pp. 426–35; Gen. G. Schmitt, "La matinée du 11 novembre 1942 à Vichy," *Revue d'histoire de la 2e guerre mondiale* (October 1962), pp. 77–80; Darlan, p. 206; Juin, p. 97.
16. Howe, pp. 171–81; Morison, pp. 161–65; Jacques Mordal, *La bataille de Casablanca* (Paris, 1952), pp. 255–62.
17. The account of negotiations in Algiers is based heavily on Schmitt; Dhers; Clark, *Events*; and Clark Papers.
18. During the evening of 10 November, Clark had argued with Darlan about rallying the fleet, which Clark was led to believe was standing by outside Toulon. Darlan said he would direct the fleet to join the Allies when the Germans entered France (Clark, *Events*, p. 18). That night Darlan sent de Laborde a telegram inviting him to rally to Algiers if the armistice was broken. As the authenticator was missing, de Laborde assumed the message to be not genuine and he disregarded it (Vulliez, p. 123). Cf. Kammerer, pp. 394–95.
19. Clark to Eisenhower, evening of 11 November, Clark, *Events*, pp. 23–24. Darlan's "invitation" in Kammerer, p. 447.
20. Eisenhower to Clark, 11 November 1942, Eisenhower Papers, 2: 698–99.
21. Kammerer, pp. 450–54.
22. Clark to Eisenhower, 12 November, Clark, *Events*, pp. 35–36. Clark gives some verbatim sequences of this "stormy session" in his memoirs (Clark, pp. 117–19), details of which are more extensive in Clark, *Events*, pp. 26–34.
23. Eisenhower to Clark, 11 November, Clark, *Events*, p. 38.
24. Kammerer, pp. 472–73; Admiral Auphan *Les grimaces de l'histoire: histoire de mes trahisons* (Paris, 1951), pp. 288–89. On 14 November, Eisenhower wrote the Combined Chiefs: "we are convinced that

Darlan is making a determined effort to get that fleet . . ." (Eisenhower Papers, 2: 709).
25. Clark, pp. 119–20; Clark, *Events*, pp. 39–40; Clark Diary; Juin, pp. 103–6; Mast, p. 290; Beaufre, pp. 157–58; Moreau Papers. Zanuck, *Tunis Expedition*, pp. 56–61 (erroneously describing meeting as 10 November). On Eisenhower's intention to visit Algiers: Eisenhower Papers, 2: 705–6.
26. Kammerer, pp. 475–76; Dhers, p. 159; Moreau Papers.
27. Clark, *Events*, pp. 41–43. See also Clark, pp. 121–23; Eisenhower Papers, 2: 706–7; Eisenhower, pp. 108–9; Butcher, pp. 190–92; Juin, pp. 107–9; Beaufre, pp. 159–62; Murphy, pp. 139–40; Howe, pp. 269–71.
28. Clark, *Events*, p. 45; Darlan, pp. 207–8; Mast, pp. 290–94; Warner, pp. 344–46; Dhers, pp. 163–68; Schmitt, pp. 175–78; Juin, p. 108; Kammerer, pp. 484–86. Kammerer concludes that Pétain secretly favored the landing, but the minute researches of Dhers and Schmitt have conclusively upset this interpretation. It is possible, however, that Darlan sincerely believed the telegram provided Pétain's sanction.

11. *The Clark-Darlan Agreement*

1. Churchill, pp. 631–32; De Gaulle, pp. 356–57; Soustelle II, pp. 19–20; Eden, pp. 403–4; Burns, pp. 295–96; Funk, pp. 43–46.
2. Eisenhower to Combined Chiefs, 14 November 1942, Eisenhower Papers, 2: 707–10.
3. Churchill, p. 632. See also Eden, pp. 403–6; PM 3/442, War Cabinet Meeting of 16 November 1942 (Public Record Office); Howard, pp. 175–77.
4. John Morton Blum, *From the Morgenthau Diaries* (New York, 1967), p. 149.
5. S. Rosenman, ed., *The Public Papers and Addresses of Franklin D. Roosevelt*, 1942 (New York, 1950): 479. See also *The Memoirs of Cordell Hull*, 2 (New York, 1948), 1199–1200; FRUS (1942), 2: 445–46; Sherwood, p. 653; Burns, pp. 297–98.
6. Eisenhower to Smith, 18 November 1942, Eisenhower Papers, 2: 732–35; Pogue, pp. 420–21; Stimson, p. 543; Leahy, pp. 134–35. British commanders did not object. Brooke wrote in his diary for 15 November regarding Darlan's taking charge: "P.M. for it. . . . In any case no alternative at present" (Bryant, p. 522). Admiral Cunningham advised the Admiralty on 22 December: "Unless we have some better and more acceptable man to put in his place, I feel we should grasp the nettle and make a declaration of some sort which will show we are backing him" (PM 3, 442, Public Record Office).
7. Roosevelt to Marshall, 2 June 1944, quoted in Forrest C. Pogue,

George C. Marshall, vol. 3, *Organizer of Victory* (New York, 1973), pp. 398–99.
8. Gabriel Kolko, *The Politics of War: The World and United States Foreign Policy, 1943–1945* (New York, 1968), pp. 64–75. For other commentaries on Roosevelt policy see Burns, pp. 286–87, 302, 359–61, 481; Robert A. Divine, *Roosevelt and World War II* (Baltimore, 1969); William L. Neumann, *After Victory: Churchill, Roosevelt, Stalin and the Making of the Peace* (New York, 1967), pp. 52–70; Raymond G. O'Connor, *Diplomacy for Victory* (New York, 1971), pp. 31–104; John L. Gaddis, *The United States and the Origins of the Cold War* (New York, 1972), pp. 1–173; John L. Snell, *Illusion and Necessity* (Boston, 1963), pp. 106–44.
9. Langer, pp. 386–98. Langer saw the policy regarding North Africa as "an unqualified success" and "in the last analysis pretty much beyond controversy" (p. 395). The classic rebuttal to Langer's thesis was Louis Gottschalk's "Our Vichy Fumble," *Journal of Modern History* (March 1948), pp. 47–56. Emphasizing the North African aspect of the Vichy policy misses the point that Anglo-American forces could have occupied Morocco and Algeria even if relations with Vichy had been broken. Darlan's cooperation is quite unrelated to the fact that the United States maintained diplomatic relations with France during the period 1940–42.
10. De Gaulle, pp. 363–81; André Kaspi, *La mission de Jean Monnet à Alger* (Paris, 1971), pp. 25–37.
11. On British support of the French Resistance, see M. R. D. Foot, *SOE in France* (London, 1966), pp. 220–22.
12. Smith, chap. 4; F. W. Deakin, *The Brutal Friendship* (London, 1962), p. 112. It should be noted that British SOE representatives were still working with Mihailovic rather than Tito, and in any case then controlled but meager resources for the eastern Mediterranean. See Howard, pp. 389–91.
13. Stalin to Roosevelt, 14 December 1942. *Stalin's Correspondence with Roosevelt and Truman, 1941–1945* (New York, 1958), p. 44.
14. Funk, p. 42.
15. Walter Lippmann, "Today and Tomorrow," syndicated feature, 19 January 1943.
16. For Darlan's forty-day "reign," see Danan, pp. 129–60; Langer, pp. 365–81; Butcher, pp. 198–226; Coles and Weinberg, pp. 34–48; Julius C. Holmes, "Eisenhower's African Gamble," *Collier's* (19 January 1946); Eisenhower Papers, 2: 711–861; Murphy, pp. 135–43; Kammerer, pp. 573–637; Chamine, *La querelle des généraux* (Paris, 1952), pp. 249–434.
17. Eisenhower Papers, 2: 739–42, 749 n.1; A. L. Funk, "The Clark-Darlan Agreement," *Journal of Modern History* (March 1953), pp. 63–65; FRUS (1942) 2: 453–57. For text of the Clark-Darlan Agreement, compared with the original "soft" armistice, see Appendix.

18. Mast, pp. 298–99; 315–59.
19. Emile Béthouart, *Cinq années d'esperance: Mémoires de guerre, 1939–1945* (Paris, 1968), pp. 145–72; Crusoe, pp. 78–86; Richard and Sérigny, pp. 143–78; Danan, pp. 130–76; Kammerer, p. 576; Kaspi, *La mission de Jean Monnet*, pp. 43–132.
20. Van Hecke, pp. 244–304; unpublished account of Bernard Pauphilet, loaned to author.
21. A. J. Liebling, *The Road Back to Paris* (New York, 1944), p. 228.
22. Funk, pp. 52–53. See also Ordioni, pp. 514–95. On 8 November 1972, the Benjamin Franklin Post (Paris) of the Veterans of Foreign Wars published an album commemorating the *Thirtieth Anniversary of the Landing of Allied Troops in North Africa*, in collaboration with the Association de la Libération Française du 8 November 1942. This volume includes statements, photographs, and memoirs of participants still living in 1972. Among the commentators: Robert Murphy, Mark Clark, General Jousse, General Monsabert, General Gruenther, José Aboulker, John Knox, Abbé Cordier, General Chrétien, Bernard Karsenty, André Achiary, Bernard Pauphilet.
23. The letter was sent to Churchill, Roosevelt, and Eisenhower via Clark. Text from Churchill, pp. 636–37. See also Butcher, pp. 206–7; Clark, pp. 126–27.
24. Eisenhower Papers, 2: 803. See also Eisenhower, pp. 110–30.
25. Attlee to Churchill, 8 December 1942, PM 3-442, Public Records Office.
26. Howard, pp. 174–79; Sir Llewellyn Woodwood, *British Foreign Policy in the Second World War*, 2 (London, 1972): 374–88; Eden, pp. 409–16; *Life* (4 February 1946).
27. See Appendix B.
28. The reader is invited to explore further the unfolding of these matters in Funk, pp. 61–147.

Bibliography

Bibliographical Note

There are no recent books in English which concentrate on political aspects of the North African invasion. There is a little volume by Peter Tompkins, published by Simon and Schuster in 1965, called *The Murder of Admiral Darlan.* This is not a work of original scholarship; it merely rehashes material from other books which, unfortunately, the author does not identify. As the author accepts uncritically a conspiracy theory of history, scholars cannot take the book seriously.

The classic in the field must be considered William Langer's *Our Vichy Gamble* (1947) based on State Department and OSS records, but not dealing much with military or French aspects. Although far from recent, Langer's book has in it a lot of information. Another classic is in French, Alfred Kammerer's *Du débarquement africain* (1949), which however has not appeared in English. Another book in English, Renée Gosset's *Conspiracy in Algiers,* came out at the end of the war. It is interesting, journalistic, but no longer widely available.

There are, of course, many good books dealing with the war which include political and diplomatic sections devoted to TORCH: notably the many, many memoirs: those of Eisenhower, Butcher *(My Three Years with Eisenhower),* Pendar, Stimson, Murphy, Clark, Alan Brooke [Bryant], Hull, Eden, Cunningham, Hopkins [Sherwood], and so on. There are many excellent histories, such as Gaddis Smith's *American Diplomacy during the Second World War* and Kenneth Davis's *The American Experience of War.* Many excellent biographies touch at aspects of this subject in certain chapters, as for example James MacGregor Burns (Roosevelt), Forrest Pogue (Marshall), and Stephen Ambrose (Eisenhower).

There are also the official military histories: George Howe's *Northwest Africa* (1957) (U.S. Army); Samuel Eliot Morison's *Operations in North African Waters* (1947) (U.S. Navy); I. S. O. Playfair's *The Mediterranean and Middle East,* vol. IV (1966) (British); S. W. Roskill's *The War at Sea,* vol. II (1956) (British). These are all excellent but rather thin on personalities and on political matters.

What most of the books in English lack is coverage of the French side. In France there are innumerable books on the subject (North Africa was, after all, French), but none available in English. Many of the participants have written memoirs: General Giraud, General Juin, Admiral Darlan (notes compiled by his son in a volume called *L'amiral Darlan parle*), General Beaufre, General Béthouart, General Mast, General Van Hecke. Furthermore, besides the work of Kammerer, some authoritative histories were produced after the war with the cooperation of participants: notably the works of Chamine, Esquer, Aboulker, Barjot, and Richard and Sérigny. In France books on the subject come out with some regularity: in recent years, Danan, *La vie politique en Alger* (1963); Robichon, *Jour-J en Afrique* (1964) (popular history); Claude Paillat, *L'échiquier d'Alger* (1966) (journalistic); Pierre Ordioni, *Tout commence à Alger, 40–44* (1972) (memoirs). None of these is available in English.

A number of significant documents pertaining to the 1942 period have now been published. Most important of these are the foreign relations papers published by the State Department in 1962, and the Eisenhower papers, published in 1970. The United States and Great Britain have now made available to researchers material which heretofore was classified. Most useful in this category have been the Roosevelt papers in the Franklin D. Roosevelt Library at Hyde Park, the records of the Combined Chiefs of Staff in the National Archives, and the Churchill papers in the Public Records Office, London. Mention should also be made of the Clark papers, made available by General Mark W. Clark, and maintained at the Citadel Library, Charleston, South Carolina.

Basic Books Cited by Abbreviated Title

Aboulker	Aboulker, José, et al. "La part de la Résistance française dans les événements de l'Afrique du Nord," *Les Cahiers Français*, August 1943.
Barjot	Barjot, Pierre. *Une réussite stratégique: le débarquement du 8 novembre 1942 en Afrique du Nord*. Paris, 1946.
Beaufre	Beaufre, André. *La revanche de 1945*. Paris, 1966.
Bryant	Bryant, Sir Arthur. *The Turn of the Tide, 1939–1943: A Study Based on the Diaries and Autobiographical Notes of Field Marshal The Viscount Alanbrooke*. London, 1957.
Burns	Burns, James MacGregor. *Roosevelt: The Soldier of Freedom*. New York, 1970.
Butcher	Butcher, Harry C. *My Three Years with Eisenhower*. New York, 1946.

Chamine	Chamine (Mme Geneviève Dumais). *Suite française: La conjuration d'Alger.* Paris, 1946.
Churchill	Churchill, Winston S. *The Second World War*, vol. 4, *The Hinge of Fate.* Boston, 1950.
Clark	Clark, Mark W. *Calculated Risk.* New York, 1950.
Clark Diary	Diary of Gen. Mark W. Clark, in General Clark's personal custody.
Clark, Events	Record of Events and Documents from the Date that Lt. Gen. Mark W. Clark entered into negotiations with Admiral Jean François Darlan until Darlan was assassinated on Christmas Eve, 1942. HQ Fifth Army, Office of the Commanding General, 22 Feb. 1943. 89 pp., mimeographed. Recorded and compiled by Lt. Jack Beardwood. Citadel Library, Charleston, S.C.
Clark Papers	Papers of Gen. Mark W. Clark, Citadel Library, Charleston, S.C.
Coles and Weinberg	Coles, Harry L., and Albert K. Weinberg. *Civil Affairs: Soldiers Become Governors.* Office of the Chief of Military History series, "U.S. Army in World War II." Washington, D.C., 1964.
Crusoe	Crusoe (Jacques Lemaigre Dubreuil). *Vicissitudes d'une victoire.* Paris, 1946.
Danan	Danan, Yves Maxime. *La vie politique en Alger de 1940 à 1944.* Paris, 1963.
Darlan	Darlan, Alain. *L'amiral Darlan parle.* Paris, 1953.
De Gaulle	De Gaulle, Charles. *The Complete War Memoirs of Charles de Gaulle.* One volume edition. New York, 1967.
Dhers	Dhers, Pierre. *Regards nouveaux sur les années quarante.* Paris, 1958.
DGFP	*Documents on German Foreign Policy, 1918–1945.* Series D, Vol. XIII. Washington, D.C., 1964.
Eden	Eden, Sir Anthony, Earl of Avon. *Memoirs of Anthony Eden*, vol. 2, *The Reckoning.* Boston, 1965.
Eisenhower	Eisenhower, Dwight D. *Crusade in Europe.* Garden City, N.Y., 1948.
Eisenhower Papers	*The Papers of Dwight David Eisenhower: The War Years.* Edited by Alfred D. Chandler, Jr., and Stephen E. Ambrose. 5 vols. Baltimore, 1970.
Esquer	Esquer, Gabriel. *8 novembre 1942, premier jour de la libération.* Paris, 1946.

France during the Occupation	*France during the German Occupation, 1940–1944.* Translated by Philip W. Whitcomb. 3 vols. Stanford, Calif., 1959.
Frierson	Frierson, William C. "Preparations for TORCH." Special Staff Study made for the War Department Historical Division. Typescript, n.d. Files of the Office of the Chief of Military History, Washington, D.C.
FRUS	*Foreign Relations of the United States.* Series edited by Historical Division of the Department of State. U.S. Government Printing Office, Washington, D.C. Citations identified by year and volume.
Funk	Funk, Arthur Layton. *Charles de Gaulle: The Crucial Years, 1943–1944.* Norman, Okla., 1959.
Giraud, *Evasions*	Giraud, Henri. *Mes évasions.* Paris, 1946.
Giraud, *Un seul but*	Giraud, Henri. *Un seul but, la victoire.* Paris, 1949.
Goodfellow Papers	Goodfellow Papers, Hoover Institution, Stanford, Calif.
Gosset	Gosset, Renée Pierre. *Conspiracy in Algiers, 1942–1943.* New York, 1945.
Gwyer and Butler	Gwyer, J. M. A., and J. R. M. Butler. *Grand Strategy,* vol. 3, parts 1 and 2. London: H. M. Stationery Office, 1964.
Howard	Howard, Michael. *Grand Strategy,* vol. 4. London: H. M. Stationery Office, 1970.
Howe	Howe, George F. *Northwest Africa: Seizing the Initiative in the West.* Office of the Chief of Military History series, "U.S. Army in World War II." Washington, D.C., 1957.
Hytier	Hytier, Adrienne D. *Two Years of French Foreign Policy: Vichy, 1940–42.* Geneva, 1958.
Jewell	Jewell, N. L. A. *Secret Mission Submarine.* New York, 1944.
Jousse	Jousse, Emile. "La libération de l'Afrique du Nord et la résistance nord-africaine," *Esprit* (1 Jan. 1945).
Juin	Juin, Alphonse. *Mémoires,* vol. 1; *Alger, Tunis, Rome.* Paris, 1959.
Kammerer	Kammerer, Albert. *Du débarquement africain au meurtre de Darlan.* Paris, 1949.
Langer	Langer, William L. *Our Vichy Gamble.* New York, 1947.
Langer and Gleason	Langer, William L., and S. Everett Gleason. *The Undeclared War.* New York, 1953.

Leahy	Leahy, William D. *I Was There.* New York, 1950.
Leighton and Coakley	Leighton, Richard M., and Robert W. Coakley. *Global Logistics and Strategy, 1940–1943.* Office of the Chief of Military History series, "U.S. Army in World War II." Washington, D.C., 1955.
Lemaigre Dubreuil	Lamaigre Dubreuil, Jacques. *Les relations franco-americaines et la politique des généraux.* Paris, 1949.
Mast	Mast, Charles. *Histoire d'une rébellion: Alger, 8 novembre 1942.* Paris, 1969.
Matloff and Snell	Matloff, Maurice, and Edwin M. Snell. *Strategic Planning for Coalition Warfare, 1941–1942.* Office of the Chief of Military History series, "U.S. Army in World War II." Washington, D.C., 1953.
Meyer	Meyer, Leo J. "The Decision to Invade North Africa (TORCH)," pp. 129–53 in *Command Decisions,* edited by Kent Roberts Greenwood. New York, 1959.
Mordal	Mordal, Jacques. *La marine à l'épreuve: de l'armistice de 1940 au procès Auphan.* Paris, 1956.
Moreau Papers	Papers and writings of Admiral Moreau, personal collection of Jacques Mordal.
Morison	Morison, Samuel Eliot. *History of United States Naval Operations in World War II,* vol. 2, *Operations in North African Waters.* Boston, 1947.
Murphy	Murphy, Robert D. *Diplomat among Warriors.* New York, 1964.
Ordioni	Ordioni, Pierre. *Tout commence à Alger, 40–44.* Paris, 1972.
Paillat	Paillat, Claude. *L'échiquier d'Alger,* vol. 1, *Avantage à Vichy, Juin 1940–Novembre 1942.* Paris, 1966.
Paxton, *Parades*	Paxton, Robert O. *Parades and Politics at Vichy: The French Officer Corps under Marshal Pétain.* Princeton, 1966.
Paxton, *Vichy*	Paxton, Robert O. *Vichy France: Old Guard and New Order.* New York, 1972.
Pendar	Pendar, Kenneth. *Adventure in Diplomacy.* New York, 1945.
Playfair	Playfair, I. S. O., and C. J. C. Molony. *The Mediterranean and the Middle East,* vol. 4, *The Destruction of the Axis Forces in Africa.* London: H.M. Stationery Office, 1966.

Pogue	Pogue, Forrest C. *George C. Marshall*, vol. 2, *Ordeal and Hope, 1939–1942*. New York, 1966.
Price	Price, G. Ward. *Giraud and the African Scene*. New York, 1944.
Richard and Sérigny	Richard, René, and Alain de Sérigny. *La bissectrice de la guerre: Alger, 8 novembre 1942*. Algiers, 1946.
Schmitt	Schmitt, Georges. *Les accords secrets franco-brittanniques de novembre-décembre 1940: histoire ou mystification?* Paris, 1957.
Sherwood	Sherwood, Robert E. *Roosevelt and Hopkins*. New York, 1948.
Smith	Smith, R. Harris. *OSS: The Secret History of America's First Central Intelligence Agency*. Berkeley, Calif., 1972.
Solborg Papers	Personal papers of Col. Robert A. Solborg.
Soustelle	Soustelle, Jacques. *Envers et contre tout*, vol. 1, *De Londres à Alger*. Paris, 1947.
Soustelle II	Soustelle, Jacques. *Envers et contre tout*, vol. 2, *D'Alger à Paris*. Paris, 1950.
Stimson	Stimson, Henry L., and McGeorge Bundy. *On Active Service in Peace and War*. New York, 1948.
Steele	Steele, Richard W. *The First Offensive 1942: Roosevelt, Marshall, and the Making of American Strategy*. Bloomington, Ind., 1973.
Van Hecke	Van Hecke, General A. S. *Les Chantiers de la Jeunesse au secours de la France*. Paris, 1971.
Vulliez	Vulliez, Albert. *Les vingt derniers jours de la Flotte*. Paris, 1963.
Warner	Warner, Geoffrey. *Pierre Laval and the Eclipse of France*. London, 1968.
Washington/Casablanca	*The Conferences at Washington, 1941–1942, and Casablanca, 1943*. Edited by the Historical Division of the Department of State in the series "Foreign Relations of the United States." Washington, D.C., 1968.

Selected Bibliography

Abetz, Otto. *Histoire d'une politique franco-allemande 1930–1950: Mémoires d'un ambassadeur*. Paris, 1953.

―――. *Pétain et les allemands: memorandum d'Abetz sur les rapports franco-allemands*. Paris, 1948.

Aboulker, José. "8 novembre 1942. La première libération trahie," *Action* (Paris), 8, 15, 22 Nov. 1946.

———. "La part de la Résistance française dans les événements de l'Afrique du Nord," *Les Cahiers Français*, August 1943.

———. "Nous, qui avons arrêté le général Juin," *La Nef*, April, 1959.

Aboulker, Marcel. *Alger et ses complots.* Paris, 1945.

Alsop, S., and T. Braden. *Sub Rosa.* New York, 1964.

Ambrose, Stephen E. *The Supreme Commander: The War Years of General Dwight D. Eisenhower.* New York, 1971.

Amé, Cesare. *Guerra segreta in Italia, 1940–43.* Rome, 1943.

Anderson, K. A. N. "Operations in Northwest Africa: Dispatch Submitted 7 June 1943," *London Gazette*, suppl. no. 37779, 6 Nov. 1945.

Annet, Armand. *Aux heures troublées de l'Afrique française 1939–1943.* Paris, 1952.

Ansky, Michel. *Les juifs d'Algérie.* Paris, 1954.

Aron, Robert. *Histoire de Vichy, 1940–1944.* Paris, 1954.

———. *Le piege où nous a pris l'histoire.* Paris, 1950.

Assmann, Kurt. *Deutsche Schicksalsjahre: Historische Bilder aus dem zweiten Weltkriege and seiner Vorgeschichte.* Wiesbaden, 1950.

Astier de la Vigerie, Jean-Bernard d'. *Henri d'Astier de la Vigerie.* Paris, 1972.

Auphan, Gabriel. *Histoire élémentaire de Vichy.* Paris, 1971.

———. *La Marine au service des français: la butte pour la vie (1940–42).* Paris, 1947.

———. *Les grimaces de l'histoire: l'histoire de mes "trahisons."* Paris, 1951.

Ballande, Henri. *De l'amirauté à Bikini: Souvenirs des jours sans joie.* Paris, 1972.

Bankwitz, Philip Charles. *Maxime Weygand and Civil Military Relations in Modern France.* Cambridge, Mass., 1967.

Barré, Georges. *Tunisie, 1942–43.* Paris, 1950.

Beaufre, André. "General Giraud's Escape," *History of the Second World War*, vol. 3, no. 11 (1967).

Belot, Raymond de. *The Struggle for the Mediterranean 1939–1945.* Princeton, 1951.

Bess, Demaree. "Our Secret Diplomatic Triumph in Africa," *Saturday Evening Post*, 26 December, 1942.

———. "The Backstage Story of Our American Adventure," *Saturday Evening Post*, 3, 10, 17 July 1943.

Béthouart, Emile. *Cinq années d'éspérance: Mémoires de guerre, 1939–1945.* Paris, 1968.

Birse, A. H. *Memoirs of an Interpreter.* London, 1967.

Blum, John Morton. *From the Morganthau Diaries*, vol. 3, *Years of War*. Boston, 1967.

Bourdan, Pierre. *Carnet des jours d'attente.* Paris, 1945.

Bourdier, Jean. *Le Comte de Paris: Un cas politique.* Paris, 1965.

Bourget, Pierre André. *Témoignages interdits sur el maréchal Pétain.* Paris, 1960.

Bouscat, Général. *De Gaulle–Giraud: histoire d'une mission.* Paris, 1969.
Bouthillier, Yves. *Le Drame de Vichy.* 2 vols. Paris, 1950–52.
Brooks, Russell. "The Unknown Darlan," *U.S. Naval Institute Proceedings,* August 1955.
Buchanan, A. Russell. *The United States and World War II.* 2 vols. New York, 1964.
Bullitt, Orville H. (ed.). *For the President, Personal and Secret: Correspondence Between Franklin D. Roosevelt and William C. Bullitt.* Boston, 1972.
Burdick, Charles B. *Germany's Military Strategy and Spain in World War II.* Syracuse, N.Y., 1968.
Cantril, Hadley. "Evaluating the Probable Reactions to the Landing in North Africa in 1942: A Case Study," *Public Opinion Quarterly,* Fall 1965.
——— (ed.) *Public Opinion, 1935–1946.* Princeton, 1951.
Catoire, Maurice. *La direction des services de l'armistice à Vichy.* Paris, 1955.
Chambe, René. "Comment fut preparée l'évasion du général Giraud," *La revue des deux mondes,* 15 April 1962.
———. "Weygand à l'heure d'Alger," *La revue des deux mondes,* 15 August, 1965.
———. *Le maréchal Juin: "Duc du Garigliano."* Paris 1968.
Childs, J. Rives. "French North Africa 1942," *New Goliards,* June 1963.
Clark, Michael K. "The Plot That Took Algiers," *Nation,* 3 July 1943.
Cole, Hubert. *Laval: A Biography.* New York, 1963.
Conn, Stetson, and Byron Fairchild. *The Framework of Hemisphere Defense.* Washington, D.C., 1960.
Cooper, Dick. *The Adventures of a Secret Agent.* London, 1957.
Courtney, G. B. "General Clark's Secret Mission to Lay Groundwork for the North African Invasion," *Life,* 28 December 1942.
Cunningham, Andrew B. *A Sailor's Odyssey.* New York, 1951.
Curel, Claude (pseud. for Claude Rosfelder). *Brancula.* Paris, 1969.
Dashiell, Samuel. *Victory through Africa.* New York, 1943.
Daugherty, W. E., and M. Janowitz. "The Darlan Story," pp. 291–98 in *A Psychological Warfare Casebook.* Baltimore, 1958.
Davis, Kenneth S. *The American Experience of War.* New York, 1965.
Deakin, F. W. *The Brutal Friendship.* London, 1962.
Delzell, Charles F. *Mussolini's Enemies.* Princeton, 1961.
De Guingand, Sir Francis. *Generals at War.* London, 1964.
De Montmorency, Alec. *The Enigma of Admiral Darlan.* New York, 1953.
Divine, Robert A. *Roosevelt and World War II.* Baltimore, 1969.
Docteur, Jules T. *La grande énigme de la guerre: Darlan, amiral de la flotte.* Paris, 1949.

Donnison, F. S. V. *Central Organization and Planning.* London: H. M. Stationery Office, 1966.
Downes, Donald C. *The Scarlet Thread: Adventure in Wartime Espionage.* London, 1953.
Dupays, P. *Débarquement allié en A. F. N., chronique historique: libération, 8 novembre–décembre, 1942.* Paris, 1953.
Erdmann, James M. *Leaflet Operations in the Second World War.* Denver, 1969.
Faivre, Mario. "Rapport du Sous-Lieutenant M. H. Faivre (MARIO), adjoint au Capitaine Pillafort, dans la préparation et l'éxécution du putsch des 7 et 8 novembre 1942," *Afrique,* March, 1945.
Farrère, Claude. *François Darlan: Amiral de France et sa flotte.* Paris, 1940.
Feis, Herbert. *Churchill, Roosevelt, Stalin.* Princeton, 1950.
Ferguson, Bernard. *The Watery Maze: The Story of Combined Operations.* New York, 1961.
Fernet, Vice-Amiral. *Aux côtes du maréchal Pétain: Souvenirs (1940–1944).* Paris, 1953.
Ferrell, Robert H. *American Diplomacy: A History.* New York, 1969.
Foot, M. R. D. *SOE in France.* London: H. M. Stationery Office, 1966.
Fourcade, Marie-Madeleine. *L'Arche de Noé.* Paris, 1968.
Fouvez, Charles. *Le mystère Weygand.* Paris, 1967.
Frizell, Bernard. *The Grand Defiance.* New York, 1972.
Frye, Alton. *Nazi Germany and the American Hemisphere.* New Haven, 1967.
Fuehrer Conferences on Naval Affairs. Brassey's Naval Annual, London, 1948.
Funk, Arthur L. "A document relating to the Second World War: The Clark-Darlan Agreement," *Journal of Modern History,* March 1953.
———. "Eisenhower, Giraud, and the Command of TORCH," *Military Affairs,* October 1971.
———. "Negotiating the 'Deal with Darlan,' " *Journal of Contemporary History,* April 1973.
———. TORCH: les opérations de diversion alliées et les renseignements de l'Axe," *Revue historique de l'Armée,* no. 4, 1973.
Gaddis, John L. *The United States and the Origins of the Cold War.* New York, 1972.
Gallagher, Charles F. *The United States and North Africa.* Cambridge, Mass., 1963.
Gallagher, Wesley. *Back Door to Berlin: The Full Story of the American Coup in North Africa.* New York, 1943.
Garder, Michel. *La guerre secrète des services spéciaux français, 1935–1945.* Paris, 1967.
Gottschalk, Louis. "Our Vichy Fumble," *Journal of Modern History,* March 1948.
Gounelle, Claude. *Le dossier Laval.* Paris, 1969.

Griffiths, Richard. *Marshal Pétain.* London, 1970.
Hayes, Carleton J. H. *Wartime Mission in Spain.* New York, 1945.
Henry-Haye, G. *La grande éclipse franco-americaine.* Paris, 1973.
Herriot, Edward. *Episodes, 1940–44.* Paris, 1950.
Higgins, Trumbull. *Winston Churchill and the Second Front, 1940–43.* Oxford, 1957.
Hitler's Table Talk. Edited by H. R. Trevor-Roper. London, 1953.
Hoare, Sir Samuel (Viscount Templewood). *Complacent Dictator.* New York, 1947.
Holmes, Julius C. "Eisenhower's African Gamble," *Collier's,* 12 January 1946.
Hougen, John H. *The Story of the Famous 34th Infantry Division.* Privately printed, 1949.
Howard, Michael. *The Mediterranean Strategy in the Second World War.* New York, 1968.
Hull, Cordell. *The Memoirs of Cordell Hull.* New York, 1948.
Ismay, Lord. *The Memoirs of Lord Ismay.* New York, 1960.
Jacques, Jean. *La Résistance française.* Algiers, 1944.
Jones, Vincent. *Operation Torch: Anglo-American Invasion of North Africa.* New York, 1972.
Kahn, David. *The Codebreakers.* New York, 1967.
Kammerer, Albert. *La passion de la flotte française.* Paris, 1951.
Kaspi, André. *La mission de Jean Monnet à Alger.* Paris, 1971.
Knight, Ridgway B. "General Clark's Secret Mission to Algeria," *Foreign Service Journal,* March 1943.
Koeltz, Louis. *Une campagne que nous avons gagné.* Paris, 1959.
Kolko, Gabriel. *The Politics of War: The World and United States Foreign Policy, 1943–1945.* New York, 1968.
Kriegstagebuch des Oberkommandos der Wehrmacht. Edited by Andreas Hillgruber. 2 vols. Frankfurt, 1963.
Kuisel, Richard F. "The Legend of the Vichy Synarchy," *French Historical Studies,* Spring 1970.
La délégation française auprès de la Commission allemande d'armistice. 5 vols. Paris, 1947–59.
Launay, Jacques de. *Le dossier de Vichy.* Paris, 1967.
Laval, Pierre. *Laval parle.* Geneva, 1948.
Lemaigre Dubreuil, Jacques. "La rentrée en guerre de la France africaine aux côtés des Alliés, le 8 novembre 1942," *T.A.M.,* 10, 17 July 1943. (Also privately printed in pamphlet form, June 1943.)
Liebling, A. J. *The Road Back to Paris.* New York, 1944.
Lockhart, Robert H. Bruce. *Comes the Reckoning.* London, 1947.
Loustaunau-Lacau, Georges. *Mémoires d'un français rébelle, 1914–1948.* Paris, 1948.
MacCloskey, Monro. *TORCH and the Twelfth Air Force.* New York, 1971.
MacDonald, Charles B. *The Mighty Endeavor.* New York, 1969.

McNeill, William H. *America, Britain, and Russia.* London, 1953.
MacVane, John. *Journey into War: War and Diplomacy in North Africa.* New York, 1943.
Martin du Gard, Maurice. *La carte impériale: Histoire de la France Outre-mer, 1940–1945.* Paris, 1949.
Medlicott, William N. *The Economic Blockade*, vol. 1. London: H. M. Stationery Office, 1959.
Melka, Robert L. "Darlan between Britain and Germany, 1940–41," *Journal of Contemporary History*, April 1973.
Melton, George E. "Admiral Darlan and the Diplomacy of Vichy, 1940–42." Ph.D. dissertation, University of North Carolina, 1966.
Michel, Henri. "Darlan et le débarquement allié en A.F.N.," *Cahiers d'histoire de la guerre*, January 1949.
———. *La seconde guerre mondiale.* 2 vols. Paris, 1968–69.
———. *Les courants de pensée de la Résistance.* Paris, 1962.
———. *Pétain, Laval, Darlan, trois politiques.* Paris, 1972.
Michel, H., and B. Mirkine-Guetzévitch. *Les ideés politiques et sociales de la Résistance.* Paris, 1954.
Mikes, George. *Darlan: A Study.* London, 1943.
Moch, J. *Rencontres avec . . . Darlan et Eisenhower.* Paris, 1968.
Moire, A. *Déportation et résistance en Afrique du Nord, 1939–1944.* Paris, 1972.
Mordal, Jacques. *La bataille de Casablanca.* Paris, 1952.
———. "Darlan, un nouveau dauphin," *Le Journal de la France*, 11 October 1971.
———. "Qui était Darlan?" *La Revue de Paris*, August 1955.
Murphy, Robert D. "Operation TORCH," *Foreign Service Journal*, November 1961.
Neumann, William L. *After Victory: Churchill, Roosevelt, Stalin and the Making of the Peace.* New York, 1967.
1942–1972: Thirty Years After . . . : Commemorative Album of the Allied Landing on North Africa. Privately printed by the Veterans of Foreign Wars, Benjamin Franklin Post 605. Paris, 1972.
Noguères, Louis. *Le suicide de la flotte française à Toulon.* Paris, 1961.
O'Connor, Raymond G. *Diplomacy for Victory.* New York, 1971.
Paillole, Commandant. "L'Afrique du Nord dans nos combats, 1940–1944," Part 1. *Bulletin de l'Amicale des anciens membres des Services de Securité Militaire et des Réseaux T. R., Bulletin de Liaison*, no. 4, December 1954.
Painton, Frederick C. "Secret Mission to North Africa," *Reader's Digest*, May 1943.
Planchais, Jean. *Une histoire politique de l'armée, 1940–1967.* Paris, 1967.
Plumyène, J. *Pétain.* Paris, 1964.
Pozzo di Borgo, Louis. *Algérie d'hier et d'aujourd'hui.* Paris, 1957.
Raïssac, Guy. *Un soldat dans la tourmente.* Paris, 1963.

Reibel, Charles. *La verité sur les origines du débarquement allié en Afrique du Nord.* Paris, 1946.
Robichon, Jacques. *Jour-J en Afrique.* Paris, 1964.
Rosenman, Samuel (ed.). *The Public Papers and Addresses of Franklin D. Roosevelt, 1942.* New York, 1950.
Rosfelder, Roger. "The Plot to Murder Admiral Darlan," *Today in FRANCE,* January-February 1972.
Roskill, S. W. *The War at Sea.* 3 vols. London: H. M. Stationery Office, 1954–61.
Roulleaux, Dugage. *Deux ans d'histoire secrète en Afrique du Nord: Alger, 1940–1942.* Paris, 1945.
Salisbury-Jones, Guy. *So Full a Glory: A Life of Marshal de Lattre de Tassigny.* London, 1954.
Schmitt, General G. "La matinée du 11 novembre 1942 à Vichy," *Revue d'histoire de la 2ᵉ guerre mondiale,* October 1962.
———. "Le général Juin et le débarquement en A.F.N.," *Revue d'histoire de la 2ᵉ guerre mondiale,* October 1961.
Schoenfeld, Maxwell P. *The War Ministry of Winston Churchill.* Ames, Iowa, 1972.
Sérigny, Alain de. *Echos d'Alger.* Paris, 1972.
Smith, Gaddis. *American Diplomacy during World War II, 1941–1945.* New York, 1965.
Snell, John L. *Illusion and Necessity.* Boston, 1963.
Stalin, Joseph. *Stalin's Correspondence with Churchill, Roosevelt, and Truman.* New York, 1958. Reprint of *Correspondence between the Chairman of the Council of Ministers of the U.S.S.R. and the President of the U.S.A. and the Prime Ministers of Great Britain during the Great Patriotic War of 1941–1945.* Vol. 2. Moscow, 1957.
Stead, P. J. *Second Bureau.* London, 1959.
Stehlin, Paul. *Témoignages pour l'histoire.* Paris, 1964.
Strawson, J. *The Battle for North Africa.* New York, 1970.
Strong, C. L. "Allo Maroc," *Bell Telephone Magazine,* September 1943.
Taylor, Edmond. *Awakening from History.* London, 1971.
Tedder, Lord. *With Prejudice.* London, 1966.
Tompkins, Peter. *The Murder of Admiral Darlan.* New York, 1965.
Trevor-Roper, H. R. *Blitzkrieg to Defeat: Hitler's War Directives, 1939–1945.* New York, 1965.
Truscott, Lucien K. *Command Missions.* New York, 1954.
Varillon, P. *Le sabordage de la flotte.* Paris, 1954.
Vernoux, Marcel. *Wiesbaden, 1940–1944.* Paris, 1954.
The War in North Africa. 2 vols. West Point, N.Y., 1945–47.
Weygand, Jacques. *Weygand, mon père.* Paris, 1970.
Weygand, Maxime. *Recalled to Service.* Garden City, N.Y., 1952.
Whiteleather, Melvin K. *Main Street's New Neighbors.* New York, 1945.
Woodward, Sir Llewellyn. *British Foreign Policy in the Second World War,* vol. 2. London: H. M. Stationery Office, 1971.
Zanuck, Daryl F. *Tunis Expedition.* New York, 1943.

Index

Aboulker, Colette, 197
Aboulker, Dr. Henri, 197, 258; authorizes insurgents to use house, 199–200, 203, 225
Aboulker, José, 174–76, 192, 197–98, 209–12, 222, 258, 279. See also Algiers Resistance movement
Aboulker, Dr. Raphael, 174, 198
Aboulker, Stéphane, 174
Achiary, André, 16, 19, 173, 175, 210, 258
Afrika Korps. See Rommel
Ain Taya, 97, 111
Alexandre, Pierre, 173, 194, 200, 258
Algeria: landings in, 93, 111–12, 212–15, 220–27
Algiers: Allied plans to attack, 100, 110–12, 132–38, 153, 157; Allied operations at, 212–15, 220–27; communications system in, 220; police force of, 172–73; strategic points in, 196–202, 215
Algiers Resistance movement: role of in Darlan assassination, 261; organization of, 172–76, 199–200, 203, 225; plans takeover of city, 171–76, 192, 197–202; *Putsch* carried out by, 203–5, 209–12, 215–17; small arms for, 42, 115, 201; stores arms in Laveysse garage, 197, 201, 207, 211; Task Groups of, 198–99, 209–12, 222–23; ultimate failure of, 220–23, 257–58. See also Five, The; French Resistance; TORCH: relations with French
ALLIANCE (Resistance network), 12, 185, 195
Allied Force Headquarters (AFHQ), 92

Anderson, Gen. Kenneth A. N., 110, 158, 243–44
Anselme, Col., 197–98, 200–201, 209, 212
ANTON (German occupation of France), 123, 241
Arabs, North African, 117, 124
Armed Forces, American: 39th Infantry, 9th Division, 111, 213, 296; 135th Infantry Regiment, 34th Division, 215; 168th Infantry Regiment, 34th Division, 111, 214, 225, 296. See also TORCH
Armed forces, British, 111, 133, 182, 224. See also TORCH
Armed forces, French, 40, 91, 94, 115, 172, 179, 199; attitudes in, 123–25, 188, 192, 247; defense of Algiers, 172, 213–15, 220–27; *Corps Franc*, 246–47, 261; modernization of, 156; service in Italy, 258. See also Giraud; Juin; Noguès; Weygand
Armed forces, German: intervention in Algeria, 221; and occupation of southern France, 123, 241; and occupation of Tunisia, 235, 239, 245
Armistice Army. See Armed forces, French
Armistice Commission, German, 179, 200
Armistice Commission, Italian, 183, 200
Armistice terms, Allied, 118–20, 235–36, 266–73
Arnold, Gen. Henry H. ("Hap"), 73, 85, 86
Assault Force. See TORCH
Attlee, Clement, 140, 260

Auphan, Adm. Paul, 236–37, 239, 246, 279

BACKBONE (operation in Spanish Morocco), 93
Baril, Col. Louis, 172, 192–93, 214–15, 224, 257
Barjot, Capt., 147
Barré, Gen. Georges, 226
Bartlett, Sydney, 19
Battet, Admiral, 206–7, 216, 222
Baurès, Gen., 47, 60
Beaufort, Maj. de, 195
Beaufre, Capt. André, 11–12, 53, 163, 168–69, 188, 279; and Gen. Giraud, 61–62, 182, 184, 229–30, 234; and Lemaigre Dubreuil, 15–17
Bègue (Vichy agent), 127
Bergeret, Gen., 195
Béthouart, Gen. Emile, 35, 176, 192–94, 237, 257
Blida airport, 111, 157, 193, 199, 224
Board of Economic Warfare. See Economic Warfare, Board of
Boisboissel, Gen., 184
Boisson, Gen. Pierre, 6, 123, 232, 259
BOLERO, 42, 66, 68, 72–74, 76–77, 92
Bône, 93, 100, 157, 186, 243
Bougie, 243
Boyd, John, 19
Bretons, Group of, 211. See also Tilly
Bringard (police officer), 173, 210
British army. See Armed forces, British
Broke, H.M.S., 111, 223–24
Brooke, Gen. Sir Alan, 73, 140
Brunel, Jean, 200–1
Bullitt, William C., 8, 282
Bulolo, H.M.S., 225, 227
Butcher, Harry C., 81, 106
Buxton, Col. Edward ("Ned"), 89

Calvet, Guy, 175. See also Cohen
Canfield, Franklin, 19
Cantril, Hadley, 95, 96
Capitant, René, 39
Carcasonne, Pierre, 20, 175
Casablanca, 93, 100, 112
Casablance Conference, 112
Cassady, Thomas J., 64
Castiglione, 97, 111, 224–25
Cease-fire, 226–27, 238–39, 242

censorship, 273
Chambe, Gen. René, 47, 49, 58
Chantiers de la Jeunesse, 53, 175, 203, 225, 261
Chapelle, Fernand Bonnier de la, 261, 275–77
Châtel, Yves, 166, 182–83
Cherchell Conference, 133, 138–44, 146–47, 149–62; assessment of, 162–64; memorandum on, 165, 167–69
Chiefs of Staff. See Combined Chiefs of Staff; Joint Chiefs of Staff
Chrétien, Col. Jean, 127–29, 178–79, 183, 204–5, 279
Churchill, Winston: and Darlan, 139–40, 251, 260–61; and Eden, 105, 141; and Eisenhower, 100, 139–40; and Roosevelt, 29–32, 72–76, 87, 98–100; and Stalin, 94; strategic thinking of, 27–32, 67, 69–70, 72–79, 96–100
civil affairs, 102–6, 109, 113, 136–38
Clark, Gen. Mark Wayne: and Churchill, 79, 96–98, 100, 139–40; and Darlan, 235–48; and Murphy, 106, 235–48; North African mission of, 143, 149–62, 186; relations with French, 139–43, 152–64, 182, 235–48; named TORCH deputy commander, 92; and TORCH planning, 111, 139–44, 228–30; and security, 187
Clark-Darlan Agreement, 118, 247–57; text of, 265–73
Clarke, Col. Brien, 155
code, U.S. diplomatic, 18, 25, 38
Cohen, André (Calvet), 210
Cohen, Guy (Calvet), 217, 175
Cole, Felix, 11, 125, 191
Collinet, Adm., 123
Combined Chiefs of Staff (CCS), 73–74, 84–86, 189
"Combat" (Gaullist Resistance Group), 212
command. See TORCH, command of
Commissariat Central (Algiers), 198, 210
Commons, House of, 78, 260
communications: in Algiers, 173–74, 212, 296 n. 7; with Vichy, 236–37; armistice terms concerning, 119, 267–68
Communists, 124

conspiracy (in Algiers). *See* Algiers Resistance movement; Five, The
Consulates, U.S., 7, 125
contingency plans, 118
convoys. *See* shipping
Coordinator of Information (COI, later OSS), 32–33, 40
Cordier, Abbé Pierre-Marie, 19, 194, 275–77
Coster, Donald, 288 n. 36
Courtney, Capt. G. B., 143
Culbert, Frederic P., 155
Cunningham, Adm. Sir Andrew, 158, 190, 250, 260

Dakar, 5, 179, 183, 232, 259
Daridan, Lt., 201
Darlan, Alain, 24, 36–37, 128, 279; illness of, 133, 180, 194
Darlan, Adm. Jean François Xavier, 5, 10, 99, 108, 123–25, 128, 131, 178–80, 194–95, 220–27, 230, 240, 243–48, 257, 265; assassination of, 261, 275–77; and cease-fire, 225–27, 238; character of, 22–25, 241–43; and Clark, 231–48; estimate of, by Americans, 140–41, 249–50, 258–60; estimate of, by British, 140, 251, 260–61; estimate of, by The Five, 133–34; and French fleet, 239–40, 243–46, 299 n. 18; asks Leahy to help France, 24, 126, 151, 209; and Murphy, 128, 206–9, 215–20, 231–48; political and strategic thinking of, 36–37, 63, 128, 179, 207–8, 220–21, 226, 233–34; considers self squeezed lemon, 259; and Weygand, 25
Dartois, Maj., 147, 157, 194, 214
d'Astier de la Vigerie, Emmanuel, 21
d'Astier de la Vigerie, François, 21, 275–76
d'Astier de la Vigerie, Henri, 19–21, 35, 127–28, 136, 146, 173, 175, 178, 192, 194, 197, 200, 205, 209–12, 234, 258, 261, 275–77
d'Astier de la Vigerie, Jean-Bernard, 276–77
"Deal" with Darlan. *See* Clark-Darlan Agreement
de Beaufort. *See* Beaufort
deception, 149–52, 195

defenses. *See* French North Africa; Armed forces, French
de Gaulle, Gen. Charles, 5, 124, 136, 140, 279; and exclusion from North Africa, 56, 83, 95, 102; and Darlan, 254, 276–77; and Giraud, 261; and Marshall, 82–84; position of, in North Africa, 95, 172
de Laborde, Adm. Jean, 243, 245, 298 n. 11
de Lattre de Tassigny, Gen. Jean, 59–60
de Rosen, Léon, 60
Dieppe raid, 94, 151
Dill, Field Marshal Sir John, 73, 86
Donovan, Col. William J., 32–33, 53, 57, 89
Doolittle, Gen. James, 89
Dorange, Maj. André, 129–31, 179, 209–10, 217–20, 237
Doyle, Col. Edward J., 225
Dreyfus, Lt. Jean, 174, 199, 222–23
Driguez, Paul, 204
Dubreuil. *See* Lemaigre Dubreuil
Dunn, James, 34
Duperré, Fort, 97, 111, 214

EAGLE. *See* Clark, Gen. Mark
Economic Warfare, Board of (BEW), 101–2, 110, 146
Eddy, Lt. Col. William, 33, 42, 72, 89–93, 95–96, 104
Eden, Sir Anthony, 104–5, 113, 139–41, 150; and Darlan, 141, 251
Eisenhower, Gen. Dwight D., 32, 73, 79, 81–83, 100, 139–41, 186–91, 227–30, 235, 247–51, 255–56, 261; and Churchill, 100, 139–40, 259; and Clark, 139–41, 244–51; and French Resistance, 93–94, 121, 139–43, 154, 181–82; and Giraud, 186–91, 228–30; becomes commander of TORCH, 92. *See also* TORCH
El Alamein, 133, 140, 179–80
election campaign, U.S., 95, 99
Esteva, Adm., 243, 250
exchange rate, 56, 118, 144–45
extraterritoriality, 120, 271

Faivre, Mario, 201–2, 276–77
Faye, Maj. Léon, 12, 169, 185
Fedala, 112

Fenard, Adm. R., 25, 36–37, 128, 133, 194, 206, 215–16, 238, 279
Fighting French. *See* Free French
Five, The, 35, 49–50, 55–56, 90–91, 127, 132–38, 198, 203, 205, 234, 257–58; and Algiers *Putsch*, 209–12; plans and objectives of, 39, 114–18, 162–66, 232, 257. *See also* d'Astier de la Vigerie, Henri; Lemaigre Dubreuil; Rigault; Tarbé de Saint-Hardouin; van Hecke
FLAGSTAFF. *See* Mast, Gen. Charles
Fleet, French. *See* Naval forces, French
Foot, Lt. J. P., 143
Fort d'Estrées, 97, 111
France. *See* Vichy France; Armed forces, French; Naval forces, French
Franco, Gen. Francisco, 4, 93
Franco-American Banking Corporation, 145
Fredendall, Gen. Lloyd R., 112
Fredj, Lt. Fernand, 174, 201
Free French, 5, 114–15, 150, 153, 276–77. *See also* de Gaulle
French Army. *See* Armed forces, French
French Navy. *See* Naval forces, French
French North Africa: censorship in, 273; defenses of, 111, 158, 179, 195, 213, 215; economic conditions in, 118, 144–46, 272; invasion of (*see* TORCH); military control in, 120–21, 269, 272; political arrangements in, 114, 119–20, 136–38, 243, 245, 247–48, 261, 270; strategic significance of, 5–6
French Resistance, 12, 40, 42, 115–16, 132–38, 155, 169. *See also* Algiers Resistance movement; de Gaulle; Five, The; Giraud
French sovereignty, 90, 101, 116–17, 136–38, 166, 232, 238, 259, 265
French West Africa, 232, 259

Gaullists, 39–40, 108, 176. *See also* Free French
Gaylord, Col. Bradford, 167
Géo Gras organization, 174, 198
Georges, Gen. Alphonse, 60
Germany, 6, 15, 179, 187, 200, 221, 227, 235; *see also* Hitler

Gibraltar, 143, 162, 167, 187, 227–30
Giraud, Bernard, 186
Giraud, Gen. Henri Honoré: escapes from Germany, 43–45, 48–49; contacts Resistance and Allies, 59–61, 64, 132, 134, 162–64, 169; leaves France, 151–53, 165–69, 176–77, 184–86; at Gibraltar, 188–91, 228–31; at Algiers, 199–200, 234–36, 240–41, 246–47; becomes High Commissioner, 261; and Allied command, 135–36, 140–41, 155–56, 168–69, 176–78, 185, 237, 250; and de Gaulle, 58–59, 232; strategic planning ("Grand Design") of, 49–51, 62–63, 132–35, 152, 165–69, 185–86, 190
Goetz (Algerian inspector of finances), 145
Great Britain: relations with French, 28, 104–5, 140–41, 251, 260–61; relations with Soviet Union, 69, 94, 254; relations with U.S., 29–32, 72–77, 105, 110–11. *See also* Churchill, de Gaulle, Eden, TORCH
Gruenther, Col. Alfred, 177
guerrillas, urban. *See* Algiers Resistance movement
GYMNAST, 30–32, 41–42, 54, 72–80, 84

Halifax, Lord, 30, 105
Hamblen, Col. Archelaus L., 143, 157
Handy, Gen. Thomas T., 96
Harriman, W. Averell, 106
Harvey, Constance, 60
Herriot, Edouard, 60
Hewitt, Adm. Henry Kent, 112
Hillenkoetter, Cmdr. R. H., 6
Hitler, Adolf, 6, 47, 93, 123, 231
Hoare, Sir Samuel, 93
Holmes, Col. Julius, 106–7, 110, 143, 161
Hopkins, Harry, 30, 72, 80, 84–86
Huiles Lesieur, 13–14, 19
Hull, Cordell, 30, 104, 251

Imbert, Lt., 209
Intelligence: Allied, 82, 152, 186; British, 7, 276; French, 99, 127, 157–58, 183–84, 195 (*see also* Chrétien); German, 187; U.S., 11, 19, 33 (*see*

also Donovan; Eddy; Solborg; TORCH)
insurgency. *See* Algiers Resistance movement
invasion currency, 145
Ismay, Gen. Sir Hastings, 73, 139–40
Italian Armistice Commission, 183, 200

Jacquin, Col., 223
Jaïs, Sub-Lt. Roger, 174, 201
Jeanneney, Jules, 60
Jewell, Lt. N. L. A., 143–44, 161–62, 167, 185–86
Jews: in North African Resistance, 172, 174–75, 211
Joint Chiefs of Staff, U.S., 32, 95–96, 101, 108, 137–38
Jousse, Maj. Emile, 12, 19, 34–35, 53, 147, 157, 172–73, 178, 192, 197–200, 209–12
Juin, Gen. Alphonse, 38, 123–24, 129–30, 171–72, 179, 183, 204–9; and defense of Algiers, 215–27, 231, 235–38
JUPITER (operation against Norway), 75

Kammerer, Alfred, 503
Karsenty, Bernard, 20, 147, 160–61, 175, 258
King, Adm. Ernest, 73, 80, 83
King, David, 19
KINGPIN. *See* Giraud
Knight, Ridgway, 19, 147
Knox, Frank, 73
Knox, John, 19, 155
Koeltz, Gen., 184, 198, 210–11, 220, 235–36, 238
Kolko, Gabriel, 253

Laurencie, Gen. de la, 60
Laval, Pierre, 6, 37, 47–48, 124, 166, 233, 236, 239, 241, 248
Lazeret, Battery of, 97, 111, 213, 226
Leahy, William D., 24–25, 28, 37, 85–86, 96, 125, 142
Lebel rifles: used by insurgents, 202, 207, 211
LeBrun, Albert, 60
Leclerc, Adm., 199, 216–17, 219
Lecoq, Squadron Chief, 204

Lemaigre Dubreuil, Jacques, 19, 61, 126, 162–63, 199–200, 234, 279; established in Algiers, 13–17; and The Five, 34–35; involved with Giraud, 10, 52–53; missions between North Africa and France, 90, 165–69, 178–85, 191; political ambitions of, 39, 136
Lemnitzer, Brig. Gen. Lyman L., 143, 155–57
Lempereur, Fort, 225
Lend-Lease, 145
LeNen, Lt., 147, 159, 161
Liebling, A. J., 258
Linarès, Col. de, 47
Lippmann, Walter, 256
Livingstone, Capt. R. P., 143, 159–61
Lorber, Col., 157
Loustaunau-Lacau, Maj., 16–17

MacArthur II, Douglas, 64
McGowan, Lt. Col. (cover name for Robert Murphy), 106
Mack, W. H. B., 103, 106, 108, 113, 188
Macmillan, Harold, 261
McNarney, Gen. Joseph, 85
Maison Blanche airfield, 111, 213–14, 222
Malcolm, H.M.S., 111, 223–24
Malta, 31, 78–79
Marshall, Gen. George C.: and civil affairs planning, 90, 103; and de Gaulle, 83–84; and French Resistance, 109; and Murphy, 101; and Roosevelt policy, 92, 137; and Soviet Union, 68; strategic thinking of, 32, 72–73, 80–87
Mason-MacFarlane, Lt. Gen., 143
Mast, Gen. Charles: comes to Algiers, 51–52, 90–91, 93; active in Resistance, 132–38; confers with Clark, 146–47, 152–57; prepares for D-Day, 168, 172, 176, 183–84, 191–93, 198, 200; during landings, 204, 209, 214–15, 217, 224–25; relieved of command, 234, 237; later career, 257
Matthews, H. Freeman, 105–6, 113, 188, 279
Mendigal, Gen., 199, 236, 238
Messelmoun, 146

Michel, Aspirant, 147, 159, 161
Michelier, Admiral P., 123
MINERVA (Giraud's escape from France), 167, 176–77, 184–86, 186–89
Mockler-Ferryman, Brigadier, 106, 155
Molotov, Vyacheslev, 65–70, 254
Monnet, Jean, 257
Monsabert, Gen. A. J. de, 172, 192–93, 234, 258, 261
Montgomery, Gen. Bernard, 96, 140, 180
Morali-Daninos, Dr., 198, 258
Moreau, Adm., 123, 195, 209, 217, 236, 238
Morgenthau, Henry, 251
Morocco, French, 93, 112, 125, 179, 192–94, 237–39, 242, 250
Morocco, Spanish, 93
Mountbatten, Lord, 70–72, 140
Murphy, Robert D.: characterized, 8–9, 109; and Cherchell Conference, 159–64, 176–78; consults in Washington and London, 90–91, 99–121; criticized, 256; and Darlan, 36–37, 178, 215–20, 227, 231–35, 247–48; and date of D-Day, 177, 191, 293 n. 6; and Eisenhower, 106–9; and French Resistance, 21, 36–41, 52; and Giraud, 136–37, 146, 182–83, 237, 247–48; instructions for, 33–34, 38, 42, 50, 102–3, 106–8, 114, 116, 129, 135, 142, 254–55; and Intelligence, 25, 33, 38; and Juin, 183–84, 205–9, 215–20; and Lemaigre Dubreuil, 14–15, 19, 132–38, 176–78; and U.S. policy, 130, 249; pre-landing conferences, 125–26, 132–38; proposes postponement of landings, 181; and Roosevelt, 9–10, 100–3, 137–38
Murphy-Weygand Agreement, 10, 18, 37, 144, 146
Muscatelli (police chief), 210, 258

Naval forces, Allied, 79, 112, 215, 223–24, 292 n. 23. See also shipping, Allied
Naval forces, Axis, 187–88
Naval forces, French: Armistice terms concerning, 119, 267–69; admiralty at Algiers, 197–98, 210; defense of North Africa by, 195, 199, 215; fleet at Toulon, 221, 230, 232, 239–40, 243, 245–46, 299 n. 18
Noguès, Gen. Auguste, 7, 82, 123–26, 176, 194, 226, 239, 242, 246–48
Norfolk House, 92, 158
North Africa. See French North Africa
North African invasion. See TORCH

occupation of North Africa: allied terms regarding, 119–20
Oran, 93, 100, 112, 194, 237, 239, 242
OSS (Office of Strategic Services), 158. See also Coordinator of Information; Donovan; Eddy; Solborg
Our Vichy Gamble (William Langer), 158, 253–54, 301 n. 9, 303

P-219 (H.M.S. Seraph), 143–44, 161–62, 167, 185–86, 292 n. 23
Painton, Frederick, 158
Paris, Henri, Comte de, 261, 275–77
Patton, Gen. George, 89, 112, 126, 237, 242
Pauphilet, Bernard, 199, 206–9, 218, 280
Pearl Harbor, 27
Pendar, Kenneth, 8, 19, 193–94, 205–9, 215–19
Pétain, Marshal Henri, 4, 40, 123–24, 131, 178, 215–16, 219–20, 235, 239–41, 249; "accord intime" with Darlan, 237. See also Vichy France
Philippeville, 100
Pillafort, Capt. Alfred, 174, 198, 200–2, 210–11, 220, 222
Pointe Pescade, 97, 111, 157, 193, 214
Porte du Theil, Gen. de la, 191, 234
Port Lyautey, 112
Pound, Sir Dudley, 140
Pretender, French. See Paris, Henri, Comte de
prisoners, political, 120, 270
Protocols of 15 June 1942, 55–56, 139, 166
public opinion, 95, 251–52, 260
Putsch. See Algiers Resistance movement

Queyrat, Jean, 146

Ramsey, Adm. Bertram, 111–12

Reid, Stafford, 19
Requin, Gen., 60
requisitioning, 120, 270
Resistance. *See* Algiers Resistance movement; de Gaulle; Five, The; French Resistance; Giraud
Revers, Gen., 127–28
Rigault, Jean, 21, 34–35, 39–40, 56, 132, 147, 162–63, 167–68, 176, 194, 208–12, 215–16, 234, 258
Rommel, Gen. Erwin, 23, 28, 70, 76, 78, 140, 151, 180
Roosevelt, Franklin D.: and Darlan deal, 257; and elections, 95; foreign policy of, 99, 137, 289 n. 51; and France, 3–4, 105, 117, 252–53; and Murphy, 9–10, 100–2, 137–38; proclamations of, 108, 110, 113; personal representatives of, 10, 103, 104; and Stalin, 253–54; strategic thinking of, 66–68, 80–82; decisions related to TORCH, 85–87, 95–100, 141; First Washington Conference, 30–32; Second Washington Conference, 72–78
Rosfelder, Roger, 276–77
Roubertie, Gen., 211, 220
Rounds, Leland, 19, 155
ROUNDUP, 42, 66, 81–86, 92, 103
Ruff, Lt., 199
Ryder, Gen. Charles W., 111, 225, 230–31, 235, 247

Safi, 112
Saint-Georges Hotel, 173–74, 197, 220, 238, 246–47
Saint-Hardouin. *See* Tarbé de Saint-Hardouin
Second front, 68–69
Security, 119, 150, 195, 248
Service d'Ordre Legionnaire (SOL) 172, 212
Sevez, General, 206, 208
shipping, 78–79, 93, 110–12, 119, 146, 187, 269
Sidi Ferruch, 97, 111, 157, 193, 209, 214, 224–25
SLEDGEHAMMER, 42, 62, 79, 81
Smith, Gen. Bedell, 73, 86, 92, 106, 139
Smuts, Field Marshal Jan, 139–40
Solborg, Col. Robert, 33–34, 42–43, 89, 90, 102, 139, 144, 280; first mission to North Africa, 11–12, 17–18; sees de Gaulle in London, 50; second mission to North Africa, 53–58; dropped from OSS, 57
Soviet Union, 65–71, 94, 254
Spain, 4, 93, 95, 121, 125, 132
Special Operations Executive (SOE), 32, 40, 50, 155
Stalin, Joseph, 94, 254
Stéphane, Roger, 289 n. 6
Stimson, Henry, 32, 73, 85, 87, 101; considers North Africa Roosevelt's "great secret baby," 76
Strategic Services, Office of. *See* OSS; Intelligence, U.S.
strategy, Allied, 81–87, 91–100, 110–12, 133, 140
STREITAXT (U-Boat group), 187–88
Strong, Gen. George V., 89–90
SUPER-GYMNAST, 31, 41, 72
Surcouf, 97, 111
Syria, 17

Tangiers, 7
Tarbé de Saint-Hardouin, Jacques, 19, 35, 90, 128, 145, 163–64, 205, 215, 234, 258
Task Forces. *See* TORCH, operations
Teissier, Jacques, 146–47, 160–61
Témime, André, 174, 258
"temporary expedient," 251–52
Théry, Father, 19
Thomas Stone (ship), 189
Thorez, Maurice (French Communist leader); referred to, 254
Tilly, Félix, 198, 211, 222
Tobruk, 76
Tompkins, Peter, 275, 303
TORCH (North African invasion): landings in Algiers, 221–25; American-British relations in, 95–99, 113–115, 140–41; Armistice terms of, 118–20, 232, 239, 257, 266–73; assault forces in, 110–13, 220–27; casualties, 242; civil affairs arrangements, 113–14, 229; command of, 86, 92, 108–9, 135–36, 139–41, 155–56, 165–69, 176–78, 182–85, 189–91, 228–30; Clark and, 152–57, 186, 235–48; Darlan and, 231–48; D-Day of, 110, 153,

155, 176–78, 183; decision to launch, 85–87; and relations with French, 132–33, 139–43, 152–57, 181, 192–94, 231–48; and Giraud, 152, 166–67, 227–30, 238–39, 244–48; intelligence and deception in, 149–52, 157–58, 195; harbor attacks in, 215, 223–24; headquarters of, 91–100, 187, 227–30; and Juin, 184; operations, 187–88, 209, 213–15, 220–27, 242 (*see also* Murphy); planning, 91–100, 107, 110–12, 123, 164, 166–67, 193; political aspects of, 99, 108, 110, 113, 137 (*see also* Roosevelt); security, 187; size of, 115, 181; strategic considerations in, 99, 231–32, 253 (*see also* Churchill, Roosevelt)

Tostain, Col., 20, 194
Transatlantic Essay Contest, 91–100
Trevor, Lt. Col. T. H., 214, 224
Tuck, Pinkney, 125
Tunisia, 93, 94, 99, 223, 235, 237, 239, 243, 245, 250, 260
Turner, Capt., 185

unconditional surrender, 253
Underground. *See* Resistance; Algiers Resistance movement
United States: position on Darlan, 142, 254–55; foreign policy of, 115–17, 120–21; and Germany, 4–5, 98; policies of, attacked by Lippmann, 256; and North Africa, 18, 144, 265–66; and France, 28, 31, 41, 102, 104–5, 115–17, 125, 130, 137–38; and United Nations, 137
Utter, John, 19

Van Hecke, Col. A. S., 20, 34–35, 191, 198, 203, 234, 258
vice-consuls, American, 18–19, 40
Vichy France, 124, 181, 215, 233, 236, 241–42, 248; Allied relations with, 40–41, 80, 99; collaboration of, 23, 179, 207–8, 221, 235; and North Africa, 114, 136–38, 179, 195, 216
Viret, Cmdr., 59
Vogl, Gen., 179
Volontaires de Place (VP), 172, 201, 204

Washington Conference, First, 29–32
Washington Conference, Second, 72–78
Watson, Capt. Lindsay, 147, 225
Welles, Sumner, 9, 30, 42, 130, 137
Welsh, Air Marshal William; referred to by Eisenhower, 244
Weygand, Gen. Maxime, 6–7, 16–18, 23, 25, 31, 46, 49, 124, 129, 163, 241
Wilson, Woodrow: influence on Roosevelt, 253
Winant, John, 106
Woodruff, Harry, 19, 219
Wright, Capt. Jerauld, 143, 167, 185

Zanuck, Daryl, 229
Zermati, Aspirant Jacques, 174, 198–99, 210
Zwilling, Colonel, 217